LEAR

4 Books In 1: The Easiest Guide for Beginners, Spanish Language, Grammar, Short Stories, the Best Lessons to Increase Your Vocabulary And Common Phrases, Even If You Start From Scratch

Living Languages

Copyright
© Copyright 2020 - **All rights reserved.**

This book may not be reproduced or transmitted in any form of electronic, mechanical, photocopy, recording, or otherwise, without the prior permission of the author. It is illegal to copy this book, post it to a website, or distribute it by any other means without permission.

Neither the publisher nor the author is engaged in rendering legal or any other professional service through this book. If expert assistance is required, the services of appropriate professionals should be sought.

The publisher and the author shall have neither liability nor responsibility to any person or entity concerning any loss or damage caused directly or indirectly by the professional by using the information in this book.

Disclaimer

The information contained in this eBook is offered for informational purposes solely, and it is geared towards providing exact and reliable information in regards to the topic and issue covered. Also, this eBook provides information only up to the publishing date.

The author and the publisher do not warrant that the information contained in this e-book is fully complete and shall not be responsible for any errors or omissions. The author and publisher shall have neither liability nor responsibility to any person or entity concerning any reparation, damages, or monetary loss caused or alleged to be caused directly or indirectly by this e-book. Therefore, this eBook should be used as a guide - not as the ultimate source.

The publication is sold with the idea that the publisher is not required to render accounting, officially permitted, or otherwise qualified services. If advice is necessary, legal or professional, a practiced individual in the profession should be ordered.

In no way is it legal to reproduce, duplicate, or transmit any part of this document in either electronic means or printed format. Recording of this publication is strictly prohibited, and any storage of this document is not allowed unless with written permission from the publisher. All rights reserved.

The author owns all copyrights not held by the publisher. The trademarks that are used are without any consent, and the publication of the trademark is without permission or backing by the trademark owner. All trademarks and brands within this book are for clarifying purposes only and are not affiliated with this document.

The trademarks that are used are without any consent, and the publication of the trademark is without permission or backing by the trademark owner. All trademarks and brands within this book are for clarifying purposes only and are owned by the owners themselves, not affiliated with this document.

TABLE OF CONTENTS

LEARN SPANISH 1

Table of Contents 5

LEARN SPANISH FOR BEGINNERS 1

Introduction 2

Chapter 1: Fundamentals of Essential Grammar 4

Chapter 2: Chronological Order In Learning the Spanish Language 27

Chapter 3: Progress of Learning the Spanish Language 34

Chapter 4: the Use of Numbers, Colors, Time and Feelings 39

Chapter 5: Spanish Language Quirks......................... 49

Chapter 6: Restaurant — Restaurante 53

Chapter 7: Professions — Profesiones 60

Chapter 8: Traveling – Viajes 66

Chapter 9: Yes, No, Please, Thanks: Basic Vocabulary 69

Chapter 10: Practice Makes Perfect 80

Chapter 11: Learn Spanish Vocabulary Efficiently 85

Chapter 12: Benefits of Learning Spanish 90

Chapter 13: Basic Conversational Phrases 97

Chapter 14: Important Lessons to Learn About the Spanish Language 100

Chapter 15: Different Ways to Interact to Improve Your Spanish Language 104

Chapter 16: Tips on How to Learn the Spanish Language for Beginners, the Easiest Way Possible ... 117

Chapter 17: Spanish Accents 133

Conclusion 141

SPANISH LANGUAGE FOR BEGINNERS 144

Introduction 145

Chapter 1. Introduction to the Spanish Language ... 146

Chapter 2. Common Spanish Phrases, Greetings, and Good Manners 154

Chapter 3. Major Spanish Grammar Lessons to Consider 227

Chapter 4. The Pronunciation Rules of Speaking Spanish 271

Chapter 5. The Progressive Tenses 286

Chapter 6. Tips to Speed up Learning 306

Chapter 7. Online Learning 321

Conclusion 333

LEARN SPANISH GRAMMAR 336

Introduction 337

Chapter 1: Pronunciation is the Key 338

Chapter 2: Forming Sentences 349

Chapter 3: Spanish Nouns 356

Chapter 4: Spanish Pronouns 387

Chapter 5: Spanish Verbs 418

Chapter 6: Spanish Adjectives 434

Chapter 7: Spanish Adverbs 448

Chapter 8: Articles 454

Chapter 9: Learning Basic vocabulary 466

Chapter 10: Conjugation and Gender Rules.............. 480

Chapter 11: Interrogative Phrases about Personal Characteristics and Information............................. 486

Chapter 12: Alphabet and Pronunciation 488

Conclusion 514

SPANISH SHORT STORIES FOR BEGINNERS 517

Introduction 518

Chapter 1: Paolo y la Sirena 520

Chapter 2: Los Cazadores Locales 528

Chapter 3: Un Ángel en La Miseria 536

Chapter 4: La Buena Madre 541

Chapter 5: Jamari, El Estudiante Serio 547

Chapter 6: El Carpintero 553

Chapter 7: El Sueño del Rey 557

Chapter 8: Luca y El Señor Tiempo 564

Chapter 9: Ella Siempre Me Supera 571

Chapter 10: La Muerte Los Sigue 584

Chapter 11: Experiencia Nocturna 598

Chapter 12: Cyril y Su Voluntad 606

Chapter 13: La Asumida Muerte de Henry, El Granjero
 612

Chapter 14: La Gran Noticia 620

Chapter 15: Salir con Los Amigos *631*

Chapter 16: El Alfarero Sabio *636*

Chapter 17: La Fiesta de Los Gnomos y Las Hadas....*642*

Chapter 18: Granja Los Villalobos *649*

Chapter 19: Los Piratas del Bufón Errante (Torpes en Tierra y en Mar)..*667*

Chapter 20: Nuevos Amigos......................................*683*

Conclusion *694*

LEARN SPANISH FOR BEGINNERS

Simple Step-by-Step Guide to Learning. A Proven Approach to Studying at Home, on the Road or in the Car Like Crazy. Have Fun Understanding and Remembering with Practice

Living Languages

Introduction

You are now on your way to learning Spanish through some funny and easy to read stories that both the young and the young at heart will love.

As you read and listen to the stories, you can let your imagination soar while you are having fun learning this foreign language. This book is set up for anyone who has not studied Spanish before or for those who want a complement to learn the language in the beginning stages.

Included as well is a breakdown of the sentence structure in Spanish so that you can understand it much more easily. Also, there is a breakdown of how to conjugate verbs in the Spanish language. This information will come in handy as you continue to learn more Spanish in the future, as well as strengthening the vocabulary this book focuses on.

The key to learning any new language is to incorporate it in as many ways as you can into your daily life.

This book is the beginning of your journey toward perfecting your Spanish skills. You will quickly and effectively improve your Spanish skills so that you can communicate with others and make traveling a lot less stressful.

With this book, you will brush up on your Spanish skills regardless of your current level. If you are brand new, don't worry! We will get you from zero to sixty in just a few lessons. Please bear in mind that learning Spanish doesn't have to be hard. All it requires is some good, old-fashioned elbow grease and a positive attitude.

If you have tried to learn Spanish or any other language for that matter, you can attest to the fact that it is a challenge. Unfortunately for some folks, they haven't had good experiences when trying to learn a new language. But fear not! This volume is intended to help you figure out the inner workings of the Spanish language. In doing so, we will unlock the keys that make the Spanish language easier to comprehend.

So, let's get started on this journey. Sure, there will be a few bumps along the way, but that is perfectly natural. In fact, the bumps along the way are perfect learning experiences, which will help cement your understanding of everything you are going to learn in this volume.

If you are already familiar with Spanish and are looking to brush up on your skills, there are plenty of new things that you are sure to discover. As a matter of fact, that is the beauty of language: just when you thought you knew something, there is always something new to discover.

Whether you are a newbie or a seasoned veteran, you will find a treasure trove of information that will enable you to develop your skills to the point where you feel comfortable having a conversation with anyone. If you are planning to travel, you will feel comfortable speaking with locals. You will be able to navigate your way through Spanish-speaking countries much easier. With our help, you won't have to struggle to get around.

Chapter 1: Fundamentals of Essential Grammar

Why Is It Essential to Learn Spanish Grammar?

Spanish language learning is very crucial to social interactions. The majority of native speakers are bilingual. In areas where English is the only formal language, like the United States, most people only speak one language. Thus, being bilingual is very important and can help you build your social network. Research has also shown that bilingual children are smarter and often perform better than their peers who only speak one language. Being conversant in another language can also improve your negotiation skills when dealing with Spanish-speaking colleagues and business partners. Be well-prepared before you begin studying the grammar. It's necessary for people to realize that language, just like culture, can be learned and unlearned. Learning a new language can also boost your confidence, thus improving your self-esteem.

Spanish grammar needs to be mastered, as this makes your written Spanish look excellent and professional. Grammar also helps in sentence construction as you combine various words and phrases to form a sentence. Spanish grammar is, therefore, very crucial for anyone who intends to learn Spanish. Getting the right tutor can help a great deal in helping someone master the language. There are also keywords that can help you understand your progress. Spanish grammar also helps us learn and understand the different punctuation marks and how they're used. If we do not learn the grammar correctly, then the words we use may completely lack meaning. In fact, the words may even mean something completely different. All non-Spanish speakers who want to learn Spanish as a foreign language need to master the correct grammar and spelling.

The Spanish language is also very useful in doing business. The world is now like a global village. Spanish-speaking countries have become a big consumer market base. In order to tap this market, one needs to understand the language and culture of the people before they can persuade them to purchase their products. Successful business relations can only be achieved when people are able to communicate effectively and efficiently. If one is able to speak to the people, he or she may learn and understand their tastes and preferences. Consumers can sometimes be very hard to please, especially if there is a language barrier. Migration has also caused people to adopt the Spanish language. This can be seen when someone relocates to a place where people speak Spanish. Learning the language can facilitate trade and help people be more confident as they exchange goods and services.

They also say that love knows no bounds. In the current generation, intermarriages are very common. Being married to a Spanish-speaking spouse can spark Spanish language learning. There are people who learn the language from their spouses so they can speak with extended family members who may not speak English. It can be very frustrating, being in the midst of people who speak Spanish when you do not speak any Spanish yourself. The urge to learn often comes naturally if you surround yourself with the right people. These are the people who motivate you to learn and are encouraging when you make mistakes. Do not be discouraged when some of the people you started learning with get ahead of you. Some people are quick at grasping new languages, while others take a while longer. Verbs, in particular, can be confusing. In the midst of confusion, do not be discouraged. Instead, move on and continue learning. Learning a new concept is a process; it does not happen overnight. Be patient with yourself, accept the challenges you face, and face your fears with courage.

There are many Spanish dialects around the world. Know and understand the dialect that the Spanish speakers in your area speak. Notice the difference between the uses of accents. Do not rush to learn the spoken Spanish slang, but master the correct Spanish speech patterns. This is because, once you are exposed to the slang, you may not be able to control yourself and may find yourself unintentionally offending someone. Spanish slang also differs from one place to another, and is a non-official mode of communication. Communication in slang may also be more common among young people when compared to the elderly. Some of the slang words, when translated literally, can mean something odd.

There are so many ways you can learn Spanish quickly; for example, by listening to music, being in the company of children who speak Spanish, having daily interactions with native speakers, or using a language app. Daily practice will also help you learn faster and master the language with ease. Form your own group sessions that are mainly dedicated to learning Spanish. You can also set goals and reward yourself if you reach your goal. For example, you can decide to master up to 100 words and their meanings. If you reach your goal, treat yourself to ice cream or coffee. Choose rewards that can motivate you. Make your learning exciting by incorporating pieces of art like flashcards; you can use these cards anytime during your free time. You can also ask friends or family to hold them as you identify them. You can try downloading games in Spanish. There is nothing quite like playing games using a new language that you are learning. You can download an English to Spanish translator, or use the Google Translate website. Whatever you choose, make sure it best suits your interests and that it is readily available. For example, you cannot use Google Translate if you do not have access to the internet. Whatever you do, make sure that you have a schedule that works for you. While some people prefer to learn a new language on the weekends, others prefer to study during the week, when they can interact with more people.

Speaking the Spanish language is easier than writing it. This is because of some special characters present in some of the spelling. These can confuse someone, especially an English speaker who is just learning Spanish. For English speakers, there are no special characters in the English alphabet. This makes it hard for them to spell some Spanish words correctly since sometimes they omit the characters. Speaking enhances learning. Taking Spanish as a foreign language should also be a privilege that one should not miss. Human beings interact with each other every day. As we interact, we influence and empower one another. It can be possible to influence someone's thinking and mindset. This can be attained using open language, which can be persuasive, paying attention to each other, and enabling us to open our hearts to strangers whom we would never have met. Speaking not only facilitates interaction, but can also bring about peace, unity, and cohesion. This is not just among family, but among any group of people who share a common goal.

Culture defines people. It highlights their belief systems, language, food, and more. Language only cements the bond. A good example is a young person staying in the United States as a foreign student. Though this student may be able to grasp the American accent and speak almost like them culturally, he is not American. This is also used to describe why some people have been assimilated into the culture.

Know when, where, and how the accents are used. Be patient as you learn this, since it may be your gateway to fully understanding the culture. While others have mastered the art of using the accent of the residents of the area where they are, others still may speak Spanish with a lot of influence from more formal Spanish grammar. They may even be affected by their mother tongue. This can make some of their pronunciation different. Whether you decide to learn an accent or retain your original accent, being able to communicate is very important. Learning Spanish can change your accent in spoken English, as well. Be conscious of the people around you. These are people whom you interact with very frequently. They will be able to tell you honestly if everything is working as well as expected in areas that require interaction, especially if your Spanish is not yet good enough.

Making a list of things that one requires and need for the entire learning program is important, as well. This will make your transition from beginner to intermediate smooth and effective. Plan ahead, keeping in mind that you need to grow in your learning and mastery of the language. Be a role model, and always be ready to help and assist others whenever you can.

Being a model student is good, as well. Be inquisitive and ask questions. Don't let opportunities pass; through these events, others are shaping you for the future. In our day to day interactions, we come across some people who do not have any plan at all. Learning Spanish does not need to be hard and difficult. As you research on the easiest and fastest way to learn, be in control of your lessons and classes. Start with the simple and most commonly used words before you go to sentences. It is easier to master the short words, and then you can use the words to create simple sentences.

Basic learning of Spanish is just to ease your communication in the language and expose you to a new world of learning that you may not be used to. Spanish speakers sometimes omit some special characters, while those who speak a foreign language are keen on all characters. This can be attributed to the background where they came from. While the Spaniards gained early exposure to the language, the others learned it as a foreign language by struggling with the lessons. Spanish culture is full of love and romance. The culture also appreciates women and their contribution to development. Most people love Spanish love songs, and they can be used to serenade women. When you serenade someone, you can sing or pay people to sing for that someone on your behalf. These special moments make learning the language worthwhile. As you learn Spanish, you can sing a love song or any other song that motivates you and encourages you. Be intelligent in your thinking, and do not be misled to believe that all Spanish-speaking natives are good. Just like any other person across the world, there are positive and negative attributes. As we learn the culture and the language, we get assimilated into their way of doing things. Through this, we also appreciate structures set to keep us on our toes. There are also people who believe that through learning the language, they will get favor from the local administrators and residents.

Lastly, Spanish grammar should be used wherever you go. Develop an interest in whatever you are doing. Try to influence your community or church. Patience is a virtue, and if you want something, ask. Learning Spanish needs a lot of patience to grasp all the needed assignments. I hope the book helps you learn about nouns and pronouns. You will also see the different sentence formations and the use of nouns and pronouns. You will also be exposed to verbs, adjectives, and adverbs. From there, you will be able to go through them and understand them. Be present and learn the various uses of verbs, and find easy ways to learn Spanish verbs. These were very important as they introduce us to the world of learning Spanish and how it can influence our thinking. The basic Spanish vocabulary introduced in this book is really important in starting to learn the Spanish language. As we learn, we need to know that we are learning the language to grow and be more diverse. People who have learned at least one foreign language appreciate diversity more. They have also experienced and appreciated different cultures besides their own and are open-minded. They are risk-takers, and some of them have the adventure of traveling. Learning Spanish is a plus since knowing the language may be a bonus asset when traveling.

Quench your adventure by learning different Spanish words today. Start slowly but steadily, and be keen on your vocabulary memorization. You do not need experience in the language when visiting Spanish-speaking countries. You only need passion and zeal to travel and explore the world. Once you have mastered simple Spanish vocabulary, and you and passed intermediate school, be an instructor, too. You can teach others at home. Speak Spanish regularly as if it is your first language. If you meet native Spanish speakers, speak to them in Spanish. This will build your vocabulary and boost your confidence. Spanish is a language spoken by many people across the globe, and its first growth has sparked a lot of interest. The language, therefore, needs to be preserved and taught from one generation to the next.

For most folks, learning a language can seem like a daunting task. The main reason behind this lies in the fact that most folks are unfamiliar with the dynamic of learning a language. Consequently, they don't really know where to begin and how to make the most of their efforts.

Hence, many language learners tend to quit after a while because they can't seem to gain enough traction. This leads to frustration as struggling with a new language is never a pleasant experience. However, much of the frustration and struggles can be avoided by learning the ropes of how languages work.

The underpinnings of any language lie in the way the language is structured. In the case of Spanish, its basis lies in the conjugation of verbs. This means that you must become familiar with the various verb conjugations in order to fully understand how to structure the different verb tenses used throughout the language.

This can be a bit complicated with Romance languages. So, French, Spanish, Italian, Portuguese, and Romanian receive the denomination of "Romance" languages since they are mainly derived from Latin, which was the language of the old Roman Empire.

Over the centuries, each one of these languages has acquired its own nuances that make it unique. While they all have the same underpinnings, the visible surface can be quite different. Thus, it is important to get a firm understanding of how these languages work.

In this book, we will predominantly focus on the present tense as it is the most widely used tense in the Spanish language. Most Spanish speakers tend to use what are known as "simple" tenses since they tend to focus on just one tense at a time.

This is a stark contrast to the English language, as most English speakers are able to weave their way in and out of various verb tenses. This can make conversation rather complex, especially when topics warrant the use of several verb tenses.

In Spanish, the infinitive form of the verbs is defined by the ending of each verb. As such, there are three main forms in which infinitive verbs end. This is what will become the basis of the conjugation for each verb.

First, you will notice that there is a singular and a plural "you." In English, "you" is used to refer to both singular and plural nouns. So, "you are a teacher" and "you are teachers" use the same subject pronoun though its function is different.

Please note that English is an outlier in this regard as virtually all languages make a distinction between the singular and plural versions of "you." As such, it is important to keep this in mind as you navigate throughout the texts and conversations you find in Spanish.

You may also encounter "vosotros" as another plural version of "you." This form tends to be considered archaic in Latin America and is not used outside of Spain. You may hear Spaniards use this form, but you will almost never hear it used in Latin America.

Another important distinction between English and most other languages, especially Romance languages, is the use of the masculine and feminine for nouns. English is a gender-neutral language. What this means is that nouns do not receive a "male" or "female" denomination. Nouns are simply referred to in a single, genderless tone.

Spanish assigns a gender to all nouns. This might get a bit tricky as determining which nouns are masculine and which nouns are feminine can be tough. But rest assured that with practice and experience, you will be able to get a firm grasp on this.

Another fundamental difference between Romance languages and English is the various ways in which you can address a person. In Spanish, there are two main forms. The most common form is "tú." This form is an informal "you". It can be used to address people of a similar age, rank or friends, family, and other acquaintances with whom you have a high degree of familiarity.

In the case of "usted," this is the formal version of "you." This form is used to refer to people who are much older than you, have a higher rank, such as an employer, or people with whom you are not very familiar, for example, new acquaintances whom you've just met.

With these fundamentals in mind, let's take a look at learning strategies that you can use throughout this book.

Consistency is the biggest success factor you will encounter when learning a language. Regardless of whether you can devote 15 minutes or 2 hours a day, the most important thing to keep in mind is that a consistent amount of time dedicated to learning will go a long way.

In this regard, most folks "binge learn," that is, they will not touch their books for days and then spend hours on end trying to make up the time. Think about it along these lines: imagine you do not go to the gym for a week, and then you decide to spend 3 hours working out on a Saturday morning. What do you think the result of that would be?

The same principle applies to language learning.

Repetition is another success factor. When you go over your lessons multiple times, you will be able to better fixate information and knowledge into your mind. After all, humans are not built to learn things instantaneously. Humans need practice and repetition before they can master any skill. That same concept applies to language.

The more practice you get, the more your skills will improve.

Keep a learning diary. Keeping a learning diary or a log of your activities will help you visualize what you are doing to help yourself learn. In other words, you are keeping track of your language learning tasks. What this does is help you to see what works and doesn't. Later on, you can always refer back to those tasks that provide you with the most value and which ones don't.

Making handwritten notes will help fixate knowledge much better. Of course, using your phone, laptop, or tablet makes life a lot easier. However, making handwritten notes enables the brain to involve more senses in the learning process. As such, individual words and grammar will permeate your mind in such a way that the mechanics of grammar, word order, and spelling will become clear in your mind.

Use a tool such as www.spanishdict.com as a grammar and conjugation reference. In addition, this tool will provide you with the pronunciation of words. Consequently, you will have a tool that can support you when you are working on your own. Furthermore, it is a great study tool or just serve as a reference when you are curious about something related to your Spanish lessons.

Now, let's look at a suggested methodology which you can use to help you get the most out of this book. Of course, this is not the only way that you can take advantage of this material. Nevertheless, this methodology is designed to help you utilize the contents of this book to the fullest.

Firstly, read each story once, all the way through. At first, it will be hard to make sense of its contents. However, as you go through the story, you will see some words which resemble English words. These words, most of the time, will basically be the same English word. For example, "responsable" and "responsible" resemble each other almost identically. And yes, they have the same meaning. Consider this: "police" and "policía." It is practically the same word. So, you can highlight, or underline, these words and make a note of them.

Next, go through the text a second time. You will see your comprehension improving significantly. You will notice how similar-looking and sounding words make the text a lot easier to understand.

After, go through the text highlighting, or underlining, words that are completely unfamiliar to you. Hopefully, there won't be that many, but there will be some of these words. This will help you to visualize how much of the vocabulary is actually new to you.

Then, you can use a tool such as www.spanishdict.com or www.wordreference.com to help you find the meaning, pronunciation, and usage of these new vocabulary items.

Once you have found translations, synonyms, and equivalent meanings, you can then run through the entire text one more time. You will find that the text is now much more comprehensible than it once was. This will enable you to make greater sense of the content in each lesson.

After you feel comfortable with the language in the lesson, you can proceed to the questions located at the end of the lesson. The questions are intended to help you gain further practice in question formation, word order, and reading comprehension. The questions have been designed to be open-ended. As such, there is no single way of answering. Nevertheless, we have taken care to provide suggested responses in order to provide you with guidance.

Once you feel confident in answering each question, you go back and give the text one more run through. You can read the text aloud for further practice. If you are shy about your pronunciation, pick a time when you are alone and go through it.

If you so choose, you can use a tool such as the Text to Speech plugin for Google Chrome to read the text for you. This will give you a great sense of how the text is pronounced. As such, you will be able to hear the perfect pronunciation and thereby help you get the right pronunciation as well.

One good tip is to have a vocabulary notebook. You can use your learning journal to write down all of the vocabulary words which you encounter on a daily basis. What this enables you to do is to keep track of all the new words that you learn on a given day. Thus, the act of writing things down by hand will help to further fixate ideas in your mind.

Lastly, watching Spanish language content on television or online will also help you to practice your listening skills while allowing you to learn more vocabulary and grammar. So, do try to make the most of the opportunities around to improve your Spanish skills.

With these tips and strategies, you will be well on your way to improving your overall Spanish skills.

Common Problems When Learning Spanish

When English speakers go about learning Spanish, they will run into some essential differences that will be challenging at first but don't necessarily have to insurmountable. As such, it is important to understand these differences in order to make them more accessible to learners.

The first big difference is gender.

Gender tends to be one of the biggest sources of frustration for Spanish learners as there is no clear rule or guideline to determine which objects are masculine and which ones are feminine. The easiest way to identify gender among nouns is by observing the article that precedes it.

For example, "el" is used for masculine, and "la" is used for feminine. So, "el sol" (the sun) is masculine, whereas "la luna" is feminine. This is a good rule of thumb to follow when you are reading a text or simply hearing a regular conversation.

However, it gets tricky when you see or think of an object, but you are unaware of the article that precedes it. In this case, it can be tough to figure out the gender of an object. Since there really is no way to determine this just by looking at the object itself, there is one way in which you can figure this out: look at the object's name.

In general, the names of masculine nouns end in "o" and feminine nouns end in "a." This is a good rule of thumb to follow, as the endings will help you figure out their gender.

For instance, these are some examples of masculine nouns:

- Carro (car)
- Niño (boy)
- Palo (stick)
- Mono (monkey)
- Zapato (shoe)

As you can see, these nouns are all masculine, given their endings. Also, there are some exceptions that you can keep an eye out for. Nouns that end in "ma" and "pa" are masculine. For example, "mapa" (map) and "problema" (problem) are masculine.

There are also some other exceptions such as:

- Papel
- Hombre
- Doctor
- Autobus
- Atún

These nouns don't have a regular "o/a" ending, yet they are considered masculine.

Regarding feminine nouns, the general rule of thumb is that they end in an "a." Here are some examples:

- Cama (bed)
- Casa (house)
- Planta (plant)
- Mamá (mother)
- Hoja (leaf)

As you can see, these are feminine nouns based on the fact that they end in "a." However, there are some exceptions, as always. Nouns that end in "ión" such as "relación" (relation), "dad/tad" such as "amistad" (friendship), and "tud" such as "solicitud" (request) are considered feminine.

Also, another good rule of thumb is that nouns can be converted into feminine by adding an "a" to it. For instance, "doctor," which is masculine, can become feminine as "doctora." Also, "enfermero" (nurse, male) would become "enfermera" (nurse, female) by simply substituting the "o" for the "a" ending.

Also, there are a couple of interesting exceptions:

- La mano (hand) is feminine despite ending in an "o."
- La radio (the radio) is feminine despite ending in an "o."
- La noche (night) is also feminine.

Please keep in mind that Spanish always uses the articles "el" and "la" to precede a noun. Conversely, English does not use this form unless the speaker is specific about the noun in question.

With this guide, you can begin to navigate your way through the world of masculine and feminine nouns. As you gain more practice and experience, you will find that it is actually rather straightforward. So, do take the time to go over them.

Another area to take into consideration is verb conjugation.

Unlike English, Spanish has a specific verb conjugation for verbs based on the subject that it agrees with and the verb tense.

This is rather simple and straightforward in the English language as verb conjugation does not necessarily imply radically modifying the verb's structure. However, Spanish does require verb endings to be changed in accordance with the subject it agrees with. But fear not, we will make this very straightforward.

The first thing to look out for is the ending of the verb in its infinitive form. As stated earlier, the infinitive form of a verb is when it has not been conjugated to agree with a subject in a particular verb tense. As such, the infinitive form of the verb is key in order to determine how it will be conjugated.

Verbs in the infinitive form in Spanish will end in one of three ways: "ar," "er" and "ir." So, let's take a look at some examples of this:

Verbs ending in "ar"

- Estar (to be)
- Jugar (to play)
- Viajar (to travel)
- Cantar (to sing)
- Firmar (to sign)

Now, let's take a look at some verbs that end in "er":

- Resolver (to solve)
- Responder (to respond)

Here is a list of some verbs ending in "ir":

- Abrir (to open)
- Cubrir (to cover)
- Sentir (to feel)
- Vivir (to live)
- Fingir (to fake)

The above examples are a small sample size of the verbs which you will encounter throughout your study of the Spanish language. As such, let's take a look at how these verbs are conjugated in the present simple tense.

Here is a chart that explains the various endings for each subject and according to the verb ending.

Subject pronoun	AR	ER	IR
Yo (I)	o	o	o

Tú (you, singular)	as	es	es
Él (he)	a	e	e
Ella (she)	a	e	e
Nosotros (we)	amos	emos	imos
Ellos (they, masculine)	an	en	en
Ellas (they, feminine)	an	en	en
Ustedes (you, plural)	an	en	en

Figure 1. Verb endings in the present simple tense.

Another significant difference between English and Spanish is the use of subjects, or lack thereof, in sentences. In Spanish, it is quite common to omit the use of a subject at the beginning of a sentence, especially when it is clear who is being referred to in the conversation. As such, speakers will often take the liberty of omitting the subject using only the proper conjugation of the verb.

Needless to say, this can cause confusion even among native Spanish speakers. The reason for this is that unless there is a clear understanding of who is being referred to, it can be very difficult to keep track of a conversation.

Let's look at an example:

"Soy de los Estados Unidos"

(I am from the United States)

In this example, the use of the from "soy" (am) is the proper conjugation for the verb "ser" (to be) in the present simple tense. However, it is rather clear that "soy" refers to "I am." hence, a Spanish speaker would be more than willing to dump "yo" (I) given the fact that it is perfectly clear that this individual is referring to themselves.

So, do keep an eye out for this type of omission as you will frequently see it throughout the text presented in this book.

On the subject of the verb "ser," the Spanish language has two versions of the verb "to be." One is "ser," and the other is "estar." As such, let's take a look at their difference and their conjugation. In essence, the difference in "ser" and "estar" lies in the fact that "ser" refers to permanent or often unchangeable attributes, whereas "estar" refers to temporary or changeable characteristics.

For example, when referring to your occupation, you can say "soy abogado" (I am a lawyer). This makes it clear that your occupation is permanent and won't be changing any time soon. On the other hand, you can say "estoy feliz" (I am happy). This is a totally changeable proposition as your mood is far more changeable than your occupation.

In addition, please bear in mind that "estar" is the verb that is used with the present continuous. It serves as the auxiliary verb that provides the tense to the "ando" and "iendo" endings of the verbs that must be conjugated in order to make the present continuous.

Now, the present continuous is used in exactly the same fashion as it is in English; the present continuous is used to indicate when there is a temporary action either happening at the time of speaking or around the time of speaking. Thus, the most important element to consider is that the present continuous is a temporary action, whereas the present simple is used to indicate more permanent actions.

Let's take a look at an example:

"Estoy practicando español."

(I am practicing Spanish).

In this example, you are indicating an action that is happening at the time of speaking. That is, you are practicing Spanish at this very moment. Also, it can refer to an action that is happening around the present. For instance, you could be practicing your Spanish with other individuals though you are not practicing Spanish right at the moment of speaking.

The present continuous is constructed with the "estar" version of to be. Furthermore, the main verb is then modified to include the "ando" or "iendo" ending.

Let's take a look at how that works.

- "ar" verbs end in "ando"
- "er" verbs end in "iendo"
- "ir" verbs end in "iendo"

Here are some examples:

"Nosotros estamos jugando fútbol."

(We are playing soccer).

"Ustedes están comiendo carne."

(You are eating meat).

"Ella está viviendo en Buenos Aires."

(She is living in Buenos Aires).

Please notice how the main conjugation happens with the verb "estar" while the main verb is conjugated to the "ando" and "endo" form. It should be noted that this ending is not specific to the subject. The agreement with the subject occurs with "estar." Therefore, the main verb does need to be transformed to suit the individual subject in question. This makes it far easier to get a grasp on this tense as you won't have to conjugate each verb based on individual subjects.

With this, we have laid the groundwork for the content in this book. We are now ready to move on to the short stories prepared for your study. Please keep in mind that nothing is ever cast in stone when it comes to language. Nevertheless, the patterns which we have laid out herein will provide you with a good head start when it comes to improving your Spanish skills.

Chapter 2: Chronological Order In Learning the Spanish Language

The following phrases and words are elementary to those who are experts in the Spanish language. But to beginners, these are important words to know because, without them, it is difficult to start a conversation with friends.

(Las siguientes frases y palabras son elementales para los expertos en lengua española. Pero para los principiantes, estas son palabras importantes para saber porque sin ellas es difícil comenzar una conversación con amigos.)

Spanish Language	English Language	Sentence Use
Hola	Hi or hello!	S: Hola, ¡Bienvenido a nuestra casa! E: Hello, welcome to our house!
Buenos días	Good morning	S: ¡Solo vine a decir buenos días! E: I just came to say good morning.
Buenos tardes	Good afternoon	S: ¡Buenas tardes! ¿Cuál es tu almuerzo para hoy? E: Good afternoon! What is your lunch for today?

Buenas noches	Good evening/Good night	S: ¡Ya me voy a dormir! ¡Buenas noches a todos!
		E: I am going to sleep already! Goodnight everyone!
¿Cómo está usted? ¿Cómo estas? (informal)	How are you?	S: Hace tiempo que no te veo. ¿Cómo está usted?
		E: I have not seen you for a while. How are you?
Muy bien	Very well	S: Mi vida esta muy bien por ahora.
		E: My life is very well for now.
Me llamo	My name is…	S: ¿Sabes como me llamo?
		E: Do you know what my name is?
Por favor	Please	S: Por favor, prestame tus oídos, necesito que escuches lo que voy a decir.
		E: Please lend me your ears, I need

		you to listen to what I am going to say.
¿Qué hora tienes? ¿Qué hora es?	What time is it?	S: Le pregunté a mi hermano qué hora es, y él respondió a las 4:00 PM. E: I asked my brother what it was, and he answered 4:00 PM.
¡Perdóneme!	Excuse me!	S: ¡Perdóneme! Yo no comí tu pastel. E: Excuse me! I did not eat your cake!

After learning the basics of the Spanish language, the next thing that must be learned is the list of things to consider:

(Después de aprender los conceptos básicos en español, lo siguiente que debe aprender es la lista de cosas a considerar).

- Since everyone's time is precious, consider making a very good schedule or calendar of activities. (Dado que el tiempo de todos es valioso, considere hacer un muy buen horario o calendario de actividades.)

- Spare a little time off every day and allot it to your Spanish Language learning. (Ahorre un poco de tiempo todos los días y asígnelo a su aprendizaje del idioma español).

- Consider what time of the day to prepare, learn, and improve one's Spanish. (Considere esa hora del día para prepararse, aprender y mejorar el idioma español.)

- Watch/repeat movies and TV shows which the learner has already watched in the past. (Mire/repita películas y programas de televisión que el alumno ya ha visto en el pasado).

When the learner has already learned the basics of Spanish, then he/she must consider this tip. Because the learner has already finished watching that particular movie or TV show, then he/she must repeat watching it, but he/she must change the language setting and do not read the subtitle.

(Cuando el alumno ya ha aprendido lo básico del idioma español, debe considerar este consejo. Debido a que el alumno ya ha terminado de ver esa película o programa de televisión en particular, debe repetir la reproducción, pero debe cambiar la configuración del idioma y no leer el subtítulo.)

Use cellular phone applications in learning new or additional Spanish vocabulary.

(Usar aplicaciones en el celular para aprender vocabulario español nuevo o adicional.)

The learner must, at all times, consider each day as a part of the learning process. The use of handy gadgets like cellphones is one of the effective ways of learning new Spanish vocabulary.

(El alumno debe considerar en todo momento cada día como un proceso de aprendizaje. El uso de dispositivos útiles como teléfonos celulares es una de las formas efectivas de aprender vocabulario nuevo en español.)

Take Spanish classes.

Here, the learner may consider enrolling in actual Spanish classes or even online Spanish classes.

(Toma clases de español.

Aquí, el alumno puede considerar inscribirse en clases reales de español o incluso en clases de español en línea.)

Don'ts of the Spanish language

On the other hand, there are things that must be considered once the learner is only a beginner in the learning process: (Por otro lado, hay cosas que deben considerarse una vez que el alumno es solo un principiante en el proceso de aprendizaje:)

Set a Very High Goal to Be Inspired in Learning the Language

That is not advisable, more particularly if the learner is only a beginner. What must be instilled into the minds of the learner is a reasonable goal to reach, not a very high goal to be inspired. Inspiration is good, but it must not be too high that the learner will find it very difficult to achieve.

In setting a deadline, it must also be reasonable. Do not make a deadline that is too short of achieving. Always remember that for beginners, the more the time that is given, the more he/she is to learn about the things that one must know in the language.

(Establezca un objetivo muy alto para inspirarse en el aprendizaje del idioma.

Eso no es aconsejable más particularmente si el alumno es solo un principiante. Lo que debe inculcarse en las mentes del alumno es un objetivo razonable para alcanzarlo, no uno muy alto para inspirarse. La inspiración es buena, pero no debe ser demasiado alta para que el alumno tenga dificultades para lograrla.

Al establecer una fecha límite, también debe ser razonable. No establezca un plazo que sea demasiado corto para cumplir. Siempre recuerde que para los principiantes, cuanto más tiempo se les de, más aprenderán sobre las cosas que uno debe saber en el idioma.)

Be Sure of Everything. Do Not Allow the Learner to Make a Mistake

This is not true. Everybody makes mistakes. People are not perfect, and once the mistake is made, it must be corrected. Being afraid of making mistakes only has a possible outcome, and that is a refusal to learn.

For instance, the learner is struggling to pronounce a certain word. He must not be discouraged because it does not mean he cannot do it through constant practice and repetition.

(Asegúrate de todo. No permitas que el alumno se equivoque.

Esto no es verdad. Todos cometen errores. Las personas no son perfectas, y una vez que se comete el error, debe corregirse. Tener miedo de cometer errores solo tiene un resultado posible, y eso es negarse a aprender.

Por ejemplo, el alumno tiene dificultades para pronunciar una palabra determinada. No debe desanimarse porque no significa que no pueda hacerlo a través de la práctica y la repetición constantes.)

Chapter 3: Progress of Learning the Spanish Language

During the first day of Spanish Language learning, the learner, which is presumed to be a beginner, is considered as a "scavenger" of words to be placed inside the bucket of vocabulary. As to the purpose of this phase, the learner is expected to collect a lot of Spanish words and phrases that he may use in the coming future.

(Durante el primer día de aprendizaje del idioma español, el alumno, que se presume que es un principiante, es considerado como un "buscador" de palabras para poner dentro del cubo del vocabulario. En cuanto al propósito de esta fase, se espera que el alumno recopile muchas palabras y frases en español que pueda usar en el futuro.)

The best way to start is to think that he/she is going to say a lot about himself or herself. At the end of Day 1, the learner must already be able to supplement answers in the Spanish language to these questions, like:

- What is my name?
- Where do I live?
- What is my hobby?
- What is the nature of my work?
- Where is my workplace?

(La mejor manera de comenzar es pensar que va a presentar mucho sobre sí mismo. Al final del día 1, el alumno ya debe ser capaz de complementar las respuestas en español a estas preguntas como:

- ¿Cuál es mi nombre?
- ¿Dónde vivo?
- ¿Cuál es mi pasatiempo?
- ¿Cuál es la naturaleza de mi trabajo?
- ¿Dónde está mi lugar de trabajo?)

It is best to learn through the use of a phrasebook. The benefit of using a phrasebook is the correct pronunciation. For instance, the learner is not quite sure of the correct pronunciation of words and phrases stated in the phrasebook, then he/she can call a Spanish-speaking friend and clarify or double check it for him/her. While seeking answers to your queries, get a pen and book and state in there all the answers.

(Es mejor aprender a través del uso del libro de frases. El beneficio de usar el libro de frases es la pronunciación correcta. Por ejemplo, el alumno no está seguro de la pronunciación correcta de las palabras y frases que figuran en el libro de frases, puede llamar a un amigo que hable español y aclare o vuelva a verificarlo. Mientras busca respuestas a sus consultas, obtenga un bolígrafo y un libro e indique todas las respuestas.)

You need to continue visiting and reading your phrasebook daily. That is one effective way of exposing your attention to the Spanish language, and slowly, you will realize that your tongue has already adapted to the language. Then the next thing that you need to do is a combination of those words. Again, try to do this daily. As you go along, you will be able to practice the word combination. Finally, use the phrasebook if you want to converse with your friend. At first, you may open it while talking to them, however, as time passes by, you will find yourself being independent of the book already.

(Debe continuar visitando y leyendo su libro de frases a diario. Esa es una forma efectiva de exponer su atención al idioma español, y lentamente se dará cuenta de que su lengua ya se ha adaptado al idioma. Luego, lo siguiente que debe hacer es la combinación de esas palabras. Nuevamente, intente hacer esto diariamente. A medida que avance, podrá practicar la combinación de palabras. Finalmente, use el libro de frases si desea conversar con su amigo. Al principio, puede abrirlo mientras habla con ellos, sin embargo, a medida que pasa el tiempo, ya se encontrará independiente del libro.)

There is one challenge to be done at the end of the week. It is difficult, but you need to do it in order to check if you have learned something for the past first week of learning Spanish. You need to find a native Spanish person whom you are going to talk to. It is difficult, challenging, and scary but you need to do it. You may use chatting via Skype or Facetime if you are not confident to talk to that person in person. Another step is talking to a native Spanish person via phone call. You need to be confident speaking Spanish because you have learned enough with this method of learning. If you are already confident with your Spanish Language, you can already initiate talking to a native Spanish speaker in person.

(Hay un desafío por hacer al final de la semana. Es difícil, pero debe hacerlo para verificar si ha aprendido algo durante la última semana de aprendizaje del idioma español. Necesita encontrar una persona española nativa con quien va a hablar. Es difícil, desafiante y aterrador, pero debes hacerlo. Puede usar el chat a través de Skype o Facetime si no está seguro de hablar con esa persona en persona. Otro paso es hablar con una persona española nativa a través de una llamada telefónica. Debe estar seguro al hablar español porque ha aprendido lo suficiente con este método de aprendizaje. Si ya tiene confianza en su idioma español, ya puede comenzar a hablar con un nativo en persona.)

If you are already done with the previous step, it is recommended to look for a Spanish Language Teacher, whom you may converse with. It is recommended because the teacher will tell you if you are right or wrong. However, in cases like this, it is believed that the teacher is always pricey. It is better if you will pay a considerable price because the teacher will be a patient one if you do. If you just ask him or her to teach you without any payment, you cannot expect a patient teacher who will understand your slow Spanish. You will never forget talking to a real person as you practice your Spanish.

(Si ya ha terminado con el paso anterior, se recomienda buscar un profesor de español, con el que pueda conversar. Se recomienda porque el maestro le dirá si tiene razón o no. Sin embargo, en casos como este, se cree que el maestro siempre es caro. Es mejor si pagará un precio considerable porque el maestro será paciente si lo hace. Si solo le pide que le enseñe sin ningún precio, no puede exigir un maestro paciente que entienda su lenta habilidad para hablar español. Nunca olvidará hablar con una persona real mientras practica su habilidad en el idioma español.)

During week number 2, you must no longer use your phrasebook. The reason is that it is only applicable for use during the first week of the learning process. The use of flashcards is the next thing that will work for your learning progress. It will be very useful in memorizing if you use flashcards instead of a phrasebook. If you are financially able, you may consider an app, which prompts if you tend to forget the vocabulary you have previously memorized.

From week number 3 onwards, you must be able to talk to a Spanish person about a topic or two. Since then, you can be able to assess yourself regarding the progress of your Spanish. Just continue to practice and go back to your learnings in order not to forget the vocabulary.

(A partir de la semana número 3 en adelante, debe poder hablar con una persona española sobre un tema o dos. Desde entonces, puede evaluarse a sí mismo con respecto al progreso de su aprendizaje del idioma español. Simplemente continúe practicando y vuelva a sus aprendizajes para no olvidar el vocabulario.)

Chapter 4: the Use of Numbers, Colors, Time and Feelings

Counting in Spanish

This is where you learn all about numbers and how to count in Spanish. Numbers are used to refer to time, to amounts, to numbers, dates, years, etc. Here we will cover ordinal and cardinal numbers and how they are used in the Spanish language:

Number	Cardinal	Ordinal
0	cero	
1	un, uno /-a	primer, primero /-a
2	dos	segundo /-a
3	tres	tercer, tercero /-a
4	cuatro	cuarto /-a
5	cinco	quinto /-a
6	seis	sexto /-a
7	siete	séptimo /-a

8	ocho	octavo /-a
9	nueve	noveno /-a
10	diez	décimo /-a
11	once	undécimo /-a
12	doce	duodécimo /-a
13	trece	decimotercero /-a
14	catorce	decimocuarto /-a
15	quince	decimoquinto /-a
16	dieciséis	decimosexto /-a
17	diecisiete	decimoséptimo /-a
18	dieciocho	decimoctavo /-a
19	diecinueve	decimonoveno /-a
20	veinte	vigésimo /-a
21	veintiuno /-a	vigésimo -a primero -a

30	treinta	trigésimo /-a
31	treinta y uno /-a	trigésimo -a primero -a
40	cuarenta	cuadragésimo /-a
50	cincuenta	quincuagésimo /-a
60	sesenta	sexagésimo /-a
70	setenta	septuagésimo /-a
80	ochenta	octogésimo /-a
90	noventa	nonagésimo /-a
100	cien	centésimo /-a
101	ciento /-a uno /-a	centésimo -a primero -a
110	ciento /-a diez	centésimo -a décimo -a
120	ciento /-a veinte	centésimo /-a vigésimo /-a
200	doscientos /-as	ducentésimo /-a

300	trescientos /-as	tricentésimo /-a
400	cuatrocientos /-as	cuadringentésimo /-a
500	quinientos /-as	quingentésimo /-a
600	seiscientos /-as	sexcentésimo /-a
700	setecientos /-as	septingentésimo /-a
800	ochocientos /-as	octingentésimo /-a
900	novecientos /-as	noningentésimo /-a
1000	mil	milésimo /-a
1100	mil ciento /-a	milésimo /-a centésimo /-a
2000	dos mil	dosmilésimo /-a
2001	dos mil uno /-a	dosmilésimo -a primero -a
1.000.000	millón	millonésimo /-a

2.000.000   dos millones   dosmillonésimo
                                    /-a

Describing With Colors

Next, we have colors. One very important note about colors is that, like all adjectives, colors are subject to the masculine-feminine agreement, as well as singular and plural agreement. This means that you need to make sure that the color agrees with the subject you are talking about.

By default, colors are masculine. But when they agree with a feminine subject, their spelling changes. For example, "vestido rosado" (pink dress) refers to a masculine noun (vestido). So, "rosado" is spelled with an "o" ending. In the case of a feminine noun, "camisa rosada" (pink shirt), "camisa" is considered feminine. As such, "rosada" now has an "a" ending in order to signal that it is feminine and not masculine.

The situation changes somewhat when you factor in singular and plural. So, "vestidos rosados" (pink dresses) agrees both in terms of gender and number. The "s" ending indicates that it is plural. In the case of "camisas rosadas," the same situation applies.

Notice also that both the adjective and noun must be singular or plural in order to maintain the proper agreement.

There are a couple of exceptions, though. Azul, gris, verde, and marrón do not change in terms of gender but do agree in terms of number. So, "botas grises" (grey boots), where "botas" is feminine plural, would be the same as "coches grises" (grey cars), where "coches" is masculine plural.

Please keep this in mind, as there are exceptions from time to time. Bear in mind that virtually all adjectives in Spanish have a singular and plural form, even if they are considered uncountable in English. For instance, "un pan" (a bread) may refer to individual unit of bread in Spanish, where "bread" is uncountable in English.

Also, in Spanish, adjectives come after nouns. So, "cielo azul" (blue sky) is the opposite of the proper English syntax. Please keep this in mind so that you can avoid confusing your interlocutors when speaking.

Telling the Time

Time is a rather straightforward topic in Spanish. However, there are a couple of differences.

For starters, time is generally based on a 24-hour clock rather than two, 12-hour clocks. So, the morning hours are expressed from "cero horas" (zero hours, or midnight) to "doce horas" (twelve hours, or midday). After midday, time is expressed as "trece horas" (thirteen hours), all the way up to "veinticuatro horas" or midnight. Once the new day begins, time is then reset to "zero hours." This distinction is made in order to avoid confusion between am and pm times.

For instance, if you have an appointment at 7 O'clock in the evening, you could express it at "diecinueve horas en punto" (nineteen hours "on point"). The expression, "on point" is used to indicate that it is the beginning of the hour or "o'clock" in English.

It is also possible to express time on a 12-hour basis. However, it is important to include the specific time of day you are referring to. So, "ten o'clock in the morning" would be "diez de la mañana." Afternoon hours would be referred to as "de la tarde." For instance, "cinco de la tarde" (17:00 or 5 pm) is referring to a time that is past midday.

Now, here is an interesting difference between English and Spanish. Spanish does not account for "evening." As a matter of fact, as soon as the sun goes down and it gets dark, the time then becomes "noche" or night. So, "seis de la tarde" would be "six in the afternoon" since the sun doesn't typically finish setting by this time. However, "siete de la noche" (seven at night) would be logical since it is normal for it to be dark around this time. So, the rule of thumb is that as soon as it is completely dark, you can begin to use "night."

This also applies to greetings, like "goodnight" or "buenas noches," which is the applicable greeting whenever it is completely dark. However, if there is still a twinge of sunlight, then it would still be proper to use "buenas tardes" (good afternoon).

Fractional portions of hours also have their own particular expressions.

- "Cuarto" refers to "quarter." So, "es un cuarto después de las dos" (it's a quarter past two) refers to 2:15. "Un cuarto para las dos," (a quater to two) refers to 1:45. Please notice the difference in the use of "después" (after) and "para" (to) when referring to time.

- Also, the use of "media" (half) makes it clear that you are talking about half hours. So, "son las tres y media" (It is three and a half) is the same as saying "half past," or 30 minutes past the hour.

- Other fractional hours can be expressed using the exact number of minutes. So, "es la una y venticinco" (it's one twenty-five) refers to 1:25.

- Please note that hours are always expressed in the plural form, except for one. Hours are feminine, but minutes are masculine. Nevertheless, your expression of time will always make reference to the feminine form and not the masculine form.

When in doubt, you can always refer to time by expressing the numbers themselves. For example, you can say, "son las cuatro y cinco" (it's four and five), that is, 4:05. You will not be questioned if you are referring to am or pm when giving the current time, but you might be asked to clarify if you are referring to a future time. So, be sure to use "de la mañana," "de la tarde," or "de la noche" in order to clarify the time of day you are referring to.

Now, let us move on to the days of the week.

- lunes (Monday)
- martes (Tuesday)
- miércoles (Wednesday)
- jueves (Thursday)
- viernes (Friday)
- sábado (Saturday)

- domingo (Sunday)

Please note that the days of the week are not capitalized in Spanish.

Also, here are the months of the year.

- enero (January)
- febrero (February)
- marzo (March)
- abril (April)
- mayo (May)
- junio (June)
- july (Julio)
- agosto (August)
- septiembre (September)
- octubre (October)
- noviembre (November)
- diciembre (December)

Just like the days of the week, months are not written with capital letters. So, a formal date such as "lunes, tres de septiembre" (Monday, September third) would not be expressed in capital letters. Also, please note that dates are written out in nominal numbers and not in ordinal numbers like in English.

With regard to years, there is no split between the digits of a year. For example, the year "2010" would be "dos mil diez," that is, "two thousand ten." So, keep this in mind any time you are talking about a year.

Here are some examples:

- 1991 (mil novecientos noventa y uno – one thousand nine hundred and ninety-one)
- 2002 (dos mil dos – two thousand two)
- 1885 (mil ochocientos ochenta y cinco – one thousand eight hundred and eighty-five)

Keep this important difference in mind when talking about years.

Expressing Feelings

Generally speaking, feelings are adjectives, which agree in gender and number. This implies that you need to be aware if you are talking about yourself or others in the singular and/or plural form.

As such, a question such as "¿Cómo estás?" (how are you?) can be replied with:

- Estoy bien. (I am fine)
- Estoy cansado/a (I am tired)
- Estoy feliz (I am happy)

Notice how "feliz" does not have a gender agreement but would have a plural agreement as "feliz" (singular) and "felices" (happy in plural form).

Chapter 5: Spanish Language Quirks

Like any language, Spanish has its quirks and foibles, but it's very straightforward in a lot of ways, so these quirks shouldn't present you with too many problems. And there certainly are not so many as you find in the English language. It's not essential to learn about them, but just being aware of them will help you to become more proficient in the language and help you to sound more like a local.

Apocopation

Apocopation is the practice of shortening some adjectives whenever they precede masculine nouns. Other than a few exceptions, apocopation never happens with feminine nouns, so as a quirky way to remind yourself when to apocopate, just say to yourself, 'Cut a bit off the male.'

You may even have been apocopating without even realizing what you were doing. For example, if you go out for a snack at lunchtime, you may well ask for 'un bocadillo.' On the other hand, if you want to eat more healthily, you may order 'una ensalada.' The masculine 'uno' (meaning one) is the most common example of apocopation, and if you speak a little Spanish each day, you're almost certain to have used it in its shortened form.

This is Spanish we're learning, so there is always something that goes against the rules and is different. Where apocopation is concerned, it's the word 'santo,' which means 'saint.' This is only shortened when it precedes certain proper nouns, but not those beginning with 'Do' or

'To.' So to be correct, you'd say 'San Juan,' and 'Santo Tomas.'

As a matter of fact, as you get used to the flow of the Spanish language, you'll find yourself automatically apocopating, simply because it sounds better as you speak. If you don't apocopate, nobody will die, so don't worry too much. However, if you do, you'll sound more like the native speakers, and ultimately, that's what you're aiming for.

Comparatives and Superlatives

Making comparisons in Spanish is very different from the English way. In English, you'd simply say 'big, bigger, biggest,' where big is the standard adjective, bigger is a comparative, and biggest is the superlative. However, it doesn't work that way in Spanish.

Taking grande (big) as an example to compare like for like, there is no equivalent in Spanish of the -er and -est comparative and superlative. Instead, the language makes use of the words más (more) and menos (less). So, bigger is más grande (literally more big), and biggest is el más grande. (The more big, literally, which sounds rather odd to English or American ears, but makes perfect sense to Spanish speakers).

While you're not likely to use superlatives all that often, you could find yourself using comparatives more frequently than you might expect. For example, when shopping for clothing and shoes, you might need to ask for a smaller or larger size in something. Here are a couple of examples to illustrate comparatives in action.

"¿Tienes esta falda en una talla más pequeña?"

(Do you have this skirt in a smaller size?)

"Quiero una talla más grande, por favor."

(I would like a larger size, please.)

Notice the word order – the noun (size) precedes the adjective (smaller/larger).

Another example of the use of comparatives is when saying one person is older or younger than another. The Spanish words for young and old are joven and viejo/vieja respectively. You may think 'más joven' is younger, and 'más viejo' is older, based on what you've just learned about Spanish comparatives, and while that is understandable, it's also wrong!

There are special comparative expressions for 'younger' and 'older', and they are 'menor que' and 'mayor que,' meaning 'younger than' and 'older than' respectively. Here are a couple of examples.

"Maria es menor que su hermano."

(Maria is younger than her brother).

"Juan es mayor que Pedro"

(Juan is older than Pedro.)

Take some time to construct a few sentences using 'menor que' and 'mayor que,' using members of your family and friends – it's great practice, and it will help you to familiarize yourself with these comparatives.

The Spanish words for best and worst are 'mejor' and 'peor.' There's nothing quirky about that, but there is a slight difference in the way they work in speech and writing. As you surely know by now, in Spanish, the adjective follows the noun.

This is not the case with mejor and peor. For example, if you are describing a shirt by color, you would say 'Mi camisa roja.' (My red shirt). However, if you were talking about your best shirt, you would say, 'Mi mejor camisa.' Here's how mejor and peor work in sentences.

"Maria es la mejor estudiante en la clase."

(Maria is the best student in the class).

"Es la peor excusa de todas."

(That is the worst excuse of all).

"Las mejores cosas en la vida son gratis."

(The best things in life are free).

"Él es el peor doctor en el hospital."

(He is the worst doctor in the hospital).

Mejor and peor can also be preceded by 'lo' to mean 'the best/worst thing,' without the need to use the noun 'cosa.

Chapter 6: Restaurant — Restaurante

cubiertos *(koo-byehr-tohs)* Masculine noun - silverware

>En los restaurantes, es importante la higiene de los cubiertos.

>In restaurants, the hygiene of cutlery is important.

mesero *(meh-seh-roh)* Masculine or feminine noun - waiter

>Los meseros son una parte fundamental en los restaurantes.

>The waiters are a fundamental part of the restaurants.

mesa *(meh-sah)* Feminine noun - table

>Las mesas deben estar impecables y correctamente adornadas con manteles.

>The tables should be impeccable and properly decorated with tablecloths.

chef *(shehf)* Masculine or feminine noun - chef

>El chef es el maestro de cocina que se encarga de elaborar los platos especiales.

>The chef is the master of the kitchen and is responsible for preparing the special dishes.

menú *(meh-noo)* Masculine noun - menu

>El menú en un restaurante debe ser diverso, claro, comprensible, y bien presentado.

> The menu in a restaurant must be understood easily and presented well.

cocina *(koh-see-nah)* Feminine noun - kitchen

> La cocina de un restaurante debe estar en buen estado y siempre limpia.
>
> The kitchen of a restaurant must be in good condition and always clean.

nevera *(neh-beh-rah)* Feminine noun - refrigerator

> Es necesario que los restaurantes tengan una nevera suficientemente amplia y bien abastecida.
>
> It is necessary that restaurants have a sufficiently large and well-stocked fridge.

plato *(plah-toh)* Masculine noun - plate

> Los platos no solo deben estar limpios, también los debe haber de todos los tamaños.
>
> The dishes must not only be clean, but they must also be of all sizes.

despensa *(dehs-pehn-sah)* Feminine noun - pantry

> La despensa de los restaurantes contiene los insumos y víveres necesarios.
>
> The restaurant's pantry contains the necessary supplies and provisions.

ayudante de cocina *(ah-yoo-dahn-teh deh koh-see-nah)* Masculine or feminine noun - kitchen assistant

Los ayudantes de cocina son los que apoyan al chef en todo momento.

The kitchen assistants are the ones who support the chef at all times.

cuchara *(koo-chah-rah)* Feminine noun - spoon

La cuchara estaba tan sucia que parecía el dedo de un mono.

The spoon was so dirty; it looked like a monkey's finger.

cuchillo *(koo-chee-yoh)* Masculine noun - knife

El cuchillo lo afilaron tanto que podías cortar las pezuñas de un rinoceronte.

The knife was sharpened so much that you could cut the hooves of a rhinoceros.

tenedor *(teh-neh-dohr)* Masculine noun - fork

La cocina estaba equipada con todo pero no tenía ni un solo tenedor.

The kitchen was equipped with everything but did not have a single fork.

vaso *(bah-soh)* Masculine noun - cup, glass

Se cortó la mano con el vaso de vidrio que se cayó de la despensa.

He cut his hand with the glass tumbler that fell from the pantry.

cuenco *(kwehng-koh)* Masculine noun - bowl

El cuenco se desbordó de agua y todo el piso quedó mojado.

The bowl overflowed with water, and the entire floor became wet.

servilleta *(sehr-bee-yeh-tah)* Feminine noun - napkin

Le gustaba dibujar, pintar y hacer garabatos en las servilletas.

He liked to draw, paint, and doodle on the napkins.

aperitivo *(ah-peh-ree-tee-boh)* Masculine noun - appetizer

Los aperitivos tienen la función de abrir el apetito.

The appetizers have the function of creating the appetite.

desayuno *(dehs-ah-yoo-noh)* Masculine noun - breakfast

El desayuno es la comida más importante del día.

Breakfast is the most important meal of the day.

postre *(pohs-treh)* Masculine noun - dessert

Hay gente que de verdad no se le debería permitir comer el postre.

There are people who really should not be allowed to eat dessert.

cena *(seh-nah)* Feminine noun - dinner

La cena debe ser ligera, sencilla, y humilde para no tener el sueño pesado.

> Dinner should be light, simple, and humble so as not to have a heavy sleep.

almuerzo *(ahl-mwehr-soh)* Masculine noun - lunch

> Muchas personas prefieren almorzar en la calle que en sus casas.
>
> Many people prefer to have lunch on the street rather than in their homes.

plato principal *(plah-toh preen-see-pahl)* Masculine noun - main dish

> La mayoría de las veces el plato principal no es tan bueno como el aperitivo.
>
> Most of the time, the main course is not as good as the appetizer.

You will always want to be able to ask for what you want to eat or drink in a restaurant. Start each sentence with:

Quiero – I want (kee ayr oh)

Quisiera – I would like (kee say ayr oh)

And don't forget your please (por favor) and thank you (gracias).

Spanish	English	pronunciation
Una mesa	a table	*oona may sah*

Una mesa para dos	a table for two	*oona may sah pah rah dohss*
Un menu	a menu	*oona may noo*
Sopa	soup	*soh pah*
Ensalada	salad	*ayn sah lah dah*
Hamburguesa	hamburger	*ahm boor gay sah*
Con salsa de tomate	with ketchup	*cohn sahl sah day toh mah tay*
Con salsa de mostaza	with mustard	*cohn sahl sah day mohs tah sah*
Con tomate	with tomato	*cohn toh mah tay*
Con lechuga	with lettuce	*cohn lay choo gah*
Una entrada	an appetizer	*oona ayn trah dah*
Un postre	dessert	*oon pohs tray*
Una bebida	a drink	*oona bay bee dah*
Cerveza	beer	*sayr vay sah*
Un café	coffee	*oon cah fay*

La cuenta the check *lah cwayn tah*

Chapter 7: Professions — Profesiones

bombero *(bohm-beh-roh)* Masculine or feminine noun - firefighter

> Los bomberos no siempre apagan el fuego, también rescatan gatos.
>
> Firefighters do not always put out the fires; they also rescue cats.

mecánico *(meh-kah-nee-koh)* Masculine or feminine noun - mechanic

> El mecánico estuvo seis horas revisando el motor de ese auto.
>
> The mechanic spent six hours checking the engine of that car.

médico *(meh-dee-koh)* Masculine or feminine noun - doctor

> El médico le dijo a su paciente que debía reposar por dos semanas.
>
> The doctor told his patient that he should rest for two weeks.

boxeador *(bohk-seh-ah-dohr)* Masculine or feminine noun - boxer

> Los boxeadores entrenan muy duro y cuidan su salud para estar en forma.
>
> Boxers train very hard and take care of their health to be fit.

abogado *(ah-boh-gah-doh)* Masculine or feminine noun - lawyer

> El abogado tuvo que investigar el caso a fondo durante ocho meses.
>
> The lawyer had to investigate the case thoroughly for eight months.

veterinario *(beh-teh-ree-nah-ryoh)* Masculine or feminine noun - veterinarian

> Ese veterinario les salvó la vida a seis animales en un día.
>
> That veterinarian saved six animals in one day.

arquitecto *(ahr-kee-tehk-toh)* Masculine or feminine noun - architect

> Se necesitaron cuatro arquitectos para revisar los planos de ese centro comercial.
>
> It took four architects to review the plans for that mall.

dentista *(dehn-tees-tah)* Masculine or feminine noun - dentist

> El dentista asistió a la conferencia de odontología que se realizó en Italia.
>
> The dentist attended the conference of dentistry that was held in Italy.

astronauta *(ahs-troh-now-tah)* Masculine or feminine noun - astronaut

> Los astronautas pasaron cinco meses reparando la estación espacial de Marte.

>The astronauts spent five months repairing the space station on Mars.

músico *(moo-see-koh)* Masculine or feminine noun - musician

>Los músicos de la banda se fueron de gira por Latinoamérica.

>The musicians of the band went on tour in Latin America.

periodista *(peh-ryoh-dees-tah)* Masculine or feminine noun - journalist

>El periodista recibió el premio Pulitzer por su reportaje sobre los emigrantes.

>The journalist received the Pulitzer Prize for his report on emigrants.

carpintero *(kahr-peen-teh-roh)* Masculine or feminine noun - carpenter

>Al carpintero le encargaron fabricar tres camas, dos sillas, y una mesa grande.

>The carpenter was commissioned to make three beds, two chairs, and a large table.

escritor *(ehs-kree-tohr)* Masculine or feminine noun - writer

>El escritor terminó de escribir su última novela y la entregó a tiempo a su editorial.

>The writer finished writing his latest novel and delivered it on time to his publisher.

actor *(ahk-duhr)* Masculine or feminine noun - actor

> El discurso de aceptación del actor en la ceremonia de entrega de los premios Oscar fue muy emotivo.
>
> The acceptance speech of the actor in the Oscar awards ceremony was very emotional.

científico *(syehn-tee-fee-koh)* Masculine or feminine noun - scientist

> La sociedad científica le otorgó el máximo galardón al científico por sus aportes a la humanidad.
>
> The scientific society gave the highest award to the scientist for his contributions to humanity.

cocinero *(koh-see-neh-roh)* Masculine or feminine noun - cook

> Para la fiesta de fin de año contrataron a los mejores cocineros del país.
>
> For the end-of-the-year party, they hired the best chefs in the country.

chofer *(choh-fehr)* Masculine or feminine noun - chauffeur

> El chofer manejó durante 14 horas seguidas, demostrando resistencia y control.
>
> The driver drove for 14 straight hours, demonstrating resistance and control.

piloto *(pee-loh-toh)* Masculine or feminine noun - pilot

> Los pilotos de aviación comercial tienen una gran responsabilidad para sus pasajeros.
>
> Commercial aviation pilots have a great deal of responsibility for their passengers.

agricultor *(ah-gree-kool-tohr)* Masculine or feminine noun - farmer

> El trabajo del agricultor es muy importante porque sin campo no hay ciudad.
>
> The work of the farmer is very important because, without a field, there is no city.

docente *(doh-sehn-teh)* Masculine or feminine noun - teacher

> Los docentes son responsables de la educación de las generaciones futuras.
>
> Teachers are responsible for the education of future generations.

camionero *(kah-myoh-neh-roh)* Masculine or feminine noun - truck driver

> Los camioneros son las personas que comen más comida chatarra en todo el mundo.
>
> Truck drivers are the people who eat the most junk food in the whole world.

enfermero *(ehm-fehr-meh-roh)* Masculine or feminine noun - nurse

> El enfermero es a veces mucho más importante que el doctor y trabaja más.
>
> The nurse is sometimes much more important than the doctor and works harder.

farmacéutico *(fahr-mah-seyoo-tee-koh)* Masculine noun - pharmacist

>Un farmacéutico es una persona sin escrúpulos que negocia la salud de la gente.
>
>A pharmacist is an unscrupulous person who negotiates the health of people.

juez *(hwehs)* Masculine or feminine noun - judge

>Es casi ciencia ficción decir que existe un juez que no sea corrupto.
>
>It is almost science fiction to say that there is a judge who is not corrupt.

padre *(pah-dreh)* Masculine noun - priest

>Ser padre de oficio significa explicar con fe lo que él mismo no entiende ni practica.
>
>Being a father by trade means explaining with faith what he does not understand or practice.

Chapter 8: Traveling – Viajes

transporte *(trahns-pohr-teh)* Masculine noun - transportation

> El transporte es cómo se transfieren los objetos y las personas.
>
> Transportation is how objects and people are transferred.

transporte terrestre *(trahns-pohr-teh teh-rrehs-treh)* Masculine noun - land transport

> El transporte terrestre es el que se realiza sobre ruedas como automóviles y motocicletas.
>
> Land transport is carried out on wheels like cars and motorcycles.

señales de tránsito *(see-nyal-ehs deh trahn-see-toh)* Plural noun - road signs

> Las señales de tránsito son los signos usados en la vía pública para dar la información correcta.
>
> Traffic signs are the signs used on public roads to give the correct information.

carreteras *(kah-rreh-teh-rah)* Feminine noun - highway

> Una carretera es una ruta de dominio y uso público construida para el movimiento de vehículos.
>
> A highway is a route of the domain and public use built for the movement of vehicles.

autopistas *(ow-toh-pees-tah)* Feminine noun - freeway

Las autopistas son aquellas que son rápidas, seguras y con un gran volumen de tráfico.

The highways are those that are fast, safe, and contain a large volume of traffic.

autobús *(ow-toh-boos)* Masculine noun - bus

El autobús es un vehículo diseñado para transportar numerosas personas por las vías urbanas.

The bus is a vehicle designed to transport many people through urban roads.

taxi *(tahk-si)* Masculine noun - taxi

Ese taxi tenía una tarifa muy alta y preferí hacer el viaje en autobús.

That taxi had a very high fare, and I preferred to take a bus trip.

tren *(trehn)* Masculine noun - train

Este tren es uno de los más rápidos del mundo y las tarifas son económicas.

This train is one of the fastest in the world, and the fees are cheap.

metro *(meh-troh)* Masculine noun - metro

Las grandes ciudades prefieren el metro subterráneo como opción de transporte.

Large cities prefer the underground metro as a transportation option.

motocicleta *(moh-toh-see-kleh-tah)* Feminine noun - motorcycle

> Las motocicletas son el medio de transporte ideal para evitar el tráfico.
>
> Motorcycles are the ideal means of transport to avoid traffic.

carro *(kah-rroh)* Masculine noun - car

> El carro del vecino tenía fallas en el motor y el parachoques roto.
>
> The neighbor's car had a broken engine and bumper.

bicicleta *(bee-see-kleh-tah)* Feminine noun - bicycle

> La bicicleta es un transporte ecológico y a la vez deportivo.
>
> The bicycle is an ecological and sporty transport at the same time.

bote *(boh-teh)* Masculine noun - boat

> Todos los fines de semana llevó a mis hijos a pasear en bote.
>
> Every weekend, he took my children for a boat ride.

ciclomotor *(see-cloh-moh-tohr)* Masculine noun - moped

> Prefiero el ciclomotor porque es mucho más rápido y seguro. I prefer the moped because it is much faster and safer.

Chapter 9: Yes, No, Please, Thanks: Basic Vocabulary

Along with the basic vocabulary that you learned in the last lesson, these are also some basic words you need to know to get by: yes, no, please, thanks.

- Yes – sí.
- No – no.
- Please – por favor.
- Thanks – gracias.

Now that you know how to say these four words, you can travel in a Spanish-speaking country without being considered rude.

Let's see a few other expressions and words that might turn out useful in case you want to make a really good impression:

- Sorry – perdón
- I am sorry – lo siento / lo lamento
- Excuse me – disculpe
- Thanks – gracias
- Thank you very much – muchas gracias
- You are welcome – de nada
- Never mind – no hay por qué

- It is fine – está bien
- Of course – por supuesto
- Of course not – por supuesto que no
- Absolutely – absolutamente
- Not at all – para nada
- For sure – sin lugar a duda / por supuesto / pero claro
- Let's use all of these in sentences:
- Yes, I also need a ticket – Sí, yo también necesito un billete
- No, I don't eat meat – No, no como carne
- Please, could you point me to the train station? – Por favor, ¿podría indicarme dónde está la estación de trenes?
- Thanks, you are very kind – Gracias, eres muy amable
- Sorry, I did not see you there – Perdón, no te vi ahí
- I am sorry, I do not have any cash on me – Lo lamento, no tengo nada de efectivo conmigo
- Excuse me, do you work here? – Disculpe, ¿usted trabaja aquí?
- Thanks, but that is not necessary – Gracias, pero eso no es necesario

- Thank you very much! It is delicious! – ¡Muchas gracias! ¡Está delicioso!

- You are welcome, I also have extra water, just in case – De nada, también tengo agua de más por si acaso

- Never mind, you would have done it for me too – No hay por qué, tú también lo habrías hecho por mí

- It is fine; I do not need anything – Está bien; no necesito nada

- Of course I want to go – Claro que quiero ir

- Of course not, that was not me – Claro que no, ese no fui yo

- Absolutely, I will be there at 7 – Absolutamente, voy a estar ahí a las 7

- Not at all, it was not trouble for me – Para nada, no fue ningún problema

- For sure, tell me what you need, and I will bring it – Por supuesto, dime qué necesitas, y yo te lo traigo

Now, let's take a look at this conversation:

When James gets back from the beach, he sees Andrea at the hostel reception:

JAMES: Excuse me, Andrea, may I ask you a question?

Disculpa, Andrea, ¿puedo hacerte una pregunta?

ANDREA: Of course, James! Whatever you need.

¡Claro, James! Lo que necesites.

JAMES: Thank you.

Gracias.

ANDREA: Don't worry, tell me

No hay de qué, dime,

JAMES: I am really sorry, but I lost my map

Lo siento mucho, pero he perdido mi mapa

ANDREA: Don't worry! We have millions

¡No te preocupes! Tenemos millones

JAMES: Are you sure?

¿Estás segura?

ANDREA: For sure, yes. Here, take one.

Por supuesto, sí. Aquí, toma uno.

JAMES: Thanks a lot, Andrea, you are the best!

Muchas gracias, Andrea, ¡eres la mejor!

ANDREA: Yes, I know!

Sí, ¡lo sé!

What's Happening? The Present Tense (Part I)

This is not meant to be a boring grammar book, so you won't be driven crazy with conjugation rules that you need to learn by heart. However, what will be explained in this lesson might actually turn to be quite useful to understand why verbs are conjugated the way they are. There is no need to memorize this, but it will inevitably happen once you start learning more and more verbs.

Some of the verbs before were irregular verbs. This means they don't follow the normal rules of conjugation. This is why a verb like ser (to be) can be conjugated into words that sound nothing like ser: eres (you are), for example—it is completely irregular. Now, luckily for you, most verbs in Spanish are actually regular. This means they follow three basic models of conjugation, depending on whether they end on -ar, -er, or -ir.

Regular verbs that end in -ar always follow the same structure and add the same letters after the 'root' of the verb. You can find the root of a verb easily. Just take -ar, -er or -ir off it in its infinitive form, and you will have the root. For the verb amar (to love), for example, the root is am-.

Amar **(to love):** yo amo tú amas / vos amás / usted ama él/ella ama / nosotros amamos / ustedes aman / vosotros amáis / ellos/ellas aman

Regular verbs that end in -er also follow the same structure and add the same letters after the root of the verb, as in the following example. For the verb temer (to fear), the root is tem-.

Temer **(to fear)** yo temo tú temes / vos temés / usted teme él/ella teme / nosotros tememos / ustedes temen / vosotros teméis / ellos/ellas temen

Regular verbs that end in -ir also follow the same structure and add the same letters after the root of the verb, as in the following example. For the verb vivir (to live), the root is viv-.

Vivir **(to live)** yo vivo / tú vives / vos vivís / usted vive él/ella vive / nosotros vivimos / ustedes viven / vosotros vivís / ellos/ellas viven

As you can see, in all cases, for the singular first-person, yo, you just need to add an o to the root of the verb: Caminar (to walk): I walk in the park – Yo camino en el parque Beber (to drink): I only drink beer – Solo bebo cerveza Partir (to leave): I leave tomorrow morning – Yo parto mañana por la mañana.

For tú, you just add -as or -es: Extrañar (to miss): Do you miss your sister? – ¿Extrañas a tu hermana?

Creer (to believe): You do not believe in magic – No crees en la magia Abrir (to open): Do you open the door? – ¿Abres la puerta?

For él or ella, you, as in English, normally add an s. In Spanish, you just have to add an a or e: Escribir (to write): She never writes – Ella nunca escribe Hablar (to talk): He talks too much – Él habla demasiado Vender (to sell): She sells her soul for a snack – Ella vende su alma por un bocadillo

For nosotros, you add either -amos, -emos or -imos: Alquilar (to rent): We rent the same apartment every year – Todos los años alquilamos el mismo piso Aprender (to learn): We never learn! – ¡Nunca aprendemos!

Asistir (to attend): Tonight we attend the party no matter what – Hoy asistimos a la fiesta de cualquier forma

For vosotros, you have to add -áis, -éis or -ís: Ayudar (to help): Why don't you help with the cleaning? – ¿Por qué no ayudáis con la limpieza?

Leer (to read): You read all day – Leéis todo el día Compartir (to share): You share everything you do on social media – Compartís todo lo que hacéis en redes sociales

Finally, for ellos, ellas, and ustedes, you have to add -an or -en to the root of the verb: Cocinar (to cook): They cook every night – Cocinan todas las noches Responder (to answer): You always answer late – Ustedes siempre responden tarde Decidir (to decide): They decide what to do with their lives – Ellas deciden qué hacer con sus vidas.

Now, let's take a look at this conversation:

James and Alex want to surprise the girls. They are cooking dinner for everybody! They are in the hostel's kitchen making some risotto with vegetables and seafood:

ALEX: How lucky you are here! I cook very bad

¡Qué suerte que estás aquí! Yo cocino muy mal.

JAMES: Do you think I am a chef or something like that? I'm not so good.

¿Crees que soy un chef o algo así? No soy tan bueno.

ALEX: We help each other.

Nos ayudamos el uno al otro.

JAMES: I learn a few things about rice while we do this.

Aprendo algunas cosas sobre el arroz mientras lo hacemos.
ALEX: Like what?

¿Qué aprendes?

JAMES: That it gets done faster while I drink beer.

Que se cocina más rápido cuando bebo cerveza.

ALEX: I miss Australian beer!

¡Extraño la cerveza australiana!

JAMES: There is a bar nearby where they sell Foster's.

Hay un bar cerca de aquí donde venden Foster's.

ALEX: Really? I'm leaving right now

¿De veras? Parto ahora mismo

JAMES: No way! You help me until we are done and after dinner, I will take you there.
¡De ningún modo! Me ayudas hasta que terminemos y después de cenar te llevo.

What's Happening?: The Present Tense (Part II)

There is another way to talk about things that are actually happening right now.

The construction of the present conjugation of verb estar + the gerund of another verb is very similar to the English present continuous: I am cooking, I am talking, I am walking.

While the English gerund always ends with -ing, the Spanish gerund ends in -ando or -endo.

Cocinar **(To cook)** yo estoy cocinando / tú estás cocinando / vos estás cocinando / usted está cocinando él/ella está cocinando / nosotros estamos cocinando / ustedes están cocinando / vosotros estáis cocinando / ellos/ellas están cocinando

Beber **(to drink)** yo estoy bebiendo / tú estás bebiendo / vos estás bebiendo / usted está bebiendo / él/ella está bebiendo / nosotros estamos bebiendo / ustedes están bebiendo / vosotros estáis bebiendo ellos/ellas están bebiendo

Escribir **(to write)** yo estoy escribiendo / tú estás escribiendo / vos estás escribiendo / usted está escribiendo / él/ella está escribiendo / nosotros estamos escribiendo / ustedes están escribiendo / vosotros estáis escribiendo / ellos/ellas están escribiendo.

These are some sentences with verb estar + gerund that you might use a lot while traveling:

- I am traveling – Estoy viajando.
- I am getting to know Spain – Estoy conociendo España.
- I am learning Spanish – Estoy aprendiendo español.
- I am taking a year off – Me estoy tomando un año sabático.
- I am falling in love with this country – Me estoy enamorando de este país.

You might use this construction a lot while making plans:

- I am leaving – Me estoy yendo (yendo is the gerund of verb ir, to go).
- I am going to your hotel – Estoy yendo a tu hotel.
- I am coming – Estoy llegando.
- Juan is calling a taxi – Juan está llamando un taxi.
- The food is arriving – La comida está llegando.

You can definitely use estar + gerund to talk about your life at present:

- I am working for a company – Estoy trabajando en una empresa.
- I am studying in university – Estoy estudiando en la universidad.
- I am saving money to travel some more – Estoy ahorrando para viajar más.
- I am thinking about quitting my job – Estoy pensando en renunciar.

Now, let's take a look at this conversation:

James and Alex's meal is ready, but the girls are nowhere to be seen:

JAMES: Do you think they are coming?

¿Crees que están viniendo?

ALEX: I don't know. I'm texting María.

No lo sé. Estoy escribiendo un mensaje a María.

MARÍA: Who are you texting?

¿A quién estás escribiendo?

JAMES: Girls! You are here!

¡Chicas! ¡Estáis aquí!

ANDREA: Yes, and we are starving.

Sí, nos estamos muriendo de hambre.

ALEX: That is great because we are waiting for you with a surprise.

Eso es genial, porque las estamos esperando con una sorpresa. ALICIA: Is that a risotto or am I hallucinating?

¿Eso es un risotto o estoy alucinando?

ALEX AND JAMES: Surprise!

¡Sorpresa!

Here are some other examples of this construction:

- Verb to buy – comprar: I am buying a surfboard – Estoy comprando una tabla de surf.
- Verb to travel – viajar: You are traveling a lot – Estás viajando mucho.
- Verb to book – reservar: We are booking a room – Estamos reservando una habitación
- Verb to talk – hablar: They are talking – Ellos están hablando.

Chapter 10: Practice Makes Perfect

We've established that you will need to create a learning program for yourself that includes immersion into both the Spanish language and culture. You already know that you should read, write, and speak Spanish every day to keep yourself on pace to meet your deadline. At this point, you should focus on getting to a point where you can communicate effectively. Be sure to break out of the self-imposed isolation that is common when studying Spanish. Once you've built up an arsenal of common and personalized phrases, it's time to practice them in the real world! If you haven't located a Spanish language partner, you'll want to find someone fast.

Practicing your Spanish will improve your functional ability to use the skills you've learned so far. Interacting with native Spanish speakers regularly can improve your new language skills dramatically. You'll hear authentic pronunciations, expansive vocabularies, and accurate grammar. Finding a consistent language partner can help you to avoid getting discouraged by not finding informational content that's exactly at your pace since you'll be able to communicate with them if something is too easy or advanced.

Traditional Methods of Practice

If you already know any Spanish speakers, reach out to them directly and ask if they would be able to go over a few things with you. Set up a video chat date with them once or twice a month, or if they are local, meet up for coffee. Being able to speak with a native Spanish speaker in person is best.

You may not know anyone personally that speaks Spanish, but there are plenty of other ways to practice. For example, there are lots of people online that you can have anything—from quick chats to full-length discussions with—entirely in Spanish. There are websites dedicated to helping you break down the barriers that typically prevent people from really understanding Spanish.

Language Exchange

In addition to typical language partners, there are Language Exchange opportunities as well. A language exchange partner is what it exactly sounds like. These are people looking for someone to practice English with, and they can be super helpful with your Spanish. You might be able to find an exchange partner that will work with you one-on-one in exchange for your help. Be sure to set up a defined time-frame for your conversations and work on English half of that time, and the other half in Spanish. There are language exchange boards and forums all over the world that you can search for. Some people will be upfront with what they need help with and how much of a time commitment they are able to dedicate. Make a post yourself and let prospective language exchange partners know what you'd like to work on and your availability.

Ask a Stranger

Don't be afraid to talk to strangers and try and grow a thick skin. If you hear people talking Spanish when you're out and about, be brave enough to ask them for the time or even directions. Chances are most people are more than happy to answer your question. It's quite possible that they will respond to you quickly and that you may not understand; don't worry, and don't get defensive! Getting defensive is way more likely to make the exchange uncomfortable than simple Spanish slip-ups. Just tell them that you're new to Spanish and ask if they can repeat what they said slowly or help you understand what they meant. While this can be a difficult thing to ask of strangers, it's a great way to get out of your comfort zone, and once you've been corrected in a real-world scenario, the chances that you'll remember the correct words for next time are very high.

Unconventional Approaches

Call Restaurants and Bakeries

There are plenty of unconventional approaches to practicing your Spanish as well. Make a list of Mexican or any Spanish speaking restaurants anywhere in the country. For example, you can call them and ask if you would need to make a reservation if you have a group of 7 people wanting to dine next weekend on Saturday at around 7:30 p.m. Have a script prepared for yourself before you call. Be sure to greet the person and then follow your script. There are a few different ways that you can ask this, so have those options ready to go and try them out on different phone calls. If they don't speak Spanish, simply move on to another number. Mix up the number of people on the reservation, the day, and the time that you're asking about. You could even actually make a reservation and then call back later that day or week and cancel it. You could also simply call to ask what hours they are open, or if they have vegetarian options. Another great way to get real-world practice is to look up Latin grocery stores or bakeries in your area. You could make up a scenario where you call or go in and ask if they make custom birthday cakes and get pricing and details.

Get On the Phone

Try calling 1-800 numbers that have Spanish menus. Look up numbers for banks, airlines, internet providers, or any company you assume would have Spanish speaking clientele. Again, have a scenario picked out, or if you're feeling bold, improvise something based on the menu options. Before going into a call, pretend that while you may just be learning Spanish, your native language isn't English. "Lo siento, no hablo ingles" (I'm sorry, I don't speak English) will help them continue to attempt communication with you in Spanish. Some companies have an online option for a live chat. This can be a great way to practice both writing and reading.

Take It to the Kitchen

If you like to cook, you can find plenty of Spanish cookbooks that will test out your reading comprehension and give your palate a new way to branch out. Watch a Spanish cooking show and attempt to recreate a dish you are interested in. You can search for recipes in Spanish by dish, or find a recipe you love and translate it yourself. Make a list of items you need and go to a Hispanic grocery store so that you can reinforce the language you're learning. When you're preparing the meal, read every step out loud so that you can get verbal practice.

Help Others

Volunteer organizations hold opportunities to interact with Spanish speakers as well. Perform a quick search for organizations that are active in your community and find out what kind of help they're looking for where you may get exposure to Spanish speakers. Some excellent volunteer programs focus on improving language skills while volunteering time towards a good cause. Make a few calls and ask the organizers if they are familiar with anything in line with your needs. Of course, giving back to underprivileged people in your community can be an advantageous experience in and of itself.

Remember to keep things light-hearted and fun. If you can learn to relax and go with the flow, you will naturally fall into the rhythm of the Spanish language. Commit to getting the most out of every opportunity you must practice, and you'll move from beginner to intermediate and to advanced in no time.

Chapter 11: Learn Spanish Vocabulary Efficiently

The format of this book has been thoughtfully set up with the beginner Spanish student in mind. It does not matter how young or old you are. There are always benefits to expanding your mind by broadening your experiences.

Firstly, you made the right choice in learning Spanish through reading short stories as it is proven to help you understand a new language more quickly as you are learning about words within context. Many make the mistake of simply learning grammar and vocabulary solely, which leads the student not to be able to hold a conversation fully.

When you are reading the story, you will be able to memorize and learn different phrases in which you can use in conversations. In fact, there are phrases in the vocabulary at the end of each story to help you learn the most important phrases. As mentioned in each chapter, it is extremely helpful to focus on the vocabulary and repeat the words and phrases until they are imprinted in your memory.

Another helpful tip is to focus on the main concepts of the stories, which will help you to learn the rest of the vocabulary due to context. This is also a great way to learn new words as you continue to read other Spanish books, which may be more advanced. If it helps you out, underline phrases and sentences you have issues with, so you can focus on these until you become more comfortable. Be sure to read when you are able to concentrate and not be interrupted.

For each of the words in the chapters about vocabulary, there is a pronunciation guide for each word and phrase, and it will indicate what type of word it is, such as masculine or feminine. The verbs which will be able to be conjugated are those which are defined as an example "to read" rather than "he or she reads." This shows it is the original form of the verb, which in turn will be conjugated depending on the subject.

There are words that have several meanings within Spanish, so pay attention to the surrounding words to ensure you are using the word in the correct context.

Afterward, you can test your comprehension of the story.

Learn Spanish More Quickly

It does not have to be difficult to learn a new language. When you set your mind to do something with determination, then it is possible to learn Spanish rather quickly. There are some methods you can use that will make learning Spanish easier for you. Again, age does not factor in this fact. The main key to learning any new concept is that you need to use and practice the language as much as possible.

There is strength in numbers when it comes to learning something new. Take the resources that you have at hand at the moment. Utilize the internet to search online for free or cheap practice sessions online or meeting in person at a neutral location with a native speaker. This will help you to understand their particular dialect, which will also help you learn Spanish more quickly, but the teacher will be able to correct your mistakes in real-time. They will also be a brilliant support system when they praise your correct pronunciation.

There are usually also local groups or online meetups which will practice a range of languages, including Spanish. This goes along the same lines as meeting with a native speaker. When you take the opportunity to speak the language, not only does it stick in your head more quickly, but you will also learn more vocabulary as well as make some new friends who can all become a support system. Of course, anyway that you can make learning a new language fun is a plus!

Another way to use the internet to learn Spanish is to search for Spanish videos or movies which subtitles as needed. When you tune your ear to listen to Spanish being spoken in the native tongue, it will help you to be able to converse with people who are from Spanish speaking countries. The bottom line with the videos is to find something which interests you so that you are more engaged. As you continue with your practices, put the Spanish subtitles onto your English speaking videos. That way, you can read what is going on in Spanish as you are listening to the audio in English.

Music is also an excellent teacher. Find some music that you really enjoy, which is sung in Spanish. Many older Spanish ballads are a good place to start if you have no idea. As with the videos, as long as you have an interest, this will get you more involved in listening and singing along to the lyrics as you create a connection with the music.

If you find that you do not have so much time to dedicate to learning and scheduling appointments with people, you can also use some methods within the comfort of your home. One way is to buy some index cards to create your own flashcards for Spanish. Simply write down the phrases or words in Spanish on one side. Then flip over the card and write down the English translation. It is also helpful to write down a sentence in context, which will help you also to learn entire sentences rather than just words.

The flashcard system is extremely helpful when it comes to learning the conjugated forms of the verbs. This system is also an aid because you are able to take the cards wherever you go so that you can study them any time you are just sitting around.

Another useful tool to use around your house or even your work in some situations is to use sticky notes to write the Spanish word on items around. This is very helpful for those who are visual learners. This is an engaging way to use the Spanish language, and it will skyrocket your learning when you are surrounding yourself with the language. Remember that practice makes perfect, and if you can incorporate Spanish more deeply into your daily life, you will learn much more quickly.

If you have a favorite Mexican restaurant, try to order your meal the best that you can in Spanish, even if you do not know all the words. Many times, people of other cultures will appreciate that you are trying to speak their language. If you continue to explain that you are learning Spanish, they may also help by speaking in Spanish with you as the meal goes along. Spanish speaking people like to help others learn their language.

Even though it is a bit of a leap, travel to a Spanish speaking country to immerse yourself more in the language. Not only will you learn to listen to several different dialects, but you will also likely find a teacher at every turn. Again, the Spanish speaking people are always helpful if you are putting in an effort to speak their language. When you are listening to Spanish speaking people, you will pick up on key phrases and words much more quickly as well.

Many people have smartphones, they are always looking for an easy app to use. These apps are usually free and are convenient and easy, as phones are quite common in today's society. Consider downloading a Spanish language learning application that will act as a supplement to this book. Not only will you broaden your language with more vocabulary, but you will also be able to converse much more easily with more words to choose from.

As you download the Spanish language application, consider also downloading an English-Spanish dictionary. This will come in handy if you are curious as to what something is called in Spanish. You can quickly use the dictionary to continue to solidify your Spanish vocabulary. You can do this anytime and anywhere, be it your house, the office, or out with your friends.

Above all, have fun with learning Spanish. It does not have to be a chore. Be sure not to get discouraged and continue to find new ways to incorporate the Spanish language into your day. Before long, speaking Spanish will become second nature, and it will be even more engaging and fun, especially when you are able to share it with your family, friends, coworkers, and business associates.

Chapter 12: Benefits of Learning Spanish

Ever wondered why you should take the challenge head-on and concentrate on learning Spanish? Having an excellent command of Spanish comes along with a bag of goodies. Here are several advantages of gaining Spanish knowledge

Benefits for the General Audience

- It introduces you to the world. Imagine being able to understand all those Spanish movies on cable TV or your favorite channel. Learning Spanish opens up new learning avenues where you will gain access to immense knowledge concerning life; for instance, you would be able to easily consume content found in Spanish books written by highly rated authors. Books that are in their original form provide more insight, unlike translated versions. Besides this, you will enjoy music from Spanish artists with comparative ease.

- Moreover, life can become easy when touring in overseas countries. Being able to understand the basic expressions and phrases will not only make your life more comfortable within the initial weeks and months but will also reduce your anxiety levels in case of any emergency. Apart from that, having the ability to give your cab driver the direction to your home and be able to offer him the correct sum of money without any assistance would also be an excellent experience.

- It provides you with employment opportunities. Understanding and speaking Spanish fluently gives you a chance to interact with more people than you had in your life. Therefore, you will become a potential asset for any employer who wishes to expand his business to international standards.

- What is more, this language is one of the six languages recognized by the United States and is the third most utilized language in the media, which increases the possibility of you being employed. Businesses are picking up everywhere, and the primary language used is Spanish.

- Therefore, to increase your chances of becoming employed at any of these businesses or companies, an understanding of Spanish puts you ahead of the competition. Besides, in most cases, it is used to advertise current job opportunities; therefore, understanding it allows you to pitch jobs.

- Also, bilinguals earn up to 30 percent bonus salary compared to monolingual counterparts. For companies that mostly deal with international customers, bilingual workers are much appreciated.

- It makes your travels and adventures enjoyable. Due to its global popularity, studying Spanish can be a worthwhile endeavor. It will enable you to easily interact with the folks from these countries while traveling there. In doing so, you gain lots of experience and knowledge from the people you interact with. Lastly, you get can definitely have a lovely time while crisscrossing these countries.

- Moreover, enjoy speaking out fluent Spanish when touring the most beautiful Spanish destinations. Such include Costa Rica, Mexico, Argentina, and Peru, among others. Besides this, it makes you a confident traveler in these countries. For instance, imagine yourself pitching a business deal in Mexico City using an English presentation while the rest speak in Spanish. After finishing your performance, you might also not be able to socialize around, and the locals might also avoid interacting with you. Another way of warming yourself to your prospective clients would be interacting with them in their language. Therefore, excellent knowledge of Spanish will enable you to win their hearts and, in the long run, make a successful business with them.

- Also, relocating to other countries becomes comfortable with the knowledge of the language. Apart from that, businesses that plan to expand to overseas markets are on a constant lookout for bilingual employees who are compensated well.

- The lack of knowledge concerning the local language of the place you are going to visit handicaps you in a way since you would experience a communication breakdown, which might not be fun after all or might end up on a bad note.

- It maintains a healthy mind. When practicing a new activity that you have never done before, your mind and body perform some form of exercise. Studying a new language such as Spanish causes a similar action. The importance of such exercises is to keep your brain at its best and also helps eliminate some issues such as the decline in the mental abilities of a person. Scientists, on their part, have discovered that people with reduced brain activities have a high chance of developing conditions such as Alzheimer's. To minimize such occurrences on your part, you can choose to learn a language such as Spanish to improve your brain activity; thus maintaining it at a tip-top condition. Besides, it was identified that bilinguals had more advanced brain functions as a result of learning more than one language. Lastly, the acquiescence of a new language enlarges your language faculties. It, thereby, increases your hippocampus volumes. The same increases the size of the cortical. This would protect your brain from adversaries such as diseases and injuries.

- Makes you a better person. Having an in-depth knowledge of a second language like Spanish broadens your knowledge concerning other people's culture, values, likes, and dislikes, among other things. These will enable you to empathize with them in times of trouble and need and be able to read cues easily. Also, being bilingual can improve your mind theory and perception; both of which are necessary emotional and social skills.

- It will make you appreciate the pop industry.

- Currently, top acts in the pop industry enlisting the Spanish language. Therefore, fluency in it will provide you access to top-notch entertainment. A lot of modern creatives have taken the dance floor by storm; for instance, it wouldn't be hard for you to hear some Pitbull music chiming from speakers in a club. Also, big restaurants and brands such as Wal-Mart and Taco Bell are not being left behind by the craze. They, too, have infused some Spanish words in their welcoming comments to attract Hispanic clients. Therefore, if you need employment from such brands or just needed marvel at the Spanish pop-ups in these facilities, then I guess that you need to put on the work boots and get it going.

- It can act as occupational therapy. Though learning a new language can be beneficial to all ages, it can be particularly helpful to the elderly, who, in most cases, have free time at their disposal. Not only can learning a new language help eliminate cognitive decline but it will also help in the development of mnemonic devices, study strategies, and other resources. Apart from that, it adds emotion to the senior citizens' lives as the challenge of learning a new language comes along with its expectations. Also, the prospects of meeting new people, traveling to new destinations, and studying new cultures can bring excitement into one's life.

- It can help you form a new romantic relationship. Being a popular language across the globe, Spanish can help you in finding a partner. Therefore, you can make efforts to learn Spanish if it interests you.

Benefits for Students

If you are a student, learning Spanish provides you with several advantages that include the following:

- There is an increased chance of getting into your desired college. Several universities require those entering their institution to have the ability to speak more than a single dialect. The same applies to everyone who wants to join before enrolling. Other programs, like postgraduate courses, require fluency in a specific dialect since relevant research might not be published in English. Knowing a second language can provide you with a competitive edge during the admission process.

- It allows you to make new friends. One of the best strategies for acquiring new friends is studying a new language. During the process of learning the skill, you will find tons of resources on the internet and offline sources. You can make friends with those you are sharing the resources with, both online and offline by having conversations concerning your shared interest in the Spanish culture and language.

- You have an increased chance of getting a scholarship to study abroad. Becoming bilingual can immensely increase the chances of you winning an award to go and study abroad. An ability to speak Spanish fluently paves the way for study opportunities at some well-known universities in Latin America. Also, students with a fluent level of Spanish are allowed to join undergraduate and graduate programs in any Spanish-speaking nations.

- Moreover, students can engage themselves in local traditions and cultures.

- It sharpens one's cognitive skills. According to a study done by a student, the study of a language increases the scores of grad and college school exams. People who have the ability to communicate using more than one language portray cognitive development in their various aspects of life. Such areas include mental flexibility, creativity, reasoning, and problem-solving. Also, studying a new language creates new neural formations in the brain and creates new connections that were not there before. Additionally, their encounter with different cultures makes them accept the diverse customs and way of life. These improve their ability to interact with people from diverse backgrounds.

Chapter 13: Basic Conversational Phrases

There are some phrases that you should know in any language. You can imagine yourself using them in real-life situations. The first will be some types of introductions. This will be useful when you have your first conversation in Spanish.

- ¡Hola! ¿Cómo te llama? – "Hello, What is your name?"
- ¿De dónde eres? – "Where are you from?"
- ¿Cómo estás? – "How are you?"
- Yo estoy bien. – "I am good."
- Por favor. – "Please."
- De nada. – "You're welcome."
- Gracias – "Thank you."

Focus on pronunciation when you speak. The better the pronunciation, the more you will sound like a native speaker.

Next, you can learn the following phrases…

- Repita por favor – "Please repeat that."
- Yo entiendo. /Yo no entiendo. – "I understand."/"I do not understand."
- ¿Qué es eso? – "What is that?"
- Yo necesito. – "I need."

- Ayúdame por favor. – "Please help me."

These phrases are useful when describing things or needing help. They can be helpful in your first conversations with other speakers.

Next, let's try these other phrases.

- ¿Por qué este? – "Why this?"
- ¿Está bien? - "Is it good?"
- ¿Cuál es? – "Which one is it?"
- ¿Cuándo llegas? – "When will you arrive?"
- ¿Cuánto cuesta? – "How much is this?"
- ¿Cuántos hay aqui? – "How many are here?"
- Yo quiero eso/esa – "I want this."(masculine/feminine)
- ¿Tú sabes? – "Do you know?"
- ¿Tú sabes llegar a…? – "Do you know the way to the…?"
- Perdóname. – "Please excuse me."
- Yo no sé porqué./Yo no sé porqué pasó eso..– "I don't know why."/"I don't know why this happened."

These are a few helpful phrases when needing to know information or traveling about.

Hopefully, in this chapter, you have learned a few helpful phrases. These phrases should help you get around, and navigate your surroundings better. When you combine them with new vocabulary that you learn, you can expand them to even more useful phrases.

These are just a few helpful phrases. You can try to make a list of your own that you want to translate. Try to imagine yourself in the real world, speaking Spanish to other people. What would you want to say? What would you like to do?

Chapter 14: Important Lessons to Learn About the Spanish Language

Adjectives

(ADJETIVO)

You are familiar with the definition of the adjective as that particular word describing a person, place, thing, or event which is the subject of the sentence. The following are known as the most common adjectives used in the Spanish language:

(Usted está familiarizado con la definición de adjetivo como esa palabra en particular que describe a una persona, lugar, cosa o evento que es el sujeto de la oración. Los siguientes son los adjetivos más comunes utilizados en el idioma español:)

ENGLISH ADJECTIVE (ADJETIVO EN INGLÉS)	SPANISH EQUIVALENT (EQUIVALENTE EN ESPAÑOL)
Beautiful	Hermoso/a
Kind	Amable
Caring	Atento/a
Thoughtful	Considerado
Wonderful	Maravilloso/a
Happy	Feliz

Inspiring	Inspirador/a

Adverbs
(ADVERBIO)

If an adjective is describing a noun which is the subject of the sentence, then the adverb is describing a verb. There are three kinds of adverbs, and you should know about this because it will help you a lot in your journey towards learning the Spanish language.

(Si un adjetivo está describiendo un sustantivo que es el sujeto de la oración, entonces el adverbio está describiendo un verbo. Hay tres tipos de adverbio y debes saberlo porque te ayudará mucho en tu viaje hacia el aprendizaje del idioma español.)

Adverbs of manner	Adverbs of frequency	Adverbs of place	Adverbs of time
Adverbio de modo	Adverbio de frecuencia	Adverbio de lugar	Adverbio de tiempo
This is the kind of adverb that describes how a particular thing or event is done.	This is the kind of adverb that describes how fast or how often the event happens.	This is the kind of adverb that describes where an action took place. Este es el tipo de	This is the kind of adverb that describes when or what time an action

| Este es el tipo de adverbio que describe cómo se hace una cosa o evento en particular. | Este es el tipo de adverbio que describe qué tan rápido o con qué frecuencia se produce el evento. | adverbio que describe dónde tuvo lugar una acción | took place. Este es el tipo de adverbio que describe cuándo o en qué momento tuvo lugar una acción. |

Prepositions
(PREPOSICIÓN)

To some, prepositions are a very scary thing to learn. However, that is not true. The preposition is just a word that connects two elements composing a sentence. (Para algunos, la preposición es algo muy aterrador de aprender. Sin embargo, eso no es cierto. La preposición es solo una palabra que conecta dos elementos que componen una oración.) For example, the following phrases or combination of words are prepositions:

ENGLISH PREPOSITION (PREPOSICIÓN INGLESA)	SPANISH PREPOSITION (PREPOSICIÓN ESPAÑOLA)
Caja de chocolates	Box of chocolates
Bolsa de dulces	Bag of candies

Nouns

(SUSTANTIVOS)

Just like the English alphabet, a noun is either the subject or the object of the sentence. The noun may be used either way, as in these examples:

(Al igual que el alfabeto inglés, un sustantivo es el sujeto o el objeto de la oración. El sustantivo se puede usar de cualquier manera, como en estos ejemplos:)

SUBJECT NOUN/ SUJETO	OBJECT NOUN/ OBJETO
The **bag** is red.	That thing which is colored red is a **bag**.

In which case, both BAG is considered as a noun, either as subject or as an object. (En cuyo caso, ambas bolsas se consideran como un sustantivo, ya sea como sujeto o como un objeto.)

Chapter 15: Different Ways to Interact to Improve Your Spanish Language

Through Social Interaction

Speaking is the most common form of human communication and a great social activity. This claim is supported by evidence coming across all fields, which intrinsically states that social interaction influences people's communication and, more specifically, in mastering a new language.

When you socialize with people who can speak Spanish fluently, it will help you to speak the language effortlessly in no time. Through people, you can learn the different pronunciations that will not be taught in books.

Speaking and interacting with native speakers will do wonders for your Spanish proficiency journey. You will get to learn pronunciations and the colloquiums of the Spanish language that will help your comprehension. It's also fun and more natural to learn a new language through interactions. Do it with people who speak it as their mother tongue because you will get real-time feedback. They will correct you when you make mistakes and also help you fix your weaknesses.

Speaking may be tough, and you can start by practicing a lot. When you are alone, and if you do come across a word that you don't understand, you can always look it up in your Spanish dictionary. If you feel uncomfortable speaking Spanish in the first instances of interacting with native speakers, then it's okay not to speak too soon. It would be advisable to find someone who sympathizes with you and is patient enough to take you slowly through the learning process. However, you shouldn't take a long time to practice speaking, or you might delay your comprehension.

It's a slow learning process, so take baby steps and be consistent with what you are doing. Try to accept the fact that you will make mistakes along the way, and that is allowed. The goal here is to keep going and visualize that, in the future, you will be speaking fluently almost as well as the natives.

Through Language Websites

For those who are not that lucky to live in a Spanish-speaking country to interact with the natives, you can try joining an online exchange program. You will find people willing to teach you Spanish, and in return, you can teach them English or a language you are fluent in. It will enable you to form a mutually beneficial relationship. You can both create a schedule, where half the time, you are teaching them your language, and the other half, you are learning Spanish. They will be your link to the Spanish world, so make an effort to maintain contact until you feel you have mastered the language

These free language websites work by connecting you to someone via text, audio, or video service to facilitate communication. After being linked by the website, you will both decide on the type of connection you are comfortable using. Here are examples of free language websites you can use to interact.

Conversion Exchange

This site provides a simple platform for you to meet someone to help you learn Spanish. There are options where you can precisely find a partner that you can communicate through videos or audio calls. You can also opt to meet with the person physically.

The Mixxer

You create a user account through the site. Once you find someone whom you can interact with and learn Spanish with, then you can exchange Skype details for video calls. This site has the option of posting your writings in Spanish, and you can have people proficient in the language correct you. So you build your Spanish language prowess, both in speech and written form.

Easy Language Exchange

It has thousands of users and also has tests that help you with your Spanish.

Papora

This website is easy to use and navigate and has the option of joining groups where you can interact as a group and help each other learn.

Speaky

This is a great website because, other than interacting with Spanish natives, it has an automated tool that will help you in translations where you don't understand.

Through Social Media

Another awesome way to interact and learn Spanish is through social media. We spend many hours a day on social media, chatting with friends and family. You could also spend this time learning and mastering your Spanish language. Here are a few ways you can optimize your time spent on social media and still learn Spanish at the same time.

Subscribe to Pages and People Who Are Proficient in Spanish

To learn Spanish on social media, start by following people who are Spanish speakers. Whether it's on Twitter, Facebook, or Instagram, it doesn't matter. And, of course, try as much as possible to interact with them. It's free, and your brain already sees this as a habit you are used to. You can practice speaking and interacting with them and get used to speaking in Spanish. These changes will have a significant impact on your language mastery skills, without realizing you will be creating a Spanish language immersion environment.

You can still keep up with your interests and hobbies like cooking or whatever you are interested in. But at the same time, you will get to improve your language skills. Remember, the key here is to interact so that your learning experience is more active and not passive. So go ahead and share posts, comment on them, and interact!

Follow Language Enthusiasts and Experts

You can follow Spanish natives or specialists in the language. You can also follow some people who teach the language or polyglots who speak Spanish fluently. These are people like Benny Lewis, on Facebook, Twitter, and Instagram. You can get a ton of advice from these language enthusiasts. YouTube is also a great platform that you can use because you can work on your listening comprehension skills while you learn.

You can learn from videos and articles they publish online. There is really good content online that can help you in mastering your Spanish language skills. They also have comment sections where you can interact with the polyglots or other learners.

Join Language Groups on Facebook

If you prefer to interact on Facebook, there are groups you can join to learn Spanish. Be sure to join as many groups as you can that are Spanish-oriented. This way, every time you visit Facebook, you will find one or two interesting posts to read in Spanish. You are also being exposed to the language every time you log in.

To top that, joining Spanish learning language groups is a great way to make new friends who speak the language. Interacting with other learners keeps you motivated and spikes your interest to continue learning. You can also post your learning goals in your group, and other members can hold you accountable and even keep motivating and pushing you. Remember to support other learners, too, and create a mutually beneficial interaction.

You can also send messages and videos with your new friends as ways of interaction. It's a great way to put your progress into practice and gauge your language prowess.

Watching YouTube Videos

Watch whatever you like watching on YouTube, but do it in Spanish. Learning to make tacos from scratch is way more fun and more authentic if the teacher is showing the instructions in Spanish. You can relax and enjoy watching your favorite sports in Spanish, and you can pick up some sports slang along the way.

YouTube is also another great way to master your pronunciation. When subscribing to these videos, you will familiarize yourself with the accents. Watch how they speak and try to repeat after them as much as possible. An excellent channel to check out on YouTube is Easy Languages; this is one of the easiest ways to learn Spanish as a beginner. They interview natives, so you have access to fresh content. It also comes with subtitles to help you understand and translate what you don't understand

Speaking Spanish with Twitter Users
Twitter is an awesome place where you can experience sarcasm and, at the same time, interact with other users. Following key people will improve your Spanish language capabilities. Comment on posts and like tweets to improve your Spanish language proficiency and fluency.

If you don't understand some tweets in Spanish, no worries. Twitter has a feature for translations. Under each tweet, you will see an icon that says 'translate.' Click on it, and you will read the translation in English or your native language.

Blogs
Reading blogs in Spanish is also another exciting way to start your interactive Spanish learning process. There are comment sections that offer you an opportunity to open conversations with Spanish learners or natives. Ask questions and exchange ideas with other people on the platform to improve your language skills. PEPPY BURRO is an awesome Spanish blog for learners, which has great cultural content and learning tips for mastering Spanish.

Through Socializing

Go out and meet people who are learning Spanish or can speak the language fluently. Clubs, music concerts, and local cultural events offer a great platform for language practice and growth. Just think about it; these events offer an entire interactive process with people who speak and also those who are learning the language.

It can be intimidating being in a crowd of people, but you should take the opportunity to go out and mingle. Use the opportunity to the fullest to speak with natives, listen to music, or even sample the Spanish cuisine. Learn how to order in Spanish and interact with natives in Spanish restaurants. Strike up a conversation with other diners or the waiter at the restaurant; your aim here is to interact and socialize.

Meet-ups in clubs or coffee shops enable you to get real-life experience on how to articulate yourself in the language. You will learn a wide array of vocabulary while you get acquainted with friends and fellow learners. If you worry that you'll stumble over your words or forget some words, don't. These mistakes are part of your learning.

Sing along to songs at a concert. Music helps you in memorizing vocabulary and phrases that are commonly used in the Spanish language.

Through Various Classroom Interactions

When you enroll in Spanish classes, it will go a long way in helping you with speaking the language fluently, not only the grammar lessons. However, learning grammar is important; but learning is achieved through students' interaction and engagement in class. You will gain more speaking, making mistakes, and struggling through the lesson. This is a topic-based approach that is used by many teachers in class, and it has proved to be very effective.

A language teacher will motivate you, guide you through the lessons, and help you work on your weak points. In the classroom, you will be free to interact and express yourself in whatever you are learning.

Through Online Courses

As much as real-life interactions are a valuable way to learn a new language, it's not possible for everyone. You could be having your reasons not to be able to interact with people at social functions. Don't worry, though. You can enroll in an online language class that lets you interact with others. The online language course will adhere to your schedule, and you can take them anytime you got some free time. Examples of online language courses are:

Fluent

This online course offers videos, music, movie trailers, and inspirational talks to help you in learning Spanish. These are all interactive methods that you can use; you get to choose how to learn and what you will use. They have fantastic grammar lessons and vocabulary learning tutorials that have Spanish content, which offers authenticity to a learner. The site contains interactive captions that enable you to tap on any word, view the image, find the definition, and also get the vocabulary and audio examples. It is available to you anywhere and at any time.

Busuu

This online language learning course helps you connect with people and engage in conversations with native speakers. It's an effective interactive resource that you can use for grammar practice and build your vocabulary.

Verbal Planet

This course offers you the option of interacting with tutors online via Skype, book your lessons, and make a schedule that suits you perfectly. It is an interactive way to learn among Spanish learners who have a busy schedule. It's a bit pricey, though; I would only recommend it if the other options haven't worked so far. But if it works for you, then it's an excellent way to invest in your Spanish learning progress. It also lets you learn faster.

Through Playing Games

The main goal of learning Spanish is to attain fluency in communication. Playing games is an efficient way; you can use it to improve your language learning skills. Games are not only engaging and fun, but they also promote learning through interactions. They also enhance your problem-solving capabilities. They give learners a break from Spanish lessons, while at the same time, improving your vocabulary. They also provide a conducive environment where gamers can freely express themselves in Spanish.

Here are some advantages of using games to learn Spanish:

- Games will promote spontaneous interactions among learners. It will help students be able to apply real experiences, jogging their memories, and helping them learn. Well-developed games allow students to apply what they have learned in the previous lessons. The spontaneity of playing games with other students gives learners a chance to speak, remember words, and make mistakes.

- Games will also motivate Spanish learners to communicate effectively. Fun in games comes with the rules and the communication between the players. And this is the kind of interaction that will help learners communicate and gain the confidence and motivation to want to continue to learn and be able to master the subject.

- Games will also give students the chance to be resilient. When trying to master a new language, being resilient is a crucial element. The games offer a healthy sense of competition, which is also suitable for learning.

If you are not an online game enthusiast, you can come up with games in the classroom that can also serve the same purpose as online games. So what are the things to consider when you want to design or find a game to play with fellow learners?

Ensure you understand that the games are for learning purposes only. Set clear guidelines and expectations. These will be your guiding force and will surely help you and other learners in the long run.

Games need to have an element of repetition to enable you to practice a lot. Practice does make you perfect.

Look for games that are challenging. These are effective in the learning process, as they will spark your interest and provide an effective learning process. Be sure to choose a game in your language level. Otherwise, it won't be of much help to choose a game that you do not understand or is too difficult to play.

Try to monitor your progress and reward yourself when you win. It serves as motivation to keep learning.

Here a few games you could try playing with your new friends or fellow students.

Pictionary

Give random names of things or places in Spanish and let one person draw what the word means or describes. It's a competent game because you get a chance to work on your fast thinking capabilities, and it also boosts your memory when it comes to vocabulary.

Two Truths and a Lie

In this game, get your friends to write down three sentences. The two sentences must be the truth, and one must be a lie. The sentences should be in Spanish. This game will widen your vocabulary, and you will get to practice pronunciations and even attempt to become fluent in Spanish.

Start-Stop

This is a great game that will test your vocabulary, especially on the topic of nouns. You can play with two or more people. You take pieces of paper and write down in columns names, places, animals, and foods. You can choose what to add. Then the one playing will start saying the alphabet when they are told to start, and once you are told to stop, you say which letter of the alphabet you stopped at. Then all the learners get a chance to write the different nouns starting with the letter. For example, if it stopped at 'd,' you think of a noun in Spanish that starts with 'd.' The one who fills the column first wins. This is a great way to interact and practice your recall capabilities.

You enjoy yourself and, at the same time, you keep learning.

Interaction through gaming is fun, and you also get to learn at the same time. You can always come up with a game of your own that you will enjoy and will help you learn.

We have seen the importance of interaction and how it helps you with learning the Spanish language. But you can also attempt to go a step further and create your interactive program. It is an ideal schedule that you could use in one week. We got everything covered from Monday to Friday. If this fits into your schedule, you are free to use it. If it doesn't, you can always create your own, one that fits perfectly with your schedule.

On Monday, you can spare an hour you will spend watching interactive videos. Try to repeat after the speakers to master the accent and pronunciation. If you hear something you didn't understand, write it down in your phrasebook and look up the meaning when you are free.

On Tuesday, spend an hour writing your thoughts in a journal. Then you can post it on social media, so you will get feedback from your Spanish friends, as well as corrections if you made any mistakes.

On Wednesday, you can attend a social event. Check out what is going on and involve yourself in a cultural event, a coffee date, or a class activity. It is a great way to interact with others who will give your language skills a well-deserved workout.

On Thursday, you can simply go online and find a game, interact with other gamers, experience adventure, and solve mysteries. This is your laid-back day but still in the company of Spanish lessons.

On Friday, go to you YouTube and subscribe to your favorite Spanish speaker. Watch their tips on learning Spanish and how they speak. Repeat after them and learn their pronunciations and vocabulary. You can also watch a cooking show and learn how to make a Spanish dish. The possibilities are limitless with YouTube; just choose what you like, then sit back and enjoy.

You can tweak the above schedule to suit your preferences and daily routine. Make the process fun so that you don't feel like it is tedious. Be consistent and stay motivated, and soon, you will be a master in the Spanish language.

The interaction will inject some fun into your learning process and kill the monotony of learning Spanish with grammar and writing. So go out, interact, and learn!

Chapter 16: Tips on How to Learn the Spanish Language for Beginners, the Easiest Way Possible

Considering the Brain Activity of the Learner

The learning process varies from one person to another. Some people are fast-learners, others are slow ones. It is because there are people who are intelligent and there are also those who are average when it comes to intellectual faculties. You may grasp a certain topic easily, while other people could hardly grasp the topic at all.

(El proceso de aprendizaje varía de una persona a otra. Algunas personas aprenden rápido, otras son lentas. Es porque hay personas que son inteligentes y también hay personas que son promedio cuando se trata de facultades intelectuales. Puede comprender un determinado tema fácilmente, mientras que otras personas difícilmente podrían comprenderlo en absoluto.)

Intelligence has been understood as the ability of one person to grasp knowledge and information and the ability to reason out and understand the topic given. Have you asked yourself why a person's intelligence and learning process vary differently? The reasons are so many, and they may be as many as sand in the ocean.

(La inteligencia se ha entendido como la capacidad de una persona para captar el conocimiento y la información y la capacidad de razonar y comprender el tema que se le ha dado. ¿Te has preguntado por qué el proceso de inteligencia y aprendizaje de una persona varía de manera diferente? Las razones son muchas, y pueden ser tantas como granos de arena en el océano.)

First, one reason why intelligence varies from person to person is their mental capacity. If have listened to your science teacher before, you have realized and learned that the size of a brain is connected with one's intelligence. But through researches which came after our lessons about science, it was explained that it is not the size of the brain but instead the folds of the lobes in the forebrain that determine one's intelligence. One good example of this is Plato, which has a smaller brain than the ordinary human. On the other hand, Albert Einstein also has an average-sized brain compared to the usual brain of a human being. You can see the folds in the lobes of the forebrain through MRI, and through that, you can study the activity of the brains.

(Primero, una razón por la cual la inteligencia varía de persona a persona es su capacidad mental. Si ha escuchado a su maestro de Ciencias, se habrá dado cuenta y habrá aprendido que el tamaño de un cerebro está conectado con la inteligencia de uno. Pero a través de investigaciones que surgieron después de nuestras lecciones sobre ciencia, se explicó que no es el tamaño del cerebro sino los pliegues de los lóbulos en el cerebro anterior lo que determina la inteligencia de uno. Un buen ejemplo de esto es Platón, que tiene un cerebro más pequeño que el humano común. Por otro lado, Albert Einstein también tiene un cerebro de tamaño promedio en comparación con el cerebro habitual de un ser humano. Puede ver los pliegues en los lóbulos del cerebro anterior a través de la resonancia magnética y, a través de eso, puede estudiar la actividad de los cerebros.)

The second probable reason why learning and intelligence vary from person to person is their genetic attribute. Humans are different from one another because not even twins are considered to be totally the same or identical. Just like our brains, no two people have identical brains. For example, the child's parents are intelligent, so it would likely appear that the child is also intelligent. Their intelligence is being passed from their generation to the generation of their children. However, have you been wondering why two siblings have different intelligence, one may be smarter than the other? It is because of their different genetic make-up.

(La segunda razón probable por la cual el aprendizaje y la inteligencia varían de persona a persona es su atributo genético. Los humanos son diferentes entre sí porque ni siquiera los gemelos se consideran totalmente iguales o idénticos. Al igual que nuestros cerebros, no hay dos personas que tengan cerebros idénticos. Por ejemplo, los padres del niño son inteligentes, probablemente parezca que el niño también es inteligente. Su inteligencia se transmite de generación en generación a sus hijos. Sin embargo, ¿se ha estado preguntando por qué dos hermanos tienen inteligencia diferente, uno puede ser más inteligente que el otro? Es debido a su diferente composición genética.)

The third probable reason is environmental influence. Again, the size of the brain of a person affects his intelligence. During the formidable years of a child, his brain gradually increases, and as it gets bigger, the child becomes more intelligent. The formidable years of a child involve the first five years of himself after birth. In this stage, there are a lot of factors affecting their brain development, leading to either higher or lower intelligence. These factors are the following: The place where the child is being raised, the proper way of treating the child, even their family's lifestyle, and the educational background of a child.

(La tercera razón probable es la influencia ambiental. Nuevamente, el tamaño del cerebro de una persona tiene el efecto en su inteligencia. Durante los años formidables de un niño, su cerebro aumenta gradualmente y a medida que crece, el niño se vuelve más inteligente. Los años formidables de un niño implican los primeros cinco años de sí mismo después del nacimiento. En esta etapa, hay muchos factores que afectan su desarrollo cerebral que conducen a una inteligencia más alta o más baja. Estos factores son los siguientes: el lugar donde se cría al niño, la forma adecuada de tratarlo, incluso el estilo de vida de su familia y los antecedentes educativos de un niño.)

The place or location where the child is being raised is one factor affecting his intelligence. The place may be the country and its norms. Sometimes, the tradition of that country affects the child's brain development and how they think in the future. For example, the child was raised in a liberated country; then, when he grows up, there is a strong chance that he will also think liberally.

(El lugar o ubicación donde se cría al niño es un factor que afecta su inteligencia. El lugar puede ser el país y sus normas. A veces, la tradición de ese país afecta el desarrollo del cerebro del niño y cómo piensa en el futuro. Por ejemplo, el niño fue criado en un país liberado, luego, cuando crezca, existe una gran posibilidad de que también piense liberalmente.)

The proper way of treating the child also has an effect on him. For example, the child's parents are not good examples or good models for their child, then the child's brain development will also be affected. Say, for instance. The mother is a prostitute then the father is a drunkard; there is a strong possibility that the child will end up growing as a loud drunkard too.

(La forma correcta de tratar al niño también tiene un efecto en él. Por ejemplo, los padres del niño no son buenos ejemplos o buenos modelos para su hijo, entonces el desarrollo del cerebro del niño también se verá afectado. Digamos, por ejemplo, que la madre es una prostituta, el padre es un borracho, existe una gran posibilidad de que el niño termine creciendo como un ruidoso y un borracho también.)

The family's lifestyle, be it poverty or richness, also has a strong effect on the brain development of a child. There are children who grow up to be more intelligent if they are poor rather than when they are rich. It is probably because poor children were taught to give more importance to education because they do not have enough money to support their education.

(El estilo de vida de la familia, ya sea pobreza o riqueza, también tiene un fuerte efecto en el desarrollo cerebral de un niño. Hubo niños que crecieron para ser más inteligentes si son pobres en lugar de cuando son ricos. Probablemente se deba a que a los niños pobres se les enseñó a dar más importancia a la educación porque no tienen suficiente dinero para mantener su educación.)

Lastly, their educational background affects the child. For example, in a family of doctors, there is a great chance that the child will also be a doctor when he grows up. Like in other professions, the work of one's parents have an effect on the child as to what course to take in college.

(Por último, su formación académica afecta al niño. Por ejemplo, en una familia de médicos, existe una gran posibilidad de que el niño también sea médico cuando crezca. Al igual que en otras profesiones, el trabajo de los padres tiene un efecto en el niño sobre qué curso tomar en la universidad.)

Time Frame in Learning How to Speak and Understand Spanish Language for Beginners

Ordinarily, formal Spanish learning would take approximately one year in order for a person to fluently speak and understand Spanish. Here are some tips that you would consider if you are learning Spanish on your own:

(Por lo general, el aprendizaje formal del idioma español tomaría aproximadamente un año para que una persona hable y entienda con fluidez el idioma español. Aquí hay algunos consejos que consideraría si está aprendiendo español por su cuenta:)

The first one is motivation. Sometimes, you will become courageous in life because you have an aim to achieve. Through that motivation, you will understand that the thing you thought was a problem has become a good motivator for you to take life seriously. For instance, why do you want to learn Spanish? One of the reasons given by people learning Spanish is because they will use it in their work. Spanish knowledge is a requirement for a particular person to qualify for a position. If you are motivated, you will have that drive to reach that goal of yours.

(El primero es la motivación. A veces, serás valiente en la vida porque tienes un objetivo que alcanzar. A través de esa motivación, comprenderá que lo que creía que era un problema se ha convertido en un buen motivador para tomarse la vida en serio. Por ejemplo, ¿por qué quieres aprender español? Una de las razones por las que las personas que aprenden español es porque lo usarán en su trabajo. El conocimiento del español es un requisito para que una persona en particular califique para un puesto. Si está motivado, tendrá ese impulso para alcanzar ese objetivo suyo.)

Another one is the focus. If you are learning other than your language at birth, then you should give it a hundred percent of focus because, without it, you will only waste your time. Even if you are interested in learning the language; if you keep on taking it lightly, then you will earn nothing from it. You have to take things seriously in order for you to learn Spanish the easiest way possible.

(Otro es el foco. Si está aprendiendo un idioma que no es su idioma natal, entonces debe concentrarse cien por ciento porque sin eso, solo perderá su tiempo. Incluso si estás interesado en aprender el idioma, si sigues tomándolo a la ligera, no ganarás nada. Tienes que tomar las cosas en serio para poder aprender español de la manera más fácil posible.)

One more tip in order to learn Spanish easily is time. You need to create a schedule of Spanish short story reading, which must be daily. Focus on your phrasebook and read it everyday. From that day on, you will be able to familiarize yourself with the Spanish vocabulary.

(Un consejo más para aprender español fácilmente es el tiempo. Debe crear un horario de lectura de cuentos en español, que debe ser diario. Concéntrese en su libro de frases y léalo todos los días. A partir de ese día, podrás familiarizarte con el vocabulario español.)

Learning the Attitude of Spanish People

The next step after the phrasebook and flashcards is the process of conversing with a Spanish person, a Spanish speaking person, or a Spanish Subject Teacher. That is the reason why you need to understand and learn the attitude of Spanish people just for the purpose of preparing yourself for a long conversation. If the person you are talking to is not that friendly, then you cannot sustain the conversation.

(El siguiente paso después del libro de frases y las tarjetas de vocabulario es el proceso de conversar con una persona española, una persona que habla español o un maestro de español. Esa es la razón por la que necesita comprender y aprender la actitud de los españoles solo con el fin de prepararse para una larga conversación. Si la persona con la que está hablando no es tan amigable, entonces no puede mantener la conversación.)

The truth is that Spanish people are naturally friendly and will give you a warm welcome if you are new to their place. However, these people are easily irritated by their visitors.

There are visitors who did some unwanted things which make these Spanish people do things which are opposite to being friendly. They may raise their brows and other similar things. One example of these is that Spanish people do not like shaking hands; they kiss each other's cheeks as a form of respect.

(La verdad es que los españoles son amigables por naturaleza y te darán una cálida bienvenida si eres nuevo en su lugar. Sin embargo, estas personas se irritan fácilmente por sus visitantes. Hay visitantes que hicieron cosas no deseadas que hacen que estos españoles hagan cosas opuestas a ser amigables. Pueden levantar las cejas y otras cosas similares. Un ejemplo de esto es que a los españoles no les gusta darse la mano, se besan las mejillas como una forma de respeto.)

Another one, Spanish people usually have a long siesta after eating lunch. That is the reason why there is a misconception that Spanish people are a lazy group of people. Actually, they are not; they are just fond of having a long siesta.

(Otro, los españoles suelen tener una larga siesta después de almorzar. Esa es la razón por la cual existe una idea errónea de que los españoles son un grupo de personas perezoso. En realidad no lo son, simplemente les gusta tener una larga siesta.)

Also, when it comes to going out of their houses for work, they usually leave the house late. That is one of the aspects of a Spanish person. They are not used to waking up early and leaving the house early. If they do it, they will only have an unproductive day. They will yawn all day, and they will think of sleeping all day.

(Además, cuando se trata de salir de sus casas por trabajo, generalmente salen tarde de la casa. Ese es uno de los aspectos de una persona española. No están acostumbrados a levantarse temprano y salir temprano de la casa. Si lo hacen, solo tendrán un día improductivo. Bostezarán todo el día y pensarán en dormir todo el día.)

Are Spanish people rude? No, they are not. They also consider their private place as sacred. You will enter it if you are trusted. Another one, Spanish people are touchy and would usually talk to you so closely. That is normal for Spanish people. They do not shake hands. Instead, they kiss the cheeks of the person they are greeting. Usually, the kiss would be from cheek to cheek.

(¿Son groseros los españoles? No, no lo son. También consideran su lugar privado como sagrado. Lo ingresarás si eres de confianza. Otro, los españoles son sensibles y por lo general te hablan muy de cerca. Eso es normal para los españoles. No se dan la mano, sino que besan las mejillas de la persona que están saludando. Por lo general, el beso sería de mejilla a mejilla.)

Other common attitudes of Spanish people are courteous, tardy (like what was mentioned a while ago), jealous, possessive, passionate, short-tempered, hospitable, and lazy. Although they are considered rude by some, Spanish people are actually courteous. They respect the elderly and their spouses. Actually, researchers say that most of the Spanish people do not have concubines. Although the women are even more prone to having paramours.

(Otras actitudes comunes de los españoles son corteses, tardías (como lo que se mencionó hace un tiempo), celosas, posesivas, apasionadas, de mal genio, hospitalarias y flojas. Aunque algunos los consideran groseros, los españoles en realidad son corteses. Respetan a los ancianos y sus cónyuges. En realidad, las investigaciones dicen que la mayoría de los españoles no tienen concubinas. Aunque las mujeres son aún más propensas a tener amantes.)

Another not so good trait of a Spanish person is that they usually fall in love (or actually not, they are just sexually attractive) with a blood relative. Just like in Chinese culture, they are prone to having an unwanted relationship with a relative. But unlike Chinese culture, that relationship is not for the purpose of fencing their wealth altogether, but for the purpose of sexual fantasies.

(Otro rasgo no tan bueno de una persona española es que generalmente se enamoran (o en realidad no, solo son sexualmente atractivos) de un pariente de sangre. Al igual que en la cultura china, son propensos a tener relaciones no deseadas con un pariente. Pero a diferencia de la cultura china, esa relación no tiene el propósito de cercar su riqueza por completo, sino el propósito de las fantasías sexuales.)

But even if they are considered as rude, there is no single record that Spanish people created a non-friendly relation with other countries. They are not considered a threat to the peace of other countries, but they are racists. That means that they do not want certain people or races to stay in their country. Two of those races are the Arabs and the North Africans. On the other hand, they love and adore the Portuguese people. When you are invited by Spanish people to enter their country, you must be very lucky. However, that is not true at all times because if one Spanish person invites an alien that is because of business and not because of friendly purposes.

(Pero incluso si se consideran groseros, no existe un registro único de que los españoles hayan creado una relación no amistosa con otros países. Si bien no se consideran una amenaza para la paz de otros países, son racistas. Eso significa que no quieren que ciertas personas o razas se queden en su país. Dos de esas razas son los árabes y los africanos del norte. Por otro lado, aman y adoran a los portugueses. Cuando los españoles te invitan a entrar en su país, debes ser muy afortunado. Sin embargo, eso no es cierto en todo momento porque si una persona española invita a un extranjero por motivos comerciales y no por motivos amistosos.)

Those are the traits of Spanish people that you must know before you approach them and start a conversation with them. Remember what they like and what they do not like. They love kissing and not shaking hands, they are kind of lazy in the morning, and they are active at night. Yes, you have read it right! They are very much active at night, but they are sleeping in the morning. Give them their personal space, and you will not get into trouble. So if you are planning to initiate a conversation with Spanish people, you better talk to them at night and over a bottle of whisky or rum. They are not actually drunkards, but they love drinking liquor and having chit-chats with their friends.

(Esos son los rasgos de los españoles que debes conocer antes de acercarte y comenzar una conversación con ellos. Recuerde lo que les gusta y lo que no les gusta. Les encanta besar y no darse la mano, son un poco flojos por la mañana y están activos por la noche. ¡Sí, lo has leído bien! Son muy activos por la noche pero duermen por la mañana. Déles su espacio personal y no se meterá en problemas. Entonces, si planea iniciar una conversación con los españoles, es mejor que hable con ellos por la noche y con una botella de whisky o ron. En realidad no son borrachos, pero les encanta beber licor y tener charlas con sus amigos.)

Spanish people also are usually well-off in life. They enjoy their lifestyle much more than Americans. They give importance to social status and family life. They are also loud, they are liberated, and they enjoy partying more than Americans do. When it comes to family, its concept is more tangible compared to other races. They give more preference to daughters compared to sons. Unlike in Australian culture wherein sons and daughters reaching eighteen years of age, Spanish eighteen-aged people are still living in the house of their parents, more particularly if they are ladies. They take care of ladies more than men.

(Los españoles también suelen ser acomodados en la vida. Disfrutan de su estilo de vida mucho más que los estadounidenses. Dan importancia al estatus social y a la vida familiar. También son ruidosos, están liberados y disfrutan más de la fiesta que los estadounidenses. Cuando se trata de familia, su concepto es más tangible en comparación con otras razas. Dan más preferencia a las hijas que a los hijos. A diferencia de la cultura australiana en la que los hijos y las hijas alcanzan los dieciocho años, los españoles de dieciocho años todavía viven en la casa de sus padres, especialmente si son mujeres. Cuidan más a las damas que a los hombres.)

As mentioned a while ago, Spanish people are usually jealous ones. Yes, that is true. Spanish people do not like to be cheated on. If they catch their partners cheating on them, they will definitely initiate break-up or divorce. Men are more faithful than women in Spain, so that means they love harder compared to women. That is the reason why they do not want to be cheated on. They feel they deserve respect and love, which is unconditional because they love truthfully. They do not want to be cheated on because they believe they do not deserve it.

They are also possessive, which means their property, their partners, and their wealth are kept privately. Another one is that Spanish people are very private in life. They are not also expressive of their love in public. Yes, they are touchy and close when talking to you, but they are not expressive of their love. That is the difference between Spanish people compared to Australian people. The latter are more expressive. They buy expensive gifts for their wives and kids but Spanish people, they just prepare food for you. They just wash your clothes, iron your pants and skirts, send you to your work, and fetch you thereafter. In other words, the Spanish people are showing their love through action and not through expensive gifts.

(Como se mencionó hace un tiempo, los españoles suelen ser celosos. Si eso es verdad. A los españoles no les gusta que los engañen. Si descubren que sus parejas los engañan, definitivamente iniciarán la ruptura o el divorcio. Los hombres son más fieles que las mujeres en España, lo que significa que aman más que las mujeres. Esa es la razón por la que no quieren ser engañados. Sienten que merecen respeto y amor, lo cual es incondicional porque aman con sinceridad. No quieren ser engañados porque creen que no lo merecen. También son posesivos, lo que significa que su propiedad, sus socios y su riqueza se mantienen en privado. Otra es que los españoles son muy privados en la vida. No son también expresivos de su amor en público. Sí, son sensibles y cercanos cuando te hablan, pero no expresan su amor. Esa es la diferencia entre los españoles y los australianos. Los últimos son más expresivos. Compran regalos caros para sus esposas e hijos, pero para los españoles, solo preparan comida para usted, simplemente lavan su ropa, planchan sus pantalones y faldas, lo envían a su trabajo y lo buscan luego. En otras palabras, los españoles muestran su amor a través de la acción y no a través de regalos caros.)

One last topic that you need to know is how Spanish wants to be respected. They want not to be disturbed when it comes to taking their siesta. The sacred hour that must be respected about them is from two to five o'clock in the afternoon. Just after their lunchtime, they need to recharge so that they have a lot of time in the evening to party and talk about business. So if you are planning to initiate a good conversation with them, don't approach them during these hours because you will get either a napping conversation partner or an angry one. It is a cliché that you must choose to disturb a drunk person rather than a person who lacks sleep.

(Un último tema que debe saber es cómo quiere ser respetado el español. Quieren no ser molestados cuando se trata de tomar su siesta. La hora sagrada que debe respetarse es de las dos a las cinco de la tarde. Justo después de la hora del almuerzo, necesitan recargarse para tener mucho tiempo en la noche para divertirse y hablar de negocios. Entonces, si planeas iniciar una buena conversación con ellos, no te acerques a ellos en estas horas porque obtendrás un compañero de conversación para la siesta o uno enojado. Es un cliché que debes elegir molestar a una persona borracha en lugar de a una persona que carece de sueño.)

Chapter 17: Spanish Accents

The Spanish language is spoken by many far and wide. In over 20 different countries, it is the official language. Many international organizations like the European Union, United Nations, World Trade Organizations, and the Commonwealth recognize it as one of the official languages of their operation. We need to understand that despite being the second largest spoken language, not all the countries that speak Spanish have the same culture. Each state has its own unique culture that defines them, but regions inside these countries can have similar cultural practices that define them. Learning a language, therefore, helps one connect with a particular culture.

There are so many accents around the world. People may speak the same language but with different accents. The Spanish language is no exception when it comes to accents. For someone who has just started learning the language, the accents can be quite hard to grasp. Spanish accents are even harder for people whose first language does not use accent marks. Typing them can also be hard if you use the classic keyboard. Pronunciation of some words always changes when you use accent marks. Accent marks can influence stress in a word, and one always needs to remember when they use them. It is also essential to know and understand the Spanish accent rules. This will enable you to understand when to use them and when to omit them. Don't get tired of accents because they are an essential part of a language that requires accent marks. The omission of accent marks can change the meaning of a word. So as you begin your journey of learning Spanish, be careful not to omit any accent marks.

When you start learning the basics in the Spanish language, understand the various dialects and accent marks. Their accents can also be called diacritics or diacritical signs or marks. They usually represent an extra glyph or just a symbol added to the letter. In the Spanish language, accents are sometimes called 'tilde.' In the English language, however, the same word can be referred to using the '~' symbol. Some Spanish native speakers usually refer to the same symbol as "la virgulilla" or just "la tilde de la eñe."

The Spanish language consists of three main types of accents. One is the tilde (ñ); this is one that people use the most and is very common. The second one is known as the acute accent (ú); this is mainly used to indicate speech that has words to be stressed on. The last type is known as diaeresis (ü). All the five vowels a, e, i, o, u can have this accent. The Spanish accents are á, é, í, ó, ú, ñ, and ü. It is important to note that Spanish words do not have circumflex or rather grave accents. They can be easily mastered and will be essential in daily conversations in Spanish. As you read on, you will discover various accents and how to use them regularly.

Pronouncing Spanish Words With Accents and Without Accents

In linguistics, stress represents a syllable and syllables of words that are pronounced with emphasis. This is essential knowledge in English, and all English speakers understand this. In Spanish, however, accents and stress are used to distinguish different words. For example, you can say, "She sent a letter" in Spanish; you can say, "ella mandó una carta." The singular form is "I sent a letter," which is translated as "yo mando una carta."

Other examples include "tu," without the accent, means "your," while the same word with accent, "tú," means "you." In a sentence, someone can use it like this: "Tú tienes un perro muy bonito." This means, "You have a cute dog." It can be used as "¿Es tu mascota?" which, in English, is translated as "Is it your pet?"

We also have words like 'té,' which means "tea," and 'te' means 'you.' In a sentence, you can say, 'I recommend you drink much tea.' In Spanish, the same sentence translates to 'Te recomiendo que tomes mucho té.'

Some words like 'cómo' can be used to mean what or how depending on the sentence construction. 'Como,' on the other hand, means 'as' or 'like.' This also varies from one sentence to the next. You can use a sentence like '¿Cómo se llama tu colega?' to mean 'What is your colleague's name?' and a continuation of the same sentence can go like, 'Is he as smart as Ronaldo?' which, if translated into Spanish, becomes '¿Es tan inteligente como Ronaldo?'

Another sentence with an accent is 'él,' meaning 'he.' The same sentence without an accent is 'el,' which means 'the.' In a sentence, you can use it this way; 'He likes wine,' which when translated to Spanish, you can write as 'A él le gusta vino.'

The last example that I will give is 'sí,' which means 'yes' with the accent. With the accent, 'si' means 'if.' In a sentence, we can use them like this:

'Sí, quiero probar el chorizo" which means 'Yes, I want to try the pork sausage.'

In those examples, we will find out that the meaning and pronunciation of the words are different. You will also discover that you are getting used to pronouncing Spanish words with accents. Once you are used to that, it will be difficult for you to pronounce words without accents. This means that you will be used to the pronunciation of stressed words in Spanish. Here are some instructions that can guide you in applying word stress:

For words ending with any vowel, letter 's,' or the letter 'n,' the stress is usually put on the syllable proceeding the last syllable or the next to the last syllable, for example, her-mo-so, which means beautiful in English. Here, the stress is put in the next syllable before the last syllable, which is the syllable 'mo.'

Another good example is com-pu-ta-do-ra; this is known as a computer in English. Here, you stress the syllable 'do.'

With words ending with a consonant other than 's' or 'n,' you must stress the last syllable.

A good example is 'fe-liz,' meaning happy in English. The stress is on the consonant '-liz.'

Another example is the word professor written in Spanish as pro-fe-sor. The stress is in the consonant 'sor.'

Accent marks help in spelling while learning the Spanish language. Spelling is the key to learning as they bring about the meaning of a word. Incorrect spelling can mean something else that is out of the topic. Be sure to follow the spelling rules keenly and consistently. Since accents influence pronunciation that makes it a key area of learning, you should not ignore it at any cost.

Some people like to refer to accents as extra symbols added to an already exciting letter to justify the meaning of differentiating two different words. All in all, the accent helps us know where to put stress, especially with regards to syllables and consonants. The Spanish accent marks in vowels make them look like this á, é, í, ó, and ú. With just a mere glance, one may think they are very insignificant and not useful. The truth, however, is that they are essential in pointing out emphasis on a particular subject. Otherwise, how will you know how important a word is if you do not put the emphasis? Every word in Spanish contains an accent. This accent is usually the syllable that is always stressed. Some of the syllables do not contain accent marks, while others have accent marks. The only crucial thing is to know and understand why and where to put accent marks. This will answer the question if the accent mark is vital in a particular sentence. Non-native speakers usually find it challenging to put the accent in sentences.

There are circumstances when accents are only used to differentiate words that are spelled the same, though they have a different meaning. For instance, they may differentiate possessive and subject and also confirmation and conditional words. The words may be pronounced the same, but when accents are put in the written text, it helps rule out the misunderstanding that may arise. Accents used merely for differentiation are also called diacritical marks.

In Spanish, vowels are divided into two types: hard vowels (a, e, and o) and weak vowels (i and u). A weak vowel can be joined with a hard one to create a one-syllable sound.

Also, two weak ones can be joined together. This is called a diphthong. Hard vowel and weak vowel can be joined together, and the stress always falls on the hard vowel. When two weak vowels join together, the stress, therefore, falls on the second vowel. Words cannot follow the rules; that is why the accent must be written. Accents are useful when you want to use formal language as you will need to look professional. In formal places, there is a need for correct spelling and grammar. It is also important to make the meaning clear. If your words do not use accents, then you will have the incorrect meaning of words, and this may be a bad thing. The formal situations can include a letter to your boss, academic publication, letter of appointment, curriculum vitae, and many other things.

People sometimes omit accents in their written Spanish. This may confuse the reader and sometimes makes the text interpretation difficult, especially to people whose first language is not Spanish. This can be quite irritating, especially to perfectionists and people who like things to be proper. Those who do like slang also hate it when accents are omitted. It can be compared to writing a text in English using the lower case while intentionally omitting all apostrophes. Native Spanish speakers, most of the time, when communicating on the internet, using emails or Facebook usually ignore the use of accents. It is just like some style they have adopted that allows one to omit them when they do not want to be formal. It is like saying stick to official orthography. Just like in English, general chatting does not require formality, and your punctuation needs not to be perfect. In this circumstance, being too formal will make your friends feel you are weird.

The native speaker has contested whether accents should be used when all letters are capital. When reading an article or a book, accents are vital as they can show the dominion of the author of the book. Omitting accents and punctuations often make text very difficult to read. This is because one will be struggling to understand what the writer meant. The accent can change the meaning and make the text more realistic. The omission can make one read twice or thrice to deduce what the text meant. Not all Spanish accents sound the same. Spanish is not different from any other language. Even in the same place or country, Spanish diversity can vary greatly. Though spoken mainly in Spain, there are still many accents and dialects, along with the other four official languages. You need to be able to understand various dialects. This is because the understanding can give you insights to move from intermediate to expert Spanish speaker.

The many dialects can influence one's accent. For example, we can look at main Spanish accents, which include Argentinean, Mexican, Northern South American, Spanish, Central American, Chilean, and the Caribbean. Mexican Spanish is spoken in the Southwestern U.S. region. This is because most Spanish speakers in that region can trace their origin from Mexico. Mexican Spanish has been influenced by indigenous languages like Tzotzil and Nahuatl and, of course, American English. There are some common words in Spanish that have the same English meaning but coming from another language. An example is chocolate, which has the same English meaning, and aguacate, which is avocado, which came from the indigenous language Nahuatl. We should also note that a lot of Mexican communities, which are purely indigenous, do not speak Spanish at all. Mexican Spanish has been known to borrow some English words. For example, Spaniards will call computer ordenador, while Mexicans would call it computadora.

Another good example is the word rentar. This is used to mean rent, while other countries use alquilar. Mexican Spanish also has a lot of exciting slang phrases and words. For example, the use of the word güey means 'dude,' while the same word literally means 'castrated bull.'

Conclusion

I hope that the contents and materials in this book have helped you to improve your overall Spanish skills. We are certain that you have put in your best effort in order to do so.

That is why my recommendation is to go back to any of the lessons which you feel you need to review and go over the content. Of course, the more you practice, the better your skills will be. Indeed, your overall skills will improve so far as you continue to practice.

So, do take this opportunity to continue building on your current skills. You will find that, over time, you will progressively gain more and more understanding of the language you encounter on a daily basis.

Given the fact that there are many resources out there that can help you to practice your listening skills, such as movies, telenovelas, and music, you will be able to put this content into practice right away.

Thank you once again for choosing this book. We hope to have met your expectations. And please don't forget to leave a comment. Other folks who are interested in learning Spanish will certainly find your reviews on this book useful.

Learning Spanish should not be hard and tiresome. Therefore, this book has provided beneficial tips to understand various Spanish accents and exposed you to some of the Spanish grammar rules. Learning Spanish will also make your travel adventure fun and exciting if you visit places where Spanish is spoken. We all have to start somewhere. Do not be discouraged if you are not learning the language as fast as you want to. Learning a new language is not easy, but it can be made fun and fast if you have the right attitude. A positive attitude motivates, and it influences learning. It will make learning the hardest lesson appear easy. It is also important to surround yourself with people who will encourage you to do more and be the best you can be. We cannot hide the fact that, in the future, the Spanish language will be widely spoken across the world, just like English.

SPANISH LANGUAGE FOR BEGINNERS

The Easiest Guide to Amaze Your Friends. Learn and Remember Words With Practical Exercises, Modern Lessons, Common Phrases, Tips and Tricks While You Travel

Living Languages

Introduction

This book will help you increase your vocabulary with modern phrases, along with their translations. It's divided into four lessons that range from common Spanish phrases and greetings to relationships and dating. These lessons include example sentences where you can see the word in action so that you can come to understand not only the meaning of a single word but also how to use it in the most appropriate context. All these terms and phrases are accompanied by their translations in English.

After gathering the basics of understanding the language, you'll then learn how a personal coach can make your learning process easy and enjoyable. Even better, you'll learn how you can get a coach, as well as the importance of including such professionals in your training. Furthermore, you'll learn about what to consider when starting Spanish-speaking lessons.

The learner is encouraged to read the book and use its information as soon as possible. Practice makes perfect, so don't feel embarrassed to use the vocabulary you're learning. On the contrary, come back to the book every time you need to remember a certain word or phrase, and then use it correctly, with confidence!

Learning a new language is a long path you need to walk in order to become proficient, but you don't need to walk alone. This book can be your companion in every situation you encounter. You have the help you need to grow your vocabulary and be able to honestly say that you truly speak a new language.

Chapter 1. Introduction to the Spanish Language

I. *Vocabulario nuevo*/New Vocabulary

Hola – hello *Qué tal?* – How's it going? *Cómo estás?* – How are you? [informal, singular]	*Cómo está usted?* – How are you? [formal, singular] *Cómo están ustedes?* – How are you? [formal, plural]
Bien, gracias. ¿Y tú? – Fine, thanks. And you? [informal, singular]	*Bien, gracias. ¿Y ustedes?* – Fine, thanks. And you? [formal, plural]
Bien – well. *Estoy bien.* – I'm well. *Mal* – not well. *Estoy mal* – I'm not well	*Regular* – So-so *Más o menos* – *more or less* *No muy bien* – Not very well
Buenos días–Good morning *Buen día* – Good day (greeting)	*Buenas tardes* – Good afternoon *Buenas noches* – Good evening, good night
Me llamo.... – My name is.... *Soy...* – I am... *Mi nombre es...* – My name is...	*Cómo te llamas?* – What's your name? [informal, singular] *Cómo se llama usted?* – What's your name? [formal, singular]

Mucho gusto – Nice to meet you	
Encantado – Pleased to meet you [speaker masculine] *Igualmente* – Likewise	*Es un placer.* – It's a pleasure *encantada* – Pleased to meet you [speaker feminine]
Gracias – Thank you! *Excelente* – Excellent!	*Muy bien, gracias* – very well, thank you! *bastante bien* – just fine
Bienvenido – Welcome [plural] *Te presento a….* – Let me introduce you to…. [informal, singular]	*Le presento a….* – Let me introduce you to…. [formal, singular]
Adiós – Goodbye *Chao* – Bye *Hasta luego* – See you later	*Hasta mañana* – See you tomorrow *Hasta pronto* – See you soon *Nos vemos* – See you
El curso – Course *Los Estados Unidos* – United States *El aspecto* – Aspect	*La lengua* – Language *El español/Castellano* – Spanish language *La cultura* – Culture
Introductorio – Introductory *Importante* – Important	*Solo* – Alone, only

Approach to Learning a New Language

Successful language learners have a positive reaction when faced with the unfamiliar. So, rather than allowing yourself to feel frustrated, confused, or annoyed when listening to Spanish, try to maintain a positive outlook and work to understand anything you can. It can help to think of communicating in Spanish as a puzzle to be solved, or an interesting challenge to be met. When you hear spoken Spanish, focus on what's being said, don't be distracted by negative thoughts, and listen for cognates, which are words that are the same or almost the same in two languages. Spanish and English share many cognates, including *curso*/course; *introductorio*/introductory; *profesor*/professor; *importante*/important; *aspecto*/aspect; *cultura*/culture; and *mucho*/much.

Spanish Language

The Spanish language, known as either español or castellano, developed in the Iberian Peninsula in the region of Castile, or Castilla in Spanish. According to the United Nations, Spanish is the third most-spoken language in the world, after Mandarin Chinese and English. Roughly half a billion people speak Spanish, which is spoken on four continents, is an official language of 20 countries, and is one of the official languages (along with English) of the U.S. territory of Puerto Rico. Spanish is also spoken more and more each year in the United States. According to the latest census data, almost 40 million people in the United States speak Spanish at home, which makes up more than 12 percent of the country's population. A 2015 report by the Instituto Cervantes, a governmental organization in

Spain that focuses on the Spanish language, concluded that there are more Spanish speakers in the United States than there are in Spain.

Varieties of Spoken Spanish

The three main differences that distinguish how Spanish is spoken in one place versus another are vocabulary, accent, and grammar. Differences in vocabulary result in different words being used in different places to refer to the same thing. To say "the computer," for example, in Latin America you'd say "*la computadora*," while in Spain it's much more common to say "*el ordenador.*"

In terms of accent, there are differences between countries and even between regions within the same country. Perhaps the most notable difference in accent among Spanish speakers relates to the way to pronounce the letter *z* and the letter *c* followed by *e* or *i*. In Latin America, the letter *z* and the letter combinations *ce* and *ci* are pronounced with an *s* sound, while in northern and central Spain this is pronounced with a *th* sound. The Spanish word for "shoe" is *zapato*, which in Madrid is pronounced as "*th*apato" and in Latin America is pronounced "sapato."

There are not many grammatical differences among regions, but there are a few, and an important one deals with the plural form of "you." In both Spain and Latin America, the word *ustedes* is the formal, plural way to say "you." However, in Spain, there's also an informal, plural way to say "you," which is *vosotros* in the masculine or *vosotras* in the feminine. But *vosotros* and *vosotras* are not used in Latin America; instead, *ustedes* is used for the plural "you" in all cases.

Despite these differences in vocabulary, accent, and grammar, hundreds of millions of Spanish speakers communicate successfully across every country where the language is spoken. Speakers of Spanish—even from different regions—understand each other extremely well.

Pronunciation of Vowels

Pronouncing words in Spanish is simpler than it is in English because when you look at a letter in Spanish, with very rare exceptions you know exactly how to pronounce the sound of that letter. One challenging aspect of Spanish pronunciation is that there are sounds in the language that don't exist in English, and these can be difficult to pronounce at first.

Each of the five vowels—a, e, i, o, u—makes just one sound in Spanish, a short sound that stays the same from beginning to end.

• A, found in the common Spanish word casa, is the easiest vowel sound to make. For the other four vowel sounds, focus on keeping the vowel sound short and uniform.

• E makes the sound pronounced in the English word "take." It's not "eyyyy." You don't close it off at the end as you often do in English.

• I makes the sound pronounced in the word "fee." It's not "iyyyy."

• O makes the sound pronounced in "toll." It's not "owwww."

- U makes the sound pronounced in "rule." It's not "uwwww."

The video lessons, audio glossaries, and speaking activities model proper pronunciation in Spanish.

Greetings

Among the very common greetings in Spanish are "hola" [hello]; "¿Qué tal?" [How's it going?]; and "¿Cómo estás?" or "¿Cómo está usted?" [How are you?]. "¿Cómo estás?" is the informal way to say "How are you?" to someone. "¿Cómo está usted?" also asks "How are you?" but is used with someone you address formally.

Three ways to introduce yourself: "Me llamo Bill" [I call myself Bill, or My name is Bill]; "Soy Bill" [I am Bill]; and "Mi nombre es Bill" [My name is Bill].

Common expressions used when you meet someone for the first time are "mucho gusto" [nice to meet you]; "encantado" [pleased to meet you, masculine form]; "encantada" [pleased to meet you, feminine form]; "Es un placer" [It's a pleasure]; and "igualmente" [likewise].

Greetings dependent on the time of day include "buenos días or "buen día" [good morning]; "buenas tardes" [good afternoon]; and "buenas noches" [good evening, or good night]. Ways to say "goodbye" include "adiós" [goodbye]; "chao" [bye]; "hasta luego" [see you later]; "hasta mañana" [see you tomorrow]; "hasta pronto" [see you soon]; and "nos vemos" [see you].

How Best to Take This Course

If your goal is to work toward proficiency in Spanish, you should watch the video lessons and engage with the other course materials as well. In order to make significant progress with your language skills, you'll need to practice what's presented in the video lessons.

When you finish a lesson, you should next listen to the audio glossary, which will give you the pronunciation and definition of all new vocabulary words. Then, it will be time to practice what you've learned. The speaking activities for each lesson are designed to help you improve your listening and speaking skills. And the workbook exercises will allow you to practice your reading and writing. You can decide if you want to do the speaking activities before or after you do the workbook exercises, but you should do both of these only after watching the video lesson and listening to the audio glossary.

If you are able to involve someone else with your studies, you are encouraged to do so. Languages are meant for social interaction, so take the course with a friend or seek out opportunities to speak Spanish with someone who already knows the language.

The more contact you have with Spanish, both within the course and beyond it, the better your progress will be.

Global Importance of the Spanish Language

Although it might seem that Spanish has gained importance in the United States only recently, in 1787 Thomas Jefferson wrote the following about the Spanish language in a letter to his nephew: "Bestow great attention on this, and endeavor to acquire an accurate knowledge of it. Our future connections with Spain and Latin America, will render that language a valuable acquisition." What was true in Jefferson's time remains true today. Spanish is a world language, and its importance now extends beyond its use in other countries to the mainland of the United States.

Chapter 2. Common Spanish Phrases, Greetings, and Good Manners

Do You Want to Speak Spanish?

The Spanish-speaking world is full of phrases, each distinct to its own region. Since Spanish is spoken in so many places around the world, this language has been shaped by the native land, culture, and customs of every country where it is present today. When it first came, almost 600 years ago to Latin America, it was already a very complex language. With the passing of time, Spanish changed to become the modern language that's spoken in this continent. These changes occurred as a result of the interaction between new cultures. Today, each Spanish-speaking country can boast of having a version of Spanish that can't be taken away. There are even some recorded instances where Spanish is mixed with the native tongue to create a very distinctive dialect.

These differences can vary wildly, from the pace to the vocabulary, and yet, it's still very easy for Spanish speakers to communicate with other Spanish speakers since these changes haven't altered the basic meanings or the sounds of the language. So, There's really no reason to despair and think that you need to learn every variation to learn Spanish. What you really need to learn is what every Spanish speaker has in common. Having this purpose in mind, common, modern phrases have been compiled to help you communicate with every Spanish speaker you run into, just like they do.

No matter where you're going or who you're talking to, these phrases are a sure way that everyone will understand you.

These useful phrases used throughout Latin America and Spain will get you started. Listed here are some of the most common and modern phrases in Spanish, along with their translations.

Spanish	English
¡Hola!	Hello!
¿Cuál es tu nombre? ¿Cómo te llamas tú?	What's your name?
Even though these phrases are quintessential in pretty much every language, people will appreciate you're speaking to them in their own language.	
Mi nombre es…/Me llamo…	My name is…
If you ever feel like answering with your full name, you can say: Mi nombre completo es…	
¿Cómo estás?	How are you?
There's another variation of this question which is getting less common but still understandable to all Spanish speakers: ¿Cómo te va? If there's ever a chance you are asked this question, you should answer: ¡Me va muy bien!	

¿Cómo estuvo tu día?	How's been your day?
Estoy bien	I'm ok
Muchas gracias	Thank you so much
Disculpa	Excuse me
¿Cuántos años tienes?	How old are you?
¿Qué hora es?	What time is it?
Tengo 23 años	I'm 23 years old
Son las 3:30 p.m.	It's 3:30 p.m.
¿Dónde vives tú?	Where do you live?
Lo siento	I'm sorry
¿De dónde vienes tú?	Where are you from?

Not to be confused with the Spanish verb "sentir" ("To feel" in English) In this case, "Lo siento" is an expression of remorse used for apologizing.

¿Cuál es tu número de teléfono celular?	What's your cellphone number?
¿Cuál es tu correo electrónico?	What's your e-mail address?
¿Cuál es tu perfil de Facebook o Instagram?	What's your Facebook or Instagram profile?

In this age of technological advances, asking for social media profiles is more common, and possibly important, than ever.

Mi número de teléfono es	My telephone number is
Mi correo electrónico es…	My e-mail address is…
Me puedes encontrar en Facebook como…	You can find me on Facebook as…
¿Estudias? ¿Qué estudias?	Do you study? What are you studying?
¿Trabajas? ¿Cuál es tu trabajo?	Do you work? What do you do?
¿Me podrías ayudar con esto?	Could you help me with this?
Tengo hambre	I'm hungry.
Tengo sueño	I feel sleepy.
¿Tienes un lápiz o lapicero?	Do you have a pen or pencil?
De nada	You're welcome.
¡Fue un placer conocerte! ¡Fue un placer conocerlo!	It was a pleasure to meet you.
¡Adiós!	Goodbye!
¡Hasta mañana! ¡Hasta pronto! ¡Hasta luego!	See you tomorrow! See you soon! See you later!

As you may have been able to see in

¿Cuál es tu pasatiempo favorito?	What's your favorite hobby?
Mi pasatiempo favorito es leer comics.	My favorite hobby is reading comics.
Me gusta ver televisión.	I like watching TV.
Me gusta hacer deporte.	I like playing sports.
¿Cuál es el tipo de música te gusta?	What kind of music do you like?
¿Cuánto cuesta esto?	How much does this cost?
Me gusta la música rock	I love rock music
Cuesta 3 dólares	It costs 3 dollars.
No sé	I don't know.
¿Entiendes?	Do you understand?
¡Qué gusto volver a verte!	It's a pleasure to see you again!
No entiendo	I don't understand.
¡Empezemos!	Let's begin!
¡Felicitaciones!	Congratulations!

these phrases, Spanish doesn't need personal pronouns to express the intended idea. This is because of verb inflections or conjugations. You see, Spanish verbs need conjugations to be used in every sentence. These conjugations are unique to every personal pronoun that is using them. So when the verbs are finally conjugated, there's no need for the personal pronoun to be present since the verb carries the inflection that is used for that particular pronoun. Fun, right?

Unlike English, there are two different ways to acknowledge the second personal pronoun:

| Tú | You |
| Usted | You |

Is there any difference? Yes.

While both are used as the second personal pronoun, "tú" is the casual form and "usted" is a more formal form. "Tú" is used when there's a measure of trust between longtime friends, family members, or a couple. "Usted" is used primarily to address important people, such as police officers, judges, or teachers. It's also used if it's the first time you meet someone as a sign of politeness.

Some cases where "usted" will be heard include the following.

Formal Greetings in Spanish

First impressions say a lot about a person. So, whether you're already a pro at Spanish or just getting started, you'll want to make sure you're well-versed in how you greet others in Spanish. Also, in Latin culture, when you greet someone it can often be a bit of a ritual. There's often hugging and cheek-kissing involved, along with numerous pleasantries. You'll definitely want to get those hellos and goodbyes perfected before your next encounter.

When you meet someone for the first time you will most probably use the formal "Usted" when addressing them. There are some exceptions e.g. meeting children, but if you are not sure, it is always safe to begin with the formal "Usted."

Here are the most common greetings:

- Hola - Hello
- Buenos días - Good morning (note: "Buenos" because "días" is masc.)
- Buenas tardes - Good afternoon (note: "Buenas" because "tardes" is fem.)
- Buenas noches - Good night (note: "Buenas" because "noches" is fem.)

This is how you introduce yourself:

- Mucho gusto - Nice to meet you.
- Me llamo Gustavo Martinez - My name is Gustavo Martinez (I call myself Gustavo Martinez).

Now let's move on to some basic examples of small talk:

1. **General Small Talk**

Cómo está usted? – How are you?

Muy bien, gracias. ¿Y usted? – Very well thank you. And you?

Buenos días Señor. ¿Es usted norteamericano? – Good morning, Sir. Are you American?

Sí, pero mi esposa es colombiana – Yes, but my wife is Colombian.

About the Language

Usted habla Español? – Do you speak Spanish?

Sí. Un poco. – Yes, a little.

Tomo clases para aprender español – I take classes to learn Spanish.

Lo leo bien pero no lo hablo muy bien – I read it well but I don't speak it very well ("lo" refers to "Spanish". See details later in this lesson).

Lo entiendo mejor que lo hablo – I undertand it better than I speak it.

Lo estudio todos los días – I study it every day.

Es difícil aprender un nuevo idioma, pero lo disfruto mucho – It is difficult to learn a new language, but I enjoy it very much.

Why and Where in Spanish

Why in Spanish – "¿Por Qué?"

"Why?" in Spanish is "por qué?", literally "for what". Let's look at a few examples:

¿Por qué quieres salir conmigo? – Why do you want to go out with me?

¿Por qué no comes más? – Why don't you eat more?

¿Por qué no te gusta? – Why don't you like it/him/her?

Me puedes decir ¿por qué? – Can you tell me why?

No entendemos por qué – We don't understand why

Pero ¿por qué? – But, why?

Note: It is important to keep in mind that "por qué?" (Two words and the second with an accent) means "why?", but "porque" (single word, no accent) means "because." This is a common mistake, so here are a few examples:

- No me gusta porque es asqueroso – I don't like it because it is disgusting.
- Voy al médico porque no me siento bien – I am going to the doctor because I don't feel well.
- No queremos estudiar porque es aburrido – We don't want to study because it is boring .
- La camisa apesta porque se cayó en la basura – The shirt stinks because it fell in the garbage.

"Where?" in Spanish – "¿Dónde?"

Let's look at some examples:

- ¿Dónde está el pato? – Where is the duck?

- ¿Dónde podemos encontrar un buen restaurante italiano? – Where can we find a good italian restaurant?
- ¿De dónde es usted? – Where are you from?
- ¿Para dónde vas? – Where are you off to?
- ¿De dónde vienes? – Where do you come from?

"From" and "Of" in Spanish
"From" in Spanish – "Desde"

There are two words that mean "from" in Spanish. Depending on the context you would translate "from" as "de" or "desde." In most cases "de" is used:

- Mi esposa es de Colombia - My wife is from Colombia.
- Ellos vienen de la misma ciudad - They come from the same city.
- Él es el rey de Inglaterra - He is the King of England.

The word "desde" also means "from" but denotes coming from one location towards/targeting another. Let's look at a few examples:

- Este canal se transmite desde Chile - This channel is transmitted from Chile
- Ella trabaja desde la casa - She works from home

- El tren viene desde Atocha - The train comes from Atocha
- Él se cayó desde el cuarto piso - He fell from the fourth floor
- Puedes oler el pollo asado desde la calle - You can smell the roast chicken from the street
- Escuché los ladrones desde el baño - I heard the thieves from the bathroom.

"Desde" is also used to mean "since":

- Aprendo francés desde el año pasado - I have been learning french since last year
- No la vemos desde hace mucho tiempo - We haven't seen her in a long time (lit. "since a long time")
- No hemos manejado desde el accidente - We haven't driven since the accident.

"Of" in Spanish – "De"

"De" is also used to mean "of" in Spanish:

- Es la mujer más bella del mundo - She is the most beautiful woman in the world (lit. 'of the world'; de + el = del).
- Ella está de mal genio - She is in a bad mood (lit. She is of bad temper).
- Él es el alcalde de Santiago - He is the mayor of Santiago.
- Este pescado no es de mar, es de río - This fish isn't from the sea, it's from the river.
- Este componente es de acero - This component is (made) of steel

- ¿Qué opina usted de la decisión? - What do you think (what is your opinion) of the agreement?
- De acuerdo - Ok (lit. "of agreement").

Where We Live

- Dónde vive usted? – Where do you live?
- Vivo en un apartamento en la Avenida Marco – I live in an apartment on Marco Avenue.
- Y ustedes? ¿Dónde viven ustedes? – And you (plural)? Where do you live?
- No vivimos aquí. Vivimos en la Ciudad de México – We don't live here. We live in Mexico City.
- Estamos aquí de vacaciones – We are here on vacation.

Where to Eat

- Hay un buen restaurante cerca de aquí? – Is there a good restaurant around here? ("cerca" – "close")
- Sí, conozco un buen restaurante mexicano en la próxima calle – Yes, I know a good Mexican restaurant on the next street.
- También conozco un buen restaurante peruano, pero está lejos – I also know a good Peruvian restaurant, but it's far.
- Gracias Señor. Usted es muy amable - Thank you sir. You are very kind.

Greetings like "good morning" or "good afternoon" are incredibly important in Spanish. As the Latin culture is more formal, going through the ritual of greeting another person is an important way of showing respect. In fact, in some parts of Latin America, you are expected to greet every person individually, even if they're in a group. That means that if you're walking along the road in a village and pass a group of five people, you'll have to say, "Good morning," five times!

"How are you?" in Spanish

After you greet someone, you'll want to ask how they are or how's it going. Here are some common questions that follow a greeting.

- Cómo estás? – How are you? (used with friends or family)
- ¿Cómo está usted? – How are you? (more formal; used with strangers, more senior persons, etc.)
- Cómo te va? – How's it going?
- Cómo has ido? – How've you been?
- Qué tal? – What's up?
- Qué pasa? – What's happening?
- Qué haces? – What are you doing?

What could you say if someone asks you one of these questions?

- Bien, gracias./Muy bien. – Well, thanks/Very well.
- Como siempre. – As always.

- Un poco cansado (for men)/Un poco cansada (for women) – A little tired.
- Estoy enfermo (for men)/Estoy enferma (for women) – I'm sick.
- Más o menos. – Okay, so-so.
- Mal. – Bad.
- Todo bien. – All good.
- Nada. – Nothing.

A common follow-up question is, ¿Y tú? – And you?

Casual Greetings in Spanish

- Hola, Estela, ¿qué tal? ¿Qué haces? – Hello, Estela, how are you? What are you doing?
- Nada, nada. Estoy enferma. – Nothing, nothing. I'm sick.
- Ah, lo siento. – Ah, sorry.
- ¿Y tú? ¿Cómo te va? ¿Bien? – How about you? How are you doing? Well?
- Sí, todo bien. – Yes, all right.

Here's another conversation. This one is much more casual. You're likely to hear this kind of conversation among young people.

Essential Phrases

The above words are extremely important. From experience, I know that the most important phrase in any language is how to say you're sorry. Others disagree. They say that there are three important phrases that you absolutely must know in any language. They are:

- Lo siento. I'm sorry.
- Te amo. – I love you.
- Necesito ayuda. – I need help.

Hmm, I can't think of a situation in which I'd need to use all three, but I'll leave it to your imagination!

How to Say Goodbye in Spanish

You can say goodbye with one of the following phrases:

- Adiós – Goodbye
- Chao – Bye
- Hasta Luego – See you later
- Hasta pronto – See you soon
- Hasta la vista – Until we see each other again
- Nos vemos – See you.

Other Common Spanish Phrases

- Buena suerte! – Good luck!
- Diviértete! – Have fun!
- Con mucho amor! – Lots of love!
- Buen viaje! – Have a good trip!
- Buen provecho! – Enjoy your meal!
- Salud! – Cheers!
- Muy bien! – Well done!
- Cuídate! – Take care! (casual)
- Cuídese! – Take care! (formal)
- Los mejores deseos para – Best wishes to…
- Felicitaciones! – Congratulations!
- Bienvenidos!/¡Bienvenidas! – Welcome!
- Feliz Cumpleaños! – Happy Birthday!

- Salud! – Bless you!
- Feliz Navidad! – Merry Christmas!
- Feliz Año Nuevo! – Happy New Year!

Salud! has two usages… You use this word when giving a toast "Cheers!" and also when someone sneezes – the Spanish equivalent of "Bless you!"

- Lo siento! – I'm sorry!

Another way to say "I'm sorry" is Perdón. This one is more of an "Excuse me" phrase. Perdón, pero dónde están los baños? "Excuse me, but where are the toilets?"

- Perdón! – Excuse me!

One expression that is milder than "Lo siento" is "Disculpeme." And when you're late for a meeting, you can say…

- Mil disculpas! – A thousand sorry's!

When you have to interrupt a meeting, say…

- Siento interrumpir. – Sorry to interrupt.

A polite way to ask someone to get out of your way, or if you're leaving a conversation, or leaving a table is to say…

- Con permiso. – Excuse me.(lit. with permission)

If someone stepped on your toes and apologized you might want to say…

- No se preocupe! – No worries!

The sooner you can talk about your everyday life in Spanish, the easier you'll find it to have real Spanish conversations.

Everyday life is different for everyone, so pay attention to the things you do throughout the day. What did you say? What did you do? Then, make your own list of words that are relevant for you so you can learn Spanish faster.

Getting to know others and talking about your interests are the bread and butter of learning a language. So you have to know how to express your hobbies!

Use these phrases as starters to get you going:

- ¿Qué te gusta hacer? – "What do you like to do?"
- Mi pasatiempo favorito es… – "My favourite pastime is…"
- ¿Cuáles son tus pasatiempos? – "What are your hobbies?"
- Qué haces en tu tiempo libre? – "What do you do in your free time?"
- Me gusta/No me gusta… – "I like/I don't like…"
- Me encanta… – "I love…"
- ¿Qué te gusta leer? – "Do you like to read?"
- ¿Que música te gusta? – "What music do you like?"
- Mi favorito es… – "My favourite is…"
- Me gusta ir… – "I like going to…"
- ¿En qué trabajas? – "What's your job?"
- ¿Te gusta tu trabajo? – "Do you like your job?"
- Trabajo en… – "I work at…"

With these phrases, you can say things like:

- Me encanta café. ¿Quieres ir a tomar una taza? – "I love coffee. Wanna go grab a cup?")
- Trabajo en la escuela. Soy profesor. – "I work at the school. I'm a teacher."

Common Questions in Spanish

Once you know your basic Spanish question words, like "¿qué?" and "¿dónde?", you can ask a whole number of things. These are some common questions you'll hear:

- ¿Cuánto cuesta? – "How much is this?"
- ¿Dónde está el baño? – "Where's the bathroom?"
- ¿Qué hora es? – "What time is it?"
- ¿Pasa algo? – "Is something wrong?"
- ¿Es esto correcto? – "Is this right?"
- Me he equivocado? – "Was I wrong?"
- ¿Me puede ayudar con esto? – "Can you help me with this?"
- Puedes traerme … por favor?" – "Can you bring me … please?"
- Puedo entrar? – "Can I come in?"
- ¿Quieres tomar una copa? – "Want to grab a drink?
- ¿A dónde deberíamos ir a comer? – "Where should we go to eat?"
- ¿Estás listo? – "Are you ready?"

Exclamations, Celebrations, and Well Wishes

It's always good to know how to wish someone well, tell them happy birthday, or what to say when toasting at happy hour. These are simple, single-use phrases you can learn quickly.

- ¡Cuánto tiempo sin verlo(a)! – "Long time no see!"
- ¡Feliz cumpleaños! – "Happy birthday!"
- ¡Buena suerte! – "Good luck!"
- ¡Alto! – "Stop!"
- ¡Salud! – "Cheers!"
- ¡Que te mejores! – "Get well soon!"
- ¡Buen provecho! – "Bon appetit!"
- ¡Cuídate! – "Take care!"
- ¡Felicitaciones! – "Congratulations!"
- ¡Bien hecho! – "Well done!"
- ¡Genio! – "Genius!"
- ¡Estupendo! – "Stupendous!" or "¡Amazing!"
- ¡Genial! – "Great!" or "Awesome!"
- ¡Increíble! – "Incredible!" or "Impressive!"

Filler Words and Phrases

Smooth out your speech with conversational connectors, sentence stretchers and filler words in Spanish.

These words and phrases give you a moment to prepare what you're going to say next. They'll help you sound more natural and fluid, like how you speak in your native language. We use these types of sayings all the time!

- A ver… – "Let's see…"
- Pues… – "Well…"
- Bueno… – "Well then…"
- Sabes? – "You know?"
- Por supuesto – "Of course"
- Por otra parte…" – "On another note…"
- Pero… – "But…"

- De verdad? – "Really?"
- Dios mio – "Oh my god"
- Entonces… – "So…"
- Asi que… – "So… About that…"

Helpful Phrases in Spanish

These are your essential phrases to fall back on when you need to express your intent, your needs, or you don't understand.

- Necesito ayuda – "I need help"
- Llámame cuando llegues – "Call me when you arrive"
- Me voy a casa – "I'm going home"
- Necesito ir a… – "I need to go to…"
- Como llego hasta ahí? – "How do I get there?"
- No lo sé – "I don´t know"
- No tengo idea – "I have no idea"
- Lo entiendes? – "Do you understand?"
- No entiendo – "I don't understand."
- Quiero… – "I want…"
- Puede hablar más despacio, por favor? – "Can you speak slowly, please?"

Funny Spanish Phrases

Add a little colour to your conversation with funny Spanish phrases and idioms! When you can use a well-known phrase like these, you sound much more natural in your everyday speech.

Ponte las pilas – "Put in your batteries." It's like telling someone to "look alive," "snap out of it," or "wake up." You say it to a person who's daydreaming.

Papando moscas – "Catching flies." Speaking of daydreaming, that's called catching flies in Spanish. Which is quite a visual: Your friend sitting there, so completely lost in thought, the flies have started to land on him or her. But he or she doesn't even notice!

Comiendo moscas – "Eating flies." Flies are popular in Spanish idioms for some reason. You use this phrase when the person talking to you is quite long-winded. It can be said about anyone who goes on tangents, or someone who can't stay on point.

Buena onda – "Good wave." This means good vibes. You can also use it to describe someone who has a positive outlook and attitude.

Me pica el bagre – "The catfish is biting me." The catfish being your stomach, and the biting being the painful ache of hunger. In other words, "I'm starved!"

Hablando del rey de Roma – "Speaking of the king of Rome." It has the same meaning as "speak of the devil" in English. You say this whenever you were just talking about someone, and then they appear.

Meter la pata – "To put a paw it in." It means "to screw up," and it's used like how we say in English, "to put your foot in your mouth."

Creerse la última coca-cola del desierto – "To think of yourself as the last Coca-Cola in the desert." This is an interesting one to me. It means you think you're better than everyone else, or you think you're hot stuff.

Tener la cola sucia – "To have a dirty tail." It comes from the idea of being sneaky like a fox. Doing something you know is wrong, but doing it anyway and trying to get away with it.

Se puso hasta las chanclas – "Puts on his flip-flops." It's like the saying "He/She put on his/her beer goggles." He or she got hammered, too drunk, trashed.

Échale ganas – "Insert desire." It means to try your best. "How bad do you want it?"

Mandar a alguien por un tubo – "Send someone through a tube." You use this to tell someone to "shove it."

Mala leche – "Bad milk." You can say this about someone who has bad intentions.

Tirar la casa por la ventana – "Throw the house out the window." Or as you would hear Donna from Parks & Rec say, "Treat yo' self." It means to splurge, spend a lot of money, or otherwise go all out for a special occasion.

Dealing With Problems

Of course, not every conversation or language exchange will go smoothly. What should you do when you don't understand something? Or if you need to ask someone for help?

It's important to know some basic phrases you can use for dealing with problems when they arise. If you need someone to speak more slowly or to repeat something, the best thing to do is just ask them!

After all, if you need someone to speak more slowly or to repeat something, the best thing to do is just ask them!

- ¿Podría ayudarle? – Can I help you?

  (poh-DREE-a ay-oo-DAR-le)

- Puede ayudarme? – Can you help me?

  (PWE-day ay-oo-DAR-may)

- Sin problema! – No problem!

  (sin prob-LAME-ah)

- Puede repetirlo! – Can you say that again?

  (PWE-day re-pet-EER-lo)

- No entiendo – I don't understand!

  (no en-tee-EN-do)

- No (lo) sé – I don't know!

  (no lo say)

- No tengo ni idea – I have no idea!

  (no TEN-go nee ee-DAY-ah)

- No hablo español – I don't speak Spanish

  (no AB-lo es-pan-YOL)

- Estoy perdido – I'm lost

    (eh-STOY per-DEE-do)

- ¿Qué significa …? – What does … mean?

    (kay sig-nif-EE-ka)

- Mi español es malo – My Spanish is bad

    (mi es-pan-yol es MA-lo)

- Puedes hablar más despacio? – Can you speak more slowly?

    (PWE-des ab-LAR mas des-PATH-ee-o).

The word "despacio" in the last phrase is interesting. Notice that the 'c' is pronounced like 'th' in this context. This is the traditional Spanish pronunciation used in Spain. However, in Latin America, people pronounced the 'c' as a 's' sound (e.g. des-PAS-ee-o).

Expressions For Special Occasions

There are a number of common expressions that are used regularly to denote special circumstances or for special occasions.

These phrases are ideal for events like birthdays, meals with friends or even for ending the conversation:

- ¡Diviértete! – Have fun!

    (di-vi-EHR-te-te)

- ¡Buen viaje! – Have a good trip!

    (bwu-en vi-AH-kay)

- ¡Buen provecho! – Bon appetit!

  (bwu-en pro-VE-choh)

- ¡Muy bien! – Well done!

  (mwee bee-en)

- ¡Cuídate! – Take care!

  (kw-EE-dah-tay)

- ¡Felicitaciones! – Congratulations!

  (fe-lis-i-ta-see-ON-es)

- ¡Bienvenidos!/¡Bienvenidas! – Welcome!

  (bee-en-ven-EE-dos/bee-en-ven-EE-das)

- ¡Feliz Cumpleaños! – Happy Birthday!

  (fe-LEES kump-lay-AN-yos)

- Salud! – Cheers!

  (Sa-LOOD).

Saying Goodbye in Spanish

Saying goodbye is never easy to do, especially when you don't know how to do it! Whether you are bidding farewell to friends you are going to see later or to somebody you will never see again, make sure you know how to say your goodbyes appropriately.

Whether you are bidding farewell to friends you are going to see later or saying goodbye to people you will never see again, Spanish has lots of different options:

- Adiós – Goodbye

    (ah-dee-OS)

- ¡Buenas noches! – Goodnight!

    (bway-nas no-ches)

- ¡Hasta luego! – See you later

    (AS-ta loo-AY-go)

- ¡Hasta pronto! – See you soon

    (AS-ta PRON-to)

- ¡Hasta mañana! – See you tomorrow

    (AS-ta man-YAN-a)

- Nos vemos – See you

    (nos VAY-mos).

The Verb "Querer" (To Want)

Once you've finished greeting someone, you'll need to be able to move on to the crux of your conversation and to do that you'll need to learn a couple of common verbs.

There are hundreds of Spanish verbs to learn and, to make your life more difficult, these verbs conjugate (change form).

This means learning a verb is never as simple as learning one word; you have to learn multiple different forms.

Having said that, you might be surprised by how far you can get only knowing one simple verb: I want.

It may not make you the most sophisticated Spanish speaker but 9 times out of 10 it will get you what you, well, want.

The verb in question is "querer" (to want) and in the first person form, it becomes "quiero" (I want).

Let's take a look at how you can use it:

- Yo quiero un menú – I want a menu

    (YO kee-EH-ro oon me-noo)

- Yo quiero un taxi – I want a taxi

    (YO kee-EH-ro oon taxi)

- Yo quiero una cerveza – I want a beer

    (YO kee-EH-ro oo-na ser-vay-za).

If you'd like to be a bit more polite (which is usually a good idea), you can also use:

- Quisiera … – I would like … (lit. I would want)

    (kee-see-eh-ra…).

Asking for & Understanding Directions

Whether you're looking for the toilet in a restaurant or trying to find a place to stay, you'll inevitably need to ask for directions at some point during your trip.

The simplest way to ask where something is, is to use "¿Dónde está?" followed by the noun you are looking for:

- ¿Dónde está el baño? – Where is the bathroom?

  (DON-day es-tah el BAH-nyo?)

- ¿ Dónde está el banco? – Where is the bank?

  (DON-day es-tah el BAN-koh?)

- ¿ Dónde está la calle [de Alcalá]? – Where is [Alcalá] Street?

  (DON-day es-tah la ka-yay de al-cal-AH?)

If you are asking someone on the street for directions, don't forget your manners! To get someone's attention, start by saying:

- Disculpe – Excuse me

  (Dis-KUL-pay)

- Con permiso/Perdóname – Excuse me

  (Con per-MEE-soh/Per-DOH-nah-may)

- Estoy perdido – I'm lost

  (eh-stoy per-DEE-doh).

Asking for directions is one thing, but it's pretty pointless if you don't know how to understand the directions that are given to you.

Memorize these phrases to help you understand what the friendly locals are trying to tell you when you ask for their help:

- Aquí – Here

    (Ah-KEE)

- Allí – There

    (ay-EE)

- A la derecha – On the right

    (A la de-RE-cha)

- A la izquierda – On the left

    (A la iz-kee-ER-da)

- Derecho – Straight ahead

    (De-RE-cho)

- En la esquina – At the corner

    (En la es-KEE-nah)

- A una cuadra – in one, two, three, four blocks

    (A oo-na kwAD-rah).

At a restaurant:

¿(Usted) sabe el menú del día de hoy?	Do you know today's menu?

At school:

| ¿Podría darme (usted) permiso para ir al baño? | Could you give me permission to go to the bathroom? |

Meeting someone for the first time:

| Me da gusto poder conocerlo a usted | It's a pleasure to meet you. |

Or just as a sign of respect or politeness:

| ¿Podría (usted) ayudarme, por favor? | Could you help me, please? |
| ¿A dónde se dirige (usted)? | Where are you going? |

You will also find many typical expressions used to greet or welcome someone. Though many are unique to their country of origin, there are some that you can use freely.

¡Bienvenido!	Welcome!
The most common of all. Use "¡Bienvenido!" when welcoming someone into your home or a meeting.	
¡Mi casa es tu casa!	My house is your house!

This expression is an invitation for someone to enter your home. It's used to make the other person feel comfortable and relaxed when visiting your home.

The first sentence uses the possessive adjective "su" as it is a somewhat formal invitation. The use of "tu" in the second one indicates a level of informality or closeness to the person being invited.

¡Pase usted!	Come on in!

Another way of inviting someone to enter your home.

¡Cuánto tiempo!	It's been a long time!

Use this phrase in an informal setting to let the person know that you're glad to see him again despite the time you haven't seen each other.

Would you like to say you enjoy certain hobbies?

Just as in English, there are many ways to say how you enjoy your free time. Here are some phrases that will help you answer the question: "¿Cuál es tu pasatiempo favorito?"

Ways to ask what activities a person engages in when he or she has free time:

¿Cuál es tu pasatiempo favorito?	What's your favorite hobby?
¿Qué te gusta hacer en tu tiempo libre?	What do you like doing when you have free time?
¿Qué haces en tu tiempo libre?	What do you do when you are free?

Ways to answer these questions:

En mi tiempo libre yo…	In my free time, I…
Mi pasatiempo favorito es…	My favorite hobby is…
A mi me gusta…	I like…

Now let's see some examples:

"¿Cuál es tu pasatiempo favorito?"

Mi pasatiempo favorito es tocar la guitarra.	My favorite hobby is playing the guitar.
Mi pasatiempo favorito es leer.	My favorite hobby is reading.
Mi pasatiempo favorito es jugar tennis.	My favorite hobby is playing tennis.

"¿Qué haces en tu tiempo libre?"

Yo juego videojuegos en mi tiempo libre	I play videogames when I'm on a break.
En mi tiempo libre juego baseball.	In my free time, I play baseball.
En mi tiempo libre escucho música.	When I'm free, I listen to music.
"¿Qué te gusta hacer en tu tiempo libre?	
A mi me gusta cantar.	I like singing.
A mi me gusta ver televisión.	I like watching television programs.
A mi me gusta ir al cine.	I like going to the movies.

Unlike English, Spanish doesn't capitalize the first letter of the days or months of the year, but it follows a similar structure.

Spanish	English
El Lunes	Monday
¿Qué harás el lunes?	What are you doing on Monday?
El Martes	Tuesday

¿Estás libre el martes?	Are you available on Tuesday?
El Miércoles	Wednesday
Te visitaré el miércoles	I'll visit you on Wednesday.
El Jueves	Thursday
¿Te puedo llamar el jueves?	Can I call you on Thursday?
El Viernes	Friday
¿Puedo visitarte el viernes?	Can I visit you on Friday?
El Sábado	Saturday
Vamos a viajar el sábado	We're traveling on Saturday.
El Domingo	Sunday

Months

Spanish	English
Enero	January
Mi papá nació en enero.	My dad was born in January.
Febrero	February
Es demasiado frío en febrero	It's too cold in February.

Marzo	March
Viajaré en marzo	I'll travel in March.
Abril	April
¿Hace calor en abril?	Is it hot in April?
Mayo	May
No nieva en mayo	Does it snow in May?
Junio	June
Te visitaré en junio.	I'll visit you in June.
Julio	July
Llueve mucho en Julio.	It rains too much in July.
Agosto	August
Me graduo en agosto.	I'll graduate in August.
Septiembre	September
Regresaré a casa en setiembre	I'll go home in September.
Octubre	October
¿Trabajarás en Octubre?	Will you work in October?
Noviembre	November
Nací en noviembre	I was born in November.
Diciembre	December

Mi hermano nació en diciembre	My brother was born in December.

Throughout the year, there might be important dates that are dear to you or those surrounding you. Whether you wish to say when you are going to travel or when your son was born, these phrases will help you tell everyone when that special event occurred.

Spanish	English
4 de enero	January 4
16 de septiembre	September 16
Martes, 13 de octubre	Tuesday, October 13
Viernes, 8 de septiembre	Friday, September 8
Domingo, 22 de mayo del 2019	Sunday, May 22, 2019
Hoy día es martes.	Today is Tuesday
Ayer fue sábado.	Yesterday was Saturday.
Mañana será jueves.	Tomorrow will be Thursday.
Hoy día es martes, 3 de julio del 2013	Today is Tuesday, July 3, 2019.
Yo nací el 3 de febrero.	I was born on February 3.
Mis padres viajaron a Italia en 2011	My parents traveled to Italy in 2011.
Mi pasaporte expiró el 10 de abril.	My passport expired on April 10.

Me casé el 5 de agosto del 2010.	I got married on August 5, 2010.
Regresaremos a casa el 23 de noviembre.	We'll go back on November 23.
Compré mi ticket de avión el 10 de marzo.	I bought my plane ticket on March 10.

Many Spanish phrases include expressions about the weather. Here are the most useful Spanish phrases you need to know.

Spanish	English
El viento	The wind
El viento sopla fuerte	The wind blows strong.
El tiempo revuelto	The unsettled weather
Mañana tendremos tiempo revuelto	We'll have unsettled weather tomorrow.
La turbulencia	The turbulence
¿Habrá turbulencia?	Will there be turbulence?
La nieve	The snow
Nevar	To snow
¿Cuándo nevará?	When will it snow?
Llover a cántaros	To rain cats and dogs

Queríamos ir al parque pero estaba lloviendo a cántaros.	We wanted to go to the park, but it was raining cats and dogs.
Llover	To rain
¿Crees que llueva mañana?	Would you say it's going to be rainy tomorrow?
Granizo	Hail
Granizar	To hail
No habrá granizo la siguiente semana	There will be no hail next week.
La inundación	The flood
Inundar	To flood
Se inundaron las casas debido a las lluvias	Houses were flooded from the rain.
El trueno	The thunder
No he escuchado ningún trueno	I haven't heard any thunder.
El tiempo El clima	The weather
Vi en la televisión que el clima de este verano será el más calido del año.	I saw on the TV that this summer's weather would be the hottest of the decade.
La temperatura	The temperature

La temperatura es muy alta	The temperature is very high.
La insolación	The sunstroke
Ten cuidado con la insolación	Be careful with sunstroke.
El sol	The sun
El sol está brillando	The sun is shining
Los chubascos de nieve	The snow showers
¿Viste los chubascos de nieve?	Did you see the snow showers?
La bruma	The sea mist
No podia ver nada debido a la brum	I couldn't see anything due to the sea mist.
El sereno	The night dew
¿Qué es el sereno?	What is the night dew?
La neblina	The mist The fog
Hay neblina pesada	There's heavy mist.
La presión alta	High pressure
La presión baja	Low pressure
Vientoso Hace viento	Windy

Hace viento hoy día	It's windy today.
Soleado	Sunny
Es muy soleado	It's very sunny.
Nevado	Snowy
Ayer fue nevado	It was snowy yesterday.
Caliente Hace calor	It's hot.
En México, hace calor casi todo el año.	It's hot in Mexico almost all year round.
Nublado	Cloudy
Ayer estuvo muy nublado	It was very cloudy yesterday.
La humedad	Humidity
La humedad es alta	Humidity is high.
Húmedo	Humid
Es demasiado húmedo	It's too humid.
El rayo	The lightning
El día soleado	The sunny day
Hoy día será un día soleado	It will be a sunny day today.
El día tormentoso	The stormy day

Mañana será un día tormentoso	It will be a stormy day tomorrow.
La tormenta	The storm
No habrá una tormenta	There won't be a storm.
La bola de nieve	The snowball
¿Quieres jugar con las bolas de nieve?	Do you want to play with snowballs?
La ola de calor	The heatwave
Habrá una ola de calor la siguiente semana	There will be a heatwave next week.
Dry	Seco
Está semana habrá tiempo seco	It will be dry this week.
El cielo despejado	The clear sky
Podemos salir porque el cielo estará despejado	We can go out because the sky will be clear.
La brisa marina	The sea breeze
No veo la brisa marina	I don't see the sea breeze.

Feelings

How would you answer if you've ever asked how you feel at the moment?

This list of common feelings will help you answer confidently and show how you really feel.

Spanish	English
Felíz	Happy
Me siento felíz	I feel happy
Triste	Sad
¿Por qué estás triste?	Why are you sad?
Preocupado	Worried
¿Estás preocupado?	Are you worried?
Enojado	Angry
Estoy enojado	I'm angry
Asustado	Afraid
Ella está asustada	She's afraid.
Alarmado	Alarmed
¿Por qué estás alarmado?	Why are you alarmed?
Emocionado	Excited
Ella está emocionada por la noticia	She's excited about the news
Asombrado	Amazed
Me siento asombrado	I feel amazed
Calmado	Calm

Ellos están calmados	They are calm
Deprimido	Depressed
No te sientas deprimido	Don't feel depressed
Desinteresado	Disinterested
Ella parece estar desinteresada	She seems to be disinterested.
Entusiasta	Enthusiastic
Nosotros estabámos entusiastas por el juego	We were enthusiastic about the game
Avergonzado	Embarrassed
ÉL está avergonzado por su comportamiento	He feels embarrassed about his behavior
Divertido	Funny
Él siempre está contando chistes; es un chico muy divertido	He's always telling jokes; he's a very funny guy
Frustrado	Frustrated
Ellos se sienten frustrados porque no podrán viajar	They feel frustrated because they will not be able to travel.
Agradecido	Grateful

Nosotros nos sentimos agradecidos por la ayuda que recibimos	We felt grateful for the help we received
Indecidido	Hesitant
No sabían que escoger, son muy indecisos	They didn't know what to choose; they were very hesitant
Impaciente	Impatient
No seas impaciente, ellos vendrán	Don't be impatient, they'll come
Indiferente	Indifferent
No le interesa saber del tema; es indiferente	She's not interested in knowing about the issue; she's indifferent
Celoso	Jealous
Está celoso porque su esposa está conversando con otro hombre	He's jealous because his wife is talking with another man
Relajado	Relaxed
Está de vacaciones, debe estar relajado.	He's on vacation; he must be relaxed.
Incómodo	Uncomfortable
Se siente incómodo en en la situación.	He feels uncomfortable in the situation.

After studying these phrases, I'm sure you will find it easier to communicate with everyone, but this is just the beginning. These common phrases will help you sound more natural to native speakers. Greetings will be the perfect introduction to any conversation or if you want to be part of one. And good manners will surely show how educated, polite, and respectful you are to your listeners.

Now, we'll move on to the next lesson. After doing a successful introduction, you now have to continue the conversation in a natural way. How can you do that? What questions can help you sound interested in others? What if you are looking for help?

Clothing - La Ropa

Shirts, blouses, and more – Las Camisas, Blusas y más
- T-shirt – La camiseta/La playera
- Shirt – La Camisa
- Polo - El Polo
- Top - El Top
- Blouse - La Blusa
- Blazer – La chaqueta de sport
- Bodysuit – Body
- Sweatshirt – La Sudadera
- Sweater – El Jersey/El Suéter
- Cardigan – El Cárdigan
- Tunic – La Túnica

Pants and shorts – Los Pantalones y pantalones cortos
- Pants – Los Pantalones
- Trousers – El Pantalón
- Jeans – Los jeans
- Linen pants – El Pantalón de lino
- Dress pants – El Pantalón de vestir
- Suit pants – El Pantalón de traje
- Shorts – El Pantalón corto
- Joggers – Joggers
- Tracksuit pants – El Pantalón de Chándal.

Dress, skirts, formal wear – Los Vestidos, faldas, y ropa formal
- Dress – El Vestido
- Skirt – La Falda
- Miniskirt – La Minifalda
- Suit – El Traje

- Tie – La Corbata
- Bowtie – La Pajarita
- Suspenders – Los Tirantes
- Tuxedo – El Smoking
- Vest – El Chaleco
- Romper – El mono
- Overalls – El Overol
- Sundress – El Vestido sin mangas
- Gown – El Vestido
- Wedding dress – El Vestido de novia.

Underwear and sleepwear – La Ropa interior y la ropa de dormir

- Underwear – La Ropa interior
- Bra – El Sostén
- Panty – La Braga
- Panties – Las Bragas
- Boxers – Los Calzoncillos
- Thong – La Tanga
- Stockings – Las Medias
- Pantyhose – La pantimedia
- Socks – Los Calcetines
- No-show socks – Los Calcetines invisibles
- Pyjamas – La Pijama
- Camisole – La Camisola
- Robe – La Bata
- Nightie – El Camisón
- Bathrobe – El Albornoz.

Swimwear and sportswear - Ropa de Baño y ropa deportiva
- Bathing suit – El Traje de baño
- Swimsuit – El Traje de baño
- Trunks – El Bañador
- Bikini – El Bikini
- One-piece swimsuit – El Traje de baño enterizo
- Pareo – El Pareo
- Sweatshirt – La Sudadera
- Hoodie – La Sudadera con capucha
- Leggings – Las Mallas
- Sports bra – El Sujetador deportivo
- Tracksuit – El Chándal.

Outerwear – Ropa de exterior
- Coat – El Abrigo
- Jacket – La Chaqueta
- Raincoat – La Gabardina
- Bomber jacket – La Cazadora
- Jean jacket – La Cazadora vaquera
- Motorcycle jacket – La Cazadora motera
- Poncho – El Poncho
- Parka – La Parka
- Shawl – El pañuelo
- Anorak – El Anorak

Footwear – El Calzado
- Flip-flops – Las Chanclas/ Las Chancletas
- Sandals – Las Sandalias
- Ballerinas – Las Bailarinas
- Loafers – Los Mocasines

- Sneakers – Las Zapatos deportivos
- Tennis shoes – Los Zapatos deportivos
- Trainers – Los Zapatos deportivos
- Heels – Los Tacones
- Flats – Los Zapatos bajos
- Boots – Las Botas
- Ankle boots – Los Botines
- Slippers – Las Pantuflas
- Espadrilles – Las alpargatas
- Dress shoes – Los Zapatos de vestir

Accessories – Accesorios
- Cap – La Gorra
- Hat – El Gorro
- Snow hat – El Gorro
- Hood – La Capucha
- Beret – La Boina
- Belt – El Cinturón
- Necklace – El Collar
- Bracelet – La Pulsera
- Watch – El Reloj
- Earrings – Los Aretes
- Ring – El Anillo
- Gloves – Los Guantes
- Mittens – Las Manoplas
- Scarf – La Bufanda
- Handkerchief – El Pañuelo
- Leggings – Los Leggings
- Sunglasses – Las gafas de sol

- Put on your shoes – Ponte los zapatos
- Put on your shirt and shorts – Ponte la camisa y un short.
- Look for your flip-flops – Busca tus chanclas
- These are your jeans – Estos son tus jeans
- I like the dress – Me gusta el vestido
- The t-shirt is red – La camiseta es roja
- The shirt I am wearing is very ugly – La camisa que estoy usando es muy fea
- What size are you looking for? – ¿Qué talla está buscando?
- A size small – Una talla pequeña
- José wears medium size clothes – José usa ropa de talla mediana
- I need a jacket – Necesito un chaqueta
- Where are my sunglasses? – ¿Dónde están mis gafas de sol?

Countries - Los Países

Germany – Alemania
Algeria – Argelia
Armenia – Armenia
Azerbaijan – Azerbaiyán
Belarus – Belarús
Belgium – Bélgica
Bosnia and Herzegovina – Bosnia y Herzegovina
Brazil – Brasil
Bulgaria – Bulgaria
Cape Verde – Cabo Verde
Cambodia – Camboya
Canada – Canadá

Vatican City – Ciudad del Vaticano
Colombia – Colombia
North Korea – Corea del Norte
South Korea – Corea del Sur
Ivory Coast – Costa de Marfil
Croatia – Croacia
China – China
Cyprus – Chipre
Denmark – Dinamarca
Egypt – Egipto
Escocia – Scotland
Slovakia – Eslovaquia
Slovenia – Eslovenia
Spain – España
United States – Estados Unidos
Estonia – Estonia
Philippines – Filipinas
Finland – Finlandia
France – Francia
Wales – Gales
Georgia - Georgia
Greece – Grecia
Hungary – Hungría
England – Inglaterra
Ireland – Irlanda
Iceland – Islandia
Italy – Italia
Japan – Japón
Kazakhstan – Kazajstán
Kyrgyzstan – Kirquistán
Latvia – Letonia
Lebanon – Líbano

Lithuania – Lituania
Luxembourg – Luxemburgo
Malaysia – Malasia
Maldives – Maldivas
Morocco – Marruecos
Mauritius – Mauritania
Norway – Noruega
New Zealand – Nueva Zelanda
Netherlands – Países Bajos
Papua New Guinea – Papúa Nueva Guinea
Poland – Polonia
Portugal – Portugal
United Kingdom – Reino Unido
Central African Republic – República Centro-africana
Czech Republic – República Checa
Romania – Rumanía
Russia – Rusia
Serbia and Montenegro – Serbia y Montenegro
South Africa – Sudáfrica
Sweden – Suecia
Switzerland – Suiza
Swaziland – Swazilandia
Thailand – Tailandia
Taiwan – Taiwán
Tajikistan – Tayikistán
Tunisia – Túnez
Turkey – Turquía
Ukraine – Ucrania

I am from Wales – Soy de Gales

I like to visit France – Me gusta visitar Francia

He is from Russia – Él es de Rusia.

Sports - Los Deportes
Chess - El Ajedrez
Athletics - El Atletismo
Badminton - El Bádminton
Basketball - El Baloncesto
Handball - El Balonmano
Baseball - El Béisbol
Boxing - El Boxeo
Championship - El Campeonato
Cycling - El Ciclismo
Cup - La Copa
Sport - El Deporte
Sportsman - El Deportista
Draw - Empate
Riding - La Equitación
Fencing - La Esgrima
Skiing - Esquí
Soccer - El Fútbol
Gymnastics - La Gimnasia
Ice Hockey - El Hockey sobre Hielo
Discus Throw - El Lanzamiento De Disco
Javelin Throw - El Lanzamiento De Jabalina
Swimming - La Natación
Match - El Partido
Modern Pentathlon - El Pentatlón
Pole Vault - El Salto con Pértiga
High Jump - El Salto de Altura
Long Jump - El Salto de Longitud
Tennis - El Tenis
Table Tennis - El Tenis de Mesa
Sailing - Vela

Volleyball - El Voleibol
Water Polo - El Waterpolo.

Places in Town - Lugares en la Ciudad

Sidewalk - La Acera
Airport - El Aeropuerto
Department Store - El Almacén
Bank - El Banco
Library - La Biblioteca
Café - La Cafetería
Brewery - La Cervecería
Shop Window - El Escaparate
School - La Escuela
Fire Station, Firehouse - La Estación De Bomberos
Railway Station - La Estación De Ferrocarril
Stadium - El Estadio
Pharmacy - La Farmacia
Gas Station - La Gasolinera
Kindergarten - La Guardería
Hospital - El Hospital
Bookshop - La Librería
Market - El Mercado
Municipality - La Municipalidad
Museum - El Museo
Stop - La Parada
Police Station - La Policía
Inn - La Posada
Restaurant - El Restaurante
Shop, Store - La Tienda.

At Home - En Casa

Cupboard - La Alacena
Carpet - La Alfombra
Pillow - La Almohada
Wardrobe, Closet - El Armario

Tile - El Azulejo
Balcony - El Balcón
Bathtub - La Bañera
Bathroom - El Baño
Bottle - La Botella
Drawer - El Cajón
Bed - La Cama
House, Home - La Casa
Kitchen - La Cocina
Computer - El Computador
Curtain - La Cortina
Room - El Cuarto
Spoon - La Cuchara
Pantry, Larder - La Despensa
Attic, Loft - El Desván
Bedroom - El Dormitorio
Shower - La Ducha
Wallpaper - El Papel Tapiz
Desk - El Escritorio
Mirror - El Espejo
Flower - La Flor
Stove, Cooker - El Fogón
Sink - El Fregadero
Tap, Faucet - El Grifo
Oven - El Horno
Garden - El Jardín
Lamp - La Lámpara
Wash Basin - El Lavabo
Book - El Libro
Key - La Llave
Flower Pot - La Maceta
Table - La Mesa

Furniture - El Mueble
Fridge - La Nevera
Paper - El Papel
Wall - La Pared
Door Handle - El Picaporte
Floor - El Piso
Iron - La Plancha
Dish - El Plato
Pen - La Pluma
Door - La Puerta
Radiator - El Radiador
Fridge - El Refrigerador
Wall Clock - El Reloj de Pared
Sheet - La Sábana
Napkin, Serviette - La Servilleta
Chair - La Silla
Armchair - El Sillón
Cellar - El Sótano
Cup - La Taza
Ceiling - El Techo
Tile - La Teja
Television - La Tele
Phone - El Teléfono
Terrace - La Terraza
Towel - La Toalla
Glass - El Vaso
Window - La Ventana
Vestibule, Hall - El Vestíbulo.

Body parts - Las Partes del cuerpo
Armpit - La Axila

Beard - La Barba
Mustache - El Bigote
Mouth - La Boca
Arm - El Brazo
Head - La Cabeza
Hips - La Cadera
Face - La Cara
Eyebrow - La Ceja
Brain - El Cerebro
Waist - La Cintura
Elbow - El Codo
Heart - El Corazón
Skull - El Cráneo
Neck - El Cuello
Body - El Cuerpo
Little Finger - El Meñique
Finger - El Dedo
Ring Finger - El Dedo Anular
Toe - El Dedo del Pie
Tooth - Diente
Back - La Espalda
Spine – La Espina dorsal
Skeleton - El Esqueleto
Stomach - El Estómago
Forehead - La Frente
Throat - La Garganta
Liver - El Hígado

Shoulder - El Hombro
Bone - El Hueso
Forefinger - El Índice
Intestines - Los Intestinos
Lips - Los Labios

Tongue - La Lengua
Hand - La Mano
Cheek - La Mejilla
Wrist - La Muñeca
Muscle - El Músculo
Thigh - El Muslo
Nose - La Nariz
Nerve - El Nervio
Occiput - La Nuca
Eye - El Ojo
Ear - La Oreja
Organ - El Órgano
Palm - La Palma
Chest - El Pecho
Hair - El Pelo
Eyelash, Lashes — La Pestaña
Foot - El Pie
Skin - La Piel
Leg - La Pierna
Sole - La Planta
Thumb - El Pulgar
Lung - El Pulmón
Fist - El Puño
Kidney - El Riñón
Knee - La Rodilla
Blood - La Sangre
Temple - La Sien
Heel - El Talón
Ankle - El Tobillo
Nail - La Uña
Womb - El Útero
Belly - El Vientre

Important Words and Phrases - Palabras y Frases Importantes

- Please - Por favor
- Thank you - Gracias
- You are welcome! - ¡De nada!
- How are you? - ¿Cómo estás?
- Good, thank you - Bien gracias
- Not too bad - Más o menos
- A little tired - Un poco cansado
- Nice to meet you - Mucho gusto
- I would like - Yo quisiera
- I do not want - Yo no quiero
- Where is? - ¿Dónde está?
- Where is the bathroom? - ¿Dónde está el baño?
- How does it cost? - ¿Cuánto cuesta?
- What time is it? - ¿Qué hora es?
- Do you have it? - ¿Tiene?
- I have - Yo tengo
- I do not have - Yo no tengo
- I understand - Yo entiendo
- I do not understand - Yo no entiendo
- Do you understand? - ¿Entiende?
- Where is the restaurant? - ¿Dónde está el restaurante?
- Where is the bank? - ¿Dónde está el banco?
- Where can I find a taxi? - ¿Dónde puedo encontrar un taxi?
- I need - Yo necesito

- I need a hotel please - Yo necesito un hotel por favor
- I'm in a hurry - Tengo prisa
- Money - Dinero
- A table for two please - Una mesa para dos por favor
- A menu - Un menú
- Do you speak spanish? - ¿Habla español?
- Where can I find someone who speak Spanish? - ¿Dónde puedo encontrar a alguien que hable español?
- Excuse me - Disculpe
- Excuse me, Where is the bathroom? - Discúlpeme, ¿dónde está el baño?
- Sorry to interrupt - Siento interrumpir
- Excuse me - Con permiso
- I'm lost - Estoy perdido
- Why? - ¿Por qué?
- How? - ¿Cómo?
- How many? - ¿Cuántos?
- How long? - ¿Por cuánto tiempo?
- Who? - ¿Quién?
- What day is it? - ¿Qué día es hoy?
- I'm hungry - ¡Tengo hambre!
- I'm thirsty - ¡Tengo sed!
- Would you like something to eat? - ¿Quieres algo para comer?
- Would you like something to drink? - ¿Quieres algo para beber?

- What would you like to eat? - ¿Qué quieres comer?
- What do you recommend? - ¿Qué nos recomienda?
- I would like coffee with cream - Me gustaría un cafecito con leche
- I would like chicken, please - Me gustaría el pollo, por favor
- I like chocolate - Me gusta el chocolate
- I do not like fish - No me gusta el pescado
- A coffee with milk - Un café con leche
- A coffee without milk - Un café sin leche
- Enjoy your food! - ¡Que aproveche!
- Delicious! - ¡Riquísimo!
- Daily Routine – Rutina diaria
- Routine - La rutina
- Tooth brush - El cepillo de dientes
- Tooth paste - El tubo de pasta/crema dentífrica.
- Comb - El peine
- Hair brush - El cepillo
- Mirror - El espejo
- Bar of soap - La barra/pastilla de jabón
- Shampoo - El champú
- Conditione - El acondicionador
- Toilet paper - El papel de higiénico
- Facial tissue - El tejido facial
- I wake up at… - Me acuesto a…
- What time do you wake up? - ¿A qué hora se acuesta?
- I get up at… - Me levanto a…
- What time do you get up? - ¿A qué hora se levanta?

- I go to sleep at… - Me duermo a…
- What time do you go to bed? - ¿A qué hora se duerme?
- I need to take a shower. - Necesito tomar una ducha.
- Do you need to take a bath? - ¿Necesita tomar un baño?
- She bathes the baby. - Ella baña al bebé.
- He washes the car. - Él lava el carro.
- He washes his face. - Él se lava la cara.
- I brush my teeth. - Me cepillo los dientes.
- Do you have toothpaste? - ¿Tiene un tubo de pasta dentífrica?
- I need a tooth brush. - Necesito un cepillo de dientes.
- What time is breakfast - ¿A qué hora se desayuna?
- I need a ride to work. - Necesito que me lleven al trabajo.
- What bus should I take? - ¿Cuál bus debo tomar?
- Can you show me where the office is, please? - ¿Por favor, muestrame dondé está la oficina?
- My birthday is in October. - Mi cumpleaños es en octubre Happy birthday! - ¡Feliz cumpleaños!
- Congratulations! - ¡Felicitaciones!
- Bless you! - ¡Salud!
- Today is August sixteenth. - Hoy es el dieciséis de agosto.
- Of course - Claro que sí
- Of course not - Claro que no
- Don't mention it - No hay de qué

- With your permission - Con su permiso
- How nice - Que bien
- Me too - A mí también
- Me neither - A mí tampoco
- I agree - Estoy de acuerdo
- No doubt about it - No cabe duda
- I have no idea - No tengo idea
- It could be - Puede ser
- On the other hand - Por otro lado
- Good idea - Buena idea
- I hope not - Espero que no
- What do you think about…? - ¿Qué piensas de…?
- What's your opinion of..? - ¿Qué opinas de…?
- I'm not entirely sure - No estoy muy seguro
- In my opinion - En mi opinión…
- What should I do? - ¿Qué debo hacer?
- Can you give me any advice? - ¿Puedes darme algún consejo?
- What do you recommend that I do? - ¿Qué me recomiendas hacer?
- What do you advise me to do? - ¿Qué me aconsejas hacer?
- Why don't you…? - ¿Por qué tú no…?
- Maybe you should… - Tal vez tú debieras…
- Maybe you could… - Tal vez tú pudieras..
- You'd better go to… - Es mejor ir a…
- You could… - Tú podrías…
- You know what might not be a bad idea…? - ¿Sabes qué podrías hacer?

- Maybe it would be a good idea to go… - A lo mejor es una buena idea ir a…
- If I were you… - Yo que tú…
- I think you should… - Creo que deberías…
- It might be a good idea… - Tal vez fuese interesante…
- You know what I think… - Sabes que encuentro…
- Well, what I do is… - Bueno, lo que hago es…
- Maybe you're right - Tal vez tengas razón
- That might be a good idea - A lo mejor es interesante hacer eso
- I'm not really sure… - No estoy muy seguro
- I'll think about it - Voy a pensarlo
- Yeah, maybe - Puede que sí
- Let's see - Vamos a ver
- I'll figure something out. - Yo me las arreglo
- My goodness! - ¡Qué fuerte!
- How awful! (lit. what barbarity!) - ¡Qué barbaridad!
- How disgusting! - ¡Qué asco!
- How horrible! - ¡Qué horror!
- No way! - ¡No me digas!
- Get out of here! - ¡Anda ya!
- Goodness me! - ¡Madre mía!
- I can't believe it - No me lo puedo creer
- Are you kidding me? - ¿Estás de coña?
- I was shocked - Me quedé asombrado
- That's incredible - Es increíble
- I couldn't believe it - Me quedé flipado.

Holidays
- Merry Christmas - Feliz Navidad
- Happy Holidays - Felices fiestas
- Christmas Eve - La Nochebuena
- Christmas - La Navidad
- Christmas Day - Día de Navidad
- New Years Eve - La Nochevieja
- New Year - Año Nuevo
- New Year's Day - Día de Año Nuevo
- Valentine's Day - Día de San Valentín
- April Fool's Day - Día de los Inocentes
- Passover - Pascua de los hebreos
- Ash Wednesday - Miércoles de Ceniza
- Good Friday - El Viernes Santo
- Lent - La Cuaresma
- Easter - La Pascua
- Mother's Day - El día de la madre
- Memorial Day - El día de Comemoración de los Caídos
- Father's Day - El día del Padre
- Independence Day - El día de la Independencia
- Labor Day - El día del Trabajo
- Columbus Day - El día de la Raza
- Halloween - La Noche de Brujas
- Thanksgiving - El día de Acción de Gracias
- Birthday - El Cumpleaños
- Wedding - La boda
- Wedding anniversary - El aniversario de boda

Traveling

- What time does the bus leave? * ¿A qué hora se va el colectivo? * a ke o-ra se ba el ko-lek-ti-bo * a ke 'ora se βa el kolek'tiβo
- Plane * avión * a-bion * a'βjon (m.s)
- Boat * bote * bo-te * 'bote (m.s.)
- Train * tren * tren * tren (m.s.)
- Ferry * ferry * fe-rri * 'feri (m.s.)
- The plane is delayed * el avión está retrasado * el a-bion es-ta re-tra-sa-do * el a'βjon es'ta retra'saðo
- The train is cancelled * *El tren se canceló* * el tren se kan-the-lo * el tren se kanθe'lo
- From what platform does the train leave for…? * ¿desde qué plataforma sale el tren? * des-de ke pla-ta-for-ma sa-le el tren * 'desðe ke plata'forma sale el tren
- The train leaves from platform no.2 * El tren sale de la plataforma número 2 * el tren sa-le de la pla-ta-for-ma nu-me-ro dos * el tren 'sale de la plata'forma 'numero ðos
- Where is…? * ¿Dónde está? * don-de es-ta * 'donde es'ta
- The dining car *vagón restaurante * ba-gon res-tau-ran-te * el βa'ɣon restaw'rante
- The sleeping car * vagón para dormir * ba-gon pa-ra dor-mir * ba'ɣon para ðor'mir
- The berths * los atracaderos * los a-tra-ka-de-ros * los atraka'ðeros

- Where can I buy the ticket? * ¿Dónde puedo comprar el boleto? * don-de pwe-do kom-prar el bo-le-to * 'donde 'pweðo kom'prar el βo'leto
- How much does a ticket to Paris cost? * ¿Cuánto cuesta el boleto a Paris? * kwan-to kwes-ta el bo-le-to a pa-rees• 'kwanto 'kwesta el βo'leto a pa'ris
- First class * Primera clase * pri-me-ra kla-se * pri'mera 'klase (f.s.)
- Second class * Segunda clase * se-gun-da kla-se * se'ɣunda 'klase (f.s.)
- One-way * Ida * i-da * 'iða (f.s.)
- Return * Vuelta * bwel-ta * 'bwelta (f.s.)
- Discount ticket * βoleto con descuento * bo-le-to kon des-kwen-to * bo'leto kon des'kwento (m.s.)
- I'd like a seat * Quisiera un asiento * ki-sie-ra un asiento • ki'sjera un a'sjento
- Aisle * al pasillo * al pa-si-io * al pa'sijo (m.s.)
- Non-smoking * para no fumadores * pa-ra no fu-ma-do-res * para no fuma'ðores
- Window * en la ventana * en la ben-ta-na * en la βen'tana (f.s.)
- Is this seat free? * ¿Está libre este asiento? * es-ta li-bre es-te a-sien-to * es'ta 'liβre 'este a'sjento
- Do I have to pay a supplement? * ¿Tengo que pagar un suplemento? * ten-go ke pa-gar un su-ple-men-to * *'tengo ke pa'ɣar un suple'mento*
- Has the 10:00 train already departed? * ¿Ya ha partido el tren de las 10:00? * ia a par-ti-do el tren de las dieθ * ja a par'tiðo el tren ðe las ðjeθ

- My luggage didn't arrive * Mi equipaje no llegó mi e-ki-pa-he no ie-go * mi eki'paxe no je'ɣo
- Speed limit * límite de velocidad * lee-mi-te de be-lo-thi-dad * 'limite ðe βeloθi'ðað
- One way * ida * i-da * 'iða *no parking* * no estacionar * no es-ta-thio-nar * no estaθjo'nar
- Where can I get a taxi? * ¿Dónde puedo conseguir un taxi? * don-de pwe-do kon-se-gir un tak-si * 'donde 'pweðo konse'ɣir un 'taksi
- Can you show me the way to…? * ¿Puedes mostrarme el camino a…? * pwe-des mostrar-me el ka-mi-no a * 'pweðes mos'trarme el ka'mino a
- Does this road lead to…? * ¿Este camino lleva a …? * es-te ka-mi-no ie-ba a * 'este ka'mino 'jeβa a
- Can you show me on this map where I am? * ¿Puedes mostrarme dónde estoy en este mapa? * pwe-des mostrar-me don-de es-toi en es-te ma-pa * 'pweðes mos'trarme 'ðonde es'toi en 'este 'mapa
- I would like to rent a car * Me gustaría alquilar un auto * me gus-ta-ree-a al-ki-lar un au-to * me ɣusta'ria alki'lar un 'awto
- How much is daily for hire? * ¿Cuánto cuesta el alquiler diario? • kwan-to kwes-ta el al-ki-ler dia-rio * 'kwanto 'kwesta el alkiler 'djarjo
- Petrol station/Station service * Estación de servicio * es-ta-thion de ser-bi-thio * esta'θjon ðe ser'βiθjo
- Fill it up, please * Llénelo, por favor * ie-ne-lo por fa-bor * 'jenelo por fa'βor
- Unleaded petrol * Gasolina sin plomo * ga-so-li-na sin plo-mo * gaso'lina sin 'plomo

- Diesel * Diesel * die-sel * 'djesel
- LPG * Gas Natural * Gas na-tu-ral * gas natu'ral
- Please check the tires * Por favor, revise los neumáticos * por fabor re-vi-se los neu-ma-ti-kos * por fa'βor re'βise los new'matikos
- Can I park here? * ¿Puedo estacionar aquí? * pwe-do es-ta-thio-nar a-ki * 'pweðo estaθjo'nar a'ki
- I have had an accident * He tenido un accidente * e te-ni-do un ak-thi-den-te * e te'niðo un akθi'ðente
- I have got a puncture * Pinché un neumático * pin-che un neu-ma-ti-ko * pin'tʃe un new'matiko
- I have run out of petrol * Me he quedado sin nafta * me e ke-da-do sin naf-ta * me e ke'ðaðo sin 'nafta
- The battery is flat * Me quedé sin batería * me ke-de sin ba-te-ria * me ke'ðe sin bate'ria
- The car doesn't start * El auto no arranca * el au-to no a-rran-ka * el 'awto no a'ranka
- I need a mechanic * Necesito un mecánico * ne-the-si-to un me-ka-ni-ko * neθe'sito un me'kaniko
- Can you fix it today? * ¿Puedes arreglarlo hoy? * pwe-des a-rre-glar-lo oi * 'pweðes are'glarlo oi.

Borders

- Where are you from? (Formal) * ¿De dónde es usted?* de don-de es us-ted * de 'ðonde es us'teð

- Where are you from? (Informal) * ¿De dónde eres? * de don-de e-res * de 'ðonde eres
- I am from... * Soy de... * soi de * soi ðe ...
- From the USA * ... de los Estados Unidos * de los es-ta-dos u-ni-dos * de los es'taðos u'niðos ...
- From the UK * del Reino Unido * del rei-no u-ni-do * del 'rejno u'niðo ...
- From Australia * de Australia * de aus-tra-lia * de aws'tralja ...
- From New Zealand * de Nueva Zelanda * de nwe-ba the-lan-da * de 'nweβa θe'landa ...
- From Germany * de Alemania * de a-le-ma-nia * de ale'manja ...
- From France * de Francia * de fran-thia * de 'franθja
- Passport * pasaporte * pa-sa-por-te * pasa'porte visa * visa * bi-sa * 'bisa
- Customs * aduana * a-dwa-na * a'ðwana
- Immigration * inmigración * in-mi-gra-thion * inmiɣra'θjon
- Purpose of visit * propósito de la visita * pro-po-si-to de la bi-si-ta * pro'posito ðe la βi'sita
- I am on holiday * estoy de vacaciones * es-toi de ba-ka-thiones * es'toi de βaka'θjones
- I am here on business * estoy de viaje de negocios * es-toi de bia-he de ne-go-thios * es'toi ðe 'βjaxe ðe ne'ɣoθjos
- I am travelling on my own * Estoy viajando solo * es-toi bia-han-do so-lo * es'toi βja'xando 'solo

- With my family * con mi familia * kon mi fa-mi-lia * kon mi fa'milja
- In a group * en grupo * en gru-po * en 'grupo
- I have a … * Tengo un … * ten-go un * 'tengo un
- Work permit * permiso de trabajo * per-mi-so de tra-ba-ho * per'miso ðe tra'βaxo
- Residency permit * permiso de residencia * per-mi-so de re-si-den-thia * per'miso ðe resi'ðensja
- Study permit * permiso de estudio * per-mi-so de es-tu-dio * per'miso ðe es'tuðjo.

Chapter 3. Major Spanish Grammar Lessons to Consider

To learn the Spanish language, you must immerse yourself in it and learn everything, including grammar. You need to learn the basic principles of Spanish grammar. It is fundamental to build a strong block in the language. Here are some of the things you should learn.

Nouns Combined With Articles

A noun is a place, person, or a thing. In Spanish, a noun is preceded by the article, but the ending can change depending on the gender of the noun. When learning this language, you should learn the articles and understand which one comes before a particular noun. The nouns are determined by gender. You cannot predict the gender of any Spanish noun, so you must master the nouns and vocabulary words to know, speak, or write the language correctly.

A good example is the word "dress." Your first guess is that this word is female, but it is wrong; "dress" is a male noun. You need to memorize the articles with a noun instead of trying to guess them. One of the great tips to use when mastering Spanish grammar is that feminine nouns mostly end with an "a," while masculine ones end with "o." They are similar to "an," "a," and "the" used in English. Examples include the following:

El, which masculine singular

La, which is feminine singular

Los, which is masculine plural

Las, which feminine plural

A noun also changes for a living thing; for example, "the dress" is "el vestido," and this never changes because it's a non-living thing. However, when referring to "the cat," you say "el gato," which changes, depending on the cat's gender.

El gato means the male cat.

La gata means the female cat.

Learning the Plurals

Spanish plurals are not different from English plurals. You simply add an "s" or "es" at the end; however, you must also change the article when writing and speaking in plural. For a noun that ends with a vowel in Spanish, you add an "s" to change to the plural. For example, "Las camas" is the plural of "la cama." It's the same thing in English where "bed" becomes "beds," for example.

A noun that ends with a consonant in Spanish requires you to add an "es" and change the article to change it into plural.

"El profesor" is changed to "Los profesores" ("the professor" becomes "the professors"). The nouns, articles, and genders help you speak correct Spanish, and you can describe events in proper grammar. These are the pillars of learning Spanish like a native and enable you to communicate effectively.

Always ask yourself what the definition of the nouns and the articles are. The gender alterations of the word define how you can write in the plural and the articles to use with it.

Asking Questions in Spanish

In every language, you need to ask questions, especially when learning. Questions are also important in real life when you need help in directions or even when you have a conversation with someone. If the locals only speak Spanish, you must know how to ask questions.

When speaking, the voice inflection helps you ask a question. This means you simply raise the voice just before you end the sentence. The whole statement becomes a question because of the change of pitch. It works perfectly when communicating in Spanish verbally.

A written question in Spanish has two question marks, indicating a rising voice. One question mark is at the beginning of a sentence and another one at the end.

For example:

"¿Qué significa esta palabra?" and it means "What does this word mean?"

In Spanish, there are interrogative words, which are also referred to as the question words. They have a unique accent that makes it easy for the reader to know they are questions and not just ordinary statements. As a Spanish learner, it will take you a lot of practice to get familiar with common question words. Here are some examples:

¿Dónde está..? And it means, Where is...?

¿Quién e..? Meaning, Who is...?

The Description Words

For you to express yourself in Spanish, you must know how to describe people, your surroundings, and places. You cannot write or speak Spanish unless you know the description words. Describing things is part of every language, and this is the part that carries most vocabularies. It's unlimited; you can enrich your language by learning as many descriptive words as you can.

Spanish descriptive sentences are not very different from English; you have to follow the same principles of grammar. The only difference is that, in Spanish, the noun comes before the adjective. This means learning to think the opposite when writing or speaking Spanish. For example:

"Manos grandes," which means "big hands."

"Pelo largo," which means "long hair."

To practice more descriptive words in Spanish, read books that you know in English but have been translated into Spanish. Since you already know the story, it will make you identify useful phrases that you can use in your descriptions. Also, you can learn more vocabulary and use them.

Learning Basic Conjugation-Verbs

At this point, you are already familiar with questions, nouns, and descriptions. You are still a newbie in Spanish but on your way to learning how to speak and read like natives. However, for you to put everything together, you must also learn about verbs, and verbs cannot be used without conjugation.

Conjugating verbs make your language fluent. But, one incorrect conjugation will alter the whole meaning of a sentence. A good example is "Yo soy de Tejas," which means, "I am from Texas." If the conjugation is changed, the sentence goes like, "Eres de Tejas," which means, "You are from Texas."

As a beginner, do not stress yourself overmastering everything at the same time. Study and try to memorize as much as possible. Start with the basic ones and advance gradually to the present tense conjugations; they are the simplest and most important. Most conversations are in the present tense, so this will be helpful and prepare you for the other tenses.

For example:

"Good morning Mary, how are you."

"I am fine, thank you."

"Glad you good, do you want to go out tonight?"

"No, I would like to stay indoors."

This conversation is an example of the everyday discussions people engage in the present tense. Present tense conjugation endings include:

"o" when speaking about yourself

"a" referring to someone else informally

"a" refereeing to someone else formally

"Emos, imos, amos" they referred to a group where you are included "an" refers to a group where you are not included.

The Stem-Changing Verbs

These are verbs consisting -ar, -ir, and -er. They are also known as shoe verbs; when a stem-changing verb is conjugated, it fits in the "shoe," and the vowel changes from single to double vowel. These groups of stem-changing verbs mainly speak about you, about someone informally or formally, or about a group where you are not included. They are the most used verbs in Spanish. So, getting familiar with them will help you get ready to learn future and past tense conjugations. As they say, practice makes perfect. Spend time practicing the conjugating stem-changing verbs, and use the shoe fitting trick so that you may know what to change.

Nouns in Spanish

Unlike English, Spanish has only 2 genders. All nouns are either masculine or feminine. Nouns like "book" which are considered to have no gender in English (neuter gender) are either masculine or feminine in Spanish.

When you learn a new word in Spanish it is important to learn what gender it is as well. For example when you learn that "mesa" means table, try to remember it as "la mesa" so you also remember that it is a feminine noun. It is hard to memorize the gender of every single word you learn so here are some general rules that will help you.

General Rules for Gender in Spanish

1. In general, nouns ending in—o are masculine and nouns ending in—a are feminine (although there are some exceptions).

- Masculine – Masculino
- The boy – El muchacho
- The boy – El chico
- The dog – El perro
- The cat – El gato
- The brother – El hermano
- The uncle – El tío
- The grandfather – El abuelo
- The book – El libro
- The dish – El plato
- The glass – El vidrio
- The car – El carro
- The chicken – El pollo
- The bull – El toro

Now some examples of feminine nouns in spanish:
- Feminine – La muchacha
- The girl – La chica
- The girl – La niña
- The dog – La perra
- The cat – La gata
- The sister – La hermana
- The aunt – La tía
- The grandmother – La abuela
- The beach – La playa
- The silver – La plata
- The table – La mesa
- The door – La puerta
- The chair – La silla

- The house – La casa

"El" and "La" are the spanish definite articles. The spanish indefinite articles are "un" and "una"

- El libro – The book
- Un libro – A book
- La playa – The beach
- Una playa – A beach
- El toro – The bull
- Un toro – A bull
- La casa – The house
- Una casa – A house

2. There are some exceptions to the rule above. The following are some exceptions to the previous rule:

Masculine
- The problem – El problema
- The system – El sistema
- The climate – El clima
- The theme – El tema
- The day – El día
- The program – El programa
- The map – El mapa
- The water – El agua

Feminine
- The hand – La mano
- The radio – La radio

3. Some nouns change their ending depending on whether they are masculine or feminine:

Masculine
- The teacher – El maestro
- The teacher – El profesor
- The dancer – El bailador
- The waiter – El mesero
- The waiter – El camarero
- The actor – El actor

Feminine
- The teacher – La profesora
- The teacher – La maestra
- The dancer – La bailarina
- The waitress – La camarera
- The actress – La actriz

Some nouns remain the same whether they are masculine or feminine:
- El periodista/La periodista – The journalist
- El socialista/La socialista – The socialist
- El pianista/La pianista – The pianist
- El dentista/La dentista – The dentist
- El piloto/La piloto – The pilot
- El novelista/La novelista – The novelist/writer
- El artista/La artista – The artist

The Plural in Spanish

Forming the plural in Spanish is pretty straightforward. Here are some general rules: 1. If the noun ends in a vowel, just add "s" to the end of the word. Note that the articles also change from "El" to "Los" for masculine nouns and from "La" to "Las" for feminine nouns. See the following examples:

Masculine

- El carro/Los carros – The car/The cars
- El hermano/Los hermanos – The brother/The brothers
- El mapa/Los mapas – The map/The maps
- El plato/Los platos – The dish/The dishes
- El libro/Los libros – The book/The books
- El vaso/Los vasos – The glass/The glasses

Feminine

- La mesa/Las mesas – The table/The tables
- La hermana/Las hermanas – The sister/The sisters
- La profesora/Las profesoras – The teacher/The teachers
- La mano/Las manos – The hand/The hands
- La puerta/Las puertas – The door/The doors
- La casa/Las casas – The house/The houses

If a noun ends in a consonant then add 'es' to the end of the word to make it plural.

Masculine

- El tenedor/Los tenedores – The fork/The forks
- El profesor/Los profesores – The teacher/The teachers
- El cantor/Los cantores – The singer/The singers

Feminine

- La ciudad/Las ciudades – The city/The cities

- La universidad/Las universidades – The university/The universities
- La cantidad/Las cantidades – The quantity/The quantities

Some common exceptions:

- El sacacorchos/Los sacacorchos – The corkscrew/The corkscrews
- El abrelatas/Los abrelatas – The can opener/The can openers
- El paraguas/Los paraguas – The paraguas/The Umbrellas

Adjectives in Spanish

Adjectives are words to describe a noun e.g. tall, small, sweet, etc. Adjectives in Spanish have to agree with the gender of the noun as well as singular or plural. For example "un hombre rico" – "a rich man," "una mujer rica" – "a rich woman," "hombres altos" – tall men, "casas lindas" – pretty/cute houses. Notice how the adjective follows the noun in Spanish, unlike English.

The following are a list of common adjectives in Spanish:

- Grande – Big
- Bonito – Pretty
- Largo – Long
- Bueno – Good
- Limpio – Clean
- Rico – Rich
- Dulce – Sweet
- Amargo – Bitter

- Joven – Young
- Gordo – Fat
- Elegante – Elegant
- Inteligente – Intelligent
- Encantador – Charming
- Pequeño – Small
- Feo – Ugly
- Corto – Short (length)
- Malo – Bad
- Sucio – Dirty
- Pobre – Poor
- Agrio – Sour
- Salado – Salty
- Viejo – Old
- Delgado – Thin
- Impresionante – Impressive
- Importante – Important
- Trabajador – Hard working

Subject Pronouns

Subject pronouns are what we usually put at the beginning of a sentence (I, you, he, she, etc). The following are the subject pronouns in Spanish:

Spanish – English
Yo – I

Tú – You (singular informal)

Usted – You (singular formal)

Él – He

Ella – She

Nosotras/Nosotros – We (males or a mixture of males and females)

Ustedes – You (plural)

Ellas/Ellos – They (males or a mixture of males and females)

Here are some things to remember:

"Tú" (you) is used to address people you know very well (good friends, relatives, children...) "Usted" (you) is used to address people you meet for the first time or are not very familiar with.

"Ustedes" is the plural form of both "Tú" and "Usted."

Now let's try a few example sentences with the subject pronouns above. We will be introducing you to the verb "hablar" which means "to speak." We will go into a lot more detail about verbs later but for now, the only thing you need to know is that verbs in Spanish change a lot more with the subject pronoun than they do in English.

- Yo hablo español – I speak Spanish
- Tú hablas inglés – You (informal) speak English
- Usted habla italiano – You (formal) speak Italian
- Él habla francés – He speaks French
- Ella habla portugués – She speaks Portuguese
- Nosotros hablamos alemán – We speak German
- Nosotras hablamos ruso – We (all females) speak Russian
- Ustedes hablan chino – You (plural) speak Chinese
- Ellos hablan hebreo – They speak Hebrew
- Ellas hablan árabe – They (all females) speak Arabic

Notice how the verb "hablar" "to speak" changed to "hablo," "hablas," "habla," "hablamos" or "hablan" depending on the subject pronoun. We cover this in a lot more detail in our section on verbs.

More on the Subjunctive Mood

We touched on the subjunctive mood in our beginners section for Verbs (Present Subjunctive of Regular Verbs and Present Subjunctive of Irregular Verbs) but there is a little more to it than what was covered there that is worth mentioning.

The subjunctive is quite frustrating for English speakers who are trying to learn Spanish but since it is used quite a bit in regular conversation, it is worth taking a little more time and trouble to understand how it works. The following section goes into a little more detail on its usage, which you as an intermediate level Spanish speaker should find very useful.

Expressions that use the Subjunctive

Here are some common expressions that require the use of the subjunctive. You have already seen some of them in the Beginner Level of this course. The following expressions take the subjunctive because they express personal feelings about something:

- Querer que – to want
- Estar contento que – to be happy that
- Alegrarse que – to be glad that
- Preferir que – to prefer that
- Temer que – to fear that
- Esperar que – to hope that
- Sugerir que – to suggest that
- Recomendar que – to recommend that
- Aconsejar que – to demand that
- Exigir que – to advise that
- Mandar que – to order that
- Rogar que – to beg
- Pedir que – to ask that.

Special Case 1: "Decir" and "Escribir"

"Decir"—to say and "escribir"—to write, are 2 verbs that may or may not use a subjunctive depending on the context. You only use the subjunctive if you are commanding someone to do something. Check out the examples below.

Subjunctive Usage

- Les digo a los niños que aprendan el subjuntivo – I tell the children to learn the subjunctive

- Ella me escribe para que yo traiga su libro – She writes me to bring her book.

Indicative Usage

- Juliana me dice que ella no viene mañana – Juliana tells me that she is not coming tomorrow
- Roberto me escribe que va a trabajar hasta el fin del mes – Roberto writes me that he will work till the end of the month.

The Subjunctive and the Negative form of a Verb

Some common personal expressions take the subjunctive only in the negative form. Watch out of the following:

- Creo que es muy fácil – I believe it is very easy
- No creo que sea muy fácil – I don't believe it is very easy
- Pienso que puedes alcanzarlo – I think you can reach it
- No pienso que puedas alcanzarlo – I don't think you can reach it

The following expressions follow the same rule. Only the negative form takes the subjunctive:

- Es cierto que – to be certain that
- Estar seguro que – to be sure that.

The Subjunctive and Impersonal Expressions

However, there are also a number of impersonal expressions that take the subjunctive, for example:

- Es importante que – it's important that
- Es necesario que – it's necessary that

- Es imposible que – it's impossible that
- Es possible que – it's possible that
- Es probable que - it's probable that
- Es bueno que – it's good that
- Es malo que – it's bad that
- Es una lástima que – it's a pity that
- Es mejor que – it's better that
- Es raro que – it's strange that

Special Case 2: "Buscar" and "Necesitar"

Verbs like "buscar" – "to look for" and "necesitar" – "to need," also take the subjunctive in the following cases:

- Conozco a un actor que habla tres idiomas – I know an actor who speaks three languages.
- Busco un actor que hable tres idiomas – I am looking for an actor that speaks three languages (Subjunctive)
- Conozco a alguien que puede ayudarnos – I know someone who can help us
- Necesito alguien que pueda ayudarnos – I need someone who can help us (Subjunctive)

Other General Cases

The following are a few more common conjunctions that also take the subjunctive:

- A fin de que – in order that
- De manera que – so that
- A pesar de que – in spite of
- A menos que – unless
- En caso de que – in case

- Sin que – without
- Con tal de que – provided that
- Para que – so that

Let's take a look at a few examples:

- Vea películas en español para que aprenda más vocabulario – Watch movies in Spanish so that you learn more vocabulary
- Te traigo mi libro para que puedas leerlo mientras tanto – I will bring my book so that you can read it in the meantime
- El nos ayudará con tal de que le digamos la verdad – He will help us, provided (that) we tell him the truth
- No iré a la playa a menos que vengas con nosotros – I won't go to the beach unless you come with us

If you want to tell someone to do something without using a command (the imperative in the Beginner Level) you can use 'que' + subjunctive

- ¡Que tenga un buen viaje! – Have a good trip!
- ¡Que vuelvan rápido! – Come back soon! (May you return soon!)
- ¡Que estés bien! - Be well!

Here are some miscellaneous examples of expressions that take the subjunctive:

- Sea lo que sea, ustedes tienen que terminar este trabajo – Be as it may, you have to finish this job
- No hay nadie en este país que tenga esta estampilla – There isn't anyone in this country who has this stamp

- No hay ningún carro que me guste aquí – There isn't a single car that I like here
- Vamos a salir hoy? Como quieras – Are we going out today? Whatever you want
- Quizás vengan pronto – Perhaps they will come soon
- Ojalá sepamos que hacer – I hope we will know what to do
- Tal vez no haya mucho tráfico – Perhaps there isn't much traffic

The Subjunctive in the Past Tense

So far we have discussed how to use the subjunctive in the present tense.

This works the same way in the future tense:

- Ella quiere que usted venga con nosotros – She wants you to come with us
- Ella querrá que usted venga con nosotros – She will want you to come with us

As you can see, the future takes the same subjunctive form as the present. The subjunctive does however, take a different conjugation in the past tense. Let's take a look at how these work for regular 'ar', 'er' and 'ir' verbs:

- Regular "ar" verb - Trabajar
- Regular "er" verb - Comer
- Regular "ir" verb - Salir

Yo trabajé, yo comi, yo salí
Tu trabajaste, tu comiste, to saliste
Usted trabajó, usted comió, usted salió
Nosotros trabajamos, nosotros comimos, nosotros salimos
Ellos trabajaron, ellos comieron, ellos salieron.
Some verbs have a slightly irregular conjugation in the past subjunctive form. These are called stem changing verbs.

Future tense
Yo trabajaré, comeré, saldré
Tu trabajarás, comerás, saldrás
Usted comerá, usted trabajará, usted saldrá
Nosotros trabajaremos, comeremos, saldremos.
Ellos trabajarán, comerán, saldrán

Verb Conjugations

- Dar – to give (Diera, dieras, diéramos, dieran)
- Poder – to be able (Pudiera, pudieras, pudiéramos, pudieran)
- Pedir – to ask (Pidiera, pidieras, pidiéramos, pidieran)
- Sentir – to feel (Sintiera, sintieras, sintiéramos, sintieran)
- Morir – to die (Muriera, murieras, muriéramos, murieran)
- Venir – to come (Viniera, vinieras, viéramos, vinieran)
- Querer – to want (Quisiera, quisieras, quisiéramos, quisieran)
- Hacer – to do, to make (Hiciera, hicieras, hiciéramos, hicieran)
- Conocer – to know, to be familiar with (Conociera, conocieras, conociéramos, conocieran)
- Caber – to fit (Cupiera, cupieras, cupiéramos, cupieran)
- Saber – to know (Supiera, supieras, supiéramos, supieran)
- Poner – to put (Pusiera, pusieras, pusiéramos, pusieran)
- Tener – to have (Tuviera, tuvieras, tuviéramos, tuvieran)
- Ver – to see (Viera, vieras, viéramos, vieran)
- Estar – to be (Estuviera, estuvieras, estuviéramos, estuvieran)

- Haber – to have (Hubiera, hubieras, hubiéramos, hubieran)
- Andar – to walk (Anduviera, anduvieras, anduviéramos, anduvieran)
- Leer – to read (Leyera, leyeras, leyéramos, leyeran)
- Caer – to fall (Cayera, cayeras, cayéramos, cayeran)
- Construir – to construct (Construyera, construyeras, construyéramos, construyeran)
- Oir – to listen (Oyera, oyeras, oyéramos, oyeran)
- Conducir – to drive (Condujera, condujeras, condujéramos, condujeran)
- Traducir – to translate (Tradujera, tradujeras, tradujéramos, tradujeran)
- Producir – to produce (Produjera, produjeras, produjéramos, produjera)
- Traer – to bring (Trajera, trajeras, trajéramos, trajeran)
- Decir – to say (Dijera, dijeras, dijéramos, dijeran).

The Verbs "ir" and "ser"

The irregular verbs "ir" – "to go" and "ser" – "to be" have the same conjugation in the past subjunctive – fuera, fueras, fueramos, fueran.

Let's take a look at a few examples using the past subjunctive:

- El maestro exigió que todos fueran a la reunión – The teacher demanded that everyone go to the meeting/be at the meeting
- Yo quería que ella se sintiera mejor – I wanted her to feel better

- Era necesario que yo estuviera con mi familia – It was necessary for me to be with my family
- Llegué mas temprano para que pudiéramos hacer algo por ellos – I arrived early so that we could do something for them
- Es posible que ellos salieran por la otra salida – It's possible that they left through the other exit
- El jefe mandó que trabajáramos este fin de semana – The boss ordered us to work this weekend
- Mis padres pidieron que yo limpiara la cocina antes de empezar la película – My parents asked me to clean the kitchen, before starting the movie

You can use the past subjunctive when you wish for something in order to be able to achieve something

- Si yo fuera más joven, lo habría hecho – If I were younger, I would have done it
- Si ella tuviera más dinero, viajaría a París – If she had more money, she would travel to París
- Si yo hubiera sabido que tú estarías aquí, te habría traído un regalo – If I knew you would be here, I would have brought you a gift
- Ojalá supiera lo que le pasó a David – If only I knew what happened to David
- Ojalá tuviera dos semanas más the vacaciones – If only I had two more weeks of vacation

You can also use 'haber' to form the present perfect subjunctive or the pluperfect subjunctive:

- Me allegro que hayas llegado – I am glad that you have arrived

- Esperamos que ustedes ya hayan comido – We hope you have already eaten
- Si yo hubiera tenido más tiempo, habría visitado a Carlos – If I had had more time, I would have visited Carlos
- Si me hubieras traído algo especial, te habría perdonado – If you had brought me something special, I would have forgiven you
- Él quería que hubieran llegado antes – He wanted them to have arrived before
- Yo habría preferido que me lo hubieras dicho antes – I would have prefered it if you had told me before

"Por" and "Para" - How to say "for" in Spanish

The terms "por" and "para" are often confused by English speakers who learn Spanish. The confusion is caused because the meaning of these terms really depends on the context. The best way to get a feel for how/when they are used is to just look at different examples.

Different Uses of "Para"

1. The easiest usage of "para" is the one that means "for" or "in order to":

- Compré este libro para usted – I bought this book for you
- Traiga su amigo para jugar fútbol con nosotros – Bring your friend to play soccer with us
- Despejé todo el cuarto para ayudarte – I cleared the whole room to help you

- Ella necesita el código para sacar el dinero – She needs the code to take out (withraw) the money
- Para nosotros hablar inglés todo el día es difícil – For us, speaking English all day is difficult

2. 'para' can also be used to say that you are going somewhere:

- Me voy para Francia – I am leaving for France
- ¿Nos vamos para la casa? – Are we leaving for home?
- El tren salió para Madrid – The train left for Madrid
- ¿Para dónde vas? – Where are you going?

3. 'para' can also be used to indicate a time limit:

- Lo vamos a terminar para mañana – We are going to finish it for/by tomorrow
- ¿Para qué fecha lo necesitas? – For/by which date do you need it?

Different Uses of "Por"

1. 'Por' can be used to indicate expressions involving time:

- Vivimos aquí por diez años – We have lived in the US for 10 years
- Lo terminaremos por Diciembre – We will finish it around December.

2. 'Por' is also commonly used to mean "through" or "by":

- Viajamos por Alemania pero sólo paramos en Berlín – We travelled through Germany but we only stopped in Berlin
- ¿Por qué no pasamos por donde Andrés a saludarle? – Why don't we pass by Andres' place to say hello
- Pasamos por el teatro pero no entramos – We passed by the theatre but we didn't go in.

3. 'Por' is also used to express something you are about to do:

- Estamos por empezar – We are about to/ready to begin
- Estamos por salir – We are about to/ready to leave.

Either "Por" or "Para"

The trickiest cases are when you can use either "por" or "para" but each one changes the meaning of the sentence. So you have to be very sure of what you mean to say before picking either one.

- Compré este libro para ti – I bought it for you (I bought the book to give to you)
- Compré este libro por ti – I bought it for you (I bought the book because of you. You were the reason I bought it but I didn't necessarily buy it to give to you. I could have bought it for myself or someone else)

In general understanding the difference between 'por' and 'para' just takes practice. Pay attention to the way native speakers use them. It's worth the effort to avoid misunderstandings. Below are a few more miscellaneous examples using 'por' and 'para':

- Usted me tomó por un idiota – You took me for a fool
- Usted puede pasar por un Latino – You could pass for a Latino
- Queda mucho por hacer – There is a lot left to be done
- Ellos me pagaron mil pesos por un día de trabajo – The paid me a thousand pesos for a day of work
- ¿Vamos por aquí or por allí? – Shall we go this way or that way?
- Saliendo del aparcamiento, otro carro nos chocó por atrás – While coming out of the parking lot, another car hit us from behind
- Manejaban a doscientos kilómetros por hora – They were driving at 200 km/hr
- Cuestan 10 pesos por docena – They cost 10 pesos per dozen.
- Lavar – to wash
- Yo lavo – I wash
- Tú lavas – You wash (singular, informal)
- Él lava – He washes
- Ella lava – She washes
- Usted lava – You wash (singular, formal)
- Nosotros lavamos – We wash
- Nosotras lavamos – We wash (feminine)
- Ellos lavan – They wash
- Ellas lavan – They wash (feminine)

- Ustedes lavan – You wash (plural).

Did you notice how the endings change with each conjugation? In the beginning, unfortunately, you will have to memorize the conjugations of the different verbs but the good news is that once you get a feeling for the pattern of how the endings of the verbs change, you will not have to memorize the conjugations anymore. When you learn a new verb, you will easily be able to figure out the conjugations.

The verb above (lavar) ended in 'ar'. There are 3 kinds of verbs in Spanish. They end in 'ar', 'er' and 'ir'. Each type has a similar pattern except for a few that are irregular and unfortunately have to be memorized. More on verbs in later chapters.

Note

"Tú" (you) is used to address people you know very well (good friends, relatives, children…) "Usted" (you) is used to address people you meet for the first time or are not very familiar with.

"Ustedes" is the plural form of both "Tú" and "Usted."

This is the way it works in Latin America. In Spain, the rules are a bit different. Since this course focuses on Latin American Spanish, we won't confuse you with too much extra material.

Present Tense: Regular Verbs

Spanish has 3 main kinds of verbs. These verbs have the endings "ar," "er" and "ir."

Examples of 'ar' Verbs

- Hablar – To speak, to talk
- Yo hablo – I speak
- Tú hablas – You speak (informal)
- Usted habla – You speak (formal)
- Él/Ella habla – He/she speaks
- Nosotros/Nosotras hablamos – We speak
- Ustedes hablan – You speak (plural)
- Ellos/Ellas hablan – They speak

Attention!!! Notice the pattern of the verbs ending in "ar." The endings change to -o, -as, -a, -amos, -an. The endings for Usted, Él and Ella are the same (-a). The endings for Ustedes, Ellos and Ellas are the same (-an).

Some examples of how to use the verb 'hablar':

- Yo hablo español – I speak Spanish
- Tú hablas muy rápido – You speak very fast (informal)
- Él habla con Rosa – He speaks to Rosa
- Nosotros hablamos inglés – We speak English
- Ellos hablan con un accento – They speak with an accent

Caminar – To walk:

- Yo camino – I walk
- Tú caminas – You walk (informal)
- Usted camina – You walk (formal)
- Él/Ella camina – He/She walks
- Nosotros/Nosotras caminamos – We walk
- Ustedes caminan – You walk (plural)

- Ellos/Ellas caminan – They walk

Some examples of how to use the verb "caminar":

- Yo camino al supermercado – I walk to the supermarket
- Tú caminas muy rápido – You walk very fast (informal)
- Ella camina todos los días – She walks every day.
- Nosotros caminamos juntos – We walk together
- Ellos caminan con los niños – They walk with the children

Tomar – To take:

- Yo tomo – I take
- Tú tomas – You take (informal)
- Usted toma – You take (formal)
- Él/Ella toma – He/She takes
- Nosotros tomamos – We take
- Ustedes toman – You take (plural)
- Ellos/Ellas toman – They take

Some examples of how to use the verb "tomar":

- Yo tomo el tren – I take the train
- ¿Tú tomas azúcar? - Do you take sugar?
- Ella toma un taxi – She takes a taxi
- Nosotras tomamos una pausa – We (feminine plural) take a break
- ¿Usted toma la medicina? – Do you take the medicine? (formal)

- Ellas toman el tren todos los días – They (feminine plural) take the train every day.

Examples of "er" Verbs

- Comer – To eat
- Yo como – I eat
- Tú comes – You eat (informal)
- Usted come – You eat (formal)
- Él/Ella come – He/She eats
- Nosotros comemos – We eat
- Ustedes comen – You eat (plural)
- Ellos/Ellas comen – They eat

Attention!!! Notice the pattern of the verbs ending in "er." The endings change to -o, -es, -e, -emos, -en. The endings for Usted, Él and Ella are the same (-e). The endings for Ustedes, Ellos and Ellas are the same (-en).

Some examples of how to use the verb "comer":

- Yo como arroz con pollo – I eat rice with chicken
- Tú comes mucha carne – You eat a lot of meat ("mucha" because carne is feminine)
- Ella come un bistek – She eats a steak
- Nosotras comemos muy temprano/tarde – We eat very early/late
- Ellas comen juntas – They (feminine plural) eat together

Beber – To drink:

- Yo bebo – I drink
- Tú bebes – You drink (informal)

- Usted bebe – You drink (formal)
- Él/Ella bebe - He/She drinks
- Nosotros bebemos – We drink
- Ustedes beben – You drink
- Ellos/Ellas beben – They drink

Some examples of how to use the verb "beber":
- Yo bebo leche – I drink milk
- Tú bebes todos los días – You drink every day
- Él bebe jugo de manzana – He drinks apple juice
- Nosotros bebemos agua con limón – We drink water with lemon
- Ellos no beben cerveza – They don't drink beer.

Note: In spoken Spanish the verb "tomar" is very often used instead of "beber." For example: Tomo una cerveza – I drink beer.

Examples of "ir" Verbs
- Escribir – To write
- Yo escribo – I write
- Tú escribes – You write (informal)
- Usted escribe – You write (formal)
- Él/Ella escribe – He/She writes
- Nosotros escribimos – We write
- Ustedes escriben – They write
- Ellos/Ellas escriben – They write

Attention!!! Notice the pattern of the verbs ending in "ir." The endings change to -o, -es, -e, -imos, -en. The endings for Usted, Él and Ella are the same (-e). The endings for Ustedes, Ellos and Ellas are the same (-en).

Some examples of how to use the verb 'escribir':
- Yo escribo una carta – I write a letter
- Tú escribes la dirección – You write the address (informal)
- Usted escribe muy bien – You write very well (formal)
- Ella escribe en la pared – She writes on the wall
- Nosotros escribimos el informe - We write the report
- Ellas escriben la historia – They (all women) write the story

Compartir – To share:

- Yo comparto – I share
- Tú compartes – You share (informal)
- Usted comparte – You share (formal)
- Él/Ella comparte – He/She shares
- Nosotros/Nosotras compartimos – We share
- Ustedes comparten – You share (plural)
- Ellos/Ellas comparten – They share.

Some examples of how to use the verb "compartir":
- Yo comparto la comida con Juan – I share the food with Juan
- Tú compartes el postre con Clara – You share the desert with Clara
- Ella comparte sus juguetes con una amiga – She shares her toys with a (female) friend.
- Nosotros compartimos el apartamento – We share the apartment.
- Ellos comparten la torta – They share the cake.

Present Tense: Irregular Verbs

There are a number of irregular verbs that are very important in order to be able to speak even basic Spanish. Since these verbs do not quite follow the pattern of conjugation that we have seen in the chapter on regular verbs, the conjugations will just have to be memorized.

We have found that repeating the conjugations of Spanish verbs out loud with examples is of great help.

Below is a list of important "ar," "er" and "ir" verbs that do not have regular conjugations, but learning these verbs will greatly increase your ability to speak and understand Spanish.

Ir – To go:

- Yo voy – I go
- Tú vas – You go
- Usted va – You go
- Él/Ella va – He/She goes
- Nosotros/Nosotras vamos – We go
- Ustedes van – You go
- Ellos/Ellas van – They go.

   Some examples of how to use the verb "ir":
- Yo voy al teatro – I go to the theatre ("a el teatro" becomes "al teatro")
- ¿Tú vas solo? – Do you go alone?
- Ella va a la escuela – She goes to school
- Nosotros vamos al supermercado – We go to the supermarket ("a el supermercado" becomes "al supermercado")

- Ellos van a la farmacia – They go to the pharmacy.

Venir – To come:

- Yo vengo – I come
- Tú vienes – You come
- Usted viene – you come
- Él/Ella viene – He/She comes
- Nosotros/Nosotras venimos – We come
- Ustedes vienen – You come
- Ellos/Ellas vienen – They come

Some examples of how to use the verb "venir":

- Yo vengo aquí todos los días – I come here every day
- Tú vienes con un amigo – You come with a friend
- Ella viene más tarde – She comes later
- Nosotras venimos aquí frecuentemente – We come here frequently
- Ellas vienen con la familia – They come with the family.

Salir – To leave/go out:

- Yo salgo – I go out
- Tú sales – You go out
- Usted sale – You go out
- Él/Ella sale – He/She goes out
- Nosotros/Nosotras salimos – We go out
- Ustedes salen – You go out
- Ellos/Ellas salen – They go out

Some examples of how to use the verb "salir":

- Yo salgo temprano – I leave early
- Tú sales tarde – You leave late
- Él sale con un amigo – He leaves with a friend
- Nosotros salimos juntos – We go out together
- Ellas salen del cine – They leave the cinema ("de el cine" becomes "del cine")

Decir – To say:

- Yo digo – I say
- Tú dices – You say
- Usted dice – You say
- Él/Ella dice – He/She says
- Nosotros/Nosotras decimos – We say
- Ustedes dicen – You say
- Ellos/Ellas dicen – they say

Some examples of how to use the verb "decir":

- Yo digo la verdad – I tell the truth
- ¿Qué dices tú? – What do you say?
- Ella dice que es cierto – She says it's true/certain
- Nosotros decimos no a la violencia – We say no to violence
- Ellos dicen mentiras – They tell lies

Hacer – To do:

- Yo hago – I do
- Tú haces – You do
- Usted hace – You do
- Él/Ella hace – He/She does
- Nosotros/Nosotras hacemos – We do

- Ustedes hacen – You do
- Ellos/Ellas hacen – They do.

Some examples of how to use "hacer":

- Hago el proyecto – I do the project
- ¿Cómo haces esto? – How do you do this?
- Ella hace una torta – She makes a cake
- Hacemos una fiesta en el hotel – We are having a party at the hotel
- Ellos hacen un buen trabajo – They do/are doing a good job.

Present Tense: Reflexive Verbs

Reflexive verbs are used to describe an action that reflects back on the subject. A good example in English is the verb 'to enjoy'. You can enjoy the food at a party but you could also just enjoy yourself in general at a party.

"To enjoy oneself" is the reflexive form of the verb "to enjoy." However, in Spanish we use reflexive verbs much more than in English, very often in cases where it seems redundant to English speakers.

For example, in English you would say "I shave every morning" but in Spanish, you say "I shave myself every morning." To English speakers the "myself" is understood and seems redundant, but in Spanish if you don't use the "myself" your listener will probably be a bit confused.

Let's take a look at a few common reflexive verbs starting with the two most common ones you will need to speak basic Spanish:

- Afeitar - Afeitarse

To shave – to shave oneself
- Lavar - Lavarse
  To wash – to wash oneself

Notice how the verb adds a "se" at the end to make it reflexive. Now let's take a look at how you conjugate reflexive verbs in the present tense by using "me," "te," "se," "nos" and "se."

Lavarse – To wash oneself:

- Yo me lavo – I wash myself
- Tú te lavas - You wash yourself
- Usted se lava – You wash yourself
- Él/Ella se lava – He/She washes himself/herself
- Nosotros/Nosotras nos lavamos – We wash ourselves
- Ustedes se lavan – You wash yourselves
- Ellos/Ellas se lavan – They wash themselves

Reflexive verbs in Spanish also use a structure which can seem rather strange to English speakers.

- Me lavo las manos – I wash my hands (lit. I wash myself the hands)
- Se lava la cara – He/She washes his/her face (lit. He/She washes herself the face)

Afeitarse – to shave oneself also follows the same pattern of conjugation: me afeito, te afeitas, se afeita, nos afeitamos, se afeitan. If you wanted to say "I shave every morning" you would say "Me afeito cada mañana."

The following are some other verbs that are used in their reflexive form:

- Caerse – To fall (me caigo, te caes, se cae, nos caemos, se caen)
- Levantarse – To get up (me levanto, te levantas, se levanta, nos levantamos, se levantan)
- Irse – To go away, to leave (me voy, te vas, se va, nos vamos, se van)
- Reirse – To laugh (me río, te ríes, se ríe, nos reímos, se ríen)
- Burlarse – To make fun of (me burlo, te burlas, se burla, nos burlamos, se burlan)
- Ponerse – To put on (me pongo, te pones, se pone, nos ponemos, se ponen).

Talking about the Past: Regular Verbs

The preterite tense in Spanish is equivalent to the simple past in English e.g. "I wrote," "I spoke," "I ate," etc. In Spanish however, the regular verbs follow a set pattern depending on whether they are "ar," "ir" or "er" verbs.

The Past Tense of "ar" Verbs

Hablar – To speak:

- Yo hablé - I spoke
- Tú hablaste – You spoke (informal)
- Usted habló – You spoke (formal)
- Él/Ella habló - He/She spoke
- Nosotros/Nosotras hablamos – We spoke
- Ustedes hablaron – You spoke (plural)
- Ellos/Ellas hablaron – They spoke

Let's look at some examples:

- Hablé con mi hermana ayer – I spoke to my sister yesterday
- ¿Le hablaste a Juan la semana pasada? - Did you speak to Juan last week?
- ¿Usted habló con el jefe esta mañana? - Did you speak to the boss this morning?
- Anoche hablamos con la familia de ella – Last night, we spoke to her family
- Ellas hablaron por teléfono por una hora – They spoke on the phone for an hour

Note: For 'ar' verbs the 'nosotros/nosotras' form is the same in the past tense (in this case 'hablamos'). Don't worry. The meaning becomes clear according to the context.

The Spanish Tenses

Learning Spanish grammar and tenses is the primary way to speak and write this language correctly. What you should know is that it is not possible to learn everything right away. Get a general idea in the initial stages, and you will understand how to learn Spanish without feeling intimidated. Take time to familiarize yourself with different tenses.

Present Tense

Speaking in the present tense means speaking or referring in the present. The present tense is exactly what you think. It's speaking in the present.

"¿Cómo estás? *Yo estoy bien.*" It means, "How are you doing? I am well."

Imperfect Tense

This tense is used to refer to actions that took place in the past, and they occurred repeatedly. It is also used when referring to something that took place over a long time. But, it's used to discuss mental or emotional actions and not physical.

"Comía pan tostado todos los días," meaning, "I ate toast every day."

Past Preterite

The preterite tense speaks about particular actions that took place in the past; they are mostly one-time occurrence events. Sometimes, they have a specific time when they start and come to an end. What's more, it is used to discuss a completed event, and it's the one used when making a list of consecutive actions. For example: "I went to the store, bought chicken, and went home." However, for you to remember preterite tense, you need to understand that this tense answers questions regarding past actions.

The Future Tense

The future tense discusses future events or things that might happen. It is used when expressing or discussing probability. Near-future is discussed using the present tense, and future tense discusses a future that is far away, for example: *"Yo ganaré la medalla de oro,"* meaning, "I will win the gold medal."

"Yo compraré ese suéter la próxima semana," meaning "I will buy that sweater next week."

Pairing Nouns and Adjectives

Adjectives, just like in English, are describing words. Examples include small, wide, round, and white, among others. Spanish adjectives are paired with nouns, and they must match with the gender and number of the nouns.

Before you give a noun to an adjective, consider the gender and number. For example, if a noun is in singular form and feminine, your adjective should match the description. For example, using the adjective red: El libro amarillo, which means "The yellow book." This sentence is singular and masculine.

La manzana amarilla, which means the yellow apple. This sentence is feminine and singular.

Los libros Amarillos, which means the books are yellow. It is masculine and plural.

The Subjunctive

The subjunctive makes English speakers find learning Spanish extremely difficult; this tense is used to discuss future, present, and past tenses. Subjunctive reflects beyond what the speaker says and expresses uncertainty and shows how the speaker feels. When using the subjunctive, you can express your desire or will, and an indicative phrase should always follow it.

Here is an example showing how to use the indicative phrase.

"Espero que Maria se vuelva profesora." This means, "I hope Mary becomes a teacher." The words "I hope that" shows the use of subjunctive and "becomes" is the subjunctive tense. This sentence presents the mood of a speaker but does not say that, indeed, Mary will become a teacher. As you advance in Spanish verb tenses, learn to pay attention when a character is narrating or telling a story for you to identify the tense they are using. You can also watch Spanish movies and soaps to practice and learn more about spoken Spanish and especially the tenses.

Learning Spanish cannot happen overnight; a lot of practice is required. The more you lay a strong foundation by learning the correct grammar, basic verbs, sounds, such as reading and speaking in Spanish, the higher the chances of mastering immaculate Spanish.

Chapter 4. The Pronunciation Rules of Speaking Spanish

Phonetic guides pronunciation in Spanish, just like any other language, such as English. However, Spanish has more character sounds than their 27 alphabets. It is not a language you can translate into based on English pronunciation rules. Actually, many rules guide your pronunciation, and a single mistake makes you sound like a foreigner trying to learn this romantic language. You will find that the intonation of different alphabetical letters is affected by their placement in a word. These are rules you have to master when reading or speaking Spanish.

Vowels in Spanish

English speakers assume that Spanish diction will be easy to grasp since the alphabet is used in the English language. It is fun to learn the little things that make Spanish intonation so different. The most notable is the vowels and the way they affect your tongue. You have to be conscious of your tongue position inside your mouth, how to twist it, or how to hold it to get the lilt right.

The most outstanding problem in vowel pronunciation is dragging the sounds, especially for new learners. This makes it wrong, and one sounds off the accent. To nail it, one should speak as if they are breathless and let the sounds come out fast and without continuous emphasis on the sound. Practicing over and over will help you get the intonation; the vowels are not meant to be pulled or pushed to the highest intonation.

In order to master the phonation, learners are advised to pay keen attention to the vowels because these are the phonetics that make up nearly the whole Spanish accent. One vowel has more than one intonation. In the beginning, the sound you will hear is your voice going off your English pronunciation. Then, with time, your tongue will learn to tilt for the Spanish language.

Key Pointers for Spanish Diction

You should learn to use your tongue around the mouth in order to say the words right by keeping the vowel intonation short. The vowels are articulated loosely on the tongue; hence, it's the reason the tongue is always moving around, searching for the right location to produce the right sound.

Vowel A

This vowel is not the easy *aah* sound in English. It is intonated correctly by placing your tongue at the far end of your mouth. The emphasis is to bring out more sharply and with deep and a little bit exaggerated accent. This vowel is very common in the Spanish language. It is a key vowel in many words in this language. Learning the diction will not be successful if you do not get this phonetic correctly from the word. Like most tips for learning Spanish, you must take your time to master diction. There is no shortcut, and you cannot use ideas borrowed from the English language to understand Spanish dictions.

Vowel E

This sound is made with the mouth open. The sound of E is fast and brief on the tongue. This vowel does shift sounds, like in English. It remains the same, whether in past or present tense. The speakers are encouraged to say it in a sharp intonation and bring out the sound of vowel E.

Vowel I

Someone who knows English finds it easy to pronunciation vowel I in Spanish because it is basically the same. There are no tongue activities, but one has to say it fast and avoid prolonging the sound. Brevity in I intonation is what makes it Spanish. In writing, it remains as I, and learners are expected to pronounce it as written.

Vowel O

The sound O is said fast and brief. The intonation does not tone the O sound. It is said with an open mouth without prolonging the phonetic sound. The learner should not involve the lips so much. The lips should be at ease and let the O sound out, almost like a gasp, but again, it should be a short sound.

Vowel U

This sound is said fast and does not involve the lips or tongue much. It is more like pronouncing the word *two* in English, but in Spanish, the lips should not be involved. The pronunciation is precise and short. Vowel U becomes complicated in intonation as you learn the Spanish vocabulary. You will note that some of the words have a silent vowel U.

How to Handle Pronunciation Challenges

Consonant Problems

Consonants make Spanish diction very distinct from other languages. They handle the letters differently without borrowing much from other languages. Some consonants are not used at all in this language, such as the letter K, which is only present in non-native words. Consonants have their own sounds but are highly influenced by the combination with other consonants and vowels. The intonations change completely from one word to another, depending on the spelling. English learners find it easier because Spanish does not have many variations as English. A learner can master these accents very fast. Learners are advised to keep the intonation short. That's the key to learning the Spanish accent. English tends to intonate the sounds very clearly, but Spanish does not.

The Spanish Brawl

You cannot learn Spanish if you do not learn the accent alongside the word intonation. Lack of twang will throw your words or phrases of meaning. A sentence can lack meaning if not said in the right style. Spanish accent is as outstanding as other languages. The natives may have a hard time understanding you even if you speak and pronounce the words without the twang.

Comparing Sound B and V

Spanish intonation has a special relationship for phonetic B and V. V sound tends to be pronounced as B all the time. This is a rule that learners have to observe keenly in order to master the diction correctly. Understanding the intonation of these sounds will affect not only your spoken Spanish but also written Spanish. The rules are quite simple. All the words that begin with either of these letters will be pronounced with a B sound. The sound should be said lightly on your lips. The B sound should not be pulled and emphasized.

Mastering C and L combination

C and L combination in Spanish is like a real measure of how good your pronunciation is. It is said fast without pulling the L, and it comes out as a deep yet light intonation of the phonetics. The C should not be clarified and lingered upon. The tongue should brush through the C to L intonation. This brings out the accent and gives you the sound of a true Spanish speaker.

The C and S Relationship

C and S are phonetics that have the same diction in most languages, and Spanish is no exception. Learners have a hard time mastering the pronunciation of these two sounds. As a general rule, C becomes S sound if the next letter is E or I, but when followed by other vowels, you have to pronounce it with K sound.

The D Sound

Spanish intonation tends to be sweet with a mark of softness, but the letter D is different. It is pronounced with a slur, like the tongue of a dazed person not able to say it right. D pronunciation is Spanish lack elegance as if it's not there. Spanish diction does not accentuate D sound at all. It is like passing the tongue on it without willing to say it. This is a mark of the Spanish accent. Learners find this intonation weird at first, especially if they are used to high pitched D sound.

Get G and J Right

This pronunciation of these sounds can get you off guard. The rules are simple, though. For starters, J becomes are loosely pronounced H. It is pronounced as if one is running out of breath. On the other hand, the letter G, when followed by the vowel u, becomes a *whoa* sound. But if the G is preceding other vowels, it remains as G sound that has to be pronounced sharply. The G diction has to come out clearly. Once you get these simple tips, you will handle G and J intonations effortlessly like a pro.

H Sound

H is only active in spelling, but in pronunciation, it does not exist. Any sound of H in Spanish is not an indication that the word has H but that there is G or J in the word. Learners should not attempt to intone the sound H in any word just because there is H in the spelling.

R Influence in Spanish Accent

R, especially when written as a double R, can be pretty hard on the tongue. It has to be intoned clearly, which means the tongue is twisted a lot. When it is a single R, the sound is given no emphasis. The way you handle the intonation of these two spellings can change the meaning of the word.

Handling L in Spanish Diction

It is great news for a person used to emphasizing phonation sounds. L should be pronounced with a rich tilt in Spanish. When it is a double L, the pronunciation shifts to sound like Y and ch, depending on the region.

Letter N

All words that begin with this letter are pronounced with the N sound, but this changes if N precedes C and G. It becomes a little hushed, and the tone of N sound comes in a distant way. You will love the little difference that this intonation gives to the conversation. The meaning of the words comes out concisely and gives you a mastery edge to the Spanish language.

The diatribe aspect of the letter N gives it a little more influence on the language. These are indication marks above the letter that alludes the pronunciation to sound like the word *nay* in English.

Letter Q
Though not used frequently, it is silent only if it precedes vowel U, but in any other spelling, it should be pronounced as K.

Sound Z
Z is usually given S sound, but it can also take TH sound. Z sound is not guided by any vowels. It depends on the native region.

Tips to Help With Proper Pronunciation
Rule number one is to watch intonation. As discussed throughout the article, you should know that intonation has a lot of influence on Spanish accents and, most importantly, the meaning of the words. Intonation can add an unwarranted twist to a sentence; it can make you sound rude, vague, or indecent.

As you learn the Spanish vocabulary, pay closer attention to the variation of accents that can only be accentuated through proper diction. Speaking to native Spanish people will give you the reality of the accent. It opens your mind and gives you the experience you need to differentiate the various spoken Spanish enunciation. This is the only way you can pronounce Spanish words without the influence of your first language.

Do not let your native language get in the way of pronouncing Spanish words. It will make you think in your language while saying the words in the Spanish language.

Speaking Spanish

Spanish was a once romance language, which has its initial roots in the Iberian Peninsula. Today, Spanish is a vast language with over millions of people spreading across the whole world, and most native speakers are within Spain and some parts of America.

Right now, Spanish is the second most spoken language in the world, coming right after the Chinese language that's Mandarin. The Spanish language has various ethnicities, which include but are not limited to Hispanics, Spaniards, and even Sahrawi. In Africa, the Spanish language is also used. But, it's not dominant like in other native states. These states are Germany and France. Equatorial Guinea is among other countries in Africa, embracing this language.

The Spanish language is an official language used in the United Nations. In addition to that, it is also the primary language in various meetings held in the European Union.

Even though the Spanish language is significant, it is not preferred in any scientific writing. Many researchers have avoided it in their studies. However, many authors undertaking humanities have decided to use it as a primary language. According to Google, the Spanish language comes third as the primary language being used by internet lovers, where English and Chinese top the list.

The Spanish language is natural to speak and master. This will only become possible if you have the determination and an urge to understand it. There are several ways in which you can learn this language freely, without undergoing much stress or frustrations. These steps will help you to develop that confidence needed in the long process of learning the Spanish language. These steps are explained in detail, as shown below.

Taking Spanish classes is the first way of knowing and understanding the Spanish language. These courses will enable you to practice those vocabularies that are new to you. Refraining from speaking other languages during Spanish lessons will eventually boost your level of confidence and, at the end of the day, increases your Spanish learning. Again, you can also have extra lessons with the educator so that you have a one-on-one discussion. For this to work to your advantage, you can have some other groups of students. The sessions need to be formed to help you in learning. You can also look for more lessons by requesting to attend some through Skype. The same will even improve your skills in mastering the Spanish language. There are several online platforms where Spanish language learning can be offered without many struggles. A good example is a Verbling site. Remember to note essential things, such as its availability. The same applies to where it's offered and even look at the price. These conditions will help in improving your ability to understand the Spanish language. The site has helpful features. They will guide you in the quest to learn how to speak the Spanish language. You'll also realize that it's easy to use.

Many studies have eventually found out that watching movies can be of great help, primarily when they have been written or edited using the Spanish language. It will even improve your listening skills, which will bring you great achievement toward your goals. These movies having a conversational dialogue are of a great deal. They will help you a lot in mastering the language without necessarily going for more lessons in Spanish literature. The move also works best for beginners. Beginners in learning the Spanish language can get a piece of wealthy information, especially from the body language and even visual cues. Since you are trying to learn and understand the language, work as hard as possible to watch content with subtitles. The same will assist you in understanding the Spanish language in a natural way. Practice makes perfect, and the more you get involved in watching and listening, the more you will be able to familiarize yourself with every aspect of the Spanish language. These aspects may refer to accent and voice tone used in Spanish. The same implies that you will be in a position to understand and undertake your confidence in speaking Spanish a little bit higher, especially when if you begin speaking. There are several places where you can get movies with excellent subtitles, and *Fluent* is just one of them. This site translates everything from videos to inspirational talks into Spanish. While watching your movies, you can listen to different intonations. The strategy will help you to comprehend the use of the Spanish language in different ways.

Listen and sing in the Spanish language. It's also another step that should be taken with a lot of significance since it helps a beginner to learn and understand the Spanish language in a natural way. The reason seems to be appended to the fact that many studies have found out that the brain can easily remember something appropriately expressed in terms of song. When you listen or have a collection of songs written and composed in the Spanish language, you will be good to go. Listening to them will automatically improve your level of understanding. The same will improve your mastering skills without many issues.

In most cases, it is better to acquire or search lyrics so that when you listen, you can also sing along. You can try as much as possible to memorize the songs and have some practice in talking and speaking. Doing this will be enjoyable, and also, it will be of great help to you in that you will be in a position of high confidence. The boost of morale will instill in you the optimism needed in learning Spanish. Just like videos, music collections are also offered on the Fluent site.

Think in Spanish. You can start doing everything in Spanish, including having thoughts in the Spanish language. Once you are in a position to do this, your confidence will shoot tremendously. You will feel nervous at first, especially when you start fumbling with words. And having increased thoughts on what to say, you will be boosting your morale in speaking this language. It is always apparent that, at the beginning stages of understanding and learning some vocabulary, people tend to do the translation in the head before pouring out what they wanted to say. The same prevents them from having a consistent flow of conversation. That could also mean you can't keep that pace required in every kind of communication. However, this will get easier with the constant exposure to the Spanish language. In the end, this becomes useful since you will be able to think without necessarily doing the translation in your head. You can also go ahead by commenting yourself in this language, even when it's just a simple word. Having your journals written in this language will be of great help as well. In this situation, all thoughts will be detailed in your journal book using the Spanish language. It also automatically trains your mind and brain not to think of anything rather than the Spanish language.

Read loudly. This is also an effective way to boost your confidence in speaking the Spanish language. You can start by reading the content very loud. This practice allows the smooth flow of words from your mouth. These words will come out naturally, thus helping you with preparation for a good flow during real conversations. You can also read books and magazines written in Spanish. Newspapers, too, contain this, and this can be a good step in learning the language. Check on the blogs and other online websites, and practice loud reading. Make yourself some challenges since they can improve your reading skills. Reading various news in Spanish is just a challenge that many people encounter. Loud reading will also assist you in understanding how to master the Spanish language. With loud reading, you'll be in a position to sharpen your mastery skills in the Spanish language. Therefore, you'll learn more about how to use the language to your advantage. Also, loud reading encourages you to take up different lessons from different packages that offer affordable units. The move is a foundation toward assisting you to become a reliable professional. In the quest to learn more about the use of verbs and adverbs, most beginners have incorporated loud reading into their programs. It's one of the ways they are learning to become pros. It's also a major strategy toward understanding the use of the Spanish language in different settings.

Practice Spanish recordings. Take time to record yourself while having a deep conversation or just a regular reading that is done in Spanish. Play your recordings to note what you missed or where you got it wrong. By doing this, you will be able to spot the areas where you really need improvement and then work on it. Do this regularly so that you can be in a position to track yourself.

Look for a "language friend." You can practice speaking the Spanish language with your friends. It is said to be a convenient and considerable way to learn the Spanish language. Having a partner who helps you in this kind of practice will also encourage and give you more inspiration in this process. You can practice this with a native friend who speaks Spanish. In this way, you will be in a high position to make more mistakes and get corrected. You will learn from the mistakes. The same will affect your morale, confidence, and skills required in Spanish language speaking. Having a conversation with a native speaker sometimes instills some fear in you. The best advice here is to avoid being shy for you to learn more. Speak out whether you are making mistakes or not. These mistakes are just small issues that will ease out with time.

Know the common mistakes in the Spanish language. Common mistakes are a hindrance not only to the Spanish language when it comes to speaking but also other words. Learning these common mistakes and understanding them will make you more comfortable in speaking the Spanish language. The same occurs because anxieties or insecurities come as a result of inadequate knowledge and a lack of awareness of this language. Getting familiarized with the Spanish language common mistakes will help you to be knowledgeable and be in a position to acquire confidence. Beginners can look at words like "por" and "para" and get their differences. Other words include "ser," "estar," and so on.

Listen carefully. This is another step that a beginner should use to learn and speak the Spanish language. The same is achieved through careful listening, especially to the native group. The same will automatically increase your confidence in speaking the Spanish language. Listening to native language speakers comes in handy with some benefits. These benefits include having a taste of the natural accent of the Spanish language and how to use Spanish words.

In many types of languages, there must be vocabulary that acts as a reference to new words. The latter applies to the Spanish language, too. For you to have confidence in speaking or having a conversation in Spanish, you must develop a new vocabulary every day. The result will make your contributions look strong, especially in Spanish. These new vocabulary words or rather new words can be derived from Spanish newspapers or internet content with the Spanish language. Use flashcards too. They are better sources of Spanish language phrases and other new words.

If you have the mindset of a beginner, you'll find it challenging to learn the Spanish language. The move is a critical condition in the long run journey of knowing and understanding the Spanish language. Be ready to learn. The later will only be possible when you can have that positive attitude toward learning and understanding Spanish speaking. Have that ambitious eagerness in you, even if the process is too difficult for you. Have faith and courage, even if you fail. What you need to know is that we learn from mistakes. These mistakes will accelerate your learning and understanding of Spanish.

The Spanish language has additional ready-made phrases. The same refers to another step taken to learn and understand the Spanish language. Having ready-made phrases will a great deal since you are in a position to back every conversation with the correct phrases needed. To enrich yourself with this, you must consider having an interest in common Spanish phrases that are used now and then. You can also do this by buying one Spanish language phrasebook from the library.

Chapter 5. The Progressive Tenses

Progressive form of the verb is used to express actions like "eating," "coming," "reading," etc. In Spanish when you say "Él habla," the translation in English could be "He speaks"or "He is speaking" depending on the context.

In Spanish if you need to specify that the action is in the process of taking place you would use the progressive form of "hablar" which is "hablando" and the indicative form of the verb "estar." That probably sounds confusing so let's take a look at the progressive forms of a few common verbs and how to use them to express activities that are/were continuous.

Although the progressive form is not used as often as it is in English, it is an important part of conversational Spanish and not all that difficult.

The Progressive Tenses and "ar" Verbs

The progressive forms of some common "ar" verbs are as follows:

Verb Progressive Form
- Hablar – To speak, hablando
- Dar – To give, dando
- Sacar – To take out, sacando
- Pagar – To pay, pagando
- Tomar – To take, tomando
- Trabajar – To work, trabajando
- Nadar – To swim, nadando.

The Progressive Tenses – "er" and "ir" Verbs

The progressive forms of some common "er" and "ir" verbs are as follows:

Verb Progressive Form
- Salir – To go out, saliendo
- Comer – To eat, comiendo
- Vivir – To live, viviendo
- Escribir – To write, escribiendo
- Decir – To say, diciendo
- Hacer – To do, haciendo
- Pedir – To ask, pidiendo

Some verbs use a "y" to form their progressive forms, as follows:

Verb Progressive Form

- Leer – To read, leyendo
- Distribuir – To distribute, distribuyendo
- Oir – To listen, oyendo
- Construir – To construct, construyendo
- Ir – To go, yendo
- Caer – To fall, cayendo
- Traer – To bring, trayendo

The Present Progressive

Now let's look at some examples. To express the present progressive, use the conjugation of "estar" in the present tense:

- Estoy trabajando en mi proyecto en este momento – I am working on my project at the moment
- No pueden contestar el teléfono. Están comiendo – Then cannot answer the phone. They are eating.
- Nos está esperando en la esquina – He/She is waiting for us at the corner
- ¿Estás marcando el número? – Are you dialing the number?
- Estamos preparando el almuerzo – We are preparing lunch

The present progressive can also be used like this:

- Leyendo el libro, me dormí – While reading the book, I fell asleep (dormir – to sleep, dormirse – to fall asleep)

- Yendo a la escuela, paré a comprar una galleta — Going to school, I stopped to buy a cookie

The Past Progressive

In the past tense, it is common to use 'estar' in the imperfect tense:

- Me estaba pidiendo un favor — He/she was asking me for a favor
- Los perros estaban ladrando — The dogs were barking
- Estábamos comprando gaseosa cuando vimos el accidente — We were buying soda when we saw the accident
- Me estaba afeitando cuando noté la sangre — I was shaving when I noticed the blood

Instant Spanish Vocabulary Category

The rule to create Spanish from English

Many English words that end with TY can be made into Spanish by changing TY to DAD.

This is a wonderful category, it is very easy to use and full of useful and versatile words.

Here are some dad words that aren't immediately obvious

Spanish — English

Habilidad — Ability

Ciudad — City

Oscuridad — Darkness

Ansiedad — Anxiety

Caridad — Charity

Igualidad – Equality

Humedad – Humidity

Libertad – Liberty

Lealtad – Loyalty

Publicidad – Advertising

Calidad – Quality

Cantidad – Quantity.

Here are 124 Spanish words that you can use instantly
Spanish – English

Anormalidad – Abnormality

Accesibilidad – Accessibility

Aceptabilidad – Acceptability

Actividad – Activity

Adaptabilidad – Adaptability

Adversidad – Adversity

Afinidad – Affinity

Agilidad – Agility

Agresividad – Aggressively

Ambiguedad – Ambiguity

Animosidad – Animosity

Ansiedad – Anxiety

Anualidad – Annuity

Aplicabilidad – Applicability

Atrocidad – Atrocity

Autenticidad – Autenticity

Autoridad – Authority

Barbaridad – Barbarity

Brevedad – Brevity

Brutalidad – Brutality

Calamidad – Calamity

Calidad – Quality

Capacidad – Capacity

Celebridad – Celebrity

Ciudad – City

Claridad – Clarity

Comodidad – Commodity

Computabilidad – Computability

Comunidad – Community

Conformidad – Conformity

Continuidad – Continuity

Creatividad – Creativity

Credibilidad – Credibility

Cristiandad – Christianity

Crueldad – Cruelty

Curiosidad – Curiosity

Debilidad – Debility

Deformidad – Deformity

Densidad – Density

Dificultad – Difficulty

Dignidad – Dignity

Deshonestidad – Dishonesty

Disparidad – Disparity

Diversidad – Diversity

Divinidad – Divinity

Domesticidad – Domesticity

Necesidad – Necessity

Negatividad – Negativity

Neutralidad – Neutrality

Normalidad – Normality

Notoriedad – Notoriety

Novedad – Novelty

Obesidad – Obesity

Objectividad – Objectivity

Obscenidad – Obscenity

Obscuridad – Obscurity

Oportunidad – Opportunity

Originalidad – Originality

Paridad – Parity

Paternidad – Paternity

Peculiaridad – Peculiarity

Perpetuidad – Perpetuity

Personalidad – Personality

Perversidad – Perversity

Piedad – Piety

Pluralidad – Plurality

Polaridad – Polarity

Popularidad – Popularity

Posibilidad – Possibility

Posteridad – Posterity

Prioridad – Priority

Probabilidad – Probability

Productividad – Productivity

Profundidad – Profundity

Promiscuidad – Promiscuity

Propiedad – Propriety

Prosperidad – Prosperity

Proximidad – Proximity

Publicidad – Publicity

Puntualidad – Punctuality

Racionalidad – Rationality

Realidad – Reality

Regularidad – Regularity

Relatividad – Relativity

Respetabilidad – Respectability

Responsabilidad – Responsibility

Seguridad – Security

Selectividad – Selectivity

Sensibilidad – Sensibility

Sensualidad – Sensuality

Serenidad – Serenity

Severidad – Severity

Sexualidad – Sexuality

Simplicidad – Simplicity

Sinceridad – Sincerity

Singularidad – Singularity

Sobriedad – Sobriety

Sociedad – Society

Solidaridad – Solidarity

Subjetividad – Subjectivity

Superficialidad – Superficiality

Superioridad – Superiority

Tenacidad – Tenacity

Tonalidad – Tonality

Totalidad – Totality

Tranquilidad – Tranquility

Trinidad – Trinity

Trivialidad – Triviality

Unidad – Unity

Uniformidad – Uniformity

Universidad – University

Vanidad – Vanity

Variedad – Variety

Velocidad – Velocity

Versatilidad – Versatility

Viabilidad – Viability

Virginidad – Virginity

Virilidad – Virility

Visabilidad – Visibility

Viscosidad – Viscosity

Vitalidad – Vitality

Volatilidad – Volatility

Voracidad – Voracity

Vulgaridad – Vulgarity

The rule to create Spanish from English

Many English words that end with ATE can be made into Spanish infinitives by changing ATE to AR.

Here are 205 Spanish verbs to use right away.

Spanish – English

Abreviar – Abbreviate

Acelerar – Accelerate

Activar – Activate

Acumular – Accumulate

Administrar – Administrate

Afiliar – Affiliate

Agitar – Agitate

Agravar – Aggravate

Agregar – Aggregate

Alienar – Alienate

Altercar – Altercate

Alternar – Alternate

Amputar – Amputate

Animar – Animate

Anticipar – Anticipate

Apreciar – Appreciate (admire)

Aproximar – Approximate

Articular – Articulate

Asesinar – Assassinate

Asfixiar – Asphyxiate

Asimilar – Assimilate

Asociar – Associate

Autenticar – Authenticate

Calcular – Calculate

Castigar – Castigate

Castrar – Castrate

Celebrar – Celebrate

Circular – Circulate

Coagular – Coagulate

Colaborar – Collaborate

Compensar – Compensate

Complicar – Complicate

Comunicar – Communicate

Concentrar – Concentrate

Confiscar – Confiscate

Congratular – Congratulate

Congregar – Congregate

Conjugar – Conjugate

Consolidar – Consolidate

Contaminar – Contaminate

Co-operar – Co-operate

Coordinar – Coordinate

Corroborar – Corroborate

Crear – Create

Culminar – Culminate

Cultivar – Cultivate

Debilitar – Debilitate

Decapitar – Decapitate

Decorar – Decorate

Dedicar – Dedicate

Degenerar – Degenerate

Delegar – Delegate

Deliberar – Deliberate

Delinear – Delineate

Demostrar – Demonstrate

Denigrar – Denigrate

Denunciar – Denunciate

Depreciar – Depreciate

Derivar – Derive

Designar – Designate

Desolar – Desolate

Deteriorar – Deteriorate

Devastar – Devastate

Dictar – Dictate

Diferenciar – Differentiate

Dilatar – Dilate

Discriminar – Discriminate

Diseminar – Disseminate

Dislocar – Dislocate

Domesticar – Domesticate

Dominar – Dominate

Donar – Donate

Duplicar – Duplicate

Educar – Educate

Elaborar – Elaborate

Eliminar – Eliminate

Emanar – Emanate

Emancipar – Emancipate

Emascular – Emasculate

Emigrar – Emigrate

Enumerar – Enumerate

Enunciar – Enunciate

Equivocar – Equivocate

Especular – Speculate

Estimar – Estimate

Estimular – Stimulate

Estrangular – Strangulate

Evacuar – Evacuate

Evaporar – Evaporate

Exagerar – Exaggerate

Exasperar – Exasperate

Excavar – Excavate

Exfoliar – Exfoliate

Exonerar – Exonerate

Expatriar – Expatriate

Exterminar – Exterminate

Fabricar – Fabricate

Facilitar – Facilitate

Fascinar – Fascinate

Filtrar – Filtrate

Fluctuar – Fluctuate

Formular – Formulate

Fornicar – Fornicate

Frustrar – Frustrate

Fumigar – Fumigate

Generar – Generate

Gesticular – Gesticulate

Graduar – Graduate

Habituar – Habituate

Hesitar – Hesitate

Humillar – Humiliate

Iluminar – Illuminate

Imitar – Imitate

Implicar – Implicate

Inaugurar – Inaugurate

Incinerar – Incinerate

Incorporar – Incorporate

Incriminar – Incriminate

Incubar – Incubate

Indicar – Indicate

Infiltrar – Infiltrate

Inflar – Inflate

Iniciar – Initiate

Inmigrar – Immigrate

Innovar – Innovate

Inocular – Inoculate

Insinuar – Insinuate

Instigar – Instigate

Interrogar – Interrogate

Intimidar – Intimidate

Intoxicar – Intoxicate

Investigar – Investigate

Irradiar – Irradiate

Irrigar – Irrigate

Irritar – Irritate

Lacerar – Lacerate

Liberar – Liberate

Liquidar – Liquidate

Litigar – Litigate

Lubricar – Lubricate

Manipular – Manipulate

Masticar – Masticate

Medicar – Medicate

Meditar – Meditate

Menstruar – Menstruate

Moderar – Moderate

Motivar – Motivate

Mutilar – Mutilate

Narrar – Narrate

Navegar – Navigate

Necesitar – Necessitate

Negar – Negate

Negociar – Negotiate

Nominar – Nominate

Obligar – Obligate

Originar – Originate

Orquestar – Orchestrate

Oscilar – Oscillate

Oxigenar – Oxygenate

Palpar – Palpate

Participar – Participate

Penetrar – Penetrate

Perforar – Perforate

Perpetuar – Perpetuate

Postular – Postulate

Precipitar – Precipitate

Predicar – Predicate

Predominar – Predominate

Premeditar – Premeditate

Proliferar – Proliferate

Pronosticar – Prognosticate

Propagar – Propagate

Radiar – Radiate

Reciprocar – Reciprocate

Recuperar – Recuperate

Refrigerar – Refrigerate

Regenerar – Regenerate

Regular – Regulate

Regurgitar – Regurgitate

Rehabilitar – Rehabilitate

Reiterar – Reiterate

Relegar – Relegate

Remunerar – Remunerate

Renovar – Renovate

Repatriar – Repatriate

Resucitar – Resuscitate

Revalidar – Revalidate

Saturar – Saturate

Segregar – Segregate

Separar – Separate

Sincopar – Syncopate

Sindicar – Syndicate

Situar – Situate

Subordinar – Subordinate

Substanciar – Substantiate

Terminar – Terminate

Tolerar – Tolerate

Triangular – Triangulate

Vacilar – Vacillate

Validar – Validate

Vegetar – Vegetate

Ventilar – Ventilate

Vibrar – Vibrate

Violar – Violate

Chapter 6. Tips to Speed up Learning

Are you in the middle of planning your trip? Did you think of everything? First aid kit, papers & documents? Very good, but what about your foreign language skills? Have you ever thought of how you'll express yourself? Unfortunately, many travelers neglect this topic and think that with English, you can get anywhere. And some also assume that you can communicate well with your hands and feet. The question that you should ask yourself is: What do I expect from my journey, and which goal do I have?

To give you a little motivation, here are five advantages of being able to express yourself in a foreign language: - You get to know the locals much more authentically - You understand the culture and attitude of people much better - You can negotiate more effectively.

You do not waste valuable time because you understand faster - You feel safer

Just to keep it short: You do not have to learn the foreign language to perfection. But you should be able to communicate properly. Here are some tips on how to learn certain basics quickly and effectively.

Are you ready? Okay, then we can start. Depending on how much time you have until the trip, you should use the time well. Which language level you achieve depends entirely on you. Here are some essential recommendations on how to learn a language.

Speak From the First Day

Unfortunately, many people follow the wrong approach when learning a language. A language is a means of communication and should, therefore, be lived rather than learned. There is no such thing as an "I am ready now." Therefore, just jump into the cold water and speak already at home from the first day on. That sounds horrible and silly? It does not matter how it sounds; with time, it will get better. It is best to set the goal not to miss a day when you have not used the foreign language in any form. Just try to implement everything you learn directly. So speak, write, and think in your foreign language.

Immerse yourself in the foreign language at home

This tip actually goes hand in hand with the first recommendation. To learn a foreign language quickly and efficiently, you have to integrate it firmly into your everyday life. It is not enough if you learn a few words from time to time and engage in grammar and pronunciation. This has to be done much more intensively. You have to dive properly into the foreign language. Just bring foreign countries to your home. By the so-called "immersion," you surround yourself almost constantly and everywhere with the learning language

Change the Language Setting on Devices

For example, you could change the menu language of your smartphone or laptop from your native language to your learning language. Since you use your smartphone or your laptop every day, you know where to find something and learn some vocabulary along the way. Of course, you can also do the same with your social networks like Facebook and Twitter. But watch out that you are always able to change back the menu language!

Use Foreign Language Media

You could, for example, get a foreign-language newspaper. If that is not available or too expensive, then there are enough newspapers or news portals where you can read news online. Probably you are already familiar with the news through your native language; then the context is easier if you read the same messages again in the foreign language. Further aids are foreign-language films or series. It's probably best to start with a movie or series that you've already seen in your native language. Slang and common phrases can make it really hard for you. If you realize that you do not understand it well, try the subtitle in a foreign language. If that does not work, then take the subtitle of your native language and try again. Even music should not be neglected in your foreign-language world. This has the advantage of teaching you a lot about pronunciation and emphasis. Incidentally, you are getting a lot closer to the culture of the country.

Learn by Taking up Classes

Spanish classes are perfect for people who are still in school and those who have ample time to take classes regularly. There are a variety of classes for your every need. There are short courses that teach the basic principles of speaking Spanish, which is perfect for ordinary tourists who need to speak conversational Spanish when abroad. There are the long term and intensive classes which are perfect for those who speak Spanish daily, like businessmen and office workers who deal with Spanish speaking clients regularly. Learning how to speak Spanish helps boost careers by opening more business opportunities for the individual.

One good (and expensive) option would be to learn Spanish abroad. A lot of schools offer Spanish classes. The biggest advantage of learning Spanish abroad is that you'll be immersed in the language no only in class but in your daily encounters. This practice will help your fluency in the language.

Learn by Self-Study

If you cannot find time and resources to take up classes, then self-studying is the way to go. There a lot of different products available in the market to suit everyone's learning needs.

If you spend most of your time in front of the computer, then there are online courses and cd-ROMs available for your needs. Many of these online courses are often free, although some of them require a certain fee. The cd-ROMs are usually available at local computer stores and the internet as well. These courses provide tutors and chat rooms for students who want to practice their lessons.

There also books to guide your learning process. These books are available in your local bookstore. These contain the basic principles of learning Spanish.

Lastly, if you learn the most through listening, then these audio lessons work best for you. They come in tapes, CDs, mp3s, and podcasts. As online courses, many of them are free, but some require a certain fee; it's just a matter of picking the best product to suit you.

Learn by Adaptation

You may think that this is a weird way to learn Spanish. According to Charles Darwin, humans, much like any mammal, adapt to the ever-changing environment.

Otherwise, they will not survive.

So, if you are a foreigner in a certain country, you are bound to adapt to their environment to survive. Learning their language is a way to adapt to the new environment. Constant exposure to Spanish will help you learn it practically.

There are many ways how to learn Spanish; it is just a matter of finding out which suits you the best. Saying the Right Words Studying how words come up in conversations in Spanish is an integral part of your learning process. For instance, an object would need you to put a "gender" on it, as this language uses the prepositions "el" and "la" specifically for items with male and female genders, respectively. If you are not yet familiar with this concept, you should refer to a reliable guide that would help you become fluent in applying this knowledge as you construct your sentences. When you start using Learn Spanish Language Fast, you will notice that repeating the ideas often would help you enhance your memory and make you remember the words easily. You could start by repeating particular words, then phrases, and then continue with properly-constructed and complete sentences that you can use in daily conversations. This way, you would be able to practice speaking the language without any trouble.

Another thing to keep in mind is that every language has a certain "rhythm" or "melody" that it follows.

The accent that comes along with it will truly help you to express yourself more clearly as you use the language.

Focus on how native speakers would use the words and their respective "tunes" when in actual conversations. This will help you identify the proper pronunciation and enunciation of the words to avoid confusion. Since some words might sound the same to you, paying attention to the correct diphthong as it is used in the language would help you determine how words vary in sound and enunciation.

One good way to start learning the language is to begin with familiarizing with Spanish words that are somewhat derivatives of English words and vice versa. As an example, the word "excellence" is translated to "Excelencia" in Spanish. As you may notice, these words are almost the same, if not for the addition of certain syllables. Nevertheless, these words can be easily related to each other by nature with which they are spelled and pronounced. Associating the words in English with that in Spanish would truly be helpful for you in your aim to learn a new language.

Probably one of the best ways to learn the language is to have someone to converse with in Spanish, just like in Learn Spanish Language Fast.

Some self-help guides could provide you with this feature: with the many language exercises, you can conduct to practice your skills in speaking Spanish.

Note that in some cases, the sentence construction in the said language is different as it is in English, and so studying it more closely would enable you to comprehend it better.

Tips

If you are interested in discovering how to learn Spanish, this article will give you some pointers to help you find the most effective language training methods for your needs. Spanish is one of the major players when it comes to world languages. So you have made a wise choice.

So, some tips to get you started! First of all, ask yourself why you want to speak Spanish, and how well you want to be able to speak it?

There are many reasons why you may want to start learning Spanish, and these could range from getting a better grade at college to learning to speak with neighbors or with distant relatives and from getting a more interesting job to making traveling abroad more fun. The level and accuracy of Spanish you need will vary according to your goals. If you just want to chat with neighbors or relatives, you'll get by even if you don't always get things right; do ask them to correct you so that you can improve.

However, it's a different story if you are aiming for a job using Spanish or you wish to pass high-level exams. You can't afford to make too many mistakes in these situations if you want to further your career.

There are probably hundreds of reasons to learn Spanish, and there are also hundreds of ways to learn.

But the best way to learn Spanish is the way that works best for you and which fulfills your needs, which is why you need to consider how well you want to be able to speak Spanish.

Everyone has to start with the basics, and you should look for a program that offers a variety of resources. Learning accurate pronunciation is essential if you want to be able to speak Spanish correctly, and building listening skills are crucial if you want to hold a conversation. There is no point in speaking excellent Spanish if you can't understand a word that is being said to you! Audio Spanish programs can be found on the internet, and you can download lessons on mp3 and then listen at odd moments during the day when you have some free time.

Basic grammar is important as it forms the structure on which the whole language is based, and once learned, you won't have much difficulty moving forward.

If you aspire to reach a high level, you absolutely must ensure that you learn grammar from the beginning. You can learn in small chunks and should choose a course which gives you exercises to practice what you've learned.

So although you can start with a basic introduction, you'll want to get a detailed grammar book as you progress.

If you are learning for holidays or talking to friends, reading and writing won't be the most important aspects of your Spanish learning program, but they shouldn't be ignored.

If you want to know how to learn Spanish well, you should concentrate on developing each of the four skills - reading, writing, speaking, and listening will complement all the other skills. And you never know, you may enjoy the language or travel to Spanish speaking countries that you decide to take your Spanish to the next level.

Tips for Learning Spanish on Your Own

Get Used to Hearing Spanish

The first step to learning any language is to familiarize yourself with its sounds and speech patterns. Audio lessons teach you how to understand spoken Spanish and most importantly, help you develop the correct accent. I'd recommend audio lessons that use "standardized" pronunciation and accent, such as the Castilian or Mexican one, which is clearer and easier for beginners.

Don't Ignore Grammar

Audio lessons make a great stepping-stone into the language, but you need to supplement them with grammar if you want to make any progress. Spanish is a lot like English in some ways but very different in others. A good grammar guide that's simple but in-depth will go a long way in helping you speak naturally and building up your vocabulary.

Brush up on Your English Grammar

Sounds weird in an article on Spanish, right? You won't find this tip anywhere else, but I speak from experience. Grammar books will often use terms like "infinitive," "transitive verb," or "conjunction." All of us probably know what they mean but aren't familiar with the technical use of the terms. Knowing your English grammar terms helps, especially since Spanish grammar terms sound a lot like English ones.

Get the Human Touch

Learning Spanish on your own instead of in a class or with a tutor means that you don't get as many chances of using the language in a real-life setting. But don't worry, there are still plenty of ways you can practice using your Spanish.

If You Have a Spanish Speaking Friend, Don't Hesitate to Ask for Their Help

You could also use your Spanish when you deal with Hispanic people in places such as restaurants or shops. Spanish speakers are usually very friendly and will encourage and help you out (just don't massacre their language too much!)

If you don't know any Spanish speakers or don't live in an area with a significant Hispanic population, then the Internet is your savior. There are plenty of language exchange sites out there. You could talk with a native speaker using instant messengers or clients such as Skype. You'll improve you're Spanish AND make a friend!

Important: Have Fun

If I could give you one tip for learning Spanish, this is it. If learning Spanish feels like a chore to you, then you'll never get anywhere. There are plenty of ways you could do this.

Language Games: There are lots of interactive games that help you brush up on your Spanish. Rocket Spanish has a great set of games that help you improve your vocabulary, grammar, and speech.

Movies: These are a fun way to get familiar with another language. You can start by watching Spanish movies with

English subtitles and later, switch to Spanish subtitles. There are some great Spanish directors—Pedro Almodovar, Alfonso Cuarón, Guillermo del Toro, and many more. You could also watch Hollywood movies dubbed into Spanish (trust me, they're a lot of fun!).

Music: Choose the kind of music you like—pop, rock, metal, folk, or whatever—and find a Spanish band in that genre. Singing along to songs is a good way to learn without boring your brains out.

Podcasts: Podcasts are a great way to learn while commuting or working out. There are podcasts for all types of learners, from beginners to advanced learners, to those who just want to pick up a few survival phrases. Download them onto your mp3 player, and you're good to go. The best part? They're usually free!

I hope these tips will help you in exploring this enchanting language. These are all common sense tips that I discovered while learning Spanish myself.

Set Clear Goals

Last but not least, an important piece of advice: Set clear goals. Without goals, you will never get where you want to go. Since you have already booked your flight, you also have a deadline, to which you have reached a goal you have set. To accomplish this, you can now place mini orders. But stay realistic with your goals, especially in relation to your mini-goals. If they are too big and not realistically achievable, you may lose your courage and give up. A good tip is also that you record your goals in writing because writing is like having a contract with yourself. It makes your goals more binding and makes you feel more obligated to stick to your schedule. Writing down also has the advantage that you have to formulate your goals more precisely and not forget them so quickly. Do not just try to formulate these goals, but really approach them and implement them.

Here are some examples of how you could define your goals:

- Learn 300 words

- Memorize 5 phrases

- Write an email in the foreign language

- Memorize important questions

- Conduct a talk online via webcam.

How can you achieve your goals?

- Set Priorities: Be sure to rank your goals by importance!

- Stay realistic: What is your current life situation?

- Start today: Do not think about tomorrow or yesterday, but start today to reach your goals! The longer you wait, the less likely you are to achieve your goals

- Change your habits: You may need to change something in your daily routine to achieve your goals. Do not hesitate and reject bad habits that get in your way!

- Reward yourself: Every time you reach a partial goal, do something good! You know best what that can be!

- Obviously, you do not have to punish yourself, but some people are more likely to do it than to be rewarded for success

- Let the imagination play: Imagine how it is when you reach your goals. What would you be capable of? What would you feel? This will motivate you immensely to work on your goals!

Humor

Do not feel sad if it does not work right away. You may be embarrassing yourself in front of a native speaker because you mispronounce a word and make a completely different sense. Nobody will blame you. For most people, it means a lot that you try to learn their language. And when they laugh, then they do not mean that. But the most important thing is: have fun getting to know a new language! After all, you do not have any pressure, as you do at school.

Mastering the foreign language of your destination country has only advantages. You will learn to understand how people of a particular region think, what fears and worries they have, and how they tackle life. You'll become more tolerant and see the world differently, and, after your journey, you'll definitely question many ways of thinking of your own culture. Of course, you will also learn a lot of new things abroad, even in foreign languages. But please take the time already and get familiar with the new language before you leave. We promise you, it's worth it!

Chapter 7. Online Learning

The quickest way to learn Spanish is by finding a teacher. If you can hire a one-on-one tutor, you should. Direct instruction, whether it be in a group class or with a private tutor, is one of the best ways to really pick up conversational Spanish. Also, having somebody insists that you do homework and will hold you accountable can keep you on track. With an experienced tutor, you can receive guidance that's tailored to you, providing a very structured approach to your personal goals. This is not the case with typical evening language classes where you will be expected to maintain the pace of the class; not very conducive to learning Spanish quickly.

This should be a fun endeavor for you, and the last thing you want is to end up in a stuffy class that takes away from the exciting discovery of new words and sentences. In most cases, these classes and tutors can be quite expensive, and since you're looking to learn quickly, you may not find many options available for the schedule you need. Take into consideration the commute as well. If you have Internet access, you can save yourself a lot of time and money.

If private tutoring and classes are out of the question, or if you want to continue learning outside of class, you can find everything you need on the internet, at the library or your local bookstore. Of course, if you have a smartphone, you have access to various instructional materials right at your fingertips.

There are plenty of both paid and free online websites and programs providing all varieties of instructional content for any level of Spanish students. You can find Podcasts, interactive websites, videos, and apps. With so many options available, it can be challenging to decide which programs are right for you. Let's look at some of the most popular online resources available.

Podcasts

Podcasts are a great way to help build your skills as they allow you to hear native Spanish speakers. Listening to Podcasts can really maximize your learning since you're able to pick up on the pronunciation and phrases they commonly use. You can listen to a podcast while performing menial tasks and passively soak up the new knowledge.

When searching for the right Podcast for you, consider how long they've been on-air. Also, look for Podcasts that break down conversations slowly for beginners so that you can understand them. While you can find Podcasts online for free, many require that you sign up or subscribe to a platform to access them.

Websites

If you prefer a more traditional approach to learning, some great websites have printable worksheets and interactive quizzes. While it is easy to find many websites that teach you the basics, it can be a challenge finding intermediate and expert Spanish level material. After you've committed some vocabulary to memory and can start stringing sentences together, check out websites that offer tests. Keep in mind most online testing will be focused on vocabulary and grammar, not necessarily speaking and listening.

Practice typing in Spanish with websites that provide a Spanish keyboard that includes accents. That way, you can save time without having to figure out how to type those accents on your standard keyboard. Just perform a search for interactive websites for learning beginners Spanish and take your pick!

Videos

Diversify your Spanish instruction arsenal with videos. You shouldn't have a hard time locating hours of content online with sites such as YouTube. Be sure to bookmark your favorite videos so that you can find them easily when it's time to review. Videos work great because you can stop, pause, or rewind when needed. When watching videos, pay careful attention to pronunciation as well as study the mouth and lip movements of Spanish speakers. Closed-captioning can be a handy feature when listening to Spanish speakers—so that you can read along and start to develop an eye for the language as well.

Try searching for a Spanish alphabet song or even children's content showing numbers, colors, and nursery rhymes that you are already familiar with. Another fun way to get in practice time is to find Spanish games. There are a wide variety of games online, and you can search for games that will target your weakest areas. Reviewing your vocabulary and practicing your translation while under pressure or finding a fun game of simple matching can reinforce what you're learning offline.

Apps

There are many Apps available on your smartphone or tablet that are entirely free for use. Look for Apps that have a very straightforward interface and are easy to use. Using language Apps can help keep you motivated with goal-setting, visual cues to stay on track, and highlighting both strong and weak points. If you're interested in creating simple sentences right away, there are interactive Apps available to get you constructing phrases right away. Keep in mind that most Apps are not meant to be stand-alone courses, but they can make for a great addition to your learning toolbox.

A simple internet search for top language apps will give you multiple lists with recommendations. Finding an app that supplies both visual and audio cues will be the most helpful, and you can even find apps that have offline learning if you find yourself getting distracted online.

- **Focus on what you need** because Spanish is considered one of the easiest languages for an English speaker to learn, you shouldn't have any trouble achieving success with a combination of online/offline materials. Even if you're not entirely convinced that you'll be able to pick up Spanish quickly, these methods are available so that you can cut to the chase and focus on learning what you need. If you have any prior knowledge, you can build on what you already know and look forward to what you still need to learn.
- To recap what we've learned in this chapter, you'll want to take advantage of as many avenues for learning that you can. While you don't want to overwhelm yourself with too much information,

having a wide array available to stimulate new thoughts can really keep you on track. Keep away from materials loaded with grammar theory to start. Instead, try to find things that build your confidence; that could mean taking quizzes in workbooks or online. You need to see results fast so that you stay motivated and continue to be inspired. Develop a strategy so that you have access to the right tool when you need it. It can be easy to get discouraged and give up; just make sure that you always start again so that you do not forget everything that you've learned.

- **Immerse Yourself.** At first, it can seem impossible to decipher the fast pace of native Spanish speakers. The series of staccato sounds makes it seem that they are speaking much faster than we do in English. How can we detect the patterns, rhythms, and nuances of the Spanish language? It is through immersing us in the language and paying attention to each sound that is made and how it relates to other sounds (and then practice making those sounds). Keep in mind that Spanish words run together, and when a word that begins with a vowel follows a word that ends with the same vowel, you only pronounce it once.

Since language is a very regional thing, the goal here is to learn a standard variety that can be understood in all Spanish speaking areas. Learning grammar and phrasing will produce an unlimited number of meaningful sentences rather than only being able to pull from the phrases you have memorized. Keep in mind that memorizing function words and phrases will help you practice the framework of

Spanish. So, how can you start immersing yourself in Spanish as a beginner? In addition to listening to Podcasts, you can watch movies, read books, listen to music, and literally surround yourself with the Spanish language. The goal here is to eat, speak, and dream in Spanish.

There are a few methods to immerse yourself in Spanish in the comfort of your home, work, and during your free time.

Sticky Note Method

With the sticky note method, you merely label all common items around your house. While you don't have to label everything, the more often you see a word, the more likely you are to remember it. It's easy to go overboard with this, but doing so can have a reverse effect. You don't want sticky notes everywhere that you'll just ignore, and you don't want to label items that you probably wouldn't talk about in general conversation.

Start by looking around your house and try to name what you see in Spanish. If you do not know a word for something, look it up and put a sticky note on it. Repeat until you remember that word by quizzing yourself before looking at the sticky note. Start referring to objects around the house and at work in Spanish.

Writing

Try writing a quick grocery list or itemized to-do list in Spanish. Keep a running list of words that you don't know and look them up. If you keep a journal, attempt to make a journal entry entirely in Spanish. This will help you learn common words that you will use in your daily life. Try and write something in Spanish every day. Writing employs our fine motor-skills and switches on our muscle memory, which helps us remember phrases and words through these repeated gestures. When you write something by hand, you are more likely to slow down and put things into your own words. If you want to kick things up a notch, practice your Spanish writing in cursive! Try and put pressure on yourself by adding some structure and challenges to your daily writing. For example, you could set a timer and write as many words and phrases that you know in Spanish within 5 minutes. Write yourself a note and don't read it until a few days later. Can you read it? Keep track of the words that you had to look up to complete a phrase or sentence.

Don't spend too much time on correct punctuation; the more you write, the easier the words will come. You can always look up the words and add the correct punctuation later. One of your goals should be to communicate in Spanish without relying on translators and dictionaries. It doesn't matter what you're writing about as long as you are putting effort into it. Try and refrain from copying directly from a translator, or you'll never commit these words to memory!

Television and Movies

Telenovelas (short Spanish soap operas) are a great way to get exposure to both the culture and body language used by native Spanish speakers. These programs typically have themes revolving around love, family, and business. Since you're watching to learn, look out for Spanish language "cognates," which are words that will have practically the same pronunciation as they do in English. For example, "absurd" in English is simply "absurdo" in Spanish.

Almost all cable providers will have a Spanish network or channels like "Telemundo." If you have a streaming device, you can find multiple shows and movies entirely in Spanish. You may be surprised to find that you understand more than you expected. Many popular movies are dubbed in Spanish, and watching some of your favorite movies in Spanish can even renew your interest in them. Overall, watching Spanish videos can be not only educational, but also engaging, exciting, and addicting!

Music

A fun way to regularly reinforce your progress and hear new vocabulary is by listening to music in Spanish. You don't have to stick to just popular music; there are Spanish radio stations that focus on cultural programming and arts as well. Also, you can find a wide variety of Spanish radio soap operas, sports, news, and healthcare issues. There are also plenty of Latin music playlists already created on popular music sites. Some Apps even include lyrics that you can follow along with to hone your listening skills.

Look up songs that you are familiar with and see if you can find a Spanish version. Remember to *listen actively* and practice imitating what you hear. Getting your ear in tune can be invaluable while learning, and you won't get that from a translation book!

Books

Physical books offer a serious advantage to online learning because you don't have to worry about downloading anything, internet connections, or dying batteries. It isn't always easy to find popular novels at the right level of beginner's Spanish. Just be brave and choose a book that challenges you but is not too complex. There are many different types of books available to the eager Spanish learner; popular fiction and nonfiction, reference materials, workbooks, dictionaries, etc. It is vital that you have a good variety of books on hand.

Imagine how satisfying it will be when you're able to turn the last page of a book and realize that you've just finished reading an entire book *in Spanish*. It's quite easy to find books both in print and online, and many books have never been translated to English—so you'll be gaining access to the information you never would come across in normal life. If you can find a book that you've already read, it can be a lot easier to follow along without having to look up every other word.

To look up words quickly or to keep on hand for on-the-spot translations, pick up a Spanish-English dictionary. These pocket-guide dictionaries are typically meant to fit in a backpack so that they are accessible when you most need them. They can be an indispensable tool for communicating while traveling or attempting to read a book written entirely in Spanish.

Starting can be tricky, but as you progress through a book, you'll notice that in most cases, the vocabulary tends to build on itself. Don't be shy to start with children's books as they can really help jump-start your understanding of the Spanish language. Find something of interest that is about half the size of a book you would typically read. You should be able to understand at least half of what the book is saying, so starting with an elementary level book will help ease you into this new reading habit.

Local Events

A quick search on social media can potentially lead to all sorts of local events in the Latin community. Look for church services, dance or cooking classes, festivals, and other events near you. Be open to meeting new people that share similar interests and hobbies. Use these as opportunities to practice speaking Spanish and observe how other Spanish speakers interact with one another. This will also give you the ability to communicate with people you would not have the chance to know.

Think in Spanish

Try and spend time thinking in Spanish. Since you're not used to it, this can feel strange at first. An excellent way to start is to think of an open-ended question (not a yes or no question) and try to give the Spanish answer. Simple questions such as "What day is it" or "how old are you" can help you understand Spanish much sooner than you think. Switch to Spanish on your favorite apps or when you use the ATM when using hashtags. In other words, utilize the language in real-life scenarios.

Remember, you must really feel like there is a reason that you're learning Spanish, or you won't really commit to it.

With the tips and methods outlined here, you will learn new things and connect with a new culture while developing invaluable language skills. The only way to swim is to get in the water. You could study swimming methods and techniques for weeks, but until you take the plunge and get in the water, you'll never learn. Don't worry about every word and phrase that you come across; it's okay to ignore the things that may be irrelevant to you.

Since you've already come up with a deadline, break that down by the day or week. Aim to achieve a certain level of competency by the end of week 1, and so on. Set a date at the end of week 2 to have your first conversation with a native Spanish speaker. It doesn't matter if you find someone to speak with online or in person. Make speaking with someone in Spanish a goal for a couple of times every week and even more frequently if you have access. You may be surprised that the conversations you attempted to have during those beginning weeks have become the cornerstones of your learning.

If you start to feel burnt out, keep in mind that just a few minutes a day is way better than not doing anything at all. Immerse yourself as much as you can, do what works for you, and fluency could be much closer than you think.

Conclusion

Thank you for making it through the end of this book. Going through this book up to the end does not, in a way, suggest that you have accomplished all your objectives. This is just a tiny fraction of the whole thing. There is a lot of information out there that you can read to become a master in the Spanish language.

The next step is to re-read the most critical sections of the book to get a mastery of the basics of the language. These will provide you with a robust foundation to lay on the proceeding levels, such as the intermediary level and so on. If you still find it challenging to hack the given basics, then it would be prudent that you reschedule your daily schedule so that you get more time to interact with difficult areas. Apart from that, you can create strict timelines in order to consume material for the maximum benefits.

Above all, you need to incorporate strict self-discipline to go through these contents at the stipulated times. You shall also learn more about the benefits of understanding the Spanish language in running your business and becoming part of other ventures. In the end, the chapters of this book will assist you in analyzing the results of becoming a fluent Spanish speaker, not only in your jurisdiction but also in your academic endeavors. At the end of the day, the manuscript shares vital information regarding what it takes to becomes an equipped learner and tutor, as well. While at it, you will realize that there are some benefits appended to understanding this language. As such, many colleges have resorted to working with educational centers at making sure that the employees they hire are not only learned but aware of the impact of understanding the Spanish language. To that end, you will also learn more about the actual history of Spanish speakers and their origin. The same implies that you'll get to understand the reasons behind aspiring to learn more about Spanish speaking. In different chapters, you will garner knowledge regarding the lessons to attend in order to learn how to speak Spanish. You shall also garner more knowledge based on how to utilize the chapters to your advantage. Of course, the chapters discuss what it takes to easily grasp more lessons about the language.

You can also separate the contents into smaller bits and consume each at a time since research reveals that dividing complex tasks into smaller individual ones, including time frames, is effective. You have higher chances of completing them successfully. Finally, if you found this book useful in any way, a review on Amazon is always appreciated!

Follow the guidelines found in this book to be able to quickly learn Spanish so that you can speak with a new set of people all over the world. Remember, it can be an asset in the workplace when you are meeting new friends or when you are traveling. Learning a new language is never going to be a waste. And you will continue to have fun with the language the more that you learn.

LEARN SPANISH GRAMMAR

How to Understand and Speak at Home, on the Road, or Traveling in the Car, Even If You're a Beginner. Common Phrases, Instruction, and Pronunciation for Conversations

Living Languages

Introduction

Spanish is quickly becoming an important element in the business and academic world.

The Hispanic population has also grown remarkably in the last decade, making it prudent for savvy business owners to learn enough of the language to interact with potential clients, possible co-workers, and employees. In a world that is rapidly becoming a global market, it is wise for anyone who wants to compete at a high level to acquire knowledge of more than one language.

This short crash Spanish grammar course will give you everything you need to start learning Spanish the right way and easily. It is made for beginners and covers the most important grammar points one needs to know.

Follow the guidelines found in this book to learn Spanish quickly and be able to speak to native speakers around the world. Remember that it can be an advantage in the workplace, meeting new friends, or when traveling.

Learning a new language is never going to be a waste. And the more you learn, the funnier you will have with the language.

Chapter 1: Pronunciation is the Key

Spanish pronunciation is really simple in comparison to other languages. The Spanish alphabet contains 27 letters, most of which are pronounced in only one way. Nonetheless, there are a few exceptions, which we will cover in this section.

Vowels

The letter **a** is always pronounced like the **a** in apricot. You will find this sound in words like *casa* (house).

The letter **e** is always pronounced as the **e** in elephant. You will find this sound in words like *verde* (green).

The letter **i** always sounds like the **i** in intelligence or the **ee** in meet (when it's stressed). You can find this sound in words like *inglés* (English), *argentino* (Argentinian), or *salir* (to go out).

The letter **o** always sounds like the **o** in tongue. You can find this sound in words like *tomate* (tomato) and *vaso* (glass).

The letter **u** always sounds like the **oo** in pool or like English **w** in water. You can find this sound in words like *luna* (moon) and *usar* (to use).

Consonants

The letter **b** in Spanish is similar to letter **b** in English, but while in English it sounds harder when it's in the beginning of a word (as in beautiful), in Spanish it's always a soft sound (as in cabin). You will find it in words like *bebé* (baby).

The letter **c** in Spanish can have three sounds: The first is like the **c** in cut. The letter **c** always sounds like this when it comes before letters a, o, u and consonants (except h), as in words like *cama* (bed), *cosa* (thing), *cuento* (tale) and *acto*.

The second **c** sound is the same as the **s** sound. It sounds like this when it comes before letters e and i, as in *cerilla* (match) or *cien* (a hundred).

The third sound is only possible when **c** comes before an **h**, just as it happens in English. The combination of **c** and **h** sounds like **ch** in change. You will find this in words like *colchón* (mattress).

The letter **d** in Spanish is similar to **d** in English (as in daisy) but softer. You can find it in words such as *dedo* (finger).

The letter **f** in Spanish sounds like **f** in English, in words such as fish. You will find this sound in Spanish words like *feliz* (happy).

The letter **g** in Spanish can have two different sounds: When it comes before letters a, o, u and consonants it sounds like a soft version of the English **g** sound in green. You can find this sound in words like *gato* (cat), *gota* (drop), *gusto* (taste) and *gracias* (thanks). You also get this sound when you have the combination of letters **gue** and **gui**. In these cases, the **u** is not pronounced, just as it happens in English in guest or guilty. You can find this sound in Spanish in words such as *guerra* (war) and *guitarra* (guitar). The **u** is only pronounced when there's a dieresis (two dots) on top of it, as in *pingüino* (penguin) or *antigüedad* (antique), but this is not very common.

The second **g** sound in Spanish is similar to the **h** sound in English word helicopter. You can find this sound when **g** comes before letters e and i, as in *gente* (people) or *girasol* (sunflower).

The letter **h** in Spanish is silent. You will normally find it at the beginning of words, such as *hielo* (ice) or *huevo* (egg), but it can also be in the middle, as in *almohada* (pillow). The only situation where **h** has a sound is in combination with **c**, as in *chocolate* (chocolate).

The letter **j** in Spanish sounds like the Spanish **g** before letters e and i. This means it sounds similar to English **h** in words like heaven. You can find this letter in words such as *jamón* (ham), *jefe* (boss) and *joven* (young).

The letter **k** is not used in many words in Spanish, but you can find it in some, like *kilo* (kilo) and *kiosco* (kiosk). The sound is the same as the sound of letter **c** when it comes before letters a, o, u and consonants, as in *cantar* (to sing).

The letter **l** in Spanish sounds exactly as letter **l** in English. You can find it in words such as *limón* (lemon) or *loco* (crazy). However, when two l's are put together, the sound changes. The combination **ll** sounds different in some Latin American countries and in Spain. In different regions, it's pronounced like the Spanish **i** or li letters, like the English **y** in yellow or **j** in jello or like the English **sh** in show.

The letter **m** in Spanish always sounds like the **m** in English, as in monster. You can find this letter in words like *miedo* (fear) or *mejor* (better).

The letter **n** in Spanish always sounds like the **n** in English, as in nonsense. You can find this letter in words like *nunca* (never) or *nada* (nothing).

Letter **ñ** sounds like the combination of letters ni, as in onion. You can find this letter in words as *niño* (kid), where the ni and the ñ sound exactly the same. Other words with the letter ñ are *contraseña* (password), *señal* (signal) and *dueño* (owner).

The letter **p** in Spanish sounds softer than the English **p**. It is actually more similar to the English **b** in because. You can find this sound in words like *perro* (dog) or *rápido* (fast).

The letter **r** has two different sounds in Spanish: The strong **r** sound is very difficult for non-Spanish speakers, so if you want to roll your **r**'s like a local, you need to try to place your tongue in the front of your palate, right behind your teeth and try to make air pass through until it sounds like an engine starting. You'll need this sound for words that start with **r**, like *rata* (rat), and for words that have a double **r**, like *perro* (dog).

The soft **r** is easier, and it sounds like the American sound for **t** in water. You'll use the soft **r** in words like *cara* (face).

The letter **s** always sounds like the **s** in snake. You'll use this sound in words like *silla* (chair) or *Sol* (sun).

The letter **t** sounds stronger than American **t** and a little bit softer than British **t**. You'll use this sound in words like *tomate* (tomato) and *techo* (roof).

The letter **v** sounds similar to English **v**, maybe a little bit softer and sometimes not really different to **b**. You'll find this sound in words like *vaca* (cow) and *vaso* (glass).

Letter **w** is not really common in Spanish. It is only used in word with a foreign origin, like those who come from English. It is pronounced like the English *w* and you'll find it in words like *kiwi* and *show*, which mean the same as in English.

Letter **x** is also not a really common word in Spanish. It sounds like a strong *c* and an *s* put together, just like in English. You'll use it in words like *taxi* (*taxi*) and *conexión* (*connection*).

Letter **y** has two different sounds: It sounds like Spanish *i* (like the *i* in *intelligence* or the *ee* in *meet*) in words like *y* (*and*) or *hoy* (*today*).

It can sound like Spanish *ll* and also sounds different in some Latin American countries and in Spain: it's pronounced like the Spanish *i*, like the English *y* in *yellow* or *j* in *jello* or like the English *sh* in *show*. You'll find this in really common words like *yo* (*I*) and *ya* (*now*).

Letter **z** is pronounced, in some countries, like an *s*; but in some others it's quite different (for example, in Spain): it sounds similar to the *th* in *with* or *throne*. You'll use the *z* in words like *cazar* (*to hunt*) and *zorro* (*fox*).

In Spanish, both nouns and adjectives are plurals. So, you need to make sure that both adjectives and nouns agree when you are constructing a sentence. While we have gone over some of the most important aspects of the plural form in previous chapters, we are now going to focus on the guidelines that come with building plurals in Spanish.

Word Ending in a Vowel

Nouns and adjectives that end in a vowel should have an "s" added to them. This applies to any noun or adjective that ends in a vowel, "a," "e," "i," "o," or "u."

Some examples include:

- Silla (chair) – sillas (chairs)
- Teléfono (telephone) – teléfonos (telephones)
- Taxi (cab) – taxis (cabs)
- Buque (boat) – buques (boats)
- Tribu (tribe) – tribus (tribes)

The same goes for words that end in a stressed vowel, that is, with a tilde at the end of it.

For example:

- Bebé (baby) – Bebés (babies)
- Papá (father) – papás (fathers/parents)
- Buró (office) – burós (offices)

However, in the case of "ú" and "í," "es" is added to make the plural form. For instance:

- Tabú (taboo) – tabúes (taboos)
- Colibrí (hummingbird) – colibríes (hummingbirds)

In this case, it is more of a pronunciation device than an orthographic one. As such, please pay attention to the words ending in "í" and "ú." The good news is that words with these endings are quite as common as the first group.

Also, the "í" ending applies to some demonyms. For example:

- Paquistaní (Pakistaní) – paquistaníes (Pakistanis)
- Iraní (Iranian) – iraníes (Iranians)
- Iraquí (Iraqi) – iraquíes (Iraqis)

While most demonyms generally end in "iego" or "és," the "í" tends to be a bit of a special case. For other demonyms, you will add the "es" ending:

- Danés (Dane) – daneéses (Danes)
- Finlandés (Finn) – finlandéses (finns)
- Irlandés (Irish) – irlandéses (Irish) Also,
- Griego (Greek) – griegos (Greeks)

All other demonyms would just have the "s" added to it.

Words Ending in Consonants

In the case of words that end in "y," the "es" ending is required to make the plural form. For instance:

- Ley (law) – leyes (laws)
- Rey (king) – reyes (kings)
- Lady (Lady, as in noble rank) – ladys (Ladies)

While the "y" ending isn't all that common, you will certainly run into a few words containing this ending.

Also, please bear in mind that all words ending in "s" (in singular form) and "x" shall have the "es" ending added to it. For example:

- Fax (fax) – faxes (faxes)
- Compás (compass) – compáses (compasses)

Given the nature of the "s" being the plural ending, there aren't many words that end in "s" in their singular form. The ones that don't generally change. For example:

- El virus – los virus
- El viernes – los viernes
- La crisis – las crisis
- El tórax – los tórax

The previous examples illustrate how these words remain the same in their singular and plural forms. In addition, words ending in "z" will have the "es" ending added but with the "z" changing to "c." For instance:

- Pez (fish) – peces (fish)
- Voz (voice) – voces (voices)
- Feroz (fierce) – feroces (fierce)

Words that end in "l," "r," n," "d," and "j," so long as they follow a vowel, will also have the "es" ending added to it.

Some examples of this rule are as follows:

- Barril (barrel) – barriles (barrels)
- Amor (loves) – amores (loves)
- Camión (truck) – camiones (trucks)
- Actividad (activity) – actividades (activities)
- Reloj (clock) – relojes (clocks)

In addition, words ending in any other consonant that isn't the ones we have listed above would simply have "s" added to it. This is mainly due to pronunciation more than any orthographic reason. Here are some examples:

- Álbum – álbums (albums)
- Bóxer – bóxers (boxers, sport)
- Cómic – cómics (comics)
- Póster – pósters (posters)
- Superávit – superávits (surpluses)

These words do not take the "es" ending in the plural form. It should be noted that these words are not nearly as common as those that take the "es" ending. Another thing to keep in mind is that most of these terms have been originally imported from other languages. As such, they tend to maintain the same structure from their original languages.

Nouns with Two or More Words and Proper Nouns

In the event of nouns that are made up of two or more words, all of the words need to become plural. This maintains the overall singular/plural structure of that noun. Consider the following examples:

- Los Estados Unidos (The United States)
- Las Naciones Unidas (The United Nations)
- Estados miembros (member states)

- Sus Majestades (Their Majesties)
- Sus Altezas Reales (Their Royal Highness)
- Buenos Aires (the city of Buenos Aires)

The above examples are generally limited to formal titles or designations. Nevertheless, each word that makes up the whole noun is plural, as it is part of the whole name, title, or designation.

Also, when you are talking about a family, the surname is not pluralized. So, if you are to the Smith family, you would have "Los Smith." By the same token, the Rodríguez family would be "Los Rodríguez." As such, surnames are never pluralized.

This previous point also applies to brand names. This is true if you are referring to various objects by the brand and not their actual name, for example, los coches Toyota (the Toyota cars). In this example, you wouldn't pluralize the brand name, as it is a proper noun just like names and surnames.

Consequently, you can pluralize the noun itself (car, in this case) but without pluralizing the brand. Here are some more examples:

- Zapatillas Nike (Nike sneakers)
- Chocolates Snickers (Snickers chocolates)
- Computadoras Dell (Dell computers)
- Relojes Omega (Omega watches)
- Gafas de sol Ray-Ban (Ray-Ban sunglasses)

Even if you referred to the items as if their brand was a noun, it would still not be pluralized. Take the example, "los Ford son muy buenos" (Fords are very good). While you would pluralize the brand name in English, you wouldn't do so in Spanish, especially if their brand name is originally from another language.

The same concept extends to the name of companies. When a company opens several branches or offices, such as in the case of banks, you won't use the company's name in the plural form. You would only limit yourself to expressing the company´s name in relation to the number of offices opened. For example, "han abierto tres nuevos Walmart en la ciudad" (Three new Walmarts have been opened). The main reasoning is that it is hard to determine what the proper plural form would be. So, it is much easier to keep the name as singular. In the event that you do hear people refer to companies and brands in the plural form, it might be due to colloquialisms from locals more than actual grammatical logic.

Chapter 2: Forming Sentences

Sentence formation in Spanish is quite similar to that in English. Spanish and English syntax are very similar despite several differences. We have spoken about these differences throughout this book. However, we are going to put them all together in this chapter.

First of all, basic sentence structure is based on the "subject + verb + object" formula. This means that you can use this basic structure to build any sentence you would like to construct. Let's see how we can build a sentence in the present simple.

- Yo juego fútbol todos los días. (I play soccer every day).

In this example, the subject is "yo" (I), the verb is "juego" (play, conjugated for the first person in present simple), and the object of the sentence, which is an adverbial phrase "todos los días" (every day).

Based on this example, you can see that building a sentence is rather straightforward. There aren't any complex rules that you need to follow in order to make sense of your ideas. As long as the verb is conjugated properly based on the tense you intend to use, you will be in good shape moving forward. This is one important point to master.

Now, let us discuss one of the main differences between English and Spanish sentence formation.

Sentences without Subject

Earlier, we talked about how it is possible to omit the subject of a sentence. In fact, it is quite common to do this, so long as it is clear about who or what you are referring to. If you omit the subject, but it is unclear who you are referring to, then you might confuse your interlocutor.

Consider this example:

- Trabajo en una oficina. (I work in an office).

The conjugation for "trabajo" makes it clear that you are referring to yourself. In this case, there is no question about who you are talking about. Hence, you can easily omit the subject because your interlocutor will be clear about who you are referring to.

Please consider this example

- Trabajo en una oficina. Mi hermano trabaja en un hospital. Mi mejor amiga trabaja desde casa. Es un buen trabajo. (I work in an office. My brother works in a hospital. My best friend works from home. It is a good job.) This example refers to three people. While this is not the issue, the actual issue lies in the "es un buen trabajo" part of the paragraph. What job are you talking about? Whose job are you referring to?

If you base your assumptions on logic, you could infer that the job you are referring to is the last one mentioned; that is, your best friend's. However, if you are referring to your job or that of your brother's, you will quickly confuse your interlocutor.

Here is a clearer version:

- Trabajo en una oficina. Mi hermano trabaja en un hospital. Mi mejor amiga trabaja desde casa. Mi trabajo es bueno. (I work in an office. My brother works in a hospital. My best friend works from home. My job is good.) As you can see, it is perfectly fine to refer to an earlier point in the paragraph. As long as you make this clear, you should have no worries about confusing your interlocutor. Nevertheless, be on the lookout in case the folks with whom you speak commit this error. While they may do it involuntarily, it may confuse you.

In that case, you can seek clarification by using questions such as:

- ¿Cuál trabajo? (Which job?)
- ¿Tu trabajo o el de tu hermano?) (Your job or your brother's?)
- ¿El trabajo de quién? (Whose job?)

There is no need to feel embarrassed when asking for clarification. Spanish culture does not frown upon asking questions. In fact, asking for clarification can be used to show genuine interest in the conversation. So, don't be afraid to ask for more information if you are not clear on something being said.

Negative Sentences

Earlier, we mentioned the use of "no" in order to build negatives. This is the case, as Spanish does not use any special auxiliaries to build negative sentences. In fact, you can simply use "no" in a regular, affirmative statement, and you should be good to go. But, there is one catch: the use of "no" needs to be in the right spot.

Let us illustrate with a couple of sentences:

- Yo no trabajo en una oficina. (I don't work in an office.)
- Yo no estoy trabajando ahora. (I am not working now.)

In both of these examples, you can see that we are using "no," following the subject and preceding the verb. This is the correct placement of "no." If you happen to place it anywhere else, then it might lead to potential confusion.

In addition, you can omit the subject of the sentence. That would look something like this:

- No trabajo en una oficina. (I don't work in an office.)
- No estoy trabajando ahora. (I am not working now.)

In this case, "no" becomes the first word of the sentence as it is indicating the negation straight away. So, as long as you place "no" before the verb, you will be making a meaningful sentence.

When responding to questions, it is optional to use "no" at the beginning of your reply or just jump right into the reply itself. Consider this question:

- ¿Quieres un café? (Do you want a coffee?)
- No, gracias. (No, thank you).

- No me gusta el café, gracias. (I don't like coffee, thank you.)
- No tomo café, gracias. (I don't drink coffee, thank you.)

In these examples, you can simply reply using "no." This makes for a much simpler way of replying in the negative form.

One other important aspect of sentence formation in Spanish is the use of time expressions.

Time Expressions

You will find that Spanish speakers use time expressions, either at the beginning or the end of a sentence. This can be somewhat confusing, given the fact that English assigns a specific placement for time expressions. In essence, the Spanish placement of time expressions depends on what the speaker is trying to get across. For example, the speaker might be more concerned about emphasizing the time expression itself. As such, that would warrant the speaker to place it at the beginning of the sentence. In other cases, the time expression itself might not be as important. So, that might motivate the speaker to place it at the end of the sentence.

Let's have a look at some examples:

- Hoy es mi cumpleaños. (Today is my birthday.)
- Mi cumpleaños es hoy. (My birthday is today.)
- Mañana trabajamos desde casa. (Tomorrow, we work from home.)

- Trabajamos desde casa mañana. (We work from home tomorrow.)
- Ella viaja la próxima semana. (She travels next week.)
- La próxima semana ella viaja. (Next week, she travels.)

In the above examples, you can see how the time expression placement can come at either the beginning or the end of the sentence. This illustrates how Spanish syntax is rather flexible. While there is a proper word order that needs to be followed, the main takeaway from this point is that even if you get the word order wrong, you should still be able to get meaning across.

So, don't worry too much about getting the exact word order right since Spanish allows you to play around with the placement of words and adverbial phrases.

However, there is one caveat. When you use the subject and verb in a sentence, make sure you don't place them at different points. Consider this example:

- Nosotros mañana viajamos. (We tomorrow travel)

In this example, the time expression "mañana" was inserted in between the verb and the subject. This placement is incorrect. While the insertion of "no," as in, "nosotros no viajamos" makes sense, the use of the time expression would be incorrect. While it is still possible that your interlocutor will get the message, it would simply sound strange and out of place. So, do take care to ensure that you don't insert time expressions in this location.

Overall, making sentences in Spanish is rather straightforward. The most complex part about it is getting the right verb conjugation. But with the guidelines we have presented in this book, you are well on your way to getting the right conjugations. As you gain more practice and experience, you will also be able to make the most of your language skills. As such, you will be able to construct solid sentences in no time.

Chapter 3: Spanish Nouns

In both English and Spanish, nouns are words used to identify a name or a person, a place, an entity, an animal, an idea, or a thing. On its own, a noun does not show any action or how it relates to other words. Nouns are your guiding force when learning Spanish. They help you name objects, places, and the world around you. Imagine the world with so much to name, and imagine if we didn't get that opportunity to name them. It would be so bland and boring. You can say that nouns contribute to bringing our world to life.

In this chapter, we shall delve deeply into the world of Spanish nouns, their types, meanings, and some of the grammar rules that accompany Spanish nouns. So stick around and be ready to learn. Let's start with some examples of nouns in English and their Spanish translations.

Places	**Lugares**
Bookstore	libreria
Museum	museo
Airport	aeropuerto
Café	café
Bank	banco
Hospital	hospital
Stadium	estadio

Bakery	panadería
Beach	playa
Zoo	zoológico
Store	tienda
Park	parque
Market	mercado
Grocery store	tienda de comestibles
Church	iglesia
Garden	jardín
Restaurant	restaurante
Factory	fabrica
Movie	película
Theater	teatro
Pastry shop	pastelería
Pool	piscina
Police station	estación de la policía
Pharmacy	farmacia
Post office	Oficina postal
Town hall	ayuntamiento

Nature and animals / Naturaleza y animales

Fish	pez

Bear	oso
Elephant	elefante
Monkey	mono
Whale	ballena
Bird	ave
Horse	caballo
Pig	cerdo/a
Duck	pato/a
Mouse	raton
Cow	vaca
Goat	cabra
Sheep	oveja
Wolf	lobo
Rooster/chicken	gallo/gallina
Cat	gato/a
Tiger	tigre
Lion	león
Skunk	mofeta
Dog	perro/a
Waterfall	cascada
Ocean	océano

River	rio
Plant	planta
Flower	flor
Jungle	selva
Forest	bosque
Rainbow	arco iris
Rain	lluvia
Pond	charca
Lightning	relámpago
Lake	lago
Fog	niebla
Sky	cielo
Mountain	montaña
Hail	granizo
Hill	Colina
Meadow/field	campo

School	**Escuela**
Student	estudiante
University	Universidad
Quiz/exam	examen

Geography	geografía
Physics	física
Algebra	álgebra
Accounting Economics	economía contable
Art	arte
Political science	ciencias políticas
Pen	lapicero
Paper	papel
Chemistry	química
Dictionary	diccionario
Book	libro
Computer	computadora
Pencil	lápiz
College	colegio
Professor	profesor
Teacher	maestro/a
Drawing	dibujo
Math	mathematics
Computer science	ciencias de la Computación
Foreign languages	idiomas extranjeros

Transportation **Transporte**

Car	coche
Airplane	avion
Bicycle	bicicleta
On foot	a pie
Boat	barco
Moped	ciclomotor
Engine	motor
Map	mapa
Wheel	rueda
Taxi	taxi
Bus	bus
Subway	subterraneo
Motorcycle	motocicleta
Directions	direcciones
Stop	parar
Acceleration	aceleración
Business	**Negocio**
Entrance	entrada
Exit	salida
Office	oficina
Check	cheque

Bill	cuenta
Price	precio
Tax	impuesto
The rent	renta
Estimate	stimación
Passport	pasaporte
Traveler's check	cheque de viajar
City	ciudad
The cost	cuesta
Baggage/luggage	equipaje
Customs	aduanas
Information	información
Currency exchange	Cambio de moneda
Pay	pagar

Clothing and body — **La ropa y el cuerpo**

Shoulder	Hombro
Finger	dedo
Arm	brazo
Heart	corazón
Mouth	boca
Waist	cintura

Neck	cuello
Head	cabeza
Face	cara
Nose	nariz
Brain	cerebro
Hair	pelo
Chest	pecho
Back	espalda
Stomach	estómago
Ear	oreja
Eye	ojo
Wrist	muñeca
Toe	dedo del pie
Leg	pierna
Shirt	camisa
Hat	sombrero
Blouse	blusa
Earrings	pendientes
Dress	vestido
Skirt	falda
Shoes	zapatos

Elbow	codo
Pants	pantalones
Socks	calcetines
Jeans	pantalones vaqueros
Swimsuit	traje de baño
Gloves	guantes
Underwear	ropa interior
Ring	anillo
Belt	correa
Coat	capa

Religion — **Religión**

God	Dios
Christianity Bishop	Obispo del Cristianismo
Bible	Biblia
Baptism	Bautismo
Angel	Angel
Cathedral	catedral
Church	Iglesia
Buddhism	Budismo
Heaven	Cielo
Faith	Fe

Hell	Infierno
Pope	Papa
Sermon	Sermón
Judaism	Judaísmo
Monastery	Monasterio
Prophet	Profeta
Temple	Templo
Protestant	Protestante

House and furniture — Casa y muebles

Apartment	apartamento
House	casa
Kitchen	cocina
Living room	sala
Room	cuarto
Hallway	vestíbulo
Bathtub	bañera
Bathroom	baño
Shower	ducha
Sink	lavabo
Closet	armario
Stairs	escaleras

Roof	tejado
Wall	pared
Window	ventana
Oven	horno
Couch	sofá
Television	television
Light	luz
Stove	estufa
Radio	radio
Desk	escritorio
Blanket	manta
Dishwasher	lavaplatos
Table	mesa
Garbage	basura
Chair	silla
Microwave	microonda

Understanding Nouns in Spanish and Their Gender Rules

The one thing you will need to know about Spanish nouns is that they have a gender. It's a tricky situation for English speakers. In English, only living things have gender, but, all non-living and living things are classified into masculine or feminine in Spanish. Gender in Spanish does not mean the nouns are male or female as compared to what they are being referred to. But in some instances, this is the case. For example, a male doctor will be masculine, while nouns that generally relate to female things, such as a female animal, are feminine.

Sometimes, you will be able to distinguish between the two by the gender they are being referred to. An excellent example is the sun. When we talk about the sun, it is usually associated with the male gender, generally. That is also the case with Spanish, where the sun is called el sol. On the other hand, the female gender is usually associated with the moon in Spanish. It's referred to as la luna.

"The" is a commonly used word in the English language as a single word. In Spanish, it is used depending on the quantity gender for which it is matched. Confused? Don't be; just remember that when a masculine noun follows the word "the" in Spanish it is **el**. When a feminine noun follows it, then it is **la**. For example:

- El señor, the gentleman (masculine)
- LA señora, the lady (feminine)

However, other nouns like table and cup may be hard to identify the gender, but if you translate it to Spanish, it's easier to know which gender they belong to. The table is **la mesa**, and the cup is **la taza**. All masculine nouns are written with an 'el' before, but for the female, it is 'la.' If it is in the plural for male, it is 'los' before the noun, and for the plural feminine, you will use 'las'. Examples:

People

The boy	el niño (singular masculine)
The boys	los niños (plural masculine)
The girl	la niña (singular feminine)
The girls	las niñas (plural feminine)

Place

The house	la casa
The houses	las casas
The restaurant	el restaurante
The restaurants	los restaurantes

Abstract ideas

The thought	el pensamiento
The thoughts	los pensamientos
The idea	la idea
The ideas	las ideas

To be able to master this part of Spanish well, there are rules we will discuss below that will make you understand this concept better. I will also use examples to make the process easier for you.

#Rule 1

In Spanish, when you are referring to living creatures, nouns that end in –o are known to be masculine, and the ones that end in –a are known to be feminine. Here are some examples:

Male monkey	el mono
Male monkeys	los monos
The male bear	el oso
The male bears	los osos
The uncle	el tio
Uncles	los tios
The grandfather	el abuelo
The grandfathers	los abuelos
The female dog	la perra
Female dogs	las perras
The female bear	la osa
The female bears	las osas
The female cat	la gata
The female cats	las gatas

Example

Where is the dog?

¿Dónde está el perro?

#Rule 2
Some nouns of non-living creatures also end with -o for masculine and -a for female gender. Look at the examples below.

Nouns ending in -o   **Nouns ending in -a**

	Masculine		**Feminine**
Roof	el techo	Flute	la flauta
Dust	el polvo	House	la casa
Dress	el vestido	Guitar	la guitará
Car	el carro	Wallet	la cartera
Egg	el huevo	Cow	la vaca
Hat	el sombrero	Office	la oficina
Book	el libro	Patience	la paciencia
Floor	el suelo	Shirt	la camisa

You should, however, avoid thinking that everything associated with the male gender will be related to the masculine noun rules or that everything associated with the female gender will automatically fall under the feminine category. For example, neckties are usually for men, but when we translate it into Spanish, it's written as **la corbata**. While on the other hand, makeup, which is associated with women, is written as **el maquillaje**.

#Rule 3

If there is a mixed gender group that is both female and male, the masculine gender will be used. Regardless of whether the ratio of women to men is higher, the gender used is male.

For example:

- 1 perro + 7 perras= 8 perros
- 1 niño + 5 niñas = 6 niños

- 3 gatos + 1000 gatas =1003 gatos

As you may have figured from the examples above in Spanish, the masculine gender is stronger than the feminine gender.

#Rule 4

This rule states that masculine nouns that end in non-vowel sounds have an alternate feminine form that ends with —a.

Examples:

Mr.	el senor
Mrs.	la señora
Male Doctor	El doctor
Female Doctor	La doctora
The Male Professor	El professor
The Female Professor	La profesora

#Rule 5

There are nouns about professions that do not change form. This does not mean that the essential element of gender disappears. It only means that if the word fails to change, the article will take full charge of specifying the gender.

	Male	**Female**
Poet	el poeta	la poeta
Athlete	el atleta	la atleta

Psychiatrist	el psiquiatra	la psiquiatra
Model	el modelo	la modelo
Soldier	el soldado	la soldado
Pilot	el piloto	la piloto

You can try doing a test where you write down all the masculine nouns and feminine nouns then check to see how much you have scored by checking which ones you got right.

#Rule 6

You may find that there are words, especially for the male articles, and others are primarily for female articles. There will be no opposite intervention from either side. If you use masculine articles with only feminine endings or the contrary, it will mess up your communication. This means that nouns that end with –ma will require you to use a masculine article. While nouns that end with –sion, –cion, –umbre, –dad, and –tud will always require you to use a feminine article. Here are a few examples to articulate this rule better.

The emblem	el emblema
The problem	el problema
The mystery	el enigma
The room	la habitación
The custom	la costumbre
The happiness	la felicidad

The exhibition	la exposición
The application	la solicitud

Please remember that learning a new language is not easy, and it may take a process. Set a daily routine for your learning, and make sure to make it fun; this will help get desirable results. Familiarize yourself with the gender rules, pick up a magazine or a newspaper, and read articles when you notice gender nouns have been used. You will realize that you will learn a lot from this exercise. You can also look for a partner to practice these gender rules with you. You should learn a lot from each other through mistakes and, definitely, through a ton of practice.

Types of Spanish Nouns

Proper Nouns (Sustantivos Propios)

These are nouns used to refer to an entity. An entity refers to buildings, cities, oceans, animals, etc. Proper nouns are written in capital letters in English, as well as Spanish. Here are some examples.

- Sia's singing is amazing/El canto de Sia es asombroso.
- The Atlantic Ocean/El Océano Atlántico
- I can't live without buying something from Versace/No puedo vivir sin comprarme algo de Versace.
- Let's go to Madrid/Vámonos a Madrid
- I am addicted to Oreos/Soy adicta a las Oreos.

- Bobbito is the cutest puppy in the world/Bobbito es el cachorro más lindo del mundo.
- Maxwell and she have been together for a very long time/Maxwell y ella han estado juntos por mucho tiempo.
- Venus can be spotted easily tonight/Venus se ve muy bien esta noche.

However, in some cases, nouns are not capitalized in Spanish. For example the days of the week.

Sunday	domingo
Monday	lunes
Tuesday	martes
Wednesday	miércoles
Thursday	jueves
Friday	viernes
Saturday	sábado

Here are ways to use them in sentences.

Which day is it, my friend?

¿Que dia es hoy, amigo?

It is Saturday.

Es sábado.

Not capitalizing months or days of the week in English is a grammatical error, but capitalizing them in Spanish is equally a grammatical error. It is best to avoid it, especially if you are going to take a Spanish exam.

Also, note that the singular days of the week, and the ones in plural that end in 's' are the same in Spanish. All you can do is change the article. For example:

- I do not have class on Friday.
- No tengo clases el viernes

- I do not have classes on Fridays.
- No tengo clases los viernes

Here is a poem for you to help you remember the days of the week. You can use it to study and practice.

7 Days in a Week

There are days in a week.

Los días de la semana son siete nada más.

If you learn this poem, then you will remember them.

Si aprendes estos poemas, los recodarás.

It's windy on Monday.

El lunes hace viento

On Tuesday, it's so hot.

El martes, que calor.

On Wednesday, it's chilly.

El miércoles hace fresco.

On Thursday, the sun comes out.

El jueves sale el sol

On Saturday, it normally does not.

El sábado normalmente no.

On Sunday, there's a rainbow.

El domingo hay un arco iris.

And you and I can go to the park.

Y varmos al parque tu y yo.

In Spanish, the days of the week have been associated with heavenly bodies.

Sunday	domingo	In Latin, it's the Lord's name.
Saturday	sábado	
Friday	viernes	In Hebrew, it's a day of rest.
Thursday	jueves	
		Venus (venus)
Wednesday	miércoles	
		Júpiter (Jupiter)
Tuesday	martes	
		Mercurio (mercury)
Monday	lunes	
		Marte (mars)
		Luna (moon)

The months in Spanish are also not capitalized.

January	enero
February	febrero

March	marzo
April	abril
May	mayo
June	junio
July	julio
August	agosto
September	septiembre
October	octubre
November	noviembre
December	diciembre

The conventions that are used to represent dates, however, are a bit different in Spanish and English. In English, the month may be written before or after the day. But in Spanish, the month is written after the day.

Example:

- Today is October fourth.
- Today is the fourth of October.

Hoy es octubre el cuarto (wrong) Hoy es el cuatro de octubre (right) In both Spanish and English, we see the year is written after the month and day. The following are examples of how to write dates in both English and Spanish.

English	Spanish
Mar-11-18	11 de marzo de 2018
Mar-02-18	2 de marzo del 2018
03/02/2018	02-03-18
Mar-02	2 de marzo
March second two thousand and eighteen	dos de marzo de dos mil dieciocho

You will find that there are a couple of things you should note when talking about dates in Spanish. In Spanish, you can use both 'de' and 'del' before writing the year. When you use 'del' when writing dates, and you write it before the year, it is usually considered more formal.

- 2 de marzo de 2018
- 2 de marzo del 2018

When you are only using numerals when writing the date in Spanish, you write the day first and then the month. It's the other way around in English; the month comes first.

- English; 03/02/2018 MM/DD/YYYY
- Spanish; 02/03/2018 DD/MM/YYYY

In English, we normally use ordinal numbers when we are talking about the date. In Spanish, on the other hand, cardinal numbers are used when talking about the date. Ordinal numbers refer to numbers that are used to put things in order like the third, second, and first (tercero, Segundo, primero).

- Yesterday was June fifteenth
- Ayer fue el quince de junio
- Hoy es el dos de marzo
- Today is March second

However, when you go to Latin America, you may find that they are using ordinal numbers to write or talk about the first of the month, even if we have discussed that cardinal numbers are typically used when writing Spanish dates.

- Hoy es el primero de marzo (Latin American Spanish)
- Today is March first.
- Today is the first of March.
- Hoy es el uno de marzo (peninsular Spanish)

When you check the rest of the dates, they are all the same; cardinals are used in both peninsular and Latin American Spanish.

Common Nouns (Sustantivos Comunes)

These are nouns used to name things, people, animals, abstract ideas, or feelings.

People

el estudiante	student
el cartero	postman
la hermana	sister

el hombre   man

Things

el libro	book
el sofa	sofa
el ordenador	computer
la mesa	table

Abstract ideas or feelings

el amor	love
la amistad	friendship
el odio	hatred
el alma	soul

Here are more examples used in sentences.

- Her boyfriend is a very loyal person/Su novio es una persona muy leal
- I love sweets/Me encantan los dulces.
- I would love to own a dog/Me encantaria tener un perro.
- There are so many planets in the galaxy that I can't count them/Hay tantos planetas en la galaxia que no puedo contarlos.
- Many people want to work as singers/Mucha gente quiere trabajar como cantantes.
- Let's go to the city that never sleeps/Vamonos a la ciudad que nunca duerme.

- I am not that much into current fashion/La moda del momento no me atrae mucho.

Abstract Nouns (los sustantivos abstractos)

These nouns mostly refer to qualities or concepts rather than beings or things. We cannot touch, taste, hear, or see these types of nouns. We also can't interact with them; however, we can think and feel about them, so they do count as meaningful, too. Examples include the following:

Fright	miedo
Intelligence	inteligencia
Virtue	virtud
Love	amor
Happiness	felicidad
Loneliness	soledad
Soul	alma
Thoughts	pensamientos
Truth	verdad

Countable and Uncountable Nouns (Sustantivos Contables y Sustantivos Incontables)

Countable nouns mainly refer to things that can be counted while uncountable nouns refer to those that cannot be counted

Movil	cellphone (countable)
Casa	house

| Tristeza | sadness (uncountable) |
| Indignacion | anger |

Here are more examples of countable nouns:

Table	mesa
Two tables	dos mesas
Three tables	tres mesas
One pencil	un lápiz
Two pencils	dos lápices
Three pencils	tres lápices

Here are more examples of uncountable nouns:

Milk	leche
Flour	harina
Detergent	detergente
Wine	vino
Ketchup	ketchup
Pepper	pimienta
Coffee	café
Politics	política
Blood	sangre

Just because a noun is uncountable, it does not mean it cannot end in –s. Look at some of the examples above.

Collective Nouns and Individual Nouns (Sustantivos Colectivos)

These are nouns that are used to represent a group of individual nouns. As you may have guessed, individual nouns are nouns that are used to refer to a single/ one entity. A few examples of collective nouns include;

Team	equipo
Multitude	multitud
Flock	rebaño
Poetry	poesía
Swarm	enjambre
Swarms	enjambres

Examples of individual nouns and their plural form are as follows.

Bee	abeja
Bees	abejas
Poem	poema
Poems	poemas
Island	isla
Islands	islas

Animated Nouns (Sustantivos Animados)

Animated nouns are a group of nouns that refer to all living things, such as animals, people, and any living creature. Some examples of animated nouns include the following:

Elf	el elfo
Dragon	el dragón
Brother	el hermano
Friends	los amigos
Neighbor	el vecino

However, you will find that there are instances where we give objects life, therefore personifying them. These are what we refer to as animated inanimate nouns. For example, cartoons and animations found in Disney channels are typical toys that are given life, and the kids identify with them, like Tom the Train or Pinocchio. Fantasy stories and books of supernatural themes also contain such objects.

Inanimated Nouns

They are used to refer to objects that have no life. It could be a place, a feeling, an idea, or a thought. Here are some examples of inanimated nouns:

Lemon	el limón
Book	el libro
Park	el parque
Anxiety	la ansiedad
Sadness	la tristeza
Wall	la pared

Toaster   el tostador

I know you may have noticed that English nouns and Spanish nouns have very similar characteristics. In some instances, there are some nouns in Spanish follow the same rules as their counterparts in English. Our beautiful words would be so meaningless and boring if we didn't have nouns to name them. I hope you have enjoyed this chapter, and you will put into practice some of the rules and memorize some of the words. Remember that the key here is to be consistent in learning, and soon, you will be on your way to mastering the Spanish language.

Chapter 4: Spanish Pronouns

Pronouns are those that are used to refer to the subject: animal, thing or person. These do not need to be accompanied by the subject in the sentence. They can take the place of the subject, and this way, the pronoun is assumed as the noun within the sentence. If we remember in English, the pronouns are: I, you, he, she, it, they, you, we.

In Spanish, there are many pronouns, and these are divided according to their use and usefulness. It usually happens that, within a sentence, the same subject must be referred to several times. The pronoun serves to avoid re-mentioning the subject and making the reading heavy. Instead of saying "María" several times in a sentence, it is preferable to say she, exactly so it happens in Spanish. We have the following pronouns: personal, reflexive, relative, possessive, indefinite, demonstrative and interrogative pronouns.

Personal Pronouns

These are the most common and simple. They are the ones we have seen several times in the practice tables of the verb. They are used to refer to the subject.

SINGULAR	*FIRST PERSON*	YO
	SECOND PERSON	TU
	THIRD PERSON	EL
	THIRD PERSON	ELLA
PLURAL	*FIRST PERSON*	NOSOTROS
	SECOND PERSON	VOSOTROS
	THIRD PERSON	ELLAS
	THIRD PERSON	ELLOS

Reflexive Pronouns

Reflexive pronouns complement reflexive verbs, agree with them in subject and number. These pronouns always refer to the subject and indicate that the action the subject performs falls on him at the same time.

- I comb my hair every morning/Me peino el cabello todas las mañanas.

- I paint my nails at night/Me pinto las uñas en las noches.

As you can see in the examples, these pronouns indicate that the action that the subject performs falls on the same subject. This is a way of not redound when speaking. The issuer performs an action that falls on him. It is very important to remember that the idea of identifying reflexive pronouns. In the first example, the sender of the message is combing his own hair. The combing action is done on himself; the same happens with the second example.

Now, we will leave you a table with the reflexive pronouns according to their personal pronoun.

YO	ME	YO ME PEINO
TÚ	TE	TÚ TE PEINAS
ÉL	SE	ÉL SE PEINA
ELLA	SE	ELLA SE PEINA
NOSOTROS	NOS	NOSOTROS NOS PEINAMOS
VOSOTROS	OS	VOSOTROS OS PEINAS
ELLOS/ELLAS	SE	ELLOS SE PEINAN

As you can see in the table, there is no need that the sentence is in first person to have a reflexive verb. There is something important to know about these pronouns in particular: their position may vary according to the need of the sentence.

Reflexive pronouns can be used before the verb:

- She combs her hair.

Verb Reflective pronouns

- Ella se peina.

Reflexive pronouns Verb

- We comb our hair.

Verb Reflexive pronouns

- Nosotros nos peinamos.

Reflexive pronouns Verb

Do you remember the verb modes? The reflexive can be placed in front of an imperative verb or attached to the verb on the verb´s back:

- Dress properly!
- ¡Arréglate!
- Focus yourself!
- ¡Te concentras!

Returning to verbs, before the infinitive pronoun, the reflexive pronoun is also added, unifying with the word:

- She does not want to comb herself/Ella no quiere peinarse
- We need to comb ourselves/Nosotros necesitamos peinarnos

The same thing happens with the gerund verb. We may attach the verb placing the reflexive pronoun at the end, or we can put it before the verb:

- He is dressing/Él se está vistiendo.
- He is dressing himself/Él está vistiendose.

Relative Pronouns

This type of pronouns is responsible for unifying two sentences or phrases. The second sentence must always qualify or add additional information to the subject named in the first sentence. This first sentence is called antecedent. This does not have to be a whole sentence. It can be from a simple name to a great phrase. This pronoun replaces the subject at the time of appearing in the second sentence.

When we add a subordinate sentence with a relative, it is usually added by placing quotes before the relative pronoun. The only exceptions to this rule are those in which very specific information will be added. Here is a table with relative pronouns: Now we will know how the different pronouns are used: The relative QUE is one of the most common relatives in the Spanish language, as seen in the table above. It can be used for person or thing no matter gender and number. Here are some examples:

- Maria dresses in clothes that belong to her sister/María se viste con ropa que es de su hermana.
- Maria, who did not finish her homework, graduated/Maria, que no terminó sus tareas, se graduó.

This relative cannot be combined directly with a preposition. To do this, it is necessary to place an article before QUE.

- Maria, the one you used to spend time with/Maria, con la que te la pasabas.

Unlike the QUE used individually, a comma must be to separate the sentences when used with an article. It must be taken into account that although the QUE is indistinct of gender and number, the article that accompanies it is not. For this reason, the article must coincide with the subject.

The next relative is QUIEN, this type of pronouns always have a person as a precedent, unlike QUE, which also accepts animal or thing, QUIEN is only usable while referring to a person, it is also indistinct for gender. However, in the plural form, an ES is added: QUIENES.

- Maria, who did not finish her homework, graduated/Maria, quien no terminaba sus tareas, se graduó.
- They were the ones who did the test. / They, who did the test.
- Ellos fueron quienes presentaron el examen / Ellos, que presentaron el examen.

As you can see, sometimes the structure order that the sentence will take depends on the pronoun you use. There are times when it is necessary to place the verb before the pronoun. Other times, it can be placed after the pronoun. These details will be polished while we get to progress more in Spanish.

The relative CUYO designates the holder that the noun accompanies, which appears explicitly in the preceding sentence. This pronoun must coincide in number and gender with the noun, as indicated in the table above. This pronoun is often used in formal or academic situations, so it is usually more present in writing and not in a day to day conversation.

- She is Maria, whose mother passed away/Ella es María, cuya madre falleció.
- He is the teacher whose classes are very good/El es el profesor, cuyas clases son muy buenas.

The next relative pronoun is the one that refers to the quantity and is similar to the English equivalent of how much/many. CUANTO has to coincide in gender and number with the subject. Its position in the sentence can also vary, although it' usually is in front of the subject. This type of pronoun is not commonly used, however, can still be used.

- Many people as they wanted to pass through/Pasaron cuantas personas quisieron.
- She brought as many dogs as she wanted/Ella trajo cuantos perros quiso.

Finally, another pronoun used to a person, animal or thing: EL CUAL and its variations; LA CUAL, LOS CUALES, LAS CUALES, referring to feminine and plural for both genders. This type of pronoun is the equivalent of the pronoun LA QUE, EL QUE, LAS QUE, LOS QUE, and exist with the sole function of giving more linguistic variety to the texts to avoid excessive repetition.

- Maria, with whom you passed it / Maria, with whom you passed it.
- Maria, con la cual te la pasabas / María, con la que te la pasabas.

Possessive Pronoun

This type of pronoun replaces the subject and refers to the possession of an object, thing or person. The possessed is linked with the holder, thanks to this pronoun. We got a table with possessive pronouns and their respective personal pronoun below.

YO	MIO
TU	TUYO
ÉL	SUYO
ELLA	SUYO
NOSOTROS	NUESTRO
VOSOTROS	VUESTRO
ELLOS	SUYO
ELLAS	SUYO

The table above reflects possessive pronouns in the singular. To convert them into plural form, an S must be added at the end of each pronoun.

For instance: TUYOS.

Also, the masculine gender pronouns are reflected in the table. To turn them into feminine, only the last letter must be changed from O to an A.

For instance: SUYA.

Here are more examples:

- Those shoes are yours/Esos zapatos son los tuyos.
- Those things are yours/Son suyas esas cosas.
- This dog is mine/Este perro es mío.

Possessive Atones Pronoun

These pronouns precede the noun and coincide with it in gender and number. We got a table of these possessive atones below:

Here some examples:

- Tomorrow, I start my course/Mañana comienzo mi curso
- Your houses are beautiful/Vuestras casas son lindas.
- Your car is new/Su carro está nuevo.

Indefinite Pronouns

Indefinite pronouns exist only to indicate the amount of the noun, it does not modify it but it can replace it, in some cases within the sentence. Indefinite pronouns are quite a lot in Spanish, but personal pronouns do not govern them as we have seen with the previous ones. Now a table with the indefinite pronouns, divided according to their possibility of variation: To vary the undefined pronouns in gender and number it is only necessary, in case you want to change it to feminine, replace the O with an A, and if you want to convert it to the plural form place an S at the end. The cases in which this cannot be done have been clarified in the table above, as is the case of the indefinite pronoun that vary only in number, these have a particular way of becoming plural.

Table with the translation of each of these pronouns:

TANTO	SO MUCH
CIERTO	CERTAIN/TRUE
MUCHO	A LOT

POCO	FEW
ALGÚN	SOME
OTRO	OTHER
TODO	ALL/EVERYTHING
DEMASIADO	TOO MUCH
BASTANTE	QUITE
CUALQUIER	WHICHEVER/ANY
QUIENQUIERA	WHOEVER/ANYONE
VARIOS	SOME
NINGÚN	NONE
ALGO	SOME
MÁS	MORE
CADA	EACH
ALGUIEN	SOMEONE

CUALQUIERA	ANYONE
NADIE	NO ONE
MENOS	LESS
NADA	NOTHING

Some of these pronouns have a particular way of appearing in Spanish. Now we will talk about them:
TODO/EVERYTHING is always accompanied by an article that must agree with the noun in gender and number. Also, it usually appears after the pronoun, but they can also appear before the verb of the sentence. Other pronouns like NADA do not need an article. For instance:

- I have everything I need/Yo tengo todo lo que necesito.
- She lost everything/Ella lo perdió todo.
- Now all that is left is this/Ahora todo lo que queda es esto.

The pronouns CUALQUIERA and CADA always refer to a totality of something, that is, a set of things.

- Each dog is different/Cada perro es diferente.
- Any dog can run/Cualquier perro puede correr.

Demonstratives Pronouns

Demonstratives pronouns help to identify a person, object or animal by referring to their physical proximity to the person who speaks, that is, if it is far away or near them. The demonstrative pronouns are governed by the adverbs of place: AQUÍ, ALLÍ Y AHÍ, which are the English equivalent of HERE AND THERE. However, you should not pay too much attention to this. These demonstrations can vary in both gender and number. Now you will see what they are and their translation into English:

Spanish:

	AQUÍ	ALLÍ	AHÍ
ESTE		AQUEL	ESE
ESTO		AQUELLO	ESO

English:

HERE	THERE	THERE
THIS	THAT	THAT
THIS	THAT	THAT

In the above table, we can see that there are three demonstrative pronouns in the middle column. The demonstrative pronouns are described in their singular masculine form, and the latter are in their singular neutral form. To change them to feminine or plural form, we do the same process as with the previous ones, we substitute the E / O for the A for feminine and add an S for plural. For instance: AQUELLAS, ESTAS, ESAS.

Below is a table with the translation of these demonstrative pronouns:

ESTE	THIS	AQUEL	THAT	ESE	THAT
ESTO	THIS	AQUELLO	THAT	ESO	THAT

Examples of the use of these pronouns:

- This man is very tall/Aquel hombre es muy alto.
- That table is very old/Esa mesa está muy vieja.
- This is a complex situation/Esta situación es compleja.
- Tomorrow I will come to this restaurant/Mañana vendré a este restaurante.

That looks very lonely/Aquello se ve muy solitario.

Interrogatives pronouns

Interrogative pronouns refer to an unknown subject, and someone wants to know it. These pronouns are used in interrogation sentences, that is, questions. These pronouns are the same as the relative ones. To help their correct differentiation, an accent mark is added:

¿QUÉ?	WHAT?
¿QUIÉN?	WHO?
¿CUÁL?	WHICH?

When a direct question is being asked, these pronouns will be accompanied by question marks, but when an indirect question is asked, the only way to differentiate them from the relative ones are the accent marks they always carry.

The pronoun QUÉ does not vary in number or gender. The pronouns QUIÉN and CUÁL vary only in the number, and an ES is added for plural form, for instance: QUIÉNES.

When the question refers to something happening to a person, it is accompanied by the indirect complement A in front of the pronoun.

For instance:

- Who got pushed?/¿A quién empujaron?

It refers to some unknown subject have been pushed. When adding this complement, it indicates the action of a verb on the unknown subject.

For most beginners in speaking Spanish, it is quite confusing to use QUÉ and CUÁL. In Spanish, these two pronouns are quite different, and you cannot replace one with the other. In order to know when each one should be used, you have to pay attention to how the sentence is structured.

QUE = absolutely identify an object.

CUAL = define or delimit an object within a set of objects.

For instance:

- What will we eat?/¿Qué comeremos? It seeks to identify something.
- Which of these cakes are we going to eat?/¿Cuál de estas tortas comeremos? It is about defining which option available will be chosen.

Some formulas can help you to structure sentences correctly with this pair of pronouns:

QUÉ + VERB	QUÉ + SUBSTANTIVE + VERB
What will we eat?	What cake do you like?
¿Qué comeremos?	¿Qué torta te gusta?

CUÁL + VERB + SUBSTANTIVE	CUÁL + VERB + VARIOUS ELEMENT
What is your cake? chocolate or vanilla?	*Which do you like more:*
¿Cuál es tu torta? chocolate o vainilla?	¿Cuál te gusta más:

Practical Exercises with Pronouns

We will do practical exercises using QUÉ and CUÁL. You will have several short sentences or phrases that you will have to complete with the two pronouns, looking for a way to solve where each one of them goes. Remember to support you from the advice we have given and review the formulas provided to you. Don't despair if at the beginning you can't do it right. That's what learning is about.

The Pronoun in Their Daily Use

Next, you will have several phrases that will be using different pronouns, identify which they are:

Ella tiene mucho frío	She is freezing
Él camina todas las tardes	He walks out every afternoon
Nosotros iremos a la playa	We will go to the beach
No, ellos se quedan	No, they stay
¿Ustedes quieren venir?	Do you want to come?
Estos son mis padres	These are my parents
Ella es mi gata	She is my cat
Mis cuadernos están rotos	My notebooks are damaged
Ese perro es suyo	That dog is yours
Ese carro es mío	That car is mine
Me miro al espejo	I look myself into the mirror
Me coloco perfume	I wear perfume

Se pintará el cabello	She/he will dye her/his hair
¿Te pondrás eso?	Will you wear that?
Creo que iré a otro lugar	I think I'll go somewhere else.

Pregúntale a quien sea	Ask anyone
Es María la que tiene que preguntarle	Maria is the one who has to ask.
Fueron cuantos quisieron	People went as much as they wanted
¿Quién es ese hombre?	Who is that man?
¿Qué quieres?	What do you want?
¿Cuál de todas esas te gusta?	Which of these do you like?
Esto tarda demasiados días	This takes too many days.
Todo pasa por algo	Everything happens for a reason.

Here is the table of correct answers from the previous exercise.

1	Which
2	What
3	What
4	What
5	Which
6	Which
7	What
8	What
9	Which
10	Which
11	What
12	What
13	Which
14	What
15	Which

In the succeeding discussion, you will be able to learn the use and importance of some pronouns, like in the English Alphabet, these are the following: (En la siguiente discusión, podrá aprender el uso y la importancia de algunos pronombres, como en el alfabeto inglés, estos son los siguientes:)

First Person (Primera Persona)	Second Person (Segunda Persona)	Third Person (Tercera Persona)
Singular (Singular)		
I (Yo)	You (Tú)	It (Eso), He (Él), She (Ella)
Plural (Plural)		
We (Nosotros/Nosotras)	You (Tú)	They (Ellos/Ellas)

English Alphabet (Alfabeto Inglés)

There is a need for you to know how to use the pronouns in the English Alphabet in order for you to make a comparison with the pronouns used in the Spanish Alphabet. You will see below thirteen rules in the proper use of pronouns. (Es necesario que sepa cómo usar los pronombres en el alfabeto inglés para poder hacer una comparación con los pronombres usados en el alfabeto español. Verá a continuación trece reglas en el uso apropiado de los pronombres.)

#Rule 1

This is similar to the abovementioned example wherein the pronoun is the subject in that particular sentence. (Regla número I. Esto es similar al ejemplo mencionado anteriormente en el que el pronombre es el sujeto en esa oración en particular.)

_____ is sinking. (Here, you are referring to the boat)

_____ se está hundiendo. (Aquí te refieres al bote)

What qualifies in the blank is the appropriate pronoun for the word "boat."

Lo que califica en el espacio en blanco es el pronombre apropiado para la palabra "barco".

You have to ask yourself, what person is the boat? Is it singular or plural?

Tienes que preguntarte, ¿qué persona es el barco? ¿Es singular o plural?

En este ejemplo, un barco es una tercera persona y es singular. Si observa la tabla mencionada anteriormente, lo que debe usarse es "Eso", por lo tanto, se está hundiendo.

#Rule 2

This is the second use of the pronoun, which is the renaming of the subject. (Regla número II. Este es el segundo uso del pronombre que es el cambio de nombre del sujeto.

It is we who are writing this literature.

Somos nosotros quienes estamos escribiendo esta literatura.

#Rule 3

This rule is similar to the second rule. If you are going to rename the subject, the verb that must be used must agree to the pronoun used. Here are some examples that will make you spot what is wrong with the "Incorrect" example. (Regla número III. Esta regla es similar a la segunda regla. Si va a cambiar el nombre del sujeto, el verbo que debe usarse debe coincidir con el pronombre usado. Aquí hay algunos ejemplos que lo harán detectar lo que está mal con el ejemplo "Incorrecto.")

Wrong Combination of Subject and Verb (Combinación Incorrecta de Sujeto y Verbo)	Correct Combination of Subject and Verb (Combinación Correcta de sujeto y Verbo)
It is I who is writing this literature. Is (I is) correct? NO. Soy yo quien escribe esta literatura. ¿Es (es) correcto? NO.	It is I who am writing this literature. Is (I am) correct? YES. Soy yo quien escribe esta literatura. ¿Es (soy) correcto? SÍ.

#Rule 4

This rule explains more about the use of pronoun as an object pronoun. In this instance, the pronoun is either direct, indirect object or the object of the preposition. (Regla número IV. Esta regla explica más sobre el uso del pronombre como pronombre de objeto. En este caso, el pronombre es un objeto directo, indirecto o el objeto de la preposición.)

His mother scolded him. (In this case, him here is the direct object, because it is being described by the word scolded.) Su madre lo regañó. (En este caso, él aquí es el objeto directo, porque lo describe la palabra regañada).

Lend me your ear. (In this instance, me is the indirect object, because it has an implied to/for appearing before the word itself. Hence, lend your ears (to) me.

Préstame tus orejas. (En este caso, yo es el objeto indirecto, porque tiene implícito a / para aparecer antes de la palabra misma. Por lo tanto, preste sus oídos (a) mí.

Is he looking at her? (In this instance, her is the object of the preposition at.) ¿La está mirando a ella? (En este caso, ella es el objeto de la preposición en.)

#Rule 5

This rule refers to some pronouns like who, which, and that. Some speakers (the ones who use grammar all the time) are confused with the use of is and are in these examples. (Regla número V. Esta regla se refiere a algunos pronombres como quién, qué y eso. Algunos oradores (los que usan gramática todo el tiempo) se confunden con el uso de is y are en estos ejemplos.)

The Use of IS After WHO El Uso De IS Después De La WHO	The Use of ARE After WHO El Uso De ARE Después De La WHO
She is the only one among those girls who is loyal to her partner. Here, what is being described by WHO is SHE that is why it must be followed by IS. Ella es la única entre esas chicas que es leal a su pareja. Aquí, lo que está describiendo la WHO es ELLA, por eso debe ser seguido por el SI.	She is one of those girls who are not loyal to their partners. Here, what is being described by WHO is THOSE GIRLS that is why it must be followed by ARE. Ella es una de esas chicas que no son leales a sus parejas. Aquí, lo que está describiendo la WHO es AQUELLAS CHICAS, por eso debe ser seguido por ARE.

#Rule 6

The pronouns that are singular must also be supported with singular verbs. To some, it is somewhat confusing but always remember that if a pronoun is singular, the verb must have an S at its end (meaning, it is singular). On the other hand, if the verb does not have an S at its end, it means it is plural. (Regla número VI. Los pronombres que son singulares también deben ser compatibles con verbos singulares. Para algunos, es algo confuso, pero siempre recuerde que si un pronombre es singular, el verbo debe tener una S al final (es decir, es singular). Por otro lado, si el verbo no tiene una S en su extremo, significa que es plural.)

Each of the kids dances gracefully. (It means that the kids "individually" classified means only one. Hence, the kid is singular, and it must be supported by a singular verb, too (dances). (Cada uno de los niños baila con gracia. (Significa que los niños clasificados "individualmente" significan solo uno. Por lo tanto, el niño es singular, y también debe ser apoyado por un verbo singular (danzas).

#Rule 7

This rule explains that in the inclusion of AS or THAN in a sentence, you must apply your mental analysis. This one example will give you a clarity of mind. (Regla número VII. Esta regla explica que al incluir AS o THAN en una oración, debe aplicar su análisis mental. Este ejemplo te dará claridad mental.)

INCORRECT USE OF AS/THAN (USO INCORRECTO DE AS / THAN)	CORRECT USE OF AS/THAN (USO CORRECTO DE AS / THAN)
I am as tired as her. Applying the mental analysis, you should complete the sentence, (I am as tired as she is) is not correct.	I am as tired as she. Applying the same analysis, you should complete the sentence, (I am as tired as she is) is correct.

#Rule 8

It must be remembered that there are known as possessive pronouns. Among these are the following: (Regla número VIII. Debe recordarse que se conocen como pronombres posesivos. Entre estos están los siguientes):

Yours, His, Hers, Its, Ours, Theirs and Whose.

You only need not be confused about the use of apostrophes. In possessive pronouns, the following are incorrect: (No necesita confundirse con el uso de apóstrofes. En pronombres posesivos, los siguientes son incorrectos:)

Your's

His'

Her's

It's

Our's

Their's

Who'se

#Rule 9

The use of an apostrophe is a must in these examples. (Regla número IX. El uso del apóstrofe es imprescindible en estos ejemplos.)

It is my own car. (It's my own car.) Es mi propio carro. (Es mi propio auto).

#Rule 10

The tenth rule is about the so-called reflexive pronouns, which are used if the subject and the object are the same person. Regla número X. La décima regla trata sobre los llamados pronombres reflexivos, que se usan si el sujeto y el objeto son la misma persona.

He carried it all by himself. (Lo llevó todo solo.)

#Rule 11

Consistency is also the key to a good grammar. For instance, you started with a singular pronoun, then the second phrase must also be singular. You try looking at this example: (Regla número XI. La consistencia también es la clave para una buena gramática. Por ejemplo, comenzaste con pronombres singulares, luego la segunda frase también debe ser singular. Intenta mirar este ejemplo:

Somebody must fix this faucet, and they must be professional enough to do the job.

Here, there is an inconsistency. Somebody is singular, and they is a plural one.

The correct construction is: Somebody must fix this faucet, and he must be professional enough to do the job.

Alguien debe arreglar este grifo, y debe ser lo suficientemente profesional como para hacer el trabajo.

Aquí hay inconsistencia. Alguien es singular y es plural.

La construcción correcta es: Alguien debe arreglar este grifo y debe ser lo suficientemente profesional como para hacer el trabajo.

#Rule 12

This rule discusses the combination of pronouns and added with a conjunction AND. Here, if you remove the AND, what will be left must still be grammatically correct. (Regla número XII. Esta regla trata sobre la combinación de pronombres y se agrega con una conjunción AND. Aquí, si elimina el AND, lo que quedará aún debe ser gramaticalmente correcto.

INCORRECT USE OF RULE XII (USO INCORRECTO DE LA REGLA XII)	CORRECT USE OF RULE XII (USO CORRECTO DE LA REGLA XII)
Him and his brother arrived early this morning. Here, if you remove "and," what will be left is no	He and his brother arrived early this morning.

longer grammatically correct. Hence, Him arrived early this morning.	Here, if you remove "and," what will be left is still grammatically correct. Hence, He arrived early this morning.

Spanish Alphabet (Alfabeto Español)

The following are some of the pronouns that are used in the Spanish Alphabet: (Los siguientes son algunos de los pronombres que se usan en el alfabeto español:)

Spanish Pronoun (Pronombre Español)	English Equivalent (Equivalente en Inglés)
PERSONAL PRONOUNS (PRONOMBRES PERSONALES)	
Yo	I
Tú	You in its singular form
Usted	You in its formal form
Él, ella	He, She
Nosotros/ nosotras	We
Vosotros/ vosotras	You in its plural
Ustedes	You in its formal form (plural)
Ellos, ellas	They

DEMONSTRATIVE PRONOUNS
(PRONOMBRES DEMOSTRATIVOS)

Éste	This
Ése	That
Éstos	These
Ésos	Those
Ésta	This in its singular feminine form
Ésa	That in its singular feminine form
Éstas	These in its plural feminine form
Ésas	Those in its plural feminine form
Esto	This in its neuter form
Eso	That in its neuter form

Chapter 5: Spanish Verbs

A verb is referred to as an action word. They explain how something is done. Verbs also describe the action, motion, or occurrence of something. In this book, you will be introduced to Spanish verbs for beginners. This will simplify it and make the verbs easy to understand and comprehend. It is vital to understand the basics of Spanish verbs and how they are formed. Spanish verbs have various components. They are known to have an inflexional verb system. The system may mean that the respective verb has a stem and root, which is followed by inflection. The root is to tell you the verb that you are using, and the inflection tells you the tense and the person it is referring to. It is crucial, thus, to learn the familiar inflections.

The Spanish language is the language´s uniqueness and South American republics, except French Guyana and Brazil. The language is also spoken in the Canary Islands, Balearic, parts of Morocco, Equatorial Guinea, and the West coast of Africa. It is mostly spoken in Arizona, New Mexico, Texas, New York City, Southern Florida, and California in the United States. The Spanish language originated from the Iberian Peninsula, and it was a dialect just spoken by Latin, which today is known as 'vulgar Latin.' This is different from classical Latin commonly used in literature. The uniqueness of the language was spread by the Visigoths, who were a Germanic group who conquered the peninsula in the fourth century at the demise of the Roman Empire.

The Visigoths were speaking Latin, and their major influence was cultural depression rather than Germanic Influence. This led to the formation of 'vulgar Latin.' This was spoken to develop isolation during the fifth century. This was how linguistics and historians pinpoint the origin of the Spanish language known by us today. After the Visigoths, the Muslim Moorish arrived. They contributed and added over 4,000 Spanish words derived from the Arabic language. They also brought about cultural influences that are clear in art, design, and Spain's architecture. The words adopted from Arabic soon lost their original pronunciation. Thus, it is correct to say that Spanish´s overall phonology or sounds are surprisingly not influenced by Arabic.

For example, a statement like 'I will work' is translated as 'trabajaré.' The first one is the root, while the second one is the inflection. Another illustration is 'vivir,' which means 'to read.' There are also verbs called the –IR, –ER, and –AR types of verbs. The meanings between these verbs are not different. –AR and –IR verbs make around 72% of Spanish verbs. The remaining 14% are –ER and –IR each. In Spanish, the infinitive forms the stem and is the basic 'to' that creates the verb. For example, 'trabajar' (infinitivo) means 'to work' (infinitive). Vivir is also an infinitive, meaning 'to live.'

Spanish verbs are also used to explain something that is happening. That is why it is a broad grammar topic that must be learned to equip the learner with basic Spanish knowledge. This can also mean that the illustrations can be used to monitor someone's progress with the language. Therefore, the instructor should strive to make the language fun and easy, as well as easy to grasp. This will make the learners develop confidence in themselves that they, too, can do it. The instructor-student relationship should be close at this point because if the learner does not learn at this point, they may never know Spanish. Also, listing key areas that can be easily forgotten can be a bonus lesson to the students.

You can also use irregular verbs to form questions. This can be very easy since the word-forming the question is an affirmative one. An inverted question mark is put at the beginning. For example, '¿vives en New York?' is translated to mean 'Do you live in New York?' Another one is '¿hablaste con Brandon?' It means 'Did you speak to Brandon?' The question mark indicates that this question needs an answer and facilitates interactions. If one is not interested in more interaction, then they should use the regular verb. The advantage of the affirmative on it ignites responses, thus facilitating continuous conversations. Through conversation, the learner can make an effort to try and maintain a conversation. This conversation buildup is one that facilitates learning.

Many things go on in our lives today. People carry out various activities, and people's actions can only be explained using verbs. A sentence is never complete without a verb. We use verbs more than we always think that we do. Learning Spanish will also expose you to so many Spanish verbs. We will be able to build on our Spanish vocabulary and learn both basic and intermediate levels to enable us to communicate better. When verbs become part of your daily routine, you don´t need to worry about how long it will take to progress.

Spanish verbs, however, are mostly written in their infinitive form. This is because the infinitive is the most basic and purest form of the verb. As you learn Spanish for beginners, you will realize that Spanish verbs are listed in an infinitive. They are also considered unprocessed raw ingredients necessary for making complicated recipes. No matter what form it is written, the verbs should form part of daily interactions and conversations.

Just like cooking without ingredients, one cannot come up with any recipe. You may succeed in fooling around, trying to find out that something is missing. Your language skills, like the dish, will not be fully developed. So that means you need to learn verbs. Start at the lowest level that you are comfortable with, and you will be guided and assisted along the way. Start memorizing the verbs you use daily.

You can try communicating in either English or Spanish without using verbs. You will feel like a small child learning to speak. Interacting with people who speak Spanish can significantly help you remember the verbs and put them into practice. Learning verbs will also help ease understanding and make communication smooth and effective. Try always to have or initiate a conversation in Spanish. Simple conversations can help one practice the verbs. This is because almost all sentences spoken must contain a verb. You may even find yourself using more verbs than you expected. Using verbs build your understanding of them to help you with conjugation. This conjugation is mostly common in regular conversations. This will develop your knowledge of the word and help in reinforcing the meaning. You can also play games in conjugation. Games provide a comfortable yet fun way of learning a language, especially verbs. You can take fun quizzes or download some games from the play store.

In the next paragraph, I am going to discuss five common but critical examples of verbs:

The verb ser means to be. It is usually used to describe useful characters like the physical description of something like 'Fresa es roja,' which, in English, means 'The strawberry is red.'

The second one on the list is **estar**, which also means to be. This, however, is used to describe conditions, places, and feelings. An excellent example in a sentence is 'Estar cansada.' This, translated into English, means 'I am tired.'

The third is 'deber.' This means to have to. It can also mean 'a must' or 'should.'

The fourth one is 'poder,' which means to be able to. This is used to describe a possibility.

The last one is 'haber,' which means to have or to be. When applied to be, it is used in the description of an object. This is to show whether the object exists or is absent. However, when translated as have, it is used as a combination with other verbs in the description of things that have not happened. However, learners need to understand that this kind of verb has an irregular conjugation, so special attention is required.

Learning Spanish verbs equip you and help you be able to participate in any conversation with ease. Learning Spanish verbs can, however, be monotonous and does not spark enthusiasm. Most language learners, even the most dedicated ones, do not feel enthusiastic about learning

Spanish verbs. However, it is vital, not only in understanding Spanish but also in speaking Spanish. You can conjugate the verbs to modify the verb and know who is doing what at a particular time. Understanding the basics can help you conjugate verb in Spanish. This, in turn, will give you more information from a single word.

This is what most English speakers find very confusing when learning Spanish. This is because, compared to Spanish, English has very few conjugations.

While in English, the verb eating in past tense takes the same form, in Spanish, each verb is differently formed. This usually depends on what one is doing, like eating, speaking, and running. When something is not clear or you need clarification, contact your tutor or your mentor.

Lack of conjugation means you will not be able to have Spanish communication. Whatever you tell others in Spanish differ in meaning depending on verb conjugation. This is the time frame, person, and intent of the action. There is a need to master various steps to master Spanish verbs to be fluent in this language. As dull as they may sound, they can be made fun to learn besides other grammar. You can start by getting as much input as you may need in Spanish. This will spark your interest and satisfy your curiosity. Be keen on what you have learned and keep repeating them whenever you get the chance. Be keen not to be discouraged if you forget most of the words. Understand that this is a normal situation. The next thing you need to learn is common conjugations and tenses. These may comprise common tenses mostly used in day to day interactions. They are simple to master and easy to remember.

As long as you have the right attitude, then you will be surprised by how much you will learn. Ever heard the say learn to speak by speaking? Well, there you have it. Talk Spanish a lot; through this, you will grasp new vocabulary every time. As you grasp new words, your spoken Spanish improves significantly. As you learn, incorporate irregular verbs too—practice writing, reading, and speaking Spanish. Record yourself, listen to the audio of people speaking Spanish.

Spend your time listening to people speaking Spanish and watch Spanish movies. Have a notebook where you can write down the verbs that you have learned. How much you learn will solely depend on your dedication and the time you have put in learning the language. You will also be familiar with the mistakes you make while speaking the language. This is because knowing the nuances of speaking a new language comes from many hours of exposure to the language. This is usually experienced when one has been exposed to a certain language since birth. So if you increase your input, the level of exposure also increases; thus, conjugation of verbs will just come naturally to you, and in no time, you will start gaining fluency.

After being exposed to the Spanish language, it is time to study the verb you intend to work on and memorize. This is not a stage of mere memorization of words. Learn the verbs from the first, second, and third-person singular tenses. Learning these will enable you to get through many conversations. This is because verb conjugations will be the most common challenge you will encounter when speaking Spanish. The rest usually comes as one improves and continues learning. Spanish words will then start popping into your mind each time you see a verb. Ensure you are exposed to the proper conjugation, as this will be the key to learning proper Spanish. This will facilitate easy and useful language mastery. Do not wait until you have grasped a lot before you can start.

Speaking Spanish at the onset of your learning goes a long way. Be keen on the tenses, and do not shy away from speaking. Making grammatical mistakes will help you learn fast. Communicating with people in a language they understand is a motivation to learn a new language. Do not fear or hold back. Believe in yourself, and realize you are your number one cheerleader. The verb conjugation is not easy, so speaking Spanish every time helps you sort everything out.

The daily study added to regularly speaking makes learning Spanish easy and fast. You will be able to sort everything out and combine targeted study with the conversations you have on a day-to-day basis. Memorization and speaking help one learn more and know which verb will work. Find creative ways to make learning fun. Do not cram your study, but find a way to master and understand the words, as well as their meaning and how they are used in a sentence. Be keen as you learn and avoid unnecessary distractions. Speak Spanish even when you do not feel like speaking it at all. You can achieve this by getting a language tutor online, finding a Spanish speaking partner, or joining a Spanish club in your community. Learning can be as cheap or as expensive as you want it to be. You will receive a more significant improvement at your learning level if you find a tutor or study with a native speaker. You will also be able to remember most of the words. This is because you will be able to remember the conversations you have each day.

There are regular Spanish verbs that are easy to memorize. You can memorize these by mastering the patterns in them, recognizing the conjugation patterns, and how they are essential in your learning. As you do this, you have to realize that most forms of verbs are irregular and cannot be mastered. Be keen on speaking and try to notice any irregularity each day. Be familiar with daily sounds. This eases memorization and reduces the stress associated with the inability to practice what you have learned. Remember that daily practice of the verbs will make them stick in your mind. Set time solely for practicing the verbs. The recommended methods of practice include three types: writing, reading, and speaking.

Reading helps you master the language and recognize the words. As you read, listen to yourself. Listening helps you know how to pronounce Spanish words. You can listen to music, news, and audio recordings in Spanish. Reading, on the other hand, provides a better way of grasping the words. It helps you pick up new conjugations and verbs. Reading is an active way of learning, while listening is a passive way of listening. Listening has a disadvantage in the sense that it can be easily zoned out. Reading helps one focus on details because you will pay close attention to what you are trying to learn.

Lack of conjugation means you will not be able to have Spanish communication. Whatever you tell others in Spanish differ in meaning depending on verb conjugation. This is the time frame, person, and intent of the action. There is a need to master various steps to master Spanish verbs to be fluent in this language. As dull as they may sound, they can be made fun to learn besides other grammar. You can start by getting as much input as you may need in Spanish. This will spark your interest and satisfy your curiosity. Be keen on what you have learned and keep repeating them whenever you get the chance. Be keen not to be discouraged if you forget most of the words. Understand that this is a normal situation. The next thing you need to learn common conjugations and tenses. These may comprise common tenses mostly used in day to day interactions. They are simple to master and easy to remember.

As long as you have the right attitude, then you will be surprised by how much you will learn. Ever heard the say learn to speak by speaking? Well, there you have it. Speak Spanish a lot; through this, you will grasp new vocabulary every time. As you grasp new words, your spoken Spanish improves significantly. Also, as you learn, incorporate irregular verbs too—practice writing, reading, and speaking Spanish. Record yourself, listen to the audio of people speaking Spanish.

Spanish verbs do not need to be such a complex subject. Be keen on all the explanations and how the words are written because the truth of the matter is once someone has mastered the grammar, it will be very easy to master all the others. Create a list and target that you intend to meet daily. The list can contain the verbs you intend to master daily. This will be like setting a goal. The goal should, therefore, be attainable. There is no need for setting a goal like 100 words in a day when, in reality, you are struggling with mastering ten words.

Language learning is a journey, so mingling with people with the same goal can help you learn the language faster than expected. Do not be discouraged when things become so complicated. Instead, associate with people who have gotten the chance to learn a new language, especially when you are older. Being in charge of your schedule also helps you take responsibility for your actions. Learning Spanish verbs does not need to be tricky if one has a reliable support system and is ready to learn the new language. Take online courses if you have to, and as you take the course, be disciplined with your study when handling the topic of verbs since it is extensive and essential.

In most situations, people always learn a foreign language when they are older. The older someone gets, the harder it is to learn a new language; so interest and attitude can contribute to faster and easier learning. You can also create a schedule that helps you keep track of your lessons and assignments.

Some people remember the lessons using flashcards. Since verbs are not so easy, flashcards can also come in handy. They are portable and can be used anywhere. That's at the dinner table, in the park, in the office, or even while driving. All you will need to do is pull one out and remind yourself what it means, and from there, construct a sentence using the verb. Describe day-to-day things that are happening around you.

Do not forget to celebrate each milestone since rewarding yourself will be the right motivation the go to the next subject. Be mindful of whatever you learn. Appreciate yourself for learning and keep watch of the mistakes and grammar area that is giving you the hardest time of all. This will encourage you more and help you not to be hard on yourself. It will also motivate you toward learning the new language. Be the best you can be, and never let anyone bring you down. Understand that you are learning the language for your own good, whether for employment, pastime, or business. Know that it will benefit you in the long run. Learning Spanish will boost your confidence, build your curriculum vitae, and bring better future networks and partnerships opportunities.

Lastly, with regards to learning Spanish verbs, master as many verbs as you can. This will make them stick to your mind and help with sentence construction and conjugation in the future. Ask for assistance from your tutor if you need help or if you are stuck.

Common Regular -AR Verbs

As you now know how to decline the Present Tense of regular -AR verbs, here's a list of 25 for you to practise with them!

- Alquilar – to rent
- Ayudar – to help
- Bailar – to dance
- Buscar – to look for
- Comprar – to buy
- Contestar – to answer
- Dejar – to allow, to leave
- Entrar (in) – to enter (into)

- Enviar – to send
- Esperar – to hope, to wait for
- Ganar – to earn, to win
- Gastar – to spend
- Llegar – to arrive
- Llevar – to wear, to carry
- Mirar – to look at, to watch
- Necesitar – to need
- Olvidar – to forget
- Pagar – to pay, to pay for

Common Regular -ER Verbs

And, here's a list of 25 regular -ER verbs with which to experiment!

- Temer – to fear
- Vender – to sell

Common Regular -IR Verbs

To finish off with, here you have 25 regular -IR verbs.

- Abrir – to open
- Admitir – to admit
- Asistir (a) – to attend (to)
- Confundir – to confuse
- Cubrir – to cover

- Decidir – to decide
- Evadir – to evade
- Existir – to exist
- Fundir – to melt
- Hundir – to sink
- Imprimir – to print
- Ocurrir – to happen
- Subir – to go up, to come up
- Unir – to unite
- Vivir – to live

In the following exercises, you have to complete either the conjugated verb or the corresponding pronoun: I am Ana´s best friend - … soy la mejor amiga de Ana

You are a great boss - Usted … un gran jefe

He is a very smart boy - Él … un muchacho muy inteligente

We are the best - ……… los mejores

You guys are always fighting - Ustedes ………. siempre peleando

They are the greatest scientists in their generation - ………. son las mejores científicas de su generación

I'm tired - ……. cansado

You are prettier each day - ……. más lindo cada día

She's sad - ……. está triste

We are in danger - ……. en peligro

You are crazy - Vosotros ……. locos

They are coming - ……. están viniendo

I'm cold - ………. frío

Do you have a lighter? - ¿………. un encendedor?

He's afraid - ………. miedo

We have what it takes - Nosotros ………. lo necesario

I'm OK, but you always have a problem - Yo estoy bien, pero ……. tienen siempre algún problema

They have a secret - Ellas ………. un secreto

I live alone - ………. solo

We live two blocks away - ………. a dos cuadras

You say she's lying? - ¿………. que ella está mintiendo?

They say it's too late - Ellos ………. que es demasiado tarde

I'm going to ask you to leave - ………. a pedirte que te marches

Let's go dancing! - ¡…………. a bailar!

I do what I can - …………. lo que puedo

You do the right thing - ………. hace lo correcto

We do everything! - ¡Nosotros …………. todo!

I love you - Te …….

We love Peruvian food - .... la comida peruana

I can't go - No .... ir

He sees what's going on - Él .... lo que sucede

I give you everything I have - Yo te .... todo lo que tengo

We give our lives for art - .... nuestras vidas por el arte

I want to eat something spicy - .... comer algo picante

Do you want to dance with me? - ¿............. bailar conmigo?

They want to travel - Ellas .... Viajar

Chapter 6: Spanish Adjectives

Adjectives are usually referred to as describing words. They are descriptive in nature and represent the noun. They are commonly used next to a noun to affect and modify the meaning. They provide a more detailed description of something or someone. Adjectives can give us a different outlook on something and can sometimes influence our perception. Just like English words, Spanish words have adjectives, too. Sometimes, people wonder where to put adjectives in words. This always confuses who learn Spanish as a second language more than those who have Spanish as their native language. In the English language, adjectives come before whatever is being described. For example, I met a tallboy. However, in the Spanish language, the adjective usually comes after whatever is being talked about, for example, 'Conocí a un chico alto' (I met a tall boy), where alto (tall) comes after the noun (chico/boy)

Spain initially established the first European settlement in the present-day United States of America in what is now called Florida. The U.S. states, governed by Mexican or Spanish governments, spoke Spanish as their ancient language. Due to the annexation of southwestern states, the official language was changed to English. Despite this, Spanish is still the language spoken by many people in those areas today. The transition from English to Spanish caused some political strife, with many in power urging that the new territories could not be American as they speak Spanish. In the United States of America today, the language rights issue is still complicated and causes many debates. English is the only official language, but the government uses the Spanish language in some states like New Mexico and California.

Studies have shown that Spanish is the most taught foreign language in the United States. In Puerto Rico, the commonwealth still maintains Spanish as the official language. Native speakers refer to the Spanish language as Castilian, and the language has become popular around the world today. It has a history that has evolved and steadily developed consistently over the centuries. Castilian traces its origin up the Castile in the top Mountain of Cantabrian, which is located in northern Spain. Here, a mixture of Latin and local dialects was spoken immediately after the Roman Empire's end. 'Vulgar Latin' spread fast as the kingdom of Castile expanded, thereby replacing the other provincial dialects.

Some adjectives end in –a or –o. No matter which syllable ends the adjective, it will be changed to match the quantity and gender of the thing being talked about. This can mean that if you add –o, it will produce masculine words while adding –a feminine. For plural, however, –s is added. For example, in the same sentence, 'I met a small boy,' the Spanish translation will be written as Conocí a un chico alto. 'I met tall girls,' on the other hand, will be Conocí unas chicas altas. You can put a personal pronoun 'Yo' at the beginning of the sentence, but it is optional. The majority of people often opt to leave it out. Other adjectives end in –e. For these activities, there is no need to change them to match the noun. A good example is Hanna compró una corbata verde, which is translated to mean 'Hanna bought a green tie.'

Unlike verbs, Spanish adjectives are easy to learn. This is because most of their forms are similar to English adjectives. You should, therefore, not be worried that your brain will be strained. Adjectives help have different ways of describing things. Spanish adjectives speed up this process and help build your Spanish vocabulary, as well. As you learn Spanish adjectives, you will be better at expressing yourself. The adjectives also build your vocabulary and help your feelings and thoughts on different situations, places, people, films, and objects. Adjectives also add color and flavor; that's why it is never dull.

Most beginner Spanish learners struggle to understand the order of adjectives. This is because they differ from English adjectives and go after the noun. For example, in English, one would say, 'She has beautiful green eyes.' In Spanish, it is translated as 'Ella tiene hermosos ojos verdes.' The direct translation of this will literally mean 'She has eyes green beautiful.' As you start learning, it gets weird, but once you get the concept, it becomes easier. Keep in mind that adjectives are feminine or masculine, plural, or singular. What this means is that when talking about plural feminine nouns, you will definitely need a plural feminine adjective.

Some Spanish adjectives change gender to match the noun. A good example is Buena / Bueno. In a sentence, we can have this example 'Una casa bonita,' which means 'A beautiful house.' In this example, it is both singular and feminine. Bonita means beautiful in singular feminine, while bonitas is plural feminine. Sometimes, it is okay to use the adjective before the noun after ignoring it for a while.

Though Spanish adjectives are more complicated than English, learners are sometimes discouraged and may be tempted to drop out of the particular program they are in. Another example that may even confuse further is that when one uses Spanish adjectives, gender is matched with the noun. After this, the number has to match, and the right order is realized. If the order is wrong, then the entire sentence will be bad. There are also many exceptions from the usual rules that people are more accustomed to.

An adjective tells us more about the noun. It may be small information of a distinct description of the noun. For example, the old clock, the ripe apple, the red ball, the hot towel, and the tall building. All these try to explain something about the particular noun. In the listed examples, words like red, old, hot, tall, and ripe, in no specific order, are adjectives. Another way to look at the adjectives is as follows: The ball is red, the clock is old, the towel is hot, the building is tall, and the apple is ripe. Therefore, the translation of the Spanish words will be as follows: La pelota es roja, el reloj es viejo, el edificio es alto, la manzana está madura, and la toalla está caliente. In these examples, however, Spanish adjectives are seen to stray from the English adjectives. Therefore, this can be termed as the first challenge with Spanish adjective that one needs to be aware of.

Other Spanish adjectives can only be used together with the verb **estar**. Other Spanish adjectives will only use **ser**, while in some, both are still used. More examples are: **Importante** is most commonly used with ser. Thus, we can write **'es importante.'** While **contento** is mostly used with **estar**, thus the right way to write it is **está contento**.

On the other hand, **frío** is used with both. So it can be es frío or **está frío**. Learners need to know that the use of any of the above named can drastically change the meaning. While Spanish adjectives use feminine and masculine nouns, English adjectives do not.

Also, you need to change the end of the adjective to match the noun where possible. Spanish adjectives are split into two main groups:

Spanish adjectives that are ending with 'o,' such as rico, corto, distinto, bajo, lógico, and distinto.

Spanish adjectives that end in any other letter besides 'o,' such as triste, difícil, capaz, and común.

Note that for all adjectives ending with o, change the end of the adjective to an 'a' when you are referring to a feminine and the 'o' to refer to male nouns. A good example can be 'a short story' in English, which is translated to 'una historia corta' in Spanish. Another example is 'the low voice,' which is translated to mean 'la voz baja.' However, for the adjectives that have an ending besides the letter 'o,' there is nothing to be done to the ending.

Spanish adjectives have similarities with the Indo-European languages. They are usually posted positive. They are also known to agree in terms of gender and the noun number that they are modifying. Spanish adjectives with the base form are commonly found in the dictionaries.

Why Is Learning Spanish Adjective Important?

Spanish adjectives facilitate gender grouping. This is because it can be categorized under male or female. This reduces the confusion that may arise due to grouping. It can also help when taking records since one can quickly tell the difference. When we are exploring culture, language forms the foundation or rather the cornerstone. This is because language provides a way that people can freely express their beliefs. Take the situation of a newborn baby; they have no exposure to any cultural thing. However, as they learn and come to terms with their surroundings, they learn the language they interact daily. After mastering the language, they start to understand arts, customs, and the nation's achievement and the particular social group they belong to. As these issues influence the children, they start forming their own world view. The shared characteristics and customs of a group can give people a sense of belonging and an identity. Language is the first and key major thing that first unites and strengthens relationships and interactions. Being able to communicate helps us discover our shared identity and beliefs. For those who love traveling, being able to understand natives' language eases communication and enhances interactions between people. If you can speak the language, it will be easy to understand and fully experience the local culture.

The Spanish language is spoken by many far and wide. In over 20 different countries, it is the official language. Many international organizations like the European Union, United Nations, World Trade Organizations, and the commonwealth recognize that of one of their operation's official languages. We need to understand that despite being the second largest spoken language, not all the

Spanish countries have the same culture. Each country has its own unique culture that defines them, but regions inside these countries can have similar cultural practices that define them. Learning a language, therefore, helps one connect with a particular culture.

Knowing the Spanish adjectives will help build your Spanish vocabulary. This, in turn, boosts your self-confidence and propels you to learn more and more. As you come to know and understand the various Spanish adjectives, you will be able to correct yourself when you are wrong.

Spanish is the fastest growing language across the globe after English and French. This means that the complex grammar we are learning is not in vain. The key lessons offer basic guidelines to the learner and expose them to what is expected of them. All the examples used should not be the only lessons for beginners.

More teachings should be incorporated from other sources, and some assignments are also given to the learners. Assignments ensure that the learner is assessed if they are progressing well. After the assessment, then it will be easier to build in their area of weakness. The examples given in this book act as a foundation of the many complex lessons ahead. Having grasped these key lessons, one should be able to understand why they need to take Spanish as a second language. You cannot underestimate the power of adverbs since they bring about a connection between verbs and adjectives.

There are a few pointers to note. The Spanish-speaking population is spreading fast, far, and wide like bush fire.

Many learning institutions are offering Spanish as a foreign language. This guide should be your foundation for Spanish fluency. After reading this book, there will be no excuse for one not to comprehend Spanish grammar.

As you learn to use the various grammar discussed in this book, start slowly and progress until you reach your goal. Let no distraction and laziness that always affect other people affect you. Make time daily to learn new adjectives.

You can also learn by pinning them in your refrigerator, hang in the wall, or just put in the study table. This sounds like a kindergarten way of learning, but it has proven very useful and efficient. Love the Spanish language, and make it a part of you. Any opportunity that you get to meet a Spanish-speaking person, use it as an opportunity to learn. Speak to them even if you will make a mistake. Be happy when they correct you because that is a good sign that you are growing and progressing well. Do not be scared of sharing your struggles since this will encourage those who want to begin learning and the ones in the process of learning. The Spanish language is a beautiful language full of love, romance, and happiness. Appreciate this fact while happily learning and being in a cheerful mood.

Learn to exchange and share materials with the people in your group. If not, you can borrow from the library or purchase materials online. There are all sorts of books about the Spanish language, which is just one of them.

There are also advanced and intermediate levels. This means that one should not just stop at the beginner level and should continue until they gain fluency. Make daily efforts to reach a goal unless you are sick or traveling.

Audio can be instrumental in helping you hear the pronunciation, especially where sentences have marks. Be your motivator; cheer yourself up even during those times when you do not believe in yourself.

Interact and mingle in the company of Spanish-speaking people. This way, you will be assimilated into their culture and be able to understand some of their practices and how they do things. Be ready to be criticized both in public and private places. This is because human beings are critical by nature. Make learning fun, and enjoy all the grammar. Ask questions when you do not understand to be guided appropriately. Know that learning is a process and takes time.

This will help you be patient, especially in adult learning. When you meet your daily goals, do not feel guilty about rewarding yourself.

While in English, they normally go before, in Spanish, adjectives are usually put after the noun or pronoun they affect. Another difference is that in Spanish, adjectives must match gender (feminine or masculine), when possible, and quantity (singular or plural).

- The beautiful car/El automóvil bello
- The ugly house/La casa fea
- The fat cats/Los gatos gordos
- My pretty cousins/Mis primas bonitas

In some cases, the adjective can be used before the noun. When you use the adjectives bueno (good), malo (bad) and grande (big), they lose the last letter if you put them before a masculine noun: A good year - Un año bueno / Un buen año A bad day - Un día malo / Un mal día A big tree - Un árbol grande / Un gran árbol

Useful adjectives

- **good** - buen/bueno/buena/buenos/buenas
- **bad** - mal/malo/mala/malos/malas
- **big** - gran/grande/grandes
- **small** - pequeño/pequeña/pequeños/pequeñas
- **fast** - rápido/rápida/rápidos/rápidas
- **slow** - lento/lenta/lentos/lentas
- **expensive** - caro/cara/caros/caras
- **cheap** - barato/barata/baratos/baratas
- **loud** - ruidoso/ruidosa/ruidosos/ruidosas
- **quiet** - silencioso/silenciosa/silenciosos/silenciosas
- **intelligent** - inteligente/inteligentes
- **stupid** - estúpido/estúpida/estúpidos/estúpidas
- **heavy** - pesado/pesada/pesados/pesadas
- **light** - liviano/liviana/livianos/livianas
- **hard** - duro/dura/duros/duras
- **soft** - suave/suaves
- **easy** - fácil/fáciles
- **difficult** - difícil/difíciles

- **strong** - fuerte/fuertes
- **rich** - rico/rica/ricos/ricas
- **poor** - pobre/pobres
- **young** - joven/jóvenes
- **old** - viejo/vieja/viejos/viejas
- **long** - largo/larga/largos/largas
- **short** - corto/corta/cortos/cortas
- **high** - alto/alta/altos/altas
- **low** - bajo/baja/bajos/bajas
- **mean** - malvado/malvada/malvados/malvadas
- **beautiful** - bello/bella/bellos/bellas
- **ugly** - feo/fea/feos/feas
- **new** - nuevo/nueva/nuevos/nuevas
- **happy** - feliz/felices
- **sad** - triste/tristes
- **safe** - seguro/segura/seguros/seguras
- **dangerous** - peligroso/peligrosa/peligrosos/peligrosas full - lleno/llena/llenos/llenas
- **empty** - vacío/vacía/vacíos/vacías
- **interesting** - interesante/interesantes
- **boring** - aburrido/aburrida/aburridos/aburridas

- **important** - importante/importantes
- **right** - correcto/correcta/correctos/correctas
- **wrong** - incorrecto/incorrecta/incorrectos/incorrectas
- **clean** - limpio/limpia/limpios/limpias
- **dirty** - sucio/sucia/sucios/sucias

Exercises

Practice matching gender and number using any adjective you want from the list.

Mi hermana .... es la más .... de la casa Me compró un regalo ....

Tus ojos son muy ....

La comida callejera es ....

Mi auto no es muy ....

Quiero ir a un lugar ....

Este lugar está ....

Yo veo el vaso medio ....

A veces sois ....

¡Qué hombre ....!

Usted es muy ....

Intenta tomar decisiones ....

Tu habitación está muy ....

Tus hijas pueden ser un poco ....

Las señoras son muy ....

Tengo un .... presentimiento

Es un .... momento

Mi bolsa es demasiado ....

Los vecinos son tan .... que no puedo dormir Los libros son ....

La montaña es ....

¡Cómo podéis ser tan ....!

Eres ....

El helado es más .... de lo que me gusta

La escuela es demasiado .... para mí

Mi abuelo es ....

Son personas ....

Creen que son hombres ....

Tus tortas son las más .... del mundo

No quiero ser tu amigo, ¡eres ....!

Tus padres son muy ....

Cuando sea ...., viajaré por todo el mundo

Tengo .... expectativas

Tienes las uñas muy ....

Tengo un pantalón ....

La película fue demasiado ....

A veces puedes ser realmente ....

Somos realmente ....

Soy ....

Tengo un .... proyecto

Fueron nuestros días más ....

Mis padres están ....

Esta es una zona ....

Chapter 7: Spanish Adverbs

Adverbs refer to words used to describe or modify verbs, adjectives, and other adverbs. Another use of adverbs is to give information concerning time, manner, place, and number. Adverbs usually answer questions like how long? When? How? How often? Where? Spanish adverbs are not variable. This, in simple terms, means they do not change according to number or gender. Their invariable nature can be attributed to the fact that they do not modify nouns.

While Spanish adjectives are variable, Spanish adverbs are usually invariable, and this is also a way of saying they never change according to the number or gender. Spanish adverbs are responsible for modifying adverbs, adjectives, and verbs. Spanish adverbs cannot, however, modify nouns. Spanish adverb usually comes after the verb that it modifies. A good example is 'cantas bien,' which means 'you sing well' in English. Adverbs can be categorized into different types. Adverb of place, for example, gives more information on the location where someone or something is. For instance, 'near' is written 'cerca' in Spanish. 'Far' is written as 'lejos' in Spanish. 'Inside' is written as 'dentro' in Spanish. Adverbs of time, on the other hand, give information on time, frequency, and duration. It is written as 'actualmente.' Adverbs of quality and degree provide us with information regarding the number, quality, and degree. They answer questions like 'to what extent' and 'how much.' For example, too much is written as 'mucho.'

In 1942, the first-ever Spanish grammar was presented by Antonio de Nebrija to Queen Isabella. The queen had a good appreciation of how the language was useful and used this in her favor as a tool to maintain power in her country during that time. From grammar, the Spanish language can be read easily with little help. This traces its way back in the 1100s, according to the documents found. Spanish royal academy was established in 1713 to help preserve the language. The academy published six volumes of Spanish dictionaries between 1726 and 1739. The first Spanish grammar book was, however, produced later in 1771. Different Spanish speaking countries came with their analogous language academy. The Association of Spanish Language Academies came up later on and was officially created in 1951. However, people need to understand that spoken Spanish is different and varies from one region to the next. Word pronunciation of similar Spanish words varies from place to place, not just in Spain but also in Spanish countries. Despite the second spoken language in the United States, Spanish speakers are many compared to those who speak Hawaiian, French, and Native American. By 2006, more than 34 million people, ages five and older, speak Spanish as their primary language.

The popularity of the Spanish language can be seen from the immigration process. The Spanish colonies from Puerto Rico and Cuba encouraged many immigrants in the 19th century from Spain. The suit was followed by Latin American countries like Uruguay and Argentina. Colombia, Mexico, Venezuela, Panama, and Chile attracted many European Spanish immigrants. The populations then preserved their language and adapted it to maintain their culture. The descendants of Spaniards continued to use the language in the United States of America. This is after Puerto Rico suddenly becomes a possession of the United States as a result of the Spanish-American war. The

Spanish and mixed Afro-Spanish/caribbean population retained their inherited Spanish language and used it as their mother tongue. They incorporated this with English when the Americans imposed the only language at that time. In the 20th century, however, over a million Puerto Ricans migrated to the United States. There are many Americans today who are bilingual and speak both languages: English and Spanish.

Anyone who would like to describe something always needs an adverb. It may be related to the direction that something is headed to or indicating frequency. Adverbs are everywhere. It is just that people do not think about them as they should. They give the details of the thing happening in the sentence. Therefore, most adverbs in English end in -ly. With the Spanish language, the suffix is —mente.

How Does One Learn Spanish Adverbs Fast And Easy?

Like any other language, to be successful at learning Spanish, one needs to be very keen. Being keen will make you master the spelling, use of the word in a sentence, and use punctuation. By this, you will not mess up your grammar and get value for your money. If you are not keen, chances are, you will miss a crucial thing that would have otherwise helped you grow. You can begin this by writing all the new words that you learn. If you do this, you might be able to learn things that you would have omitted. Check the punctuation and spelling. Look if there is any distinctive character.

Have the right attitude when learning the lessons. This can take you far, you will be a pro in the Spanish language and before you even know it. The right approach helps in learning verbs and in mastering the Spanish language as a whole. Attitude is what motivates learning. And it has also been said that attitude defines you. After you develop a positive mindset, it is time to start working on your goals. Avoid associating with negative people as they are only good at reminding you how everything is bound to fail. Attitude also determines the mindset. If the mindset is right, you will feel strong enough to overcome their fear and be ready to face the future with courage.

Have a notebook and write anything that you can describe. This will help the learner to write down important notes that are necessary for references. It will also help the learner keep records of the lessons. They can also design their homework schedule and work toward achieving that. Record-keeping is essential when one is learning a foreign language. It can also help you write down questions that are to be addressed by your tutor. This is important; when a lesson is going on, you do not need to interrupt with questions. You can write your thoughts and the new words that you have learned. The notebook can act as your new Spanish language diary.

Speak up and interact more. Get out of your comfort zone. You cannot just learn a language by writing and reading. Improve your verbal skills and be ready to meet new people. Meeting Spanish-speaking people help you incorporate various elements of their culture into your own. They will be very supportive of you and may even help you grow. Appreciate their way of life. Celebrate their traditions and heritage. Be keen during your interaction with them and how they understand your speech. Believe in yourself, and if you are not sure of what you are doing or what to say, politely ask. Do not be shy; have self-confidence by believing in yourself. Being overconfident may also be harmful, especially when you have been doing things you think were right.

Write a short description of things in Spanish, then check with your tutor. Start looking for a tutor if you have none. There are various tutors online with affordable rates and are available 24/5. These tutors have a flexible schedule and can work at your convenience. Tutors help you keep track of your progress, help you grow, and develop a curriculum suitable for you, depending on your language level. It is not easy to learn a new language on your own. This is because, in most situations, we listen to people speaking, then we copy them. Through repetitions, the words stick in our mind and form the language. It has been proven that language can be learned and unlearned. If you discover a language and fail to keep practicing in saying it, forget, you will forget. This is a natural thing that has been proven through extensive research. Converse with your tutor more. You can even take the risk of turning your Goggle search engine into Spanish.

No one forced you to learn. You did this of your own free will. Understand that no one forced you to learn. You started this because you wanted to. It might be because you need to do this, so, you can solve some problems one day. It may also be because you have a passion for traveling and planning to visit a Spanish-speaking country. Again, you may be in an interracial relationship and just learning for fun. No matter the reason for learning, be keen on the rules, follow the rules, and avoid confrontations.

Chapter 8: Articles

In Spanish, names are usually accompanied by an article, except the proper names like José or María. On the other hand, if we talk about a car or house, they are accompanied by their respective article. Articles, like many pronouns, vary by gender and number and must match the noun they precede. Articles are divided into two categories: the definite and the indefinite.

Definite Articles

Definite articles are those that refer to a specific thing: La casa, a specific object. The two definite articles that exist are: LA for feminine and LO for masculine. To turn them into a plural form, an S is added at the end. Example: LAS, LOS.

The only opportunity in which the use of an article for a proper name is permissible is when we refer to a group, for instance, if we refer to several people with the name Maria, we can say: Las Marías, adding an S at the end of the proper name.

Another use that can be given to certain articles is when we use the noun in a general way, for example:

- The pictures help decorate any place/Los cuadros ayudan a decorar cualquier lugar.
- It's two O'clock/Son las dos en punto.
- See you tomorrow at one in the afternoon/Mañana nos vemos a la una de la tarde.

To name parts of the body:

- The hand/la mano
- The foot/el pie
- The face/la cara

Indefinite Articles

The indefinite are also two articles only: UN for the masculine and UNA for the feminine. Like the others, they become plural when an S is added at the end. In the case of UN, OS is added instead: UNOS, UNAS.

- Some girls are running/Unas niñas están corriendo
- Some dogs are barking/Unos perros están ladrando.

A particular use given to these indeterminate articles is to accompany an amount:

- There are a few extra kilograms/Hay unos kilogramos extra.
- I have a pair of shirts/Tengo un par de camisas.

Contracted articles

These articles are a few words that can be contracted in Spanish as it happens in English. This contraction in Spanish occurs because the article begins with a vowel and the word that precedes it ends with a vowel, this often occurs with the letter A, the word DE and the article EL.

With this graphic you will understand better:

- Stay inside the car/Quédate dentro de el carro - This use is incorrect.

- Stay inside the car/Quédate dentro del carro -This is the correct use.
- We go to the restaurant/Vamos a el restaurante - Incorrect use.
- We go to the restaurant/Vamos al restaurante - Correct use.

There is another last article that is used for neutral words, this is the LO. Unlike the other articles, this never accompanies nouns, it only accompanies adjectives that modify the subject. Example:

That's the good thing about you/Eso es lo bueno de tí.

The simple thing of living with you/Lo simple de vivir contigo.

Exercises

___ carro

___ casa

___ perro

___ gato

___ patos

___ bueno

___ malo

___ mejor

___ sonido

___ animales

___ Marías

___ vecinos

___ países

___ Lápiz

___ matemáticas

Articles usage in everyday life:

Los sábados los tengo libre	I am free on Saturdays
¿Qué es lo que pasa?	What is happening?
Eres lo mejor del mundo	You are the best in the world
Necesito las instrucciones	I need the instructions
Pasame las frutas	Pass me the fruits
Quiero tener un perro	I want to have a dog
Hay unas botas lindas en la tienda	There are some nice boots in the store
Tengo un par de minutos libres	I have a couple of free minutes
El desayuno estaba caliente	Breakfast was hot
Llegaré una hora tarde	I'll be an hour late
¿Tienes un mapa?	Do you have a map?
Necesito un pasaje de regreso	I need a return ticket
Me duele la cabeza	I got a headache
¿Cómo llego a un hospital?	How do I get to a hospital?

Respuestas correctas a la práctica anterior:

El carro

La casa

El perro

El gato

Los patos

Lo bueno

Lo malo

Lo mejor

Un sonido

Los animales

Las Marías

Los vecinos

Los países

El lápiz

Las matemáticas

To some, articles are not that important because the noun may exist even without it. But it is very important because it determines noun identity whether it is masculine, feminine, or neuter.

Usually, in the English Alphabet, articles are the whether it is singular or plural.

In Spanish, it must first be determined whether the noun is feminine, masculine, or neuter. In the case of the feminine, the article is **La** or **Las** when plural. In the case of masculine, the article is **El** or **Los** in the case of plural. Neuter only has Lo in its singular.

It must be noted that if the noun ends in *a* or *as*, then it is always presumed that the noun is feminine. On the other hand, if the noun ends in *o* or *os*, then it is always presumed that the noun is masculine.

Para algunos, los artículos no son tan importantes porque el sustantivo puede existir incluso sin él. Pero es muy importante porque determina la identidad del sustantivo, ya sea masculino, femenino o neutro.

Por lo general, en el alfabeto inglés, los artículos son generalmente si es singular o plural. En español, primero se debe determinar si el sustantivo es femenino, masculino o neutro. En caso de femenino, el artículo es La o Las cuando está en plural. En caso de masculino, el artículo es El o Los en caso de plural. Neutro solo tiene Lo en su singular.

Cabe señalar que si el sustantivo termina en a o as, siempre se presume que el sustantivo es femenino. Por otro lado, si el sustantivo termina en o u os, siempre se presume que el sustantivo es masculino.

In case of a word ending in a vowel, the proper way of constructing is to put s after the noun as well as the article. For example, the word is Apple, it means that in Spanish, it will become **Manzana**. In case of plural, it will be added with an S at the end of the word or noun, thus **Manzanas**. (En el caso de una palabra que termina en una vocal, la forma correcta de construir es poner s después del sustantivo y del artículo. Por ejemplo, la palabra es Apple, significa que en español se convertirá en Manzana. En caso de plural, se agregará con una S al final de la palabra o sustantivo, por lo tanto, Manzanas.)

If the word is ending with a consonant, the usual thing done by Spanish people is to add es or s. For instances, the word **canción**. If you will be translating it into plural, the word will become **canciones**. (Si la palabra termina con una consonante, lo habitual que hacen los españoles es agregar es o s. Por ejemplo, la palabra cancion. Si va a traducirlo al plural, la palabra se convertirá en canciones.)

You will be able to distinguish English and Spanish when it comes to the use of articles. You have to look at these examples and tips which may be very useful in your Spanish Language lesson:

Usually, in the English Alphabet, the most used article is THE. It is different in the Spanish Language because there are actually four articles in it that you need to understand and use properly. These are EL, LOS, LAS, and LA.

There are instances wherein the English Alphabet, the use of the article is omitted, but in the Spanish Language, there must always be an article to make the sentence formal and make it formal. Without it, it will be a mere slang word or combination of words.

You will find here examples or short stories using articles. Again, it is narrated in the English Language, and it is translated to the Spanish Language for a better understanding of the lesson.

There are stories in the Spanish Language that you may want to read repeatedly because they are considered priceless since what you need to do is just to open your eyes and start reading. Some may find it boring, but to a learner, it is really a must. You need to start it by yourself, and when you are already fluent with some basic words in the Spanish Language, then the next thing to do is to create a group or circle of friends and start having a conversational discussion with them. You may start with the very popular story of the vain mouse or little mouse to be specific. (Hay historias en español que es posible que desee leer una y otra vez porque se consideran invaluables, ya que lo que debe hacer es abrir los ojos y comenzar a leer. Algunos pueden encontrarlo aburrido, pero para un alumno, es realmente imprescindible. Debes comenzar por ti mismo y cuando ya domines algunas palabras básicas en español, lo siguiente que debes hacer es crear un grupo o círculo de amigos y comenzar una conversación con ellos. Puede comenzar con la historia muy popular del ratón vano o ratoncito para ser específicos.)

In that story, the little mouse is so vain that all her suitors are being criticized, mocked, and rejected simultaneously. She fell attractive to a good looking cat. She immediately said yes to the cat's proposal, and to her surprise, it turned out that there is no food to eat together during their first picnic date. Instead, what was offered as food is the little vain mouse herself. Because of that, she was so afraid and shouted at the top of her voice, asking for help. Luckily, she was followed by her suitor, her neighbor mouse who rescued her from the dark plan of the cat. (En esa historia, el ratoncito es tan vanidoso que todos sus pretendientes son criticados, burlados y rechazados simultáneamente. Ella se sintió atractiva para un gato guapo. Inmediatamente dijo que sí a la propuesta del gato, y para su sorpresa, resultó que durante su primera cita de picnic, no hay comida para comer juntos. En cambio, lo que se ofreció como alimento es el pequeño ratón vanidoso. Debido a eso, tenía mucho miedo y gritó en voz alta, pidiendo ayuda. Afortunadamente, fue seguida por su pretendiente, su ratón vecino que la rescató del oscuro plan del gato.)

In another Spanish short story, you will find here the use of articles. This is the story of the Ugly Woman. Here, you will not only get to see the correct use of articles in Spanish short stories, but you will also be able to understand the meaning of regret which may come at the end of a decision you have made. (En otro cuento español, encontrará aquí el uso de artículos. Esta es la historia de la mujer fea. Aquí, no solo podrá ver el uso correcto de los artículos en cuentos cortos en español, sino que también podrá comprender el significado del arrepentimiento que puede surgir al final de una decisión que haya tomado.)

This is the story of Siguanaba, which used to be a very beautiful woman. However, she was swallowed whole by her dream and lack of love and empathy towards her son. She only has a single son, and yet she did not show any interest in keeping his son. She found a man she thought could give her everything she needs – love, sexual desires and wealth. That was why she made the biggest decision of her life, is to leave her son alone. Her son does not have food to eat from then on. He does not have shelter to stay in during the time that rain persists. However, that decision of her will only leave her with an outcome which she will surely regret. One day, the known God punished her by switching her face from the very beautiful and attractive one into a very ugly face. The curse includes her appearance along the highway. She will slowly walk towards the river, and she appears beautifully and gracefully. However, the man being seduced has already focused his attention on her, she will turn into a monster with a very ugly face.

(Esta es la historia de Siguanaba, que solía ser una mujer muy hermosa. Sin embargo, su sueño la tragó por completo y la falta de amor y empatía hacia su hijo. Ella solo tiene un hijo único y, sin embargo, no mostró ningún interés en mantener a su hijo. Encontró a un hombre que pensó que podría darle todo lo que necesita: amor, deseos sexuales y riqueza. Esa fue la razón por la que tomó la decisión más importante de su vida, y esa es dejar a su hijo solo. Su hijo no tiene comida para comer desde entonces, no tiene refugio para quedarse durante el tiempo que persiste la lluvia. Sin embargo, esa decisión de ella solo la dejará con un resultado del que seguramente lamentará. Un día, el Dios conocido la castigó cambiando su rostro del muy hermoso y atractivo por uno muy feo. La maldición incluye su apariencia a lo largo del camino y ella caminará lentamente hacia el río, y se ve hermosa y con gracia. Sin embargo, durante el tiempo en que el hombre que está siendo seducido ya ha centrado su atención en ella, ella se convertirá en un monstruo con una cara muy fea.)

On the other hand, her son has been awarded by the known God with a youthful appearance which will last as long as he lives. He has been blessed because of the sacrifices he has undergone with under the hands of her mother. The hunger he has suffered turned out to be a blessing this time because the known God also blessed him with abundance and happiness of the heart. (Por otro lado, su hijo ha sido premiado por el Dios conocido con una apariencia juvenil que durará tanto como él viva. Ha sido bendecido por los sacrificios que ha sufrido bajo las manos de su madre. El hambre que ha sufrido resultó ser una bendición esta vez porque el Dios conocido también lo bendijo con abundancia y felicidad del corazón.)

These two short stories may be elementary and kid-like, but these surely help you find the articles in the sentence, and now, you already know how to construct the sentences properly. Next time, you will be put in a conversation with a Spanish friend, and you will notice that you will no longer find it so difficult compared to the first time you started conversing with them. (Estas dos historias cortas pueden ser elementales y parecidas a las de un niño, pero seguramente te ayudarán a encontrar los artículos en la oración y ahora, ya sabes cómo construir correctamente las oraciones. La próxima vez, se le pondrá a conversar con un amigo español, y notará que ya no le resultará tan difícil en comparación con la primera vez que comenzó a conversar con ellos.

Chapter 9: Learning Basic vocabulary

Learning vocabulary is one of the most fun and most difficult parts of learning a language. When learning a new language, it is important to remember that you will be learning MANY new words. A child does this with ease and can absorb new information like a sponge. But as you get older, it might get a little more difficult but that doesn't mean it is impossible. There are a few ways to pick up vocabulary easier.

Clump words together. Perhaps there are words you can use for eating, comer, tenedor, cuchilla, restaurante, servidor, el baño, lavarse las manos, pagar la billete, salir, sentarse, por favor, gracias, de nada. These are a few vocabulary words that are associated with eating. They are translated as, "to eat", "fork", "knife", "restaurant", "server", "the bathroom", "wash your hands", "pay the bill", "leave", "to sit down", "please", "thank you", and "you're welcome." Do you see how the words all fit a situation in where you could be in a restaurant? Even by doing this, you can learn some words that fit in many situations, like **salir, por favor, gracias, sentarse, pagar, de nada** (to leave, please, thank you, to sit, to pay, your welcome).

Keep a dictionary with you at all time. This is easier to do in today's digital age. Repetition is key, so the more you are able to access the meaning of a word, the better it will be to understand and remember it.

Try to tell a story to someone or yourself, or even write one. This is an excellent way to learn vocabulary. Even if it is a simple story. Stories invoke in us emotional responses. A big part of learning is emotional, as part of the brain that processes emotions is thought to be connected to the learning center of our brain. You can see how, Yo conduzco mi bicicleta, or "I ride my bike", then, Yo conduzco mi bicicleta a la tienda, or "I ride my bike to the store", then, Yo conduzco mi bicicleta a la tienda para comprar manzanas, cebollas, y pollo cáda día, or "I ride my bike to the store to buy apples, onions, and chicken every day", then, Yo conduzco mi bicicleta a la tienda para comprar mazanas, cebollas, y pollo cáda día porque mi abuelita está enferma, or "I ride my bike to the store to buy apples, onions, and chicken every day because my grandma is sick." You can see how your sentence, can become more intricate, and then finally a story that invokes your emotion and is fun to write. You will learn many new vocabulary words this way.

Mnemonics. One way to remember vocabulary is to create a mnemonic device or a memorization tool. There may seem a bit complicated at first, but can be a useful tool. For example, the phrase, qué pasa, calabaza, or in English, "What's up, pumpkin?" is easy to remember, because it uses a rhyming type mnemonic. Another type of mnemonic would be to create a sort of memory type of game-like mnemonic. For example, **salir**, is pronounced "sal-lear", and you can think of a man named "Sal", "leaving", which almost sounds like the last part in **salir**, the lear, sound. It can be a stretch for your brain, but they can be helpful to create meaningful memories of words too.

Listen to audiotapes. Language is spoken. So, therefore, it can be helpful to hear an audiotape and to hear the actual language being spoken. It will resonate in the language centers of your brain. It will also help tremendously in pronunciation at first. Most audiotapes that focus on vocabulary will also try clumping or storyline techniques, which will be helpful.

With these techniques, you can manage learning vocabulary a bit easier. It may be difficult, but try to make it as fun as possible. Also, try learning words that you will frequently use. Vocabulary is the center of any language, but you don't need to know it if you are trying to learn fast take, for example, the words **poni y caballo**, or in English, "pony and horse". You don't frequently need to say pony. You can just say horse and a speaker will understand. Or the Spanish words, **supermercado, departamento, y tienda**. They mean supermarket, department, and store in English, respectively. To speak Spanish you don't really have to know all of those words. The word **tienda** is fine, which covers all of the others; the others are just more detailed. That comes with time, but even some native speakers won't know all of those words. Keep it simple, fun, and expect to learn a lot, and you will be just fine.

Learners, who are mostly beginners, need to create their personal phrasebook if they want to learn the Spanish Language in less than a year. The purpose of a phrasebook is to serve as a bucket full of Spanish words or vocabulary. You will see here the basic vocabulary in the Spanish Language that you can use in your Course. (Los estudiantes, en su mayoría principiantes, deben crear su libro de frases personal si quieren aprender el idioma español en menos de un año. El propósito del libro de frases es servir como un cubo lleno de palabras o vocabulario en español. Verá aquí el vocabulario básico en español que puede usar en su curso.)

English Vocabulary	Spanish Equivalent
COLORS	
Blue	Azul
Red	Rojo
Yellow	Amarillo
Green	Verde
Violet	Violeta
Pink	Rosa
Orange	Anaranjado
Brown	Marrón
Black	Negro
White	Blanco
Purple	Morado
MUSIC	
Drums	Tambores
Trumpet	Trompeta
Guitar	Guitarra
Piano	Piano

Lyrics	Letra
Organ	Órgano

FOOD

Honey	Miel
Milk	Leche
Potatoes	Papas
Chicken	Pollo
Egg	Huevo
Avocado	Aguacate
Beef	Carne de res
Peanut	Maní
Candy	Dulce
Pear	Pera
Grape	Uva

RELATIONSHIP

Mom	Mamá
Dad	Papá
Son	Hijo
Daughter	Hija
Daughter-in-law	Nuera
Husband	Marido

Wife	Esposa
Grandma	Abuela
Grandpa	Abuelo
Uncle	Tío
Aunt	Tía

These words can be elementary to those Spanish-speaking people, but to those who are only beginning to learn about the Spanish Language, these will be of great help. It is just the same with a toddler who could not leave his or her parents during the first day of school. There is always separation anxiety. So, instead of immediately proceeding with the Spanish Language proper, you should also help yourself by collecting words and writing it in the phrasebook. (Puede parecer que estas palabras son elementales para las personas de habla hispana, pero para aquellos que recién comienzan a aprender sobre el idioma español, serán de gran ayuda. Es lo mismo con un niño pequeño que no pudo dejar a sus padres durante el primer día de clases. Siempre hay una ansiedad por separación. Entonces, en lugar de continuar inmediatamente con el idioma español, también debe ayudarse a sí mismo recolectando palabras y escribiéndolas en el libro de frases.)

The best advice that could be given to you when learning the Spanish Language is considered your time. Time is of the essence, so it must always be treasured, and this should not be wasted. A schedule or calendar of your activities must be prepared and practiced regularly. You should spare an hour or two in your everyday schedule. That spared time must be devoted to learning the Spanish Language. If you are lucky enough to finish the hour without any difficulty, and you still have time and energy, you may consider going back to your phrasebook. It pays to read your phrasebook over and over again because, as the cliché goes, practice makes perfect.

(El mejor consejo que se le puede dar cuando se trata de aprender español es considerar su tiempo. El tiempo es esencial, por lo que siempre debe ser atesorado, y esto no debe desperdiciarse. Se debe preparar y practicar regularmente un cronograma o calendario de sus actividades. Debe dedicar una o dos horas en su horario diario. Se debe dedicar ese tiempo libre al aprendizaje del idioma español, y si tiene la suerte de terminar la hora sin ninguna dificultad, y aún tiene tiempo y energía, puede considerar volver a su libro de frases. Vale la pena leer tu libro de frases una y otra vez porque, como dice el cliché, la práctica hace la perfección.)

If your sole purpose is to learn the Spanish Language´s basic vocabulary you should think of some ways other than reading. Watching TV shows and movies is a good move, particularly if you have already previously watched those movies and shows. But what is important to note is to change its Language setting to Spanish Language and disable the subtitle. By doing so, you will be able to test yourself if you have truly learned even the basic of the Spanish Language. (Si su único propósito es aprender el vocabulario básico del idioma español, debe pensar en otras formas además de la lectura. Ver programas de televisión y películas es un buen movimiento, especialmente si ya ha visto esas películas y programas anteriormente. Pero lo que es importante tener en cuenta es cambiar su configuración de idioma a idioma español y deshabilitar los subtítulos. Al hacerlo, podrás ponerte a prueba si realmente has aprendido incluso lo básico del idioma español.)

In learning basic vocabulary, your cellular phone must be given importance this time because it is not only used as a form of communication. There are applications that you may use in order to collect words that you may use in your Spanish Language Course. Instead of using your cellular phones to capture the moments, you may use it in searching for a phone application that you may find over the web. (Al aprender vocabulario básico, su teléfono celular debe tener importancia esta vez porque no solo se usa como una forma de comunicación. Hay aplicaciones que puede usar para recopilar palabras que puede usar en su curso de español. En lugar de usar sus teléfonos celulares para capturar los momentos, puede usarlos para buscar una aplicación de teléfono que puede encontrar en la web.)

However, even if you have your own means in learning the language, it is still imperative to enroll in a formal Spanish Class. You may enroll in an actual class-type discussion or through online. (Sin embargo, incluso si tiene sus propios medios para aprender el idioma, es imperativo inscribirse en una clase formal de español. Puede inscribirse en una discusión real de clase o en línea.)

On the other hand, some points must be avoided when learning about the Basic Spanish Language.

You cannot avoid your excitement and your eagerness to learn the language the fastest way you can. As such, you set a very high goal and consider all obstacles as mere challenges towards the achievement of your goal. It may sound like a positive one, but the truth is that it is not good and definitely not advisable. (Por otro lado, también hay algunos puntos que deben evitarse al aprender sobre el idioma español básico. No puede evitar su entusiasmo y su entusiasmo por aprender el idioma de la manera más rápida posible. Como tal, establece una meta muy alta y considera todos los obstáculos como simples desafíos para alcanzar su meta. Puede sonar positivo, pero la verdad es que no es bueno y definitivamente no es aconsejable.)

This is the same as setting a deadline or a due wherein you are already fit to converse with a Spanish-speaking person or friend. A month is an impossible deadline setting. A month is just too little and too narrow for you to learn all the things and important grammatical usage of a Spanish Language. Even a quarter is also unachievable. The best deadline or timeline to be set is a minimum of 1 year or even less than a month, and a maximum of 2-3 years. Through that, you will be able to totally grasp everything that you should know about the Spanish Language. It is similar to a four-year bachelor's course wherein the first two years are all basics, and the last two years will be devoted to reviewing all the lessons learned in the first two years. (Esto es lo mismo que establecer una fecha límite o un plazo en el que ya está en condiciones de conversar con una persona o amigo de habla hispana. Un mes es una fecha límite imposible. Un mes es demasiado pequeño y demasiado limitado para que aprenda todas las cosas y el uso gramatical importante de un idioma español. Incluso una cuarta parte también es inalcanzable. El mejor plazo o plazo para establecer es un mínimo de 1 año o incluso menos de un mes, y un máximo de 2-3 años. A través de eso, podrás comprender totalmente todo lo que debes saber sobre el idioma español.

Es similar a un curso de licenciatura de cuatro años en el que los dos primeros años son todos básicos, y los últimos dos años se dedicarán a revisar todas las lecciones aprendidas en los primeros dos años.)

Another thought to avoid is being a hundred percent sure that everything will work out just fine. If, for instance, a certain activity does not carry a sure win when it comes to learning the language, you should not indulge – that is a big NO. Always think that in everything that you do, there will always be a time that you will not get a hundred percent sure win. There will always be obstacles, challenges, and a lot of frustrations. You should not give up and be open about it. (Otro pensamiento a evitar es estar cien por ciento seguro de que todo saldrá bien. Si, por ejemplo, una determinada actividad no conlleva una victoria segura cuando se trata de aprender el idioma, entonces no debe permitirse el lujo de hacerlo, es un gran NO. Siempre piense que en todo lo que haga, siempre habrá un momento en que no obtendrá una ganancia cien por ciento segura. Siempre habrá obstáculos, desafíos y muchas frustraciones. No debes rendirte y ser abierto al respecto.)

Another Useful Tip In Learning the Basic Vocabulary In the Spanish Language (Otro Consejo Útil Para Aprender El Vocabulario Básico En La Lengua Española)

Suppose you have already used all your energy in learning the basic vocabulary in the Spanish Language, then you should consider some of these friendly tips, which are mere additions to the above discussion:

Try finding a place of comfort. Some people find it so comfortable to read while lying down. Although it is not advisable because it may cause a lot of pressure in your eyes and neck or nape if that is your favorite position while reading, consider some useful tips and precautions. But then again, you have to remember that it must not be for a long period of time.

There are also some people who find it so comfortable to ride a bus, and while traveling from home to work and vice versa, there will be no idle time but instead, a time devoted to reading a lot. But then, you have to remember that you need to rest once in a while in order to avoid excessive pressure in your eyes.

Once you have established your most comfortable place and position, you should proceed with your vocabulary properly. Ask yourself questions like, Is my knowledge about the Spanish Language, particularly my vocabulary, enough to sustain a conversation? Am I already prepared for a lengthy discussion with a client or a friend? If your answers are all yes, then let yourself practice more because practice makes perfect as the cliché goes.

Is My Knowledge About the Spanish Language, In Particularly My Vocabulary, Enough To Hold On A Conversation?

This may be known through a tool that makes you either a winner in the vocabulary collection scheme or a not-so-winner.

The ultimate test is the phrasebook, and once you got to be familiar with the phrasebook, you will surely realize the lesser need of a phrasebook. It means you can already transact or converse with another friend even without referring to the phrasebook from time to time.

Another is the use of personalized flashcards. It may be used to combine words that may be found in the phrasebook. These word combinations, phrases, or sentences are being written in an instrument known as the flashcards. You may paste in on your door or walls because these may help you memorize the word combination, phrases, or sentences with the Spanish Language.

Always remember that if your aim is memorizing, then you do not need the phrasebook. What you need is the flashcard.

Si ya ha utilizado toda su energía para aprender el vocabulario básico en el idioma español, entonces debe considerar algunos de estos consejos amigables que son meramente adicionales a la discusión anterior:

1. Intenta encontrar un lugar de comodidad. Hay personas a quienes les resulta muy cómodo leer mientras se acuestan. Aunque no es aconsejable porque puede causar mucha presión en los ojos y el cuello o la nuca, pero si esa es su posición favorita mientras lee, considere algunos consejos y

precauciones útiles. Pero, de nuevo, debe recordar que no debe ser por un largo período de tiempo.

También hay algunas personas a las que les resulta tan cómodo viajar en autobús y mientras viajan de casa al trabajo y viceversa, no habrá tiempo de inactividad, sino un tiempo dedicado a leer mucho. Pero luego, debe recordar que necesita descansar de vez en cuando para evitar una presión excesiva en los ojos.

2. Una vez que haya establecido su lugar y posición más cómodos, debe continuar con su vocabulario apropiado. Hágase preguntas como: ¿Mi conocimiento sobre el idioma español, particularmente mi vocabulario, es suficiente para mantener una conversación? ¿Ya estoy preparado para una larga discusión con un cliente o un amigo? Si todas sus respuestas son afirmativas, entonces permítase practicar más porque, como dice el cliché, la práctica hace la perfección.

"¿Es Mi Conocimiento Sobre El Idioma Español, En Particular Mi Vocabulario, Suficiente Para Sostener Una Conversación?

Esto puede conocerse a través de una herramienta que lo convierte en un ganador en el esquema de recopilación de vocabulario o en uno no tan ganador.

La prueba definitiva es el libro de frases, una vez que se familiarice con el libro de frases, seguramente se dará cuenta de la menor necesidad de un libro de frases.

Significa que ya puede realizar transacciones o conversar con otro amigo, incluso sin consultar el libro de frases de vez en cuando.

Otro es el uso de tarjetas flash personalizadas. Puede usarse para combinar palabras que se pueden encontrar en el libro de frases. Estas combinaciones de palabras, frases u oraciones se escriben en un instrumento conocido como tarjetas flash y puede pegarlas en su puerta o paredes porque pueden ayudarlo a memorizar la combinación de palabras, frases u oraciones con el idioma español.

Recuerde siempre que si su objetivo es memorizar, entonces no necesita el libro de frases. Lo que necesitas es la tarjeta flash.

Chapter 10: Conjugation and Gender Rules

The most difficult part of learning Spanish for beginners is the conjugation of verbs and gender rules. Most languages have conjugations of verbs that follow a pattern, like past tense, future tense, present progressive, imperative, informal/formal etc. Spanish also contains only a few verbs, out of the many thousands of possible verb conjugations. And like most romance languages, Spanish has masculine and feminine words as well. Spanish has these few qualities, and they are very important in learning the language.

So, let's begin with basic gender rules. Every noun has a gender in Spanish. There is, unfortunately, no pattern to determine which noun is masculine or feminine in Spanish. When we say a noun is masculine or feminine, the word usually ends in -o, or -a, respectively, and is proceeded by el, for "the", or la, for "the" depending on the gender. These are called "articles" in language study. There are also los, for plural male nouns, and las, for plural feminine nouns. Some words follow something called "Natural Gender." That is to say, a word that is implying something feminine, like "girl", chica, or masculine like "boy", chico. There is also a something called "grammatical gender", for example, el color, "color", which is masculine, or la visita, or "the visitor", which is always feminine, no matter if the visitor is male or female.

Another way to consider masculine or feminine words are if they end in -o, or -a. Such as el concerto, "the concert", or la pintura, "the painting."

But keep in mind "grammatical gender" is pretty hard to preconceive, such as el raton, "the rat" which is masculine, or, la flor, "the flower", which is feminine.

Any adjectives used to describe nouns must always agree with the respective gender of the noun. For example, la pintura bonita, "the pretty picture", or el perro bueno, "the good dog." And remember always adjectives after, and articles, singular or plural before, and following the appropriate gender rules. But again, you should learn each word and its gender correspondingly as you go.

Verb conjugation is the second most difficult factor when learning basic Spanish. It can be a bit complicated! There are three types of verbs, not including irregular ones in Spanish. The "-er" verbs, the "-ir" verbs, and the "-ar" verbs.

There are, also, the many tenses, but mainly, the six, present, imperative, imperfect, preterite or past tense, future, and conditional.

These can be divided further into subjunctive and indicative.

Subjunctive means what is being thought about in mind, and indicative means what is actually happening, but that isn't that important for now.

We'll focus on the indicative and a few important tenses.

Take an "-er" verbs, aprender, "to learn", trabajar, "to work", and vivir, "to live." Take a look at the following tables for trabajar in the present tense.

They are divided into the verb form for "I" do something or Yo, "You" do something, or Tú(informal), Ustéd(formal), "He/She/It", or Él/Ella/Eso/Esa, does something "We", do something, or Nosotros, "They" do something (informal), or Vosotros, and "They" do something, formal, Ustedes/Ellos/Ellas

The part of a verb that is conjugated in Spanish is the suffix. The same goes for the "-ir", "-ar" and "-er" verbs. It is also good to remember the past tense for "–ir" and "–er" are the same as you will see.

We can also mention that the indicating party or "pronoun" is not necessary for Spanish.

Present tense of **Trabajar** (to work):

Yo trabajo	Nostoros trabajamos
Tú/Ustéd trabajas	Vosotros trabajaís
Él/Ella/Eso/Esa trabaja	Ellos/Ellas/Ustedés trabajaran

In the preterite or past tense:

Yo trabajé	Nostoros trabajamos
Tú/Ustéd trabajasté	Vosotros trabajasteís
Él/Ella/Eso/Esa trabajó	Ellos/Ellas/Ustedés trabajaron

And finally, the present tense of Vivir (to live):

Yo vivo	Nosotros vivimos
Tú/Ustéd vivés	Vosotros vivís
Él/Ella/Eso/Esa vivé	Ellos/Ellas/Eso/Esa viven

In the preterite or the past tense:

Yo viví	Nosotros vivimos
Tú/Ustéd viviste	Vosostros vivisteís
Él/Ella/Eso/Esa vivío	Ellos/Ellas/Eso/Esa vivieron

Present tense of **Aprender** (to learn):

Yo aprendo	Nosotros apredemos
Tu/Ustéd aprendés	Vosotros aprendeís
Él/Ella aprendé	Ellos/Ellas/Ustedés aprenden.

The past tense for **Aprender** will follow the same type as **Vivir**, keeping in mind that all that changes is the "-er" part or suffix.

Now take some time to explain the different tenses: The present tense is the most common and the one you will be mostly using. It is actions that are taking place in the here and now.

The preterite or past tense is simple enough, and are the actions that have already occurred.

The future tense is something that will happen in the future. The conditional tense is used for words that will happen in the future.

The imperfect describes past actions that are continuously happening.

The imperatives are commands to other people.

There are also irregular verbs.

There aren't that many but a few, and unfortunately, some of the most important verbs are irregular.

They are conjugated differently. You will have to look them up to learn them, but some of them are ser, to be, (indifinitely) estar, to be (in a temporary state), haber (to do), and ir (to go).

They are not complicated but are required that you memorize them. You can find that in the additional resources part of the book.

There are many Spanish tenses, which can become very complicated with all the different, sometimes complicated meanings and uses.

As you grow as a Spanish learner, you can focus more on these tenses, but just getting the basics down can be hard enough, and all you should focus on in the beginning.

You can get by mostly with the present and future tenses, which aren't too hard to learn, then the other five or six main tenses, followed by many others. Remember, keep it simple at first so as not to overwhelm yourself.

Chapter 11: Interrogative Phrases about Personal Characteristics and Information

Asking about personal information is one of the most important things you will need to do especially when meeting someone new. We have already discussed the essential "¿Cuál es tun ombre?" (what is your name?) question.

However, it might be unclear why "cuál" which means "which" is used in Spanish as opposed to "what". The matter is that "cuál" is used to ask information about name, surname, telephone number, address, etc. Since it is and open-ended question, your interlocutor would be able to respond with their respective information.

So, if your question is "¿cuál es tu apellido?" you can get a response such as "mi apellido es López", or simply "López". The type of response will essentially boil down to the level of formality you are looking using.

Other questions you will find useful are:

- ¿Cuántos años tienes? (How old are you?)
- ¿Cuál es tu nacionalidad? (What is your nationality?)
- ¿Cuál es tu trabajo? (What do you do?)
- ¿En dónde vives? (Where do you live?)

These questions will help you get the information you need from people you meet in addition to providing your information.

For example:

¿Cómo se escribe tu nombre? Mi nombre es Fernando. F-E-R-N-A-N-D-O.

¿Cómo se escribe tu apellido? Mi apellido es López. L-Ó-P-E-Z.

¿Cuántos años tienes? Tengo veinte (20) años.

¿En dónde vives? Vivo en Madrid.

Also, these questions use the present simple as you are asking for factual information. As such, there is no need to use any other verb tenses unless you were making specific questions about the past or the future. In such cases, you would need to use the respective tense to get the right information you are looking for.

On the whole, any time you are asking for personal information, the present simple will be enough for you to make a meaningful question. Later on, you can begin to ask and answer questions about the past or the future based on your conversation´s nature for instance, during a job interview. In that case, it would make perfect sense to use the past tense.

So, do take the time to go over the sample questions we have provided for you. They will help you get to know people better, and will also be very useful when providing your own information You will find them useful when meeting new people or perhaps just travelling through from one place to another.

Chapter 12: Alphabet and Pronunciation

Learning the Spanish Alphabet involves three processes: First, you have to know the English Alphabet (a-z with the inclusion of ch, ll, ñ, and rr); Second, you have to know its Spanish equivalent; and Third, you have to learn some friendly tips on how to pronounce it correctly. (Aprender el alfabeto español implica tres procesos: primero, debe conocer el alfabeto inglés (a-z con la inclusión de ch, ll, ñ y rr); Segundo, debes saber su equivalente en español; y Tercero, debes aprender algunos consejos amigables sobre cómo pronunciarlo correctamente.)

The first thing for you to do is start from letter a – i: (Lo primero que debe hacer es comenzar desde la letra a - i:)

English Alphabet (Alfabeto Inglés)	Spanish Equivalent (Equivalente Español)	Friendly Tips on How to Pronounce it Correctly (Consejos Amigables Sobre Cómo Pronunciarlo Correctamente)
A	A	In pronouncing this letter, you must say A as in Ah, which is the same sound you make (Al pronunciar esta letra, debe decir A como en Ah, que es el mismo sonido

		que hace al aceptar algo.)
B	BE	The proper way of pronouncing the letter is just like the same with the letter B in the English Alphabet. (La forma correcta de pronunciar la letra es exactamente igual con la letra B del alfabeto inglés.)
C	CE	It is spelled as CE, but it is pronounced as Se (like the sound of letter S in English Alphabet). Another tip is that in some parts of Spain, it is pronounced as The/Thi (like the sound of Th in the word Thick) (Se deletrea como CE pero se pronuncia como Se (como el sonido de la letra S en alfabeto inglés). Otro consejo es que en algunas partes de

			España, se pronuncia como The / Thi (como el sonido de Th en la palabra Thick)
	CH	CHE	This is no longer considered as a letter in the English Alphabet, but since it is most often used in Spanish conversation, it is still included in this list. It is pronounced as Che/Chi (like the sound of the word Cheese).
			(Esto ya no se considera como una letra en el alfabeto inglés, pero como se usa con mayor frecuencia en la conversación en español, todavía se incluye en esta lista. Se pronuncia como Che / Chi (como el sonido de la palabra Queso)

D	DE	It is pronounced as the letter D of the English Alphabet. It is the same sound used in words like Then, The or They. (Se pronuncia como la letra D del alfabeto inglés. Es el mismo sonido usado en las palabras Then, The o They.)
E	E	If you are going to pronounce this letter, think that it is the same sound you make in clarifying a certain statement. (Eh? Can you please say it again?) (Si va a pronunciar esta letra, piense que es el mismo sonido que hace al aclarar cierta afirmación. (¿Eh? ¿Puedes decirlo de nuevo?)
F	EFE	It is the same sound you use in the English Alphabet F

		only that it is has a letter E at the end. (Es el mismo sonido que usa en el alfabeto inglés F solo que tiene una letra E al final.)
G	GE	When pronounced, it resembles the sound of letter H in English Alphabet and followed by an English letter E. (Cuando se pronuncia, se asemeja al sonido de la letra H en alfabeto inglés y seguido de una letra en inglés E.)
H	HACHE	The correct pronunciation of this is Ah-Che which means it must be silent H. (La pronunciación correcta de esto es Ah-Che, lo que significa que debe ser silencioso H.)
I	I	In pronouncing the letter, it is just the

| | | same with the letter E only that it is shorter than Ee. (Al pronunciar la letra, es igual con la letra E solo que es más corta que Ee.) |

Now, you need to practice using it in a sentence.

(Ahora, necesita practicar su uso en una oración.)

English Alphabet (Alfabeto Inglés)	Spanish Equivalent (Equivalente Español)	Sentence Use (Uso de Oraciones)
A	A	¿A dónde vas? (Where are you going?)
B	BE	La biologia es mi materia favorita. (Biology is my favorite subject.)

C	CE	Mi casa es simple. (My house is simple.)
CH	CHE	Me encanta chatear con mi amigo. (I love chatting with my friend.)
D	DE	Quiero hacer dieta pero también quiero comer mucho. (I want to diet but I also want to eat a lot.)
E	E	No use un signo de exclamación, parece que está enojado. (Do not use an exclamation point, it seems that you are angry.)
F	EFE	Ella es famosa. (She is famous.)
G	GE	Ella tiene una gran boda. (She

		has a great wedding.)
H	HACHE	El hambre es visible hoy en día. (Hunger is visible today.)
I	I	Me gusta construir un imperio. (I like to build an empire.)

Then, continue from letters j – q:

(Luego, continúe de las letras j – q:)

English Alphabet (Alfabeto Inglés)	Spanish Equivalent (Equivalente Español)	Friendly Tips on How to Pronounce it Correctly (Consejos Amigables Sobre Cómo Pronunciarlo Correctamente)
J	JOTA	The proper way of pronouncing it is like the letter H in the English Alphabet.

		Remember that even if is spelled as J however, it does not mean that it should be pronounced as Judge. (La forma correcta de pronunciarlo es como la letra H en el alfabeto inglés. Recuerde que incluso si se deletrea como J, sin embargo, no significa que deba pronunciarse como Juez.)
K	CA	It is not used regularly in the Spanish Language, but for purposes of learning Spanish Grammar, it is pronounced like the English K. (No se usa regularmente en

		español, pero con el propósito de aprender gramática española, se pronuncia como el inglés K.)
L	ELE	The correct pronunciation of this letter is just the same as the letter L in the English Alphabet. However, it is slightly raised to the mouth roof or has a letter E at the end. (La pronunciación correcta de esta letra es la misma con la letra L en alfabeto inglés. Sin embargo, está ligeramente elevado al techo de la boca o

		tiene una letra E al final.)
LL	ELLE	Like Ch, LL is no longer considered as included in the English Alphabet. But, for the purpose of Spanish Grammar, it is still included in this list. It is important because some words contain Ll like yellow. When it comes to proper pronunciation, it resembles the letter J of the English Alphabet. (Al igual que Ch, LL ya no se considera incluido en el alfabeto inglés. Pero, a los efectos de la gramática

		española, todavía se incluye en esta lista. Es importante porque algunas palabras contienen Ll como amarillo. Cuando se trata de una pronunciación adecuada, se asemeja a la letra J del alfabeto inglés.)
M	EME	This is just the same with the English Alphabet M. (Esto es lo mismo con el alfabeto inglés M.)
N	ENE	It is pronounced similarly with the English Alphabet N. (Se pronuncia de manera similar

		con el alfabeto inglés N.)
Ñ	EÑE	For the correct pronunciation of this letter, it is similar to the Ni in the English word Onion. (Para la pronunciación correcta de esta letra, es similar con el Ni en la palabra inglesa Onion.)
O	O	This is a short version of the English Alphabet O. (Esta es una versión corta del alfabeto inglés O.)
P	P	You have to hold your breath and breathe out minimally as you pronounce the letter P in English

		Alphabet. (Debe contener la respiración y exhalar mínimamente mientras pronuncia la letra P en alfabeto inglés.)
Q	CU	In order for you to properly pronounce this letter, you have to combine K of the English Alphabet and the letter U of the same English Alphabet. (Para poder pronunciar correctamente esta letra, debe combinar K del alfabeto inglés y la letra U del mismo alfabeto inglés.)

For a better understanding of the Spanish Alphabet, it is important to test our ability by using these letters in sentences: (Para una mejor comprensión del alfabeto español, es importante probar nuestra habilidad mediante el uso de estas letras en oraciones:)

English Alphabet (Alfabeto Inglés)	Spanish Equivalent (Equivalente Español)	Sentence Use (Uso de Oraciones)
J	JOTA	Soy español pero hablo japonés. (I am Spanish but I speak Japanese.)
K	CA	Puedo caminar 1 kilómetro. (I can walk 1 kilometer.)
L	ELE	Uso la lámpara si no hay corriente. (I use the lamp if there is no power.)
LL	ELLE	Se llama felicidad. (It is called happiness.)

M	EME	Eres tan magnifico. (You are so magnificent.)
N	ENE	Amo nadar. (I love swimming.)
Ñ	EÑE	Tengo miedo de ñus. (I am scared of wildebeest.)
O	O	¿Que es la ocasion? (What is the occasion?)
P	P	Me gusta el pimiento rojo. (I like red pepper.)
Q	CU	¿Por qué te pones rojo? (Why do you wear red?)

Then the last batch of letters in the Spanish Alphabet is from r – z:

(Entonces el último lote de letras en el alfabeto español es de r - z:)

English Alphabet (Alfabeto Inglés)	Spanish Equivalent (Equivalente Español)	Friendly Tips on How to Pronounce it Correctly (Consejos Amigables Sobre Cómo Pronunciarlo Correctamente)
R	ERE	It sounds like the letter R in the English Alphabet, only that it is slightly touching the roof of the mouth. Aside from that, there is a letter E at the end of the word. (Suena como la letra R en el alfabeto inglés, solo que toca ligeramente el paladar. Aparte de eso, hay una letra E al final de la palabra.)

RR	DOBLE ERE	Again, just like the Ch and the Ll, Rr is not included in the letters of the English Alphabet. But for purposes of learning the Spanish Language, there is a need for it to be understood. It is a little difficult, but with practice, everything will be easier. For instance, the word butter, the Tt is similar to the Rr. When pronounced using the American pronunciation, you have to remember how did you pronounce the Tt in the middle of the word butter, that will be how you will pronounce words with Rr too. (Nuevamente, al igual que Ch y Ll, Rr no está incluido en las letras del

		alfabeto inglés. Pero para aprender el idioma español, es necesario que se entienda. Es un poco difícil pero con práctica, todo será más fácil. Por ejemplo, la palabra mantequilla, el Tt es similar al Rr. Cuando se pronuncia usando la pronunciación americana, debe recordar cómo pronunció el Tt en el medio de la palabra mantequilla, así también pronunciará las palabras con Rr.)
S	ESE	When pronounced, it is similar to the English Alphabet S. (Cuando se pronuncia, es similar con el alfabeto inglés S.)
T	TE	It is almost the same with the

		English Alphabet T however in Spanish it is shorter and softer, touching the teeth with the tongue and immediately released. (Es casi lo mismo con el alfabeto inglés T, sin embargo, en español es más corto y suave, toca los dientes con la lengua y se libera de inmediato.)
U	U	It is very much simple to understand since it is similar to Oo, as in the case of word food. (Es muy simple de entender ya que es similar con Oo como en el caso de la palabra comida.)
V	VE	It was discussed in letter B of the Spanish Alphabet that it is similar to

		this V in English Alphabet. There is less breathing, and there is only a slight touch of the tongue to the teeth. (En la letra B del alfabeto español se discutió que es similar con esta V en el alfabeto inglés. Hay menos respiración y solo hay un ligero toque de la lengua a los dientes.)
W	DOBLE VE	It is being pronounced as Dob-leh Be. However, in the English Alphabet, it is similar to the English Alphabet W. (Se pronuncia como Dob-leh Be. Sin embargo, en el alfabeto inglés, es similar con el alfabeto inglés W.)
X	EQUIS	It is very easy to pronounce this letter, as it is only

			pronounced ks. For instance, in the word socks, the last two letters of which (ks) is the sound of X in the English Alphabet. (Es muy fácil pronunciar esta letra, ya que solo se pronuncia ks. Por ejemplo, en la palabra calcetines, las dos últimas letras (ks) son el sonido de X en alfabeto inglés.)
Y	I GRIEGA		The sound of this letter is Ee Gryeh-gah. It sounds like the letter Y of the English Alphabet. But at the end of the word, it may sound like I (pronounced as Hay) and Ye. (El sonido de esta carta es Ee Gryeh-gah. Suena como la letra Y del alfabeto inglés. Pero al final de la palabra, puede

		sonar como I (pronunciado como Hay) y Ye.)
Z	ZETA	It is pronounced as Se-tah or the letter S of the English Alphabet. However, in some parts of Spain, they pronounce it as Th like in the word Thick or Thin. (Se pronuncia como Se-tah o la letra S del alfabeto inglés. Sin embargo, en algunas partes de España, lo pronuncian como Th como en la palabra Grueso o Fino.)

Now, you should use this last batch of letters in the Spanish Alphabet in a sentence in order for you to practice the word pronunciation: (Ahora, debe usar este último lote de letras en el alfabeto español en una oración para poder practicar la pronunciación de la palabra:)

English Alphabet	Spanish Equivalent	Sentence Use

(Alfabeto Inglés)	(Equivalente Español)	(Uso de Oraciones)
R	ERE	Eres tan raro. (You are so weird.)
RR	DOBLE ERE	Es irrevocable, con i al principio. (It is irrevocable, with I at the beginning.)
S	ESE	Es un lugar sagrado. (It is a sacred place.)
T	TE	¿Usas productos de tabaco? (Do you use tobacco products?)
U	U	Ella es tan ubicua. (She is so ubiquitous.)
V	VE	No hay vacantes en esta oficina. (There are no vacanies in this office.)
W	DOBLE VE	Te gusta el whiskería? (Do you like whiskey?)

X	EQUIS	Me encanta tocar el xilófono. (I love playing the xylophone.)
Y	I GRIEGA	Mi sueño es viajar en un yate. (My dream is to travel on a yacht.)
Z	ZETA	Me gustaría ir al zoológico. (I would like to go to the zoo.)

How Interactions Build Spanish Language Mastery

As much as it's important to memorize the words, it's also important to learn to speak. Fluency in the Spanish language can be achieved through various methods, but in this chapter, we will focus on interaction as a way of mastering the Spanish language.

We communicate every day through conversations, phone calls, social media, text, and emails. Interaction is how we communicate and exchange ideas. So you might say that language is inherently interactive. We may define interaction as two people or things that have an influence or affect each other. In this context, two or more people exchange ideas and information and influence each other positively.

Interacting with other people and our environment is how we learned our native languages as babies. Also, listening and interacting with those around us help form our vocabulary and knowledge. Interaction works when learning a new language because it is simple, and it's natural.

There is a theory in language that when learning a new language as an interactive process between a learner and a native speaker, communication and fluency are easily achieved. The native speaker modifies the language and makes it easier for you as a beginner to learn the language. The proficient speaker will use known vocabulary, speaking slowly and clearly. The native speaker will adjust the topic, avoid idioms, and use simpler grammatical structures. In this way, the input facilitates you with a better understanding of the Spanish language.

When interacting with a proficient speaker, you get a chance to ask questions in areas that you haven't understood. It helps you in the comprehension of the language. Interactions of this kind help in language facilitation, and evidence will be seen in the long run as your grammar accuracy, and Spanish fluency improve.

Conclusion

You know how difficult it can be for anyone to learn a foreign language. But you dared take the first step towards fluency by having this book in your hands and actively reading it. This book is the tool you needed to solidify what you previously learned, and that's going to be very useful for you.

Practice and imitate how these structures, how the verbs, nouns, adjectives, and expressions are used in the way they appear in these conversations.

Most of the time, that person will be delighted to hear another person trying to learn and speak their language. They will surely help you if you really express yourself in a very kind, respectful and polite manner.

Finding Spanish-speaking friends is a great way to test your new language skills. Any Spanish-speaking friends you might have will likely be more than willing to help you practice what you have learned in this book. Also, this type of practice and exposure will enable you to play with the language to become comfortable with going off-script. This will allow you to truly begin to communicate through the use of what you have actually learned.

We are confident that you found the content in this book useful in any situation. In fact, don't be surprised if you get caught in learning Spanish. You might even choose to pursue your learning even further.

It is important to keep in mind that you do not need to study two or three hours a day. Of course, if you can spare that much time, your skills will skyrocket in a relatively short period of time. But if you are busy like most folks, taking 15 or 20 minutes out of your day to go over these conversations will make a great start. You can always ramp up the time devoted to Spanish study as your schedule allows it.

Another important recommendation is to keep a vocabulary notebook. This can be a regular notebook or just a small notepad. Even if you are paperless, it certainly helps to write things down. The science behind this is that writing words will help your brain fix them in your memory. So what it does is it forces your brain to take physical note of it. This is the main reason children write things over and over again.

SPANISH SHORT STORIES FOR BEGINNERS

The Best Way to Learn a Language, Improve Your Vocabulary Gradually and Quickly at Home, on the Road, in Travel or in the Car Like Crazy with Common Phrases

Living Languages

Introduction

Perhaps you are new to Spanish and are looking for an entertaining challenge. Or maybe you have been learning for a while and simply want to enjoy reading whilst growing your vocabulary. Either way, this book is the biggest step forward you will take in your Spanish this year.

If you are brand new to learning Spanish, you will find that mastering this beautiful language is not nearly hard as might have thought it would have been. If you have studied Spanish before, you will find this volume to be useful in improving your overall proficiency with the language.

For most folks, learning another language is a dream. In other cases, it might be a necessity due to professional reasons. For other folks, they are just keen on picking up useful language before heading off on a trip. Whatever your individual motivations are, you will find this book to be both useful and informative.

Overall, learning languages boils down to practice and dedication. In short, the more time and dedication you are able to give a language, the faster you will be able to learn it. Now, there are some folks who have a natural ability for learning a language. This knack makes it somewhat easier to pick up new words and phrases.

That is why this book has been designed to revolve around your schedule and your lifestyle. You won't have to take classes or cut out other important activities from your life in order to study Spanish. These lessons can be studied and reviewed on the fly. So, whether you're standing in line at the bank or just have a few minutes on your hands while you are grabbing a coffee, you can use these lessons to brush up on your Spanish.

Chapter 1: Paolo y la Sirena

Paolo es un niño que vive en Italia en la costa de un lago. Incluso la gente y los botes que pasan pueden ser vistos desde su casa. Cuando hay buen clima y el sol sale, a Paolo le gusta jugar con sus dos hermanos Marco y Pietro en la orilla.

Frecuentemente juegan a la pelota y el mejor siempre es Pietro. Va a ser un futbolista profesional cuando crezca.

En cambio, cuando no hay buen clima, Paolo se queda en casa y desde la ventana admira las olas del lago que rompen en las rocas.

Paolo es un niño al que a veces le gusta estar solo, ama ir al lago y caminar recogiendo los caparazones que el lago le da.

Un día vio una sirena salir del agua e ir hacia él. Paolo se acerca a ella y ve que esta llorando y está muy triste. Paolo le pregunta: "¿Por qué estás triste?"

"Porque mi papá me dejó sola", dijo la sirena.

"No te preocupes, vivo cerca de aquí y hoy puedes venir a mi casa, comer y descansar conmigo."

Paolo se llevó a la sirena a su casa. Tan pronto como su mamá vio a la sirena, la abrazó y comenzó a halagarla. Nunca había visto una sirena viva, por lo tanto estaba muy emocionada.

Tan pronto como el papá de Paolo la vio, se preocupó porque no estaba en el agua, e inmediatamente la llevó a la piscina afuera de la casa.

Paolo entró en la piscina en el agua, y comenzó a jugar con la sirena. Finalmente, estaba tranquila y había dejado de llorar.

"¿Estás feliz ahora?" Preguntó Paolo

"Sí, me siento mejor ahora, pero siempre pienso en mi papá", respondió la sirena.

"La piscina es hermosa, pero prefiero quedarme con mis amigos peces en el lago", agregó.

Al escuchar esto, Paolo corrió a la tienda de animales para comprarle un pequeño pez dorado. Cuando regresó a casa, le dijo a la sirena:

"¿Te sientes mejor ahora? Puedes ser la amiga de este pez dorado."

La sirena comenzó a cantar felizmente y Paolo entendió que se sentía mucho mejor.

"Estoy más feliz que antes, pero aún sigo un poco triste porque pienso en mi papá; amaba jugar conmigo, y yo con él. También extraño las rocas y las algas del lago", replicó la sirena.

Tan pronto como Paolo escuchó estas palabras, se dirigió a la tienda de mascotas y compró rocas y algas para poner en la piscina. En cuanto regresó a casa le dijo a la sirena:

"¿Estás feliz ahora que también tendrás las piedras y algas que extrañabas?"

"Si, me siento mejor pero aún no estoy feliz porque el lago es mi casa."

"Ok, entonces te llevaré al lago y me despediré de ti; ¿estás feliz ahora?"

"Me siento mejor, pero no estoy feliz porque te extranaré; ¿por qué no vienes y vives conmigo en el lago?"

Paolo pensó en lo agradable que sería vivir en el lago, podría conocer a todos los peces y jugar con ellos, podría jugar en las olas, pero entonces pensó en lo triste que se sentiría sin su mamá y papá. Entonces dijo:

"Gracias sirena, pero no iré contigo."

La sirena volteó su cola y desapareció en medio del agua.

Esa noche, antes de ir a dormir, la mamá le preguntó a Paolo, "¿Eres feliz?"

"Me siento mejor, pero extraño a la sirena" y puso el caparazón cerca de su oído para escuchar el sonido del lago y se durmió pensando en ella.

Ejercicio

Ok, ahora hagamos un ejercicio rápido: te haré 5 preguntas. Trata de responder y luego de las preguntas, te daré las respuestas.

Preguntas
1) ¿Cuál es el nombre de los hermanos de Paolo?
2) ¿Qué hizo Paolo cuando vio a la sirena llorando?
3) ¿Por qué lloraba la sirena?
4) ¿Qué hizo el papá de Paolo cuando Paolo y la sirena llegaron a casa?
5) ¿Qué le compró a la sirena para hacerla feliz cuando extrañaba a sus amigos?

Respuestas
1) Marco y Pietro
2) Le dijo que fuera a su casa
3) Porque extrañaba a su papá
4) La llevó afuera, a la piscina
5) Un pez dorado

Paolo and The Siren

Paolo was a young boy who lives in Italy along the shore of a lake. Even the people and boats passing by could be seen from his house. When the weather was nice, and the sun was out, Paolo liked to play with his two brothers Marco and Pietro on the lakeside.

They often played ball, and the best was always Pietro. He would grow up to be a professional footballer.

When the weather was bad, Paolo remained at home instead, and from the window, he admired the waves of the lake that break on the rocks.

Paolo was sometimes a child who liked to be alone, and he loved walking by the lake and picking up the shells that the lake gave him.

One day he saw a siren come out of the water and come towards him. Paolo approached her and saw that the siren was crying and was very sad. Paolo asked her: "Why are you sad?"

"Because my dad left me alone," said the siren.

"Don't worry, I live near here, and tonight you can come to my house, eat and rest with me."

Paolo took the siren to his home. As soon as his mother saw the siren, she hugged her and started to compliment her. She had never seen a live siren, so she was very excited.

As soon as Paolo's father saw her, he began to worry because she was not in the water and immediately took her to the pool outside the house.

Paolo entered the pool and started playing with the siren. Finally, she was quiet, and she wasn't crying anymore.

"Are you happy now?" asked Paolo.

"Yes, I feel better now, but I always think about my dad," the siren answered.

"The pool is beautiful, but I prefer to stay with my fish friends in the lake," she added.

Upon hearing this, Paolo ran to the pet shop to buy her a small goldfish. When he got home, he put it in the pool with the siren and said:

"Are you feeling better now? You can become a friend of this goldfish."

The siren started to sing happily, and Paolo understood that she felt much better.

"I'm happier than before, but I'm still a little sad because I think of my dad; he loved playing with me, and me with him. Also, I miss the pebbles, and the seaweed of the lake," replied the siren.

As soon as Paolo heard these words, he went to the pet shop and bought pebbles and seaweed to put in the pool. Immediately once he returned home, he said to the siren:

"Are you happy now that you also have the pebbles and the seaweed you missed?"

"Yes, I feel better, but I'm still not happy because the lake is my home."

"Ok, then I'll take you back to the lake and I'll say goodbye; will you be happy then?"

"I will feel better, but I'm not happy because I'll miss you. Why don't you come and live with me in the lake?"

Paolo thought about how nice it would be for him to live in the lake. He could meet all the fish and play with them, he could play in the waves, but then he thought how sad he would be without his mother and father. So, he said:

"Thank you, siren, but I won't come with you."

The family took her to the lake, and the siren turned the tail and disappeared into the middle of the water.

That night, before going to bed, the mom asked Paolo:

"Are you happy?"

"I feel better, but I miss the siren," then he put the shell near to his ear to hear the sound of the lake, and he fell asleep thinking about her.

Exercise

Ok, let's now start a quick exercise: I am going to ask you 5 questions. Try to reply, and after the questions, I will give you the answers.

Questions
1) What are the names of Paolo's brothers?
2) What did Paolo do when he saw the siren crying?
3) Why was the siren crying?
4) What did Paolo's father do as Paolo and the siren arrived home?
5) What did Paolo buy for the siren in order to make her happy when she was missing her friends?

Answers
1) Marco and Pietro
2) He told her to come to his house
3) Because she was missing her father
4) He took her into the pool outside
5) A goldfish

Chapter 2: Los Cazadores Locales

Érase una vez, tres cazadores que se hicieron amigos. Se conocieron en el bosque durante una de las expediciones anuales de cacería de la comunidad. Cada uno admiraba las habilidades de caza del otro, y por esa razón, se hicieron buenos amigos. Uno de los tres aún era un cazador novato.

Siempre preferían cazar en el bosque mas denso y oscuro de la comunidad, donde los árboles con formas complejas y superpuestas formaban una canoa extensa. El bosque contenía muchos animales salvajes, grandes y pequeños, que lo hacían uno de los bosques más peligrosos de la región. Los árboles altos y gigantes del bosque con sus grandes hojas y ramas prevenían que la luz del sol penetrara el bosque, dandole a la atmósfera una apariencia oscura y terrorífica.

Los tres amigos cazaban juntos para alimentarse, no como deporte. Cada uno tenía su preferencia de carne, y cada uno rezaba para que sus balas caras nunca fallaran cuando apretaran el gatillo.

Para cazar en un bosque como ese, había que ser cuidadoso. Para tener éxito, el lugar de caza tenía que permitirle a los cazadores permanecer sin ser vistos. También tenían que estar cerca uno del otro para poderse comunicar ya que la visibilidad estaba limitada. Para iluminar, evitaban usar luz blanca, ya que asustaba a los animales. En cambio, hacían uso de los lentes de visión nocturna.

David, Micheal y Lucas se habían encontrado temprano un viernes y decidieron cazar la semana siguiente. Hicieron como acordaron. Ese día, caminaron dentro del bosque oscuro hasta que llegaron a un punto donde se escondieron. Luego de muchas horas esperando, ni un animal se cruzo con ellos.

"Micheal y Lucas, esta noche no se ve prometedora." Dijo David.

"¿Qué te hace decir eso?" Pregunta Michael.

"Porque no hemos visto ni un animal desde que llegamos." Responde David.

Lucas replica "No te olvides, David, que siempre hay que tener paciencia cuando cazamos tanto como necesitamos las balas para disparar."

"¿Por cuánto tiempo ejercitamos esta paciencia?" Pregunta David.

"¡Por el tiempo que haga falta para tener éxito!" Dice Lucas.

David era el novato entre ellos. En su espera, pasó algo de tiempo antes de que de pronto, vieran una manada de cerdos pasando ruidosamente a través de un camino estrecho en el bosque.

"Hey David" dijo Micheal, "ve hasta allá y mata tantos cerdos como quieras" anunció.

"Sabes muy bien que no me gustan los cerdos salvajes", David agregó.

"Entonces sugiero que cambiemos de lugar", dijo Micheal, saltando del espacio oculto con gran agilidad mientras los otros le siguieron. Entonces, un león que no habían notado a tiempo, ya estaba corriendo en su dirección.

"¡Dispara! ¡Dispara! Gritó Lucas, quien rápidamente intentó apuntar al animal salvaje rápidamente. Antes de que hubiese podido disparar, la bala de David ya había hecho lo necesario.

Estaban obviamente emocionados por su presa. David sabía muy bien que su éxito era resultado de la paciencia.

"Precisamente, la paciencia realmente paga", dijo David.

Ejercicio

Ok, ahora hagamos un ejercicio rápido: te haré 6 preguntas. Trata de responder y luego de las preguntas, te daré las respuestas.

Preguntas
1) ¿Cuál es el nombre del cazador novato?
2) ¿En qué ocasión los 3 cazadores se hicieron amigos?
3) ¿Por qué tenían que evitar el uso de la luz blanca?
4) Comida o deporte, ¿por cuál piensas que ellos cazaban?
5) ¿En qué tipo de bosque preferían cazar?

6) ¿Qué instrumento ayudaba a su visión?

Respuestas
1) DAVID
2) La expedición anual de caza
3) Porque asustaba a los animales
4) COMIDA
5) Bosque denso y oscuro
6) Lentes de visión nocturna

The Local Hunters

Once upon a time, there lived three hunters who became friends with one another. They met in the forest during one of their community's annual hunting expeditions. Each admired the hunting skills of the other, and for that reason alone, they became good friends. One of the three was still an amateur hunter.

They always preferred hunting in the thickest and darkest forest of the community, where trees with complex overlapping shapes formed an endless expanse of the canoe. The forest contained many wild animals, big and small, that made it one of the most dangerous forests within the entire region. The tall, giant trees of the forest, with their gigantic leaves and branches, prevented daylight from penetrating the forest, giving the atmosphere a scary, dark appearance.

The three friends hunted together for food, not for sport. Each had his individual choice of meat, which they prayed their expensive bullet would not miss whenever the trigger was pulled.

To hunt in such a forest, one had to be careful. To succeed, the hunting location had to be such that the hunters could remain unseen. They also had to stay near to each other so that they could easily communicate since visibility was limited. For lighting, they avoided the use of white light, for it scared away animals. Instead, they made use of night vision goggles.

David, Michael, and Lucas had met earlier on a Friday and decided they would hunt the following week. They did as they had agreed. On the very day, they walked deep into the dark forest until they reached a spot where they made their hiding place. After many hours of waiting, not a single animal had crossed their path.

"Michael and Lucas, tonight doesn't seem very promising." Said, David.

"What makes you say that?" Asked Michael.

"Because we have not seen a single animal since we arrived." Answered David.

Lucas replies "Do not forget, David that we always need patience when hunting, as much as we need our bullets to shoot."

"How long are we going to exercise this patience for?" Asked David.

"For as long as we need to, to succeed!" Said Lucas.

David was the amateur among them. They waited for quite a long time before they suddenly saw a swine of pigs passing noisily across a narrow path in the forest.

"Hey David," said Michael, "go over there and shoot as many pigs as you wish," he announced.

"You know very well that I don't like wild pigs," David added.

"Then I suggest we change location," said Michael. Jumping out of the hidden spot with great agility while the others followed. Suddenly, a lion which they hadn't noticed in time was already rushing towards their direction.

"Shoot! Shoot!" Shouted Lucas, who very quickly tried to aim at the fast-approaching wild animal. Before he could pull his trigger, David's bullet had already done the needful.

They were all obviously excited about their prey. David knew quite well that their success came as a result of patience.

"Indeed, patience really pays off," said David.

Exercise

Ok, let's now start a quick exercise: I am going to ask you 6 questions. Try to reply, and after the questions, I will give you the answers.

Questions
1) What is the name of the amateur hunter?
2) On what occasion did the three hunters become friends?
3) Why did they have to avoid the use of white light?
4) Food or sport, which do you think they hunted for?
5) What type of forest did they prefer to hunt in?

6) What instrument aided their view?

Answers
   1) David
   2) Annual hunting expedition
   3) Because it scared away animals
   4) Food
   5) Thick dark forest
   6) Night vision goggles

Chapter 3: Un Ángel en La Miseria

Después de la muerte de sus padres, Fátima empezó a dormir en las calles sucias de Calcuta, juntos con muchos otros niños malnutridos y desamparados que compartían el mismo destino.

Cuán despiadada es la vida a veces. Fátima duerme bajo el puente con casi nada para comer. Usa ropa sucia que son mas trapos que vestidos. Los niños de la calle son propensos a muchos retos y todo tipo de abusos.

La educación de Fátima se ha detenido abruptamente del día a la noche. Todavía le cuesta creer que todo lo que sonaba lograr ha sido tirado a la basura luego del repentino fallecimiento de sus padres en un tren descarrilado. Muchos de sus amigos luchan con sus traumas entre hombros decaídos y ojos débiles que parecen estar conquistados por la derrota.

A pesar de tener el corazón roto, Fátima no va a dejar que la tristeza se apodere de ella. No ha perdido la fe y aun cree que su cruel condición no implica una sentencia de muerte. Toma coraje compartiendo lindas historias con sus amigos y ayudándolos en cualquier forma que pueda.

Su gran intelecto nunca le ha fallado. A veces, recoge libros de la basura y absorbe alegremente el conocimiento en ellos.

Otros niños de la calle la admiran y la ven como la mas confiable y brillante de todos.

"Siempre me he preguntado porqué eres diferente del resto de nosotros", habló una voz conocida para Fátima.

"¿Cómo logras mantener la esperanza sin ver el mundo con manos indefensas como muchos hacemos?" la voz concluyó.

"Bueno", comenzó Fátima, "a veces cometemos el error de compararnos con otras personas. Hacerlo, da la falsa impresión que tienen todo, pero nadie lo tiene. Todos somos seres humanos atravesando los mismos retos. La fuerza viene cuando aceptas ser la razón de la felicidad de otro, que es lo que yo busco lograr", explicó.

Muy satisfecho, el curioso preguntador abrazo a Fátima. "Gracias", dijo, "muchas gracias" repitió entusiasta, "he aprendido algo maravilloso hoy", anunció, suspirando de alivio.

"Debemos buscar el progreso, en vez de permitirnos estar atormentados por el odio. Somos muy útiles y hermosos a nuestra manera" Fátima le informó, sintiéndose bien de nuevo por haber dado vida a uno de sus amigos.

Ejercicio

Ok, ahora hagamos un ejercicio rápido: te haré 5 preguntas. Trata de responder y luego de las preguntas, te daré las respuestas.

Preguntas
1) ¿Qué le pasó a los padres de Fátima?
2) ¿Dónde duerme Fátima?
3) ¿Qué recoge Fátima a veces de la basura?
4) Los niños de la calle sufren de todo tipo de abusos. ¿Verdadero o falso?
5) ¿Qué le gusta compartir a Fátima con sus amigos?

Respuestas
1) Murieron en un tren descarrilado
2) Bajo el puente
3) Libros
4) Verdadero
5) Lindas historias

Angel in the Squalor

After the passing away of her parents, Fatima began sleeping in the dirty streets of Kolkata, together with many other malnourished and neglected children who shared a similar fate.

How merciless life can be sometimes. Fatima sleeps under a bridge with hardly anything to eat. She wears dirty clothes that are more like rags than apparel. Street children are often prone to extreme challenges of all kinds, especially physical abuse and molestation.

Fatima's education has come to an abrupt halt overnight. She still finds it hard to believe that all that she dreamt of achieving has now been thrown into the mud following the sudden demise of her parents in a train wreck. Many of her friends struggle with the trauma with stooped shoulders and weak eyes that seem to acknowledge defeat.

Though broken-hearted, Fatima won't allow her sorrow to take absolute hold of her. She hasn't lost faith in life and still believes that her cruel condition doesn't imply a death sentence. She takes courage in sharing sweet stories with her friends and helping them in whatever little ways she can.

Her bright intellect has never failed her. Sometimes she picks books out of waste bins and happily absorbs the knowledge contained therein.

She is looking upon by other street children as the most reliable, and by far the most brilliant, of them all.

"I have always wondered why you are different from the rest of us," spoke a familiar voice, "how do you manage to keep hope alive without watching the world and feeling helpless as most of us do?" the voice concluded.

"You see," started Fatima, "we sometimes make the mistake of comparing ourselves with other people. Doing so gives the wrong impression that they have it all, but no one does. We are all human beings going through the same universal challenges. Strength comes when one accepts that being the reason for another's happiness is what you want to achieve," she explained.

Deeply satisfied, the curious questioner embraced Fatima. "Thank you," she said, "thank you so much," she repeated enthusiastically, "I have learned something wonderfully new today." She announced, breathing a sigh of relief.

"We must strive for progress rather than allow ourselves to be tormented by self-hate. We are all very useful and beautiful in our own ways," Fatima informed her, feeling good again that she had given life to one of her formerly dejected friends.

Exercise

Ok, let's now start a quick exercise: I am going to ask you 5 questions. Try to reply, and after the questions, I will give you the answers.

Questions
1) What happened to Fatima's parents?
2) Where does Fatima sleep?
3) What does Fatima sometimes pick out from waste bins?
4) Street children suffer from physical abuse and molestation. True or False?
5) What does Fatima like sharing with her friends?

Answers
1) Died in a train wreck
2) Under the bridge
3) Books
4) True
5) Sweet stories

Chapter 4: La Buena Madre

Mamá estaba cansada de las noticias. También de la avena que comía con la boca llena. Su ansiedad era principalmente porque ya no viajaría mas a China. Con sus maletas ya empacadas, la razón por la que cambio de idea al último minuto aún era desconocida. Había querido viajar a uno de los sitios históricos de China, incluyendo el primer puente de China conocido como el puente Zhaozhou el cual fue construido 1400 años atrás. Se decía que era el puente mas antiguo del mundo.

El sol estaba caliente. Mamá se acomodo en la silla que estaba en la esquina izquierda del porche. Se veía absorbida en sus pensamientos. Tenía tres hijos, pero John era con quien inicialmente había planeado su viaje. Aparte de ella, John era quien de hecho había recibido las noticias de la cancelación con shock e indignación. John estaba ocupado pasando las páginas de una de las revistas de niños que su madre compraba al menos dos veces a la semana para ayudarlo a ganar conocimiento y mejorar su vocabulario. Se negó a voltear cuando escuchó el sonido de los pasos de mamá, ni cuando notó que lo estaba viendo; presionó sus labios como signo externo de protesta.

Mamá podía claramente leer el lenguaje corporal de su hijo. Sabia que John no estaba feliz de que ella hubiese cancelado su viaje. Todo era culpa de ella. Si hubiese explicado a John porque tomó esa medida tan drástica, tal vez hubiese entendido.

"Si yo fuese un niño pequeño", dijo la madre, "no me comportaría de esta manera con mi madre" dijo, doblando sus dedos delgados. "Habíamos planeado ir a Hong Kong antes de ir al territorio principal de China, pero hay continuas protestas en Hong Kong" dijo ella, mirando a John quien estaba desanimado.

"Hoy en las noticias, los protestantes estaban usando bombas de petróleo como arma. Hong Kong es ahora en caos, con cientos de tiendas destruidas. No me gustaría llevarte a ninguna dirección que no sea segura. Considera cuan peligroso hubiese sido, y reconoce que actué de buena fe." Concluyó.

"Mamá", lloró John, "¿que pasará cuando te asegures de que la violencia ha terminado?" preguntó, alzando su cabeza.

"¿Qué más, John?", dijo mamá con un suspiro de alivio, "entonces no tendremos razón para quedarnos", explicó.

John, un niño de 6 años, recuperó la esperanza luego de la promesa de su madre. Estaba convencido de que un día despertaría con mejores noticias acerca de Hong Kong.

Ejercicio

Ok, ahora hagamos un ejercicio rápido: te haré 5 preguntas. Trata de responder y luego de las preguntas, te daré las respuestas.

Preguntas
1) ¿Por qué la mamá de John canceló su viaje?
2) ¿Cuál es el nombre del puente que a la mamá de John le hubiese gustado ver si hubiese viajado?
3) ¿Cuántos niños tenía la mamá de John en total?
4) ¿Por qué John presionaba sus labios?
5) ¿Cuántos años tenía John?

Respuestas
1) Por las protestas violentas en Hong Kong
2) Puente Zhaozhou
3) TRES
4) Porque estaba molesto
5) 6 años

The Good Mother

Mother was sick of the news and was also sick of the tasty oatmeal that she had taken a mouthful of. Her anxiety was mostly because she wouldn't be traveling to China anymore. Her stuff was already packed up, but the reason why she had changed her mind at the last minute was as yet unknown. She had wanted to travel to some of the historic sites in China, including China's first bridge known as the Zhaozhou Bridge, which was constructed 1,400 years ago. It was said to be the oldest bridge in the world.

The sun was hot. Mother settled herself comfortably in the deck-chair that was on the left corner of the veranda. She actually looked absorbed in thought. She had three children, but John was the one she had initially planned to travel with. Beside her was John who had received the news of the cancellation with utter shock and indignation. John was busy flipping through one of his children's magazines, which his mother bought him at least twice a week to help him gain knowledge and improve his vocabulary. He refused to turn his gaze when he heard the clacking sounds of mother's footsteps, but rather when he noticed mother was looking at him, he pursed his lips as an outward sign of protest.

Mother could clearly read her son's body language. She knew John wasn't happy she had canceled their journey. It was all her fault. If she had explained to John why she took the drastic measure, perhaps he would have understood.

"If I were a little boy," said the mother, "I wouldn't behave this way to my mother," she said, folding her slim fingers. "We had planned to visit Hong Kong before traveling to mainland China, but there is an ongoing series of demonstrations in Hong Kong," she said, looking at John who was in a dejected mood.

"On the news today, the protesters were making use of petrol bombs as a weapon. Hong Kong is now in a state of chaos with hundreds of shops destroyed. I wouldn't like to take you anywhere that is not safe. Consider how dangerous it would be, and understand that I acted in good faith," she concluded.

"Mother," cried John, "what happens when you are sure the violence is over?" He asked, raising his head half way.

"What else, John," mother said with a sigh of relief, "we will then have no reason to stay away," she explained.

John, a boy of six, regained hope after his mother's assurances. He was convinced he would wake up one morning with better news about Hong Kong.

Exercise

Ok, let's now start a quick exercise: I am going to ask you 5 questions. Try to reply, and after the questions, I will give you the answers.

Questions
1) Why did John's mother cancel her journey?
2) What is the name of the bridge John's mother would have liked to see if she had traveled?
3) How many children did John's mother have in total?
4) Why did John purse his lips?
5) How old was John?

Answers
1) Because of the violent protests in Hong Kong

2) Zhaozhou Bridge
3) Three
4) He was angry
5) Six years old

Chapter 5: Jamari, El Estudiante Serio

Jamari es un estudiante egipcio que llegó al Reino Unido hace tres años persiguiendo la carrera de sus sueños. Estudia en la universidad de Wolverhampton, en Reino Unido. Está estudiando arquitectura y quiere ser uno de los mas grandes arquitectos de todos los tiempos.

Jamari nació y se crio en Turquía. Antes de decidir tomar arquitectura, había admirado profundamente los maravillosos edificios de la era bizantina que encontraba por todas las calles de Estambul, en Turquía

Hagia Sofia fue lo que mas impresiono a Jamari. El edificio es uno de los mas famosos y espectaculares de la era bizantina. Su construcción comenzó entre los anos 532 y 537 a.C. Originalmente fue usado como catedral, y luego como mezquita durante la era Otomana.

En 1931, estuvo cerrado al público y fue reabierto como museo en 1935. En el año 2015, el ministerio de cultura y turismo de Turquía lo listó como la atracción turística mas visitada en la República de Turquía.

Jamari siempre se había preguntado como una obra de arquitectura tan impresionante había sido posible para los arquitectos que operaban cuando la tecnología era menos avanzada y sofisticada. Jamari se enorgullece mucho de las tres pirámides localizadas en Gaza. También esta al tanto de uno de los mejores arquitectos de los tiempos modernos, como Antonio Gaudi, quien diseñó la prestigiosa Sagrada familia, una catedral en Barcelona con columnas como árboles, de una estética remarcable. También sabe de Frank Lloyd Wright, un nativo de

Wisconsin quien uso geometría como elemento importante de su diseño más famoso, Casa de la cascada. Jamari es uno de los más brillantes y entusiastas de sus amigos. Cuando hizo su viaje al Reino Unido, tenía grandes cosas en mente. Simplemente quería ser el mejor.

"¿Qué es la arquitectura?" su padre le había preguntado en broma durante una de sus vacaciones escolares.

"Papá", sonrió, "es el arte o práctica de diseñar y construir edificios." Jamari respondió con confianza perceptible. "¿Alguna otra pregunta?" dijo Jamari.

"No por hoy", dijo su papá riendo.

Ejercicio

Ok, ahora hagamos un ejercicio rápido: te haré 5 preguntas. Trata de responder y luego de las preguntas, te daré las respuestas.

Preguntas
1) ¿Qué está estudiando Jamari en el Reino Unido?
2) ¿Cuál es el nombre del edificio que mas inspiro a Jamari mientras estaba en Turquía?
3) ¿Dónde creció Jamari?
4) ¿Qué edificio diseño Antonio Gaudi?
5) Jamari es un nativo de Israel. ¿Verdadero o Falso?

Respuestas
1) ARQUITECTURA
2) Hagia Sofia
3) Turquía
4) CATEDRAL
5) FALSO

Jamari, the Serious Student

Jamari is an Egyptian student who arrived in the UK three years ago, in pursuit of his dream career. He studies at the University of Wolverhampton, United Kingdom. He is studying architecture and wants to become one of the greatest architects of all time.

Jamari was raised in Turkey. Before he decided to go for architecture as a course, he had deeply admired the magnificent buildings of the Byzantine era, which he found scattered across the streets of Istanbul in Turkey.

The Hagia Sophia made the most impression on Jamari. The building is one of the most famous and most spectacular edifices of the Byzantine era. Its construction took place within the years 532 and 537 AD. Originally used as a cathedral, it was later used as a mosque during the Ottoman epoch.

In 1931, it was closed to the public and re-opened as a museum in 1935. In the year 2015, the Turkish Cultural and Tourism Ministry listed it as the most visited tourist attraction site in the Republic of Turkey.

Jamari had often wondered how such an outstanding architectural masterpiece was possible for architects who operated when technology was less advanced and sophisticated. Jamari takes great pride in the three Pyramids, which are located in his birthplace of Gaza. He is also mindful of some of the best architects of modern times such as Antonio Gaudi, who designed the prestigious La Sagrada Familia, a cathedral in Barcelona with tree-like columns of remarkable aesthetics. He also knows about Frank Lloyd Wright, a native of Wisconsin, who used geometry as an important element of his design in his most famous work, Falling Water.

Jamari is one of the brightest and most zealous amongst his mates. When he made his journey to the UK for studies, he had great things in mind. He simply wanted to be the best.

"What is architecture?" His father had jokingly asked him during one of his school holidays.

"Dad," he smiled, "it is the art or practice of designing and constructing buildings," Jamari answered with perceptible confidence.

"Any more questions?" inquired Jamari.

"No more today," said his dad, laughing.

Exercise

Ok, let's now start a quick exercise: I am going to ask you 5 questions. Try to reply, and after the questions, I will give you the answers.

Questions
1) What course is Jamari studying in the UK?
2) What is the name of the building that most inspired Jamari while in Turkey?
3) Where did Jamari grow up?
4) Which building did Antonio Gaudi design?
5) Jamari is a native of Israel. True or False?

Answers
1) Architecture
2) Hagia Sophia
3) Turkey

4) Cathedral
5) False

Chapter 6: El Carpintero

Había una vez un carpintero con una larga barba. Solía trabajar todo el día, y en la noche cuando llegaba a casa le gustaba descansar cerca de la chimenea. Su nombre era Alex, y tenía 60 años, estaba muy cansado y su piel estaba llena de arrugas.

En la noche luego de la cena, solía relajarse en el sofá mientras veía televisión y fumaba un cigarro.

Era un cálido día de julio, y Alex estaba trabajando en el bosque como siempre, cuando tuvo una idea fantástica.

"Construiré una máquina con madera que trabaje en mi lugar, para por fin poder dejar de trabajar y descansar", dijo Alex.

Inmediatamente se puso a trabajar, pero la situación se volvió peor, la máquina era difícil de construir y los días de trabajo de Alex se volvieron aun mas largos.

Finalmente, en agosto, Alex terminó de construir su maquina perfecta, y al día siguiente haría una prueba. El día que cambiaría su vida, por fin podría dejar de trabajar y disfrutar de su familia.

Durante la noche, Alex se sintió muy mal y murió. Había trabajado muy duro en su vida, y su cuerpo estaba cansado. Su esposa Bárbara decidió donar la máquina creada por su esposo a una asociación en África.

La máquina era perfecta y trabajó continuamente por 10 años. La asociación pudo construir 20 escuelas en África con el dinero ganado por la máquina de Alex.

Ejercicio

Ok, ahora hagamos un ejercicio rápido: te haré 5 preguntas. Trata de responder y luego de las preguntas, te daré las respuestas.

Preguntas
- **1)** ¿Cuántos años tenia Alex?
- **2)** ¿Por qué decidió dejar de trabajar?
- **3)** ¿En qué mes decidió construir la máquina?
- **4)** ¿En qué mes terminó la máquina?
- **5)** ¿Cómo se llama la esposa de Alex?

Respuestas
- **1)** 60
- **2)** Decidió construir una máquina
- **3)** JULIO
- **4)** AGOSTO
- **5)** Bárbara

The Carpenter

Once upon a time, there was a carpenter with a long beard. He used to work all day, and in the evening when he came home, he loved to rest near the fireplace. His name was Alex and he was 60, he was very tired and his skin was full of wrinkles.

In the evening after dinner, he used to relax on the sofa while watching television and smoked a cigarette.

It was a hot July day, and Alex was working on some wood as usual when at some point he had a fantastic idea.

"I will build a machine from wood that will work in my place, so I can finally stop working and rest," Alex said.

He immediately got to work, but the situation became worse, the machine was difficult to build and Alex's days at work became even longer.

Finally, in August, Alex finished building his perfect machine, and the next day there would be the big test. The day that would change his life, he could finally stop working and enjoy being with his family.

During the night, Alex felt very bad and died. He had worked too hard in his life, and his body was tired. His wife Barbara decided to donate to a charity association in Africa, the machine created by her husband, Alex.

The machine was perfect and worked continuously for 10 years. The association was able to build 20 schools in Africa with the money earned from Alex's machine.

Exercise

Ok, let's now start a quick exercise: I am going to ask you 5 questions. Try to reply, and after the questions, I will give you the answers.

Questions
    1) How old was Alex?
    2) What did he decide to do to stop working?
    3) In what month did he decide to build the machine?
    4) In what month did he finish the machine?
    5) What is the name of Alex's wife?

Answers
    1) 60
    2) He decided to build a machine
    3) July
    4) August
    5) Bárbara

Chapter 7: El Sueño del Rey

En un pueblo pequeño llamado Elim, vivía un rey quien gobernaba sobre un poderoso reino. Era muy reverenciado por su gran amabilidad y sabiduría. Era amado por todos sus súbditos, y cuidaba de ellos como un padre haría con sus hijos. Su esposa murió de una enfermedad misteriosa hace mucho. Ella lo dejó viudo sin heredero al trono.

Sus amigos y asociados cercanos frecuentemente le aconsejaban casarse de nuevo, pero él se negaba. Aparte de su sabiduría profunda, era conocido por mantener la justicia y admirado por las buenas reglas que implementaba, las cuales todos amaban obedecer. Su semblante le hacía parecer como alguien que encontró la felicidad en el progreso de su reino. Difícilmente se veía absorto en pensamientos deprimentes o amenazadores.

Sólo la realidad de no tener un heredero perturbaba su paz. Una vez, se levantó de su sueño en medio de la noche y declaró que tenia que encontrar un vidente que lo guiara para tomar la decisión correcta sobre su sucesor. Cuando el vidente fue, su consejo era simple. Tan simple que el rey no lo creía.

"¿Qué le aconsejó el vidente, sabio rey?", pregunto un emisario bien intencionado, quien dió al rey una visita de cortesía

"Él dijo que la solución estaba dentro de mi", respondió el rey con incredulidad.

"Oh rey, no soy ignorante de la profundidad de su dolor y confusión en ese asunto", dijo el emisario "pero ¿cómo entenderá usted el significado de las palabras del vidente si no ve hacia adentro? Debe retener su habilidad de confiar incluso cuando es muy difícil de hacerlo", concluyó el emisario.

"Gracias, noble emisario", respondió el rey. "No estoy sorprendido de escucharlo hablar así, se que tiene mi bienestar en mente."

"Oh, sabio rey." Dijo el emisario. "mi sincero agradecimiento por el reconocimiento. Realmente espero que en las próximas semanas encuentre la clave de las palabras del vidente que seguramente le causarán una alegría inmensa."

Días después de la partida del emisario, el rey soñó y se vió a si mismo coronando a un joven rico y sabio. Rico, sabio y amable como si mismo. Temprano en la mañana, el rey abrió los ojos con una sonrisa cautivadora en su rostro.

"El vidente estaba en lo correcto, la solución ha estado dentro de mi. Mil gracias al emisario. Sus palabras amables realmente me ayudaron" contempló. Conocía perfectamente el rostro que había visto en sus sueños, en la vida real. Era una revelación que continuamente le daba alegría y confianza de que bajo el liderazgo de su amable heredero, el reino siempre se mantendría siempre próspero y en paz.

Ejercicio

Ok, ahora hagamos un ejercicio rápido: te haré 5 preguntas. Trata de responder y luego de las preguntas, te daré las respuestas.

Preguntas
1) Nombre del reino sobre el cual el rey reinaba
2) ¿Qué hacia el rey para que todo el mundo amara obedecerlo?
3) ¿Qué le ocurrió a la esposa del rey?
4) ¿Cuál era la única cosa que perturbaba al rey?
5) ¿Qué decidió el rey cuando se despertó en medio de la noche?

Respuestas
1) ELIM
2) REGLAS
3) Murió de una enfermedad misteriosa
4) No tener un heredero al trono
5) Encontrarse con un vidente

The King's Dream

In a small town called Elim lived a king who ruled over a mighty kingdom. He was revered for his great kindness and wisdom. He was loved by all his subjects, and he cared for them like a father would do for his children. His wife had died from a mysterious illness long ago. She left him a widower with no heir to the throne.

His friends and close associates often advised him to remarry, but he refused. Apart from his deep wisdom, he was known for upholding justice and admired for the good rules he made, which everyone loved to obey. His countenance portrayed him as one who found happiness in the overall progress of his kingdom. He hardly had any depressing or menacing thoughts.

Only the reality of not having an heir disturbed his peace. Once he roused himself from sleep in the middle of the night and avowed that he must find a seer who could guide him in making the right decision about his successor. When the seer came, his advice was simple. So simple that the king did not believe it.

"What did the seer advice you, wise king?" Enquired a well-meaning emissary who was paying the king a courtesy visit.

"He said that the solution was inside of me," responded the king, as he shuddered in disbelief.

"Oh king, I am not ignorant of the depth of your pain and confusion in this matter," said the emissary, "but how do you grasp the meaning of the words of the seer if you fail to look inwards. You must retain your ability to trust even when it is very difficult to do so," concluded the emissary.

"Thank you, noble emissary," replied the king, "I am not surprised to hear you speak thus. I know that you have my well-being at heart."

"Oh, wise king," said the emissary, "I heartily appreciate the acknowledgment. I do really hope that in the following weeks, you shall find the key to the seer's words which will surely cause you immense joy."

Days after the emissary departed, the king dreamt and saw himself crowning a rich and wise youth. Rich, wise, and kind just like him. Early in the morning, the king opened eyes with a captivating smile on his face.

"The seer was correct; the solution has been in me. A thousand thanks to the emissary. His kind words really helped me," he contemplated. He knew perfectly the face he had seen in his dream, in real life. It was a revelation that continuously gave him joy, happiness, and the confidence that under the leadership of the kind heir, the kingdom would forever remain peaceful and prosperous.

Exercise

Ok, let's now start a quick exercise: I am going to ask you 5 questions. Try to reply, and after the questions, I will give you the answers.

Questions
1) Name the kingdom over which the king ruled.
2) What did the king make that everybody loves to obey?
3) What happened to the king's wife?

4) What was the only thing that troubled the king?
5) What did the king decide when he awoke in the middle of the night?

Answers
1) Elim
2) Rules
3) She died from a mysterious illness
4) No heir to the throne
5) To meet a seer

Chapter 8: Luca y El Señor Tiempo

Luca era un niño muy curioso y amaba hacer preguntas. Un día, cuando comía, le preguntó a su papá cómo medir el tiempo. Le dijo:

"Papá, quiero saber cómo se mide el tiempo. ¿Cómo puedo saber qué tan largo es un minuto?, ¿Qué tan larga es media hora?, ¿Qué tan largo es un día?"

Su papá le dijo:

"Luca, te contaré la historia de un señor llamado Tiempo. Vivía en un país muy lejano. Era un buen caballero, pero siempre estaba molesto. Si alguien le preguntaba porqué estaba molesto, respondía que estaba molesto y preocupado porque los días eran todos iguales. Él quería que pasaran de otra manera, y no siempre igual. Cada día buscaba maneras de controlar el tiempo para tener días largos y cortos.

Un día, tuvo una idea genial, pero necesitaba ayuda y llamo a su mejor amigo Pedro. Le dijo a Pedro lo que quería hacer, y juntos decidieron pedir ayuda a otros amigos. Sara, Christine, y Pablo también llegaron. Todos juntos decidieron que la duración de los días cambiaría.

Pedro comenzó a hablar con el viento.

"Viento, mañana soplarás mas fuerte para hacer que los días fluyan mas rápido."

Pablo comenzó a hablar con la luna.

"Luna, a partir de mañana te despertarás mas temprano para que la noche sea más larga y el día más corto."

Christine comenzó a hablar con el sol.

"Sol, mañana te irás a dormir temprano porque el día será más corto."

Sara comenzó a hablarle a la noche.

"Noche, mañana serás más larga porque la luna se despertará antes."

El señor Tiempo comenzó a hablarle al día.

"Día, mañana serás más corto porque mis amigos y yo así lo decidimos."

"Perfecto. Ahora que le dijimos a todos lo que necesitábamos que hicieran, podemos comenzar a jugar y hacer lo que más nos gusta" dijo el señor Tiempo.

Los 5 amigos todavía hablaban y discutían que hacer, y ya la noche había llegado. La luna brillo alto en el cielo, el sol ya se había puesto y el viento había dejado de soplar.

"Tuvimos éxito amigos" exclamo el señor Tiempo.

"¡Hoy el día duro mucho menos que ayer!"

Todos celebraron y entendieron que el secreto del tiempo es simple:

Cuando estás ocupado haciendo cosas divertidas, la noche llega pronto, pero cuando haces cosas aburridas, el señor Tiempo decide que el día durará mucho... mucho más que en los días divertidos.

Ejercicio

Ok, ahora hagamos un ejercicio rápido: te haré 3 preguntas. Trata de responder y luego de las preguntas, te daré las respuestas.

Preguntas
1) ¿Cuál es el nombre del niño que preguntó a su papá qué era el tiempo?
2) ¿Qué le pidió Pablo a la luna?
3) ¿Qué le pidió Pedro al viento?

Respuestas
1) LUCA
2) Que se despertara temprano
3) Que soplara más fuerte

Luca and Mister Time

Luca was a very curious boy and loved to always ask questions. One day, as he ate, he asked his Dad how to measure time. He said:

"Dad, I want to know how time is measured. How can I tell how long a minute is? How long is half an hour? How long is a day?"

His father then told him:

"Luca, today I will tell you the story of a gentleman called Time. He lived in a very distant country. He was a good gentleman, but he always went around angry. If someone asked him why he was angry, he replied that he was angry and bored because the days were all the same. He wanted at any cost that they would be different and not all the same. Every day he looked for ways to control time so that he could have longer days and shorter days.

One day he had a wonderful idea, but he needed help, and then he called his best friend, Pedro. He told Pedro what he wanted to do, and together they decided to get help from other friends. Sara, Christine, and Pablo also arrived. All together they decided that the duration of the days would change.

Pedro started talking to the wind.

"Wind, tomorrow you will blow harder to make the days flow faster."

Pablo started talking to the moon.

"Moon, from tomorrow on you will wake up earlier so the night will be longer and the day shorter."

Christine started talking to the sun.

"Sun, tomorrow you will go to bed early because the day will be shorter."

Sara started talking to the night

"Night, tomorrow you will be longer because the moon will wake up sooner."

Mr. Time started talking to the day.

"Day, tomorrow you will be shorter because my friends and I have decided so."

"Perfect now that we've told everyone what we need them to do, we can start playing and doing what we like most." Mr. Time said.

The 5 friends were still talking and discussing what to do, and already the night had arrived. The moon shone high in the sky, the sun had already set, and the wind had stopped blowing.

"We have succeeded my friends," exclaimed Mr. Time.

"Today, the day lasted much less than yesterday!"

Everyone celebrated and understood that the secret of time was simple:

When you're busy doing fun things, the night comes right away, but when you do something that is not fun, Mr. Time decides that the days will last longer... much more than fun days.

Exercise

Ok, let's now start a quick exercise: I am going to ask you 3 questions. Try to reply, and after the questions, I will give you the answers.

Questions
1) What was the name of the child who asked his father what time was?
2) What did Pablo ask the moon to do?
3) What did Pedro ask the wind to do?

Answers
1) Luca
2) To wake up early
3) To blow

Chapter 9: Ella Siempre Me Supera

Conozco a una chica desde pequeños; al ser mi vecina nos criamos prácticamente juntos. Todos los días jugábamos juntos.

¿Cómo llegué a tener una relación de amistad con ella? Pues la respuesta es simple.

"¡Se mi amigo!" Gritó enfrente de mí.

No la conocía para ese entonces, era la primera vez que nos mirábamos. Tenía alrededor de unos seis años. Solamente sabía que ella era mi vecina, pero nada más allá de eso.

Por supuesto no supe cómo responder a su pedido; uno no simplemente se lanza y le pide a otra persona que formen una amistad. En lo absoluto. Era vergonzoso, pero ella… ¡Sonreía! Sonreía con una gracia que se contagiaba.

A pura vista se podía notar que ella era una de esas chicas energéticas que siempre está feliz y jugando. Yo por otro lado era… un poco más apático. No era como si me desagradara, como dije antes, no la conocía. Simplemente… no sentía la misma emoción que ella.

"¿Por qué?" Le pregunté sin pensarlo.

No buscaba ser grosero o alejarla, solo… me interesaba saber el por qué me buscaba a mí en específico.

"No hay más niños en esta calle" Me respondió sin perder su sonrisa. "Y parece que también quieres divertirte, así que juguemos."

Ciertamente no tenía amigos en aquel entonces, y no era un problema. Aun no comenzaba a ir a la escuela, y como ella lo había dicho, no había más niños en esa calle. Pero aun así… la idea de jugar junto a una niña… usualmente no era lo común.

"No creo que quieras jugar conmigo", le respondí. "Yo no juego con muñecas como tú, tampoco a la casita o cosas así."

"¡Yo tampoco!" Respondió.

Me tomó de la mano y me estiró con fuerza.

"Juaguemos a las escondidas." Me dijo. "Esta vez yo cuento, anda a esconderte."

Era como si ignorara todos los peros que pusiera y tomara únicamente las partes donde yo aceptaba, las cuales no eran ninguna.

Se puso en la pared y comenzó a contar. Para ese momento una idea pasó por mi cabeza—'Vuelve a casa'—Nadie me podía obligar a estar ahí con ella, bueno, quizá mamá o papá lo hubieran hecho, pero ellos no estaban ahí. Podía simplemente abandonarla en lo que ella contaba y volver a la comodidad de casa. Pero…

Terminé escondiéndome no muy lejos de ahí. Sentí que volver a casa no era lo correcto, aun si solo era un niño egoísta, tenía un corazón y una conciencia, la cual me estaría matando por dejarla ahí después de estar tan animada respecto al jugar.

Pasaron los minutos, cada vez se hacía más tarde. Ella no me encontraba, me comencé a preguntar si era que me había escondido muy bien… o quizá ella se aburrió. Si me dejó ahí, no hubiera sido extraño; después de todo, yo me había negado muchas veces y quizá eso la cansó. Pensé que quizá lo hacía para darme una lección.

Pero entonces, miré nuevamente su rostro.

"¡Te encontré!" Gritó llena de alegría.

Sentí como si esas palabras tuvieran más de un significado. No solo me había encontrado de mi escondite, sino…

Algo movió mi corazón, y por primera vez en mucho tiempo, pude sonreír también de felicidad.

Nuestra amistad se afinó con el tiempo. Resultó que terminamos en la misma escuela primaria, en la misma aula, y sentados uno al lado del otro.

Aquello hizo llevadera la escuela, ella siempre hacia algo entretenido o me contaba cosas extrañas. Regularmente la regañaban por no callarse en clase. Pero aun así volvía a contarme más y más cosas.

Secundaria también estuvimos juntos; éramos inseparables. Al lugar que ella fuera, yo también estaba ahí.

Seguía siendo mi vecina, por lo que frecuentaba mucho mi casa. Mi madre la adoraba, y mi padre daba indirectas de que yo ya estaba creciendo y que estaba orgulloso de mi.

Muchos de los comentarios los ignoraba. Lo único que hacíamos era… jugar en mi habitación, mirar películas, leer algunos comics; se convirtió en mi mejor amiga.

Aquello no duró mucho. Las cosas comenzaron a cambiar, y ella lo notó. Muchos hablaban de nosotros a las espaldas.

De que era extraña la relación que llevábamos, que no estaban del todo seguros si un hombre y una mujer se podían llevar tan bien. Y ella dio el siguiente paso.

"Prácticamente ya lo somos, ¿no?" Me preguntó energética como siempre.

"¿A qué te refieres?" Le pregunté.

"¡Somos pareja!" Respondió tomando la delantera.

"¿¡Lo somos!?" Aquello me sorprendió.

Pero viendo la relación que llevábamos, era comprensible. Todos a nuestro alrededor lo pensaban igual. Entonces… solo debíamos hacerlo "Formal." Ella no me desagradaba en lo absoluto, disfrutaba estar con ella todo el tiempo. Me entendía mejor que nadie más, y creía yo también lo hacía.

Una vez más… me superó. Tomó las riendas y dijo lo que yo no hubiera podido decir.

"¿Algo cambiara?" Le pregunté.

Nunca tuvimos una pareja, por lo que no comprendíamos que era serlo.

"No lo creo." Respondió alegre. "Solo que así puedo decir felizmente que te quiero."

Decía las cosas más vergonzosas sin pensárselo. Pero eso no me desagradaba.

Llegamos a preparatoria. Nuevamente fuimos a la misma. Seguíamos siendo pareja de lo más normal. Bueno, quizá no tan normal. Parecíamos hermanos o amigos por cómo nos comportábamos. Pero no había otra forma de hacerlo, siempre estuvo a mi lado, la confianza estaba a otro nivel. Bromear con ella de cualquier cosa era el pan de cada día.

Elegimos la misma universidad, la misma carrera. A ambos nos gustaban las mismas cosas, queríamos estudiar lo mismo y trabajar juntos en los proyectos que teníamos a futuro.

Lo que me llevó a pensar que quizá… me faltaba dar un paso más allá. Ella dio los primeros dos; ella forjó nuestra amistad, ella inicio nuestra relación. Y al pensar en mi futuro, ella siempre estaba ahí. Yo… quería ser el que diera el siguiente paso.

El día de la graduación llegó. Nos graduamos con honores, éramos el equipo dinamita. Nada nos podía detener.

Era hora de comenzar la vida adulta. Y aun ella no daba el siguiente paso. Quizá… ella no lo quería dar. Comencé a dudar, aun si yo quería darlo, quizá ella en realidad no. Quizá estaba aburrida de nuestra relación y quería terminarlo.

Pero por más que intentaba mirar un futuro sin ella… me era imposible. La conocí desde pequeña y nunca se apartó de mi lado. Quería decírselo, que deseaba que nunca estuviéramos separados de la vida del otro. Aun si ella no lo miraba de la misma forma… no quería guardar esos sentimientos.

"Yo… quería pedirte algo", le dije.

"¿Qué podría ser?" Preguntó confundida.

Tome el valor que me faltaba. Era el momento. Esta vez yo… sería quien daría el siguiente paso, no quería que ella me superara una vez más.

"Lo he estado pensando durante un largo tiempo… quizá tu no sientes lo mismo, pero yo… en verdad lo quiero", dije. "Han sido unos largos años, y no los cambiaria para nada. Has alegrado mi vida de una forma que no te puedes imaginar, y por lo mismo… quiero que estés en todo lo que está por venir. Por favor… ¡CASATE CONMIGO!"

Con una expresión de sorpresa, quedó en silencio.

Pensé que quizá, después de todo, ella no…

"¿No lo estábamos ya?" Preguntó confundida.

"¿Eh?" No comprendí su respuesta.

"Me adelante un poco y rente un departamento", me dijo. "¡Por supuesto que yo también quiero que estés en mi futuro!"

¿Un departamento? Ella… yo… no pude aguantar las lágrimas de felicidad.

Una vez más… ella… me superó.

"Me alegro de haberte encontrado…"

She Always Beats Me

I've known a girl since childhood; being my neighbor, we grew up practically together. Every day we played together.

How did I get to have a friendship with her? Well, the answer is simple.

"Be my friend!" shouted in front of me.

I didn't know her at that moment; it was the first time we looked at each other. She was about six years old. I only knew that she was my neighbor, but nothing more than that.

Of course, I did not know how to respond to that request; one does not simply launch and ask another person to form a friendship. At all. It was embarrassing, but she… was smiling! She smiled with a grace that was spread.

In a plain glance, you could tell that she was one of those energetic girls who is always happy and playing. I, on the other hand, was… a little more apathetic. It wasn't like I disliked it; as I said before, I didn't know her. I just… didn't feel the same emotion as her.

"Why?" I asked without thinking.

I was not looking to be rude or away, just… I was interested to know why she was looking for me specifically.

"There are no more children in this street." She answered without losing her smile. "And it seems that you also want to have fun, so let's play."

I certainly had no friends at the time, and it wasn't a problem. I wasn't going to school yet, and as she had said, there were no more children in that street. But even so… the idea of playing with a girl… was usually not common.

"I don't think you want to play with me," I replied. "I don't play with dolls like you, or the house or things like that."

"Me neither!" Answered.

She took me by the hand and stretched me hard.

"Let's play hide and seek." She told me. "This time I count, go hide."

It was as if she ignored all the buts and took only what I accepted.

She got on the wall and started counting. By that time, an idea went through my head—'Go back home'—No one could force me to be there with her, well, maybe mom or dad would have done it, but they weren't there. I could simply abandon her while she counts and returns to the comfort of home. But…

I ended up hiding not far from there. I felt that returning home was not the right thing; even if I was just a selfish child, I had a heart and a conscience, which would be killing me by leaving her there after being so animated about playing.

The minutes passed, each time it was getting later. She was not there; I began to wonder if it was that I had hidden very well… or maybe she got bored. If she left me there, it would not have been strange; after all, I had refused many times, and maybe she got tired. I thought maybe she was doing it to teach me a lesson.

But then, I looked at her face again.

"I found you!" She shouted full of joy.

I felt as if those words had more than one meaning. Not only had I found myself in my hiding place, but...

Something moved my heart, and for the first time in a long time, I could also smile with happiness.

Our friendship was refined over time. It turned out that we ended up in the same elementary school, in the same classroom, and sitting next to each other.

That made the school bearable; she always did something entertaining or told me strange things. They regularly scolded her for not shutting up in class. But she still told me more and more things.

In high school, we were together too; we were inseparable. Wherever she went, I was there too.

She was still my neighbor, so I frequented my house a lot. My mother loved her, and my father gave hints that I was already growing up and that he was proud of me.

Many of the comments I ignored them. All we did was... play in my room, watch movies, read some comics; she became my best friend.

That did not last long. Things began to change, and she noticed. Many talked about us behind our backs. That the relationship we were having was strange, that they were not entirely sure if a man and a woman could get along so well. And she took the next step.

"Practically, we already are, right?" She asked me energetically as always.

"What do you mean?" Asked.

"We're a couple!" She responded by taking the lead.

"We are!?" That surprised me.

But seeing the relationship we had, it was understandable. Everyone around us thought the same. So... we just had to do it "Formal." She didn't dislike me at all; I enjoyed being with her all the time. She understood me better than anyone else, and I thought I did too.

Once again... it surpassed me. She took the reins and said what I could not have said.

"Will something change?" I asked.

We never had a partner, so we didn't understand what it was.

"I do not think so." She replied cheerfully. "Only that way, I can happily say that I love you."

She said the most embarrassing things without thinking about it. But that didn't displease me.

We arrived in high school. Again, we went to the same. We were still the most normal couple. Well, maybe not so normal. We looked like brothers or friends because of how we behaved. But there was no other way to do it, she was always by my side, trust was on another level. Joking with her about anything was the daily bread.

We choose the same university, the same career. We both liked the same things, we wanted to study the same and work together on the projects we had in the future.

Which led me to think that maybe... I had to go one step further. She gave the first two; she forged our friendship; she started our relationship. And when thinking about my future, she was always there. I... wanted to be the one to take the next step.

Graduation day arrived. We graduated with honors; we were the dynamite team. Nothing could stop us.

It was time to start adult life. And she has not taken the next step yet. Maybe... she didn't want to give it. I started to doubt; even if I wanted to give it, maybe she didn't really. Maybe she was bored with our relationship and wanted to end it.

But as much as I tried to look at a future without her... it was impossible. I knew her since she was little, and she never left my side. I wanted to tell her that I wished we never be apart from each other's life. Even if she didn't look at it in the same way... I didn't want to save those feelings.

"I... wanted to ask you something," I told.

"What could it be?" Asked, confused.

I take the courage I was missing. It was the moment. This time I... would be the one to take the next step; I didn't want her to beat me once more.

"I've been thinking about it for a long time... maybe you don't feel the same, but I... I really want it." I said. "Many years have passed, and I wouldn't change them at all. You have brightened my life in a way that you cannot imagine, and for the same... I want you to be in everything that is to come. Please... marry me!"

With an expression of surprise, she fell silent.

I thought maybe, after all, she didn't...

"Weren't we already?" Asked, confused.

"Eh?" I didn't understand her answer.

"I go ahead a little and rent an apartment." She told me. "Of course I want you to be in my future too!"

A department? She... I... I couldn't stand the tears of happiness.

Once again... she... beat me.

"I'm glad to have found you..."

Quiz

Questions
1) Yo _____ con la chica del vecindario.
    a. Jugué
    b. Canté
    c. Peleé
2) ¿Qué edad tenía la niña cuando nos miramos por primera vez?
    a. 6
    b. 10
    c. 2
3) ¿Por qué fue difícil imaginar un futuro sin ella?
    a. La conocía desde que era pequeña

b. No pude conseguir a nadie
c. Ella me amaba

Answers
1) a
2) a
3) a

Vocabulario (Vocabulary)

Amistad – Friendship; **Gritó** – Shouted; **Vecina** – Neighbor; **Vergonzoso** – Embarrassing; **Grosero** – Rude; **Tampoco** – Neither; **Contar** – Counting; **Abandonarla** – Abandon; **Significado** – Meaning; **Cambiar** – Change.

Chapter 10: La Muerte Los Sigue

La autopista estaba vacía, no había ningún signo de algún automóvil o camión cerca. Las luces se encendían y apagaban. A la distancia, una tormenta iluminaba la noche, y el viento comenzaba a mover las copas de los árboles violentamente. Las primeras gotas comenzaron a mojar el pavimento. En medio de la carretera tres jóvenes corrían desesperados saliendo del bosque sin razón alguna. El terror se reflejaba en sus rostros y ellos no podían hacer otra cosa que correr y gritar.

De pronto, los tres jóvenes cayeron muertos sin ningún signo de violencia. En sus caras se podía ver la sorpresa de quien no esperaba que la muerte llegue tan rápido. Tenían futuro, un trabajo y toda una vida por delante, pero ahora sus cuerpos estaban en la carretera. Los animales del bosque cercano miraban a la distancia a esas tres posibles presas, pero sabían muy bien que entrar en el bosque podía significar la muerte. Cada vez que alguien cruzaba las cuevas del bosque moría, estar mucho tiempo en ellas era fatal.

Al día siguiente con la tormenta ya muy lejos y todos los signos ya secos y olvidados, la policía rodeaba la escena del crimen, marcaban con tiza el borde de los cuerpos y sacaban fotografías a todo lo que parecía interesante o digno de investigación. Como siempre sucedía en estos casos, los camiones de noticias estaban alrededor tratando de sacar la mejor imagen de los cuerpos y luego emitirla en el horario principal. Los periodistas trataban de sacarle información a los policías, quienes estaban bajo un estricto pacto de silencio. No es que no tenían información, solo que lo mejor en estos casos era esperar que algún vocero o representante de la fuerza policíaca hiciera declaraciones cuando tuviese todos los datos.

Sin embargo, a pesar de los mejores intentos de la policía, no podían encontrar ninguna pista o ningún motivo por el cual tres cuerpos jóvenes estaban en la carretera sin signos de violencia. Sin ningún tipo de solución a la vista, el fiscal que llevaba el caso decidió tragar su orgullo y llamar a un viejo conocido - El detective McHeartley.

En su oficina el detective estaba descansando, sus pies apoyados encima del escritorio, cerca de una caja de pizza sucia y vacía. En el sillón su gato descansaba, durmiendo encima del sombrero y en una esquina su fiel chaqueta estaba colgada del perchero. Era una tarde tranquila de domingo y el detective no tenía ninguna tarea que hacer. De hecho, ni siquiera tenía un hogar al que volver, excepto esa oficina donde dormía, trabajaba y vivía toda la semana. En medio de la tranquilidad, sonó el teléfono. El ruido hizo que tanto el detective como su mascota se despertaran asustados. Desesperado, el detective atendió rápidamente el teléfono, él sabía que en un caso de investigación cada segundo es importante. "¿Hola? ¿Quién es?" prácticamente gritó al auricular "Sí, soy yo. ¿Dónde? Estoy a doce horas de distancia en autobús. No lo sé, tengo otros planes para hoy." Su gato lo miró con cara de fastidio. "¿Me van a pagar un avión privado? Bueno, está bien, allí estaré."

Tomó su chaqueta, su portafolio y para conseguir su sombrero tuvo que pedirle por favor a su gato que se moviera de encima de él. "Por favor, tengo que irme." Finalmente, después de darle una mirada asesina el gato se movió de encima del sombrero. "Te prometo que te traeré algo de regreso. ¿Atún? ¿Pollo? ¿Qué te parece?" El gato lo miró, solo apoyó su cabeza en la mano del detective para indicarle que podía irse en paz. "La vecina tiene las llaves, así que ella va a cuidarte un rato."

Rápidamente se dirigió al aeropuerto donde lo esperaban los representantes de la policía y subieron todos a un avión privado. Mientras estaba en vuelo, McHeartley tuvo la posibilidad de leer toda la información del caso. Vio todas las fotos y toda la información recopilada por los incansables miembros de la fuerza policíaca. Otro extraño caso. Era el tipo de caso que seguía al detective, el último caso fue en el fin del mundo y fue bastante particular. No podía sacarse de encima la sensación de que este caso no iba a ser tan simple como ese.

Al aterrizar, los policías lo subieron a un coche patrulla, y fueron hacia la escena del crimen. Los periodistas y el alcalde estaban esperándolo, visiblemente nerviosos. Las elecciones eran en una semana y si el alcalde no resolvía el problema con rapidez posiblemente perdería todos los votos. El alcalde recibió con manos temblorosas al detective McHeartley y lo guio hacia una carpa de la policía donde se llevaba a cabo toda la coordinación de la investigación.

Dentro de la carpa había una mesa blanca, una silla y copias de todas las fotos que ya había visto en el viaje hacia la escena del crimen. También tenía encima de la pila un sobre marrón que decía "Informe Forense." McHeartley lo abrió, esperando encontrar la respuesta rápido y volver a su oficina, pero en realidad era una sola hoja con un texto debajo que decía "No hay información suficiente para llegar a una conclusión, tan solo se hallaron huellas, estuvieron caminando durante tres días seguidos." El detective suspiró. Iba a ser una larga noche. Llamó a un asistente, pidió el café más negro que pudieran encontrar para mantenerse despierto.

Afuera, la prensa estaba atenta a cada movimiento. Después de todo, no todos los días el detective McHeartley, el héroe del caso del avión perdido, visitaba la ciudad. Y ciertamente esto significa que era un caso muy importante. Las horas pasaban y por supuesto, los ánimos eran bastante malos. Después de todo, cuando se transmite las 24 horas del día la misma noticia queda realmente muy poco que informar si no hay noticias nuevas. Pasaron días llenos de tensión, todos se sorprendían porque el detective contrató a especialistas de todo tipo para investigar la zona donde encontraron muertos a los jóvenes, así como informes de muertes extrañas en el pasado que hubiesen ocurrido en el pueblo.

En cuanto el detective McHeartley llamó a conferencia de prensa en la puerta de la carpa, todos los periodistas agradecieron esas noticias nuevas, ya que significaba que al menos el final la tortura estaba cerca. Finalmente podrían saber qué había pasado con los tres cuerpos, quién era el culpable, y en particular qué pasos se tomarían para apresarlo porque las personas de ese pueblo adoraban el drama. Sin embargo, lo que los recibió no fue exactamente lo que esperaban.

"Hola, buenas tardes", dijo McHeartley frente al micrófono instalado en un atril. "Los llamé a conferencia de prensa porque sé exactamente qué pasó con los cuerpos de los jóvenes. Sin embargo…", hizo una pausa que duró años, "creo que no es lo que ustedes esperaban escuchar."

Los periodistas estaban en el borde de sus asientos. McHeartley continuó, "los tres jóvenes no fueron asesinados por naves espaciales, o por agentes secretos del FBI o cualquiera de esas teorías conspirativas que se comentaron mucho en la prensa en estos días. Los tres jóvenes murieron intoxicados y según las huellas estuvieron corriendo alrededor de tres días."

El Alcalde no pudo detener su lengua y dijo "¿Quién lo ha hecho Señor detective? ¡Esto es un hecho *siniestro*! Deberíamos suspender las elecciones" gritó para que el candidato adversario no le ganara.

"¿Usted piensa suspender las elecciones porque el culpable de la muerte de los jóvenes fue un hongo?" preguntó McHeartley enfadado porque lo había interrumpido.

Silencio en la sala. La noticia fue tan fuerte que se podía sentir el silencio en los hogares donde las familias y curiosos seguían la transmisión. "Así es ¡sorpréndanse! Los tres murieron intoxicados por un hongo maligno que se encuentra en el bosque de este pueblo", añadió tristemente. "Me pareció extraño que unos jóvenes tan sanos murieran sin signos de violencia, así que pensé que fueron envenenados por algo y analicé todas las plantas del bosque que está cerca de la carretera. Efectivamente la prueba del hongo mortal dio positiva."

Un periodista tuvo mucha curiosidad al respecto y dijo "Entonces ¿Por qué según las huellas estuvieron corriendo alrededor de tres días seguidos? ¡Me parece que algo más tuvo que haberlos perseguido!" McHeartley lo miró fijamente, "Lo único que los siguió fue la muerte. Verá mi querido reportero, cuando alguien consume un hongo tóxico la persona alucina, cada quien a su manera. Pudieron estar perdiendo la cabeza poco a poco. Los tres jóvenes comenzaron a perder la respiración cuando estaban en lo profundo del bosque e intentaron salir a la civilización. Los tres estaban de campamento y posiblemente entraron a las cuevas del bosque que están infectadas con el hongo." El silencio fue increíble en la sala de conferencias. "Lamentablemente", añadió con un poco de tristeza, "si hubieran llevado algún teléfono de emergencia, esto se podría haber solucionado porque los efectos del hongo se eliminan con una inyección para las alergias." El alcalde miraba del otro lado de la sala de conferencias sin poder creerlo. Todo indicaba que el detective McHeartley era tan eficiente como se decía. Los rastros del veneno del hongo habían estado matando a muchas personas en medio del bosque.

Ahora el alcalde estaba sin posibilidades de ganar las elecciones. Todo era culpa del bajo presupuesto, la falta de entrenamiento y de los muy bajos sueldos que pagaba a los guardabosques. Como pudo, trató de escapar, para no verse arrinconado por la prensa.

El detective se bajó del atril y procedió a buscar su chaqueta y su sombrero. Otro caso resuelto, pensó. Antes de coger el autobús hacia el aeropuerto le compró 10 latas de atún a su gato como se lo había dicho antes de irse de casa porque el detective McHeartley era un hombre que hacía todo lo que prometía.

The Death Follows Them

The highway was empty, there was no sign of a car or truck nearby. The lights turned on and off. In the distance, a storm illuminated the night, and the wind began to move the treetops violently. The first drops began to wet the pavement. In the middle of the road, three young men ran desperately out of the forest for no reason. Terror was reflected on their faces, and they could do nothing but run and scream.

Suddenly, the three young men fell dead without any sign of violence. On their faces, you could see the surprise of those who did not expect death to arrive so quickly. They had a future, a job, and a lifetime ahead, but now their bodies were on the road. The animals of the nearby forest looked at the distance to those three possible prey but knew very well that entering the forest could mean death. Every time someone crossed the forest caves, died; being in them for a long time was fatal.

The next day with the storm far away and all the signs already dry and forgotten, the police surrounded the crime scene, marked with chalk the edge of the bodies, and took photographs of everything that seemed interesting or worthy of investigation. As always happened in these cases, news trucks were around trying to get the best image of the bodies and then broadcast it at the main time. The journalists tried to get information from the police, who were under a strict pact of silence. Not that they had no information, only that the best thing in these cases was to wait for a spokesman or a police force representative to make statements when he had all the data.

However, despite the best attempts by the police, they could not find any clue or any reason why three young bodies were on the road without signs of violence. Without any solution in sight, the prosecutor who was carrying the case decided to swallow his pride and call an old acquaintance—Detective McHeartley.

In his office, the detective was resting, laying his feet on the desk, near a dirty and empty pizza box. In the armchair, his cat was resting, sleeping on the top of the hat, and in one corner, his faithful jacket was hanging from the coat rack. It was a quiet Sunday afternoon, and the detective had no homework to do. In fact, he didn't even have a home to return to, except that office where he slept, worked, and lived all week. Amid the tranquility, the telephone rang. The noise caused both the detective and his pet to wake up scared. Desperate, the detective quickly answered the phone; he knew that in an investigation case, every second is important. "Hello? Who is it?" He practically shouted at the headset "Yes, it's me. Where? I am twelve hours away by bus. I don't know, I have other plans for today." His cat looked at him with an annoyed face. "Will they pay me a private plane? Well, that's fine. I'll be there."

He took his jacket, his wallet, and to get his hat, he had to ask his cat to move on top of him. "Please, I have to go." Finally, after giving him a murderous look, the cat moved from above the hat. "I promise I will bring you something back. Tuna? Chicken? How about it?" The cat looked at him, just rested his head on the detective's hand to indicate that he could leave in peace. "The neighbor has the keys, so she will take care of you for a while."

He quickly went to the airport where police representatives were waiting for him, and all got on a private plane. While in flight, McHeartley had the ability to read all the information in the case. He saw all the photos and all the information collected by the tireless members of the police force. Another strange case. It was the kind of case that followed the detective, the last case was at the end of the world, and it was quite particular. He could not get rid of the feeling that this case was not going to be as simple as that.

Upon landing, the policemen put him on a patrol car and went to the crime scene. The journalists and the mayor were waiting for him, visibly nervous. The elections were in a week and if the mayor did not solve the problem quickly he would probably lose all the votes. The mayor greeted Detective McHeartley with trembling hands and guided him to a police tent where all the coordination of the investigation was carried out.

Inside the tent was a white table, a chair, and copies of all the photos he had already seen on the trip to the crime scene. He also had a brown envelope on top of the stack that said "Forensic Report." McHeartley opened it, hoping to find the quick answer and return to his office, but in reality, it was a single sheet with a text below that said "There is not enough information to reach a conclusion, only footprints were found, they were walking for three days straight "The detective sighed. It was going to be a long night. He called an assistant, asked for the blackest coffee they could find to stay awake.

Outside, the press was attentive to every movement. After all, not every day Detective McHeartley, the hero of the lost plane case, visited the city. And this certainly means that it was a very important case. The hours passed, and of course, the moods were pretty bad. After all, when the news is broadcast 24 hours a day, the same news is really very little to report if there is no new news. They spent days full of tension; everyone was surprised because the detective hired specialists of all kinds to investigate the area where they found the young people dead, as well as reports of strange deaths in the past that had occurred in the town.

As soon as Detective McHeartley called a press conference at the door of the tent, all the journalists thanked those new news since it meant that at least the end was near torture. Finally, they could know what had happened to the three bodies, who was the guilty, and in particular what steps would be taken to capture him because the people of that town adored the drama. However, what received them was not exactly what they expected.

"Hello, good afternoon," McHeartley said in front of the microphone installed in a music stand. "I called you to a press conference because I know exactly what happened to the bodies of the young people. However..." He paused for years," I think it's not what you expected to hear. "

The journalists were on the edge of their seats. McHeartley continued, "The three young men were not killed by spacecraft, or by secret FBI agents or any of those conspiracy theories that were widely discussed in the press these days. The three young people died intoxicated, and according to the tracks, they were running for about three days."

The Mayor was unable to stop his tongue and said "Who has done it, Lord Detective? This is a sinister fact! We should suspend the elections," he shouted so that the opposing candidate would not win.

"Do you plan to suspend the elections because the culprit in the death of the youth was a fungus?" McHeartley said angrily because he had interrupted him.

Silence in the room. The news was so strong that silence could be felt in homes where families and curious people followed the transmission. "That's right, surprise yourself! The three died intoxicated by an evil fungus found in the forest of this town," he added sadly. "It seemed strange to me that such healthy young people died without signs of violence, so I thought they were poisoned by something and analyzed all the plants in the forest near the road. Indeed, the deadly fungus test was positive."

A journalist was very curious about it and said "Then why, according to the tracks, were they running for about three days in a row? It seems to me that something else must have pursued them!" McHeartley stared at him, "The only thing that followed them was death. You will see, my dear reporter; when someone consumes a toxic mushroom, the person hallucinates, each in his own way. They could be losing their heads little by little. The three young men began to lose their breath when they were deep in the forest and tried to go out to civilization. All three were camping and possibly entered the caves of the forest that are infected with the fungus." The silence was incredible in the conference room. "Unfortunately," he added with a bit of sadness, "if they had taken an emergency phone, this could have been solved because the effects of the fungus are eliminated with an allergy injection."

The mayor looked across the conference room without being able to believe it. Everything indicated that Detective McHeartley was as efficient as he said. Traces of the fungus poison had been killing many people in the middle of the forest.

Now the mayor was unable to win the elections. It was all the fault of the low budget, the lack of training, and the very low salaries he paid to the rangers. As he could, he tried to escape so as not to be cornered by the press.

The detective got off the lectern and proceeded to look for his jacket and his hat. Another case resolved, he thought. Before catching the bus to the airport, he bought 10 cans of tuna from his cat as he had said before leaving home because Detective McHeartley was a man who did everything he promised.

Quiz

Questions
1) ¿Dónde fueron encontrados los cuerpos?
    a. En una iglesia
    b. En medio del campo
    c. En una autopista
    d. En sus casas
2) ¿Qué decía el informe forense?
    a. Que habían caminado por tres días seguidos
    b. Decía la causa de la muerte
    c. Decía que habían sido raptados por extraterrestres
    d. Daba toda la información necesaria

3) ¿Cuál es la mascota de McHeartley?
    a. Un oso
    b. Un gato
    c. Un ave
    d. Un perro
4) ¿Por qué murieron los jóvenes?
    a. Por intoxicación de un hongo
    b. Por la picadura de un mosquito
    c. Fueron asesinados
    d. No se sabe
5) ¿Cuántas latas de atún le compró el detective a su mascota?
    a. 5
    b. 10
    c. 3
    d. 9

Answers
1) c
2) a
3) b
4) a
5) b

Vocabulario (Vocabulary)

Autopista – Highway; **Automóvil/Camión** – Car/truck; **Copas de los árboles** – Tree crows; **Gotas** – Drops; **Pavimento** – Pavement; **Carretera** – Road; **Policía** – Police; **Escena del crimen** - Crime scene; **Fotografías** – Pictures; **Información** – Information; **Pacto de silencio** – Pact of silence; **Vocero** – Spokesman; **Declaraciones** – Statements; **Intentos** – Try; **Orgullo** – Pride; **Oficina** – Office; **Escritorio** – Desk; **Gato** – Cat; **Encima** – Over; **Esquina** – Corner; **Fiel** – Faithful; **Domingo** – Sunday; **Hogar** – Home; **Semana** – Week; **Mascota** – Pet; **Desesperado** – Desesperate; **Auricular** – Handset; **Fastidio** – Nuisance; **Ánimos** – Moods; **Transmite** – Transmit; **Noticias** – News; **Días llenos de tensión** – Days filled with tensión; **Tortura** – Torture; **Cuerpos** – Bodies; **Culpable** – Guilty; **Apresarlo** – Arrest; **Micrófono** – Microphone; **Atril** – Lectern; **Asesinados** – Murdered; **Naves espaciales** – Spaceships; **Agentes secretos** – Secret agents; **Siniestro** – Sinister; **Candidato** – Candidate; **Hongo** – Fungus; **Transmisión** – Broadcast; **Conferencia** – Conference; **Indicaba** – Indicate; **Rastros del veneno** – Traces of poison; **Posibilidades** – Possibilities; **Presupuesto** – Budget; **Entrenamiento** – Training; **Sueldos** – Salaries; **Arrinconado** – Concerned.

Chapter 11: Experiencia Nocturna

Era tarde en la noche. No podía ver el ojo de mi aguja con claridad. La gente se movía por la calle concurrida mientras estaba batallando con mi máquina de coser. Algunos iban a sus casas y otros estaban de compras. Estaba cansada. Sí, lo estaba; no porque mi tienda fuese caliente, casi oscura y tranquila. Era porque mis pies ya eran pesados y débiles. No quería dejar la tienda. Había demasiados trabajos por hacer, muchas prendas que coser. No había nada agradable excepto la dulce fragancia que se elevaba de un bouquet de rosas cercano. Mientras oscurecía más y más, encendí la lámpara para ayudar a mi visión. Quién hubiese sabido que alguien estaba en la tienda, si no fuese por los rayos de la lámpara.

Vi una sombra por la ventana. La puerta se abrió y un cliente entró. Era uno de esos cuyas prendas debían haber estado listas el día anterior. Estaba vestido con un abrigo negro y pesado, y un sombrero de lana. Casi inmediatamente se quitó su abrigo y sombrero, y los colgó en un perchero. Parecía estar apurado.

"¿Dónde está mi esmoquin, John?" pregunto

No me podía mover. No podía hablar. No sabia que decir. En el silencio del momento, las manecillas ansiosas del reloj se podían escuchar. Comencé a vacilar en el fondo.

"Está casi listo, señor" dije con voz inestable.

"¿Casi listo?" repitió, sus ojos viéndome como rayos.

"No puedo tolerar tu excusa" lamentó. "¿No debía haber estado listo ayer?" preguntó molesto. En mi vergüenza, no encontré palabras para responder.

"¡Respóndeme, John!" demandó rápidamente. Yo sabía que él tenía razón, pero era claro que había fallado en cumplir.

"Lo siento mucho, señor" respondí

"Tus disculpas no son necesarias. Me has decepcionado mucho. Escucha, tengo una ocasión estatal mañana, y el Duque de Edimburgo personalmente me ha invitado. ¿Qué le digo? Odio las excusas" dijo.

Aun así, no podía decir nada. Simplemente no podía encontrar las palabras correctas. Evite su cara tanto como pude. Sin poder tolerar la incomoda atmósfera, estaba confiado en que las prestigiosas prendas estarían listas antes del día siguiente. Era la misma razón por la que me había quedado trabajando en sobretiempo.

"Señor" finalmente dije, "lamento no haber cumplido con el tiempo acordado. Pero le aseguro que su trabajo estará listo esta noche."

Por algunos momentos, no supe que estaba pasando por su mente. Mantuvo un silencio digno. Un silencio que me atormentó mas que sus palabras molestas.

"John" dijo con indiferencia "¿me estas dando tu palabra de que el saco estará listo esta noche?"

"Lo prometo" dije. Sir Williams tomó su abrigo y sombrero con facilidad y se fue majestuosamente de mi taller. Sir Williams era uno de los mas respetados hombres del estado de Edimburgo. Aunque luego cumplí mi promesa, pero no sin dificultad interna, dolor y arrepentimiento.

"Perdóneme, señor, por el retraso" rogué cuando le presente el saco del traje temprano la mañana siguiente. Me vio y me dio una sonrisa genuina que elevó mi confianza.

Ejercicio

Ok, ahora hagamos un ejercicio rápido: te haré 5 preguntas. Trata de responder y luego de las preguntas, te daré las respuestas.

Preguntas:
1) ¿Qué producía el aroma de la tienda?
2) ¿Qué llevó a Sir Williams a la tienda del sastre?
3) ¿Por qué Sir Williams estaba preocupado?
4) ¿Por qué el sastre estaba avergonzado?
5) ¿Cuál era el nombre del sastre?

Respuestas:
1) Un bouquet de rosas

2) Un saco de traje
3) Porque el saco no estaba listo a tiempo
4) Porque falló en entregar el saco a tiempo
5) JOHN

The Night Experience

It was late in the evening. I couldn't see the eye of my needle clearly. People were moving up and down the busy street while I was battling with my sewing machine. Some were heading home while others were obviously shopping. I was tired. Yes, I was, not because my shop was hot, nearly dark, and quiet. It was rather because my feet were already heavy and weak. I didn't want to leave the shop. There were just too many works to do, many clothes to sew. There was no object of delight except the sweet elevating fragrance drifting from a nearby bouquet of roses. As it darkened more and more, I lit the lamp to aid my vision. Who would have known that someone was in the shop if not for the rays of the lamp?

I saw a shadow by the window. The door opened, and a customer came inside. He was one of those whose clothes should have been ready the previous day. He was dressed in a heavy black cover coat and a woolen hat. Almost immediately, he removed his coat and hat and hung them on a standing coat rack. He seemed to be in haste.

"Where is my dinner jacket, John?" he questioned.

I was motionless. I became speechless. I just didn't know what to say. In the dead silence of the moment, the eager hands of the wall clock could be heard tick-tocking. I began to waver at heart.

"It's nearly ready Sir," I said in an unstable voice.

"Nearly ready?" he repeated. His eyes were flashing on me like extreme rays from lightning.

"I cannot bear your excuse" he lamented, "Was it not supposed to be ready yesterday?" he questioned angrily. In my shame, I found no words to reply.

"Answer me, John!" he quickly demanded. I knew he was telling the truth, but it was clear that I failed to meet up.

"I am so sorry, Sir," I replied.

"Your sorry is not needed. You have caused me great disappointment. Listen, I have a state occasion to attend tomorrow, and the Duke of Edinburgh personally invited me. What do I say? I hate excuses." he cried.

I still couldn't say anything. I just couldn't find the right words. I avoided his face as much as I could. Notwithstanding the awkward atmosphere, I had confidence the prestigious clothes would be ready before the following day. It was the very reason why I stayed overtime.

"Sir," I finally spoke, "I am sorry that I couldn't meet up at the agreed time. But I assure you that your work will be ready tonight.

For some moments, I didn't know what was going on his in mind. He kept a dignifying silence. A silence that tormented me more than his angry words.

"John," he said with sheer indifference, "Are you giving me your word that the jacket will be ready tonight."

"I promise," I said. Sir Williams pulled his coat and hat with great ease and walked majestically out of my workshop. Sir Williams was one of the few most respected statesmen in Edinburgh. Though I later fulfilled my promise but not without inner havoc, pain, and regret.

"Forgive me, Sir, for the delay," I begged when I presented him the suit jacket early the following morning. He looked at me and gave me a genuine smile that boosted my confidence.

Exercise

Ok, let's now start a quick exercise: I am going to ask you 5 questions. Try to reply, and after the questions, I will give you the answers.

Questions
1) What produced the fragrant in the shop?
2) What brought Sir Williams to the tailor's shop?
3) Why was Sir Williams worried?
4) Why did the tailored ashamed?
5) What was the name of the tailor?

Answers
1) A bouquet of roses
2) Suit Jacket
3) The suit jacket was not ready on time
4) He failed to deliver on time.
5) John

Chapter 12: Cyril y Su Voluntad

Parecía un buen día. Temprano en la mañana del Jueves. Cyril y yo estábamos juntos. El papá de Cyril era el alcalde de Nueva York. Era una ciudad muy poblada. También era referida como la capital comercial del mundo.

Cyril tenía la libertad de moverse sin su guardia de seguridad personal. Era un hombre de negocios joven y rico. Nunca le faltaba nada. El personalmente estaba manejando una de las compañías manufactureras de su padre. Era un hombre de voluntad fuerte.

Era el ultimo año de los estudiantes de post grado en la prestigiosa universidad de Harvard. Cyril me llamó "Kay." La vida no era tan cómoda para mi como lo era para Cyril. Cyril me ayudaba con algunos dólares cuando podía. Eramos muy amigos. Discutíamos cualquier cosa que nos molestara. Discutíamos todo.

"Me gustaría hacer mi post grado en Harvard" dijo Cyril mirándome.

"Buena idea" respondí rápidamente.

"Cuéntame sobre Harvard, Kay" pidió educadamente.

Tomé un tiempo para reflexionar, y empecé.

"Harvard es la institución educativa mas antigua de los Estados Unidos. Es una de las universidades mas prestigiosas del mundo."

Cyril escuchaba con mucha atención.

Yo sabía que simplemente estaba tras el mejor estándar y reputación.

Nunca había comprometido la calidad.

"Cyril" dije, "es bueno si quieres inscribirte en un post grado. Harvard seguramente será el mejor lugar para ti."

"¿Por que lo piensas?" preguntó.

"En Harvard, hay algo que se conoce como la Escuela de Economía de Harvard. Esta hecha para el beneficio de los ejecutivos de negocios" expliqué.

Cyril estaba concentrado en nuestra conversación. Era todo oídos, definitivamente.

Yo sabía que él estaba analizando la idea que compartió conmigo.

Había una señal de satisfacción y apreciación viniendo de él.

Parecía haber obtenido información vital de nuestra conversación.

"¿Tienes idea de cuánto cuesta entrar en el programa de negocios?" preguntó, aun viéndome.

Nuevamente tomé tiempo para reflexionar. No quería decir nada de lo que no estuviese seguro.

Sabía que era hora de tomar una decisión para Cyril, orientado a la acción. Tal vez el costo podría determinar su siguiente linea de decisión.

"El pago anual es aproximadamente 72 dólares. Cuando otros gastos se agregan, el total es ciento seis mil." Expliqué.

Cyril me vio con desconcierto.

"¿Cómo sabes todo esto?" preguntó con curiosidad.

"No olvides que mi amigo Bill esta actualmente cursando en la escuela de negocios de Harvard" dije.

"No es cara" dijo riendo, "Gracias por la larga explicación" agregó.

"Siempre un placer" dije con una sonrisa.

Exercise

Ok, ahora hagamos un ejercicio rápido: te haré 6 preguntas. Trata de responder y luego de las preguntas, te daré las respuestas.

Preguntas
1) ¿Quién era el padre de Cyril?
2) ¿Cual era la relación entre Cyril y Kay?
3) ¿Quién era Bill?
4) ¿Cyril estaba manejando una compañía?
5) Cyril se movía sin su guardia de seguridad. ¿Verdadero o falso?
6) ¿De qué universidad estaban hablando Cyril y Kay?

Respuestas
1) El alcalde de Nueva York
2) Mejores amigos
3) Un amigo de Kay
4) SÍ
5) VERDADERO

6) HARVARD

Cyril and His Will

It looked like a good day. In the early hours of Tuesday. Cyril and I were together. Cyril's father was the mayor of New York. It happened to be a densely populated city. It was also referred to as the commercial capital of the world.

Bill had the freedom to move about without his personal security guard. He was a rich and young businessman. He never was in lack. He personally was managing one of his father's manufacturing company. He was a man of strong will.

I was a final year master's student at the prestigious Harvard University. Cyril called me "Kay." Life was not as comfortable for me as it was for Cyril. Cyril helped me with some dollars whenever he could. We were best friends. We discussed anything that bothered us. We discussed everything.

"I will like to run my master's degree in Harvard," said Cyril looking at me intently.

"Good idea" I quickly responded.

"Tell me about Harvard, Kay" he requested politely.

I took some time to reflect, then I began.

"Harvard is the oldest institution of learning in the United States. It is one of the most prestigious universities in the world."

Cyril was listening with keen interest.

I knew he simply after the best in standard and reputation.

He had never compromised quality.

"Cyril," said I, "It is a good thing if you wish to enroll in a master's degree program. Harvard will surely be the best place for you."

"Why do you think so," he asked.

"At Harvard, there is something known as the Harvard Business School. It is made for the benefit of business executives" I explained.

Cyril was engrossed in our conversation. He was definitely all ears.

I knew he was analyzing the idea he shared with me.

There was a sign of satisfaction and appreciation gleaming from his countenance.

He seemed to have obtained vital information from our discussion.

"Do you have an idea how much it costs to enroll in the business program?" he asked, still looking at me.

Again, I took my time to reflect. I didn't want to say what I wasn't sure about.

I knew it was about decision time for the action-oriented Cyril. Perhaps the cost could determine his next line of decision.

"The annual tuition is approximately seventy-two dollars. When other costs are added, it totals up to a hundred and six thousand." I explained.

Cyril looked at me with disbelief.

"How do you know all these?" he asked curiously.

"Do not forget that my friend Bill is currently enrolled at Harvard Business School," I said.

"It's not expensive," he said laughing, "Thanks for the lengthy explanation" he added.

"Always my pleasure," I said with a soft hearty smile.

EXERCISE

Ok, let's now start a quick exercise: I am going to ask you 6 questions. Try to reply, and after the questions, I will give you the answers.

Questions
1) Who was Cyril's father?
2) What was the relationship between Cyril and Kay?
3) Who was Bill?
4) Was Cyril managing a company?
5) Cyril moved without his security guard. True or False?
6) Which university was Cyril and Kay talking about?

Answers
1) The mayor of New York
2) Best friends
3) A Kay's friend
4) Yes
5) TRUE
6) HARVARD

Chapter 13: La Asumida Muerte de Henry, El Granjero

En una ciudad donde todos amaban las flores, vivía un anciano llamado Henry.

Cultivaba flores exquisitas de raros colores y aromas.

En toda la comunidad, solo algunas personas conocían el arte de cultivar flores.

Las flores de Henry eran las más buscadas porque solo vendía flores frescas y sanas.

Aunque era conocido por cultivar distintos tipos de flores, era popular por sus cultivos de girasoles, lirios blancos y rosas rojas.

"Me pregunto cuando van a aprender todo lo que intento enseñarles" decía su abuela hace años, cuando Henry aun era un niño.

Era quien había enseñado a Henry todo sobre los cultivos de flores.

"Ahora tienes 30. Debes hacer tu propia granja" le dijo una vez a Henry.

Desde entonces, Henry había hecho mucho dinero con su negocio de cultivo de flores.

Era grandemente admirado por todos, por su naturaleza cariñosa y generosa.

Tenía una esposa y 5 hijos. Ninguno de sus hijos lo ayudaba en la granja.

Para cumplir con la demanda, contrató trabajadores diligentes que lo asistían con los retos de cultivar, desherbar, hacer crecer y cortar flores.

Un día, mientras iba a la granja, una serpiente lo mordió.

Un transeúnte que lo reconoció rápidamente acudió a su rescate y lo ayudó a llegar a su casa.

Henry pidió que llamaran a su doctor. El doctor vino pronto.

"Me mordió una serpiente de camino a la granja ayer" explicó Henry.

"¡Oh! Lo lamento" dijo el doctor, "tu salud será restaurada. Estoy aquí para minimizar tu dolor y ayudarte a recuperarte."

"Exactamente por lo que te quería aquí" dijo Henry. Henry sufría de dolor y agonía severos.

"Hubieses muerto si hubieses demorado un segundo mas en buscarme. Hiciste bien, Henry. Vas a estar bien." aseguró el doctor.

Pronto Henry empezó a recuperarse. Estaba satisfecho con la velocidad de su recuperación.

Desafortunadamente, su familia le daba poca o nada de atención. Eran indiferentes a sus predicamentos. Su esposa estaba mas interesada en atender fiestas y reuniones sociales. Amaba su joyero mas de lo que amaba a su esposo.

Pronto Henry se recuperó. Estaba en duda por el abandono total que experimentó de su familia. Armó un gran plan para ayudarlo a superar su gran duda.

"Tu padre esta muerto" declaró uno de los granjeros que fue a llevar el mensaje a la esposa de Henry y a sus hijos acerca de la tragedia. El trabajador se veía confundido y preocupado.

"¿Cómo murió?" preguntó la esposa de Henry con aparente falta de interés y simpatía.

"Se desplomó justo cuando íbamos a empezar a desherbar" explicó uno de los granjeros.

Los trabajadores que llevaron el supuesto cuerpo de Henry descubrieron claramente una alegría oculta y felicidad maliciosa entre los miembros de la familia de Henry.

"¡Aha!" anunció Henry, levantándose de pronto. "Lo he visto todo" dijo en voz fuerte. Su cara suave se transformó inmediatamente en un semblante severo.

Aterrorizados profundamente, su esposa e hijos lo vieron sin poderlo creer.

"¿Era un plan o estamos viendo un fantasma?" se preguntaron. Los trabajadores entendieron lo que había ocurrido. Era un plan colectivo.

"Nunca me han querido" le dijo Henry a su familia. "Querían que me muriera para poder heredar mi fortuna. Lo fingí. Lo hice para saber cuanto amor me tienen" dijo. Todos se quedaron inmóviles como si estuviesen muertos y sin vida. Ninguno dijo ni una palabra. "Y mi herencia cuando esté escrita no los tendrá a ningunos como beneficiarios. Todos ustedes no se merecen nada" declaró Henry.

Henry después dejo a su familia y vivió en las mismas habitaciones que una vez proveyó para sus trabajadores.

Ejercicio

Ok, ahora hagamos un ejercicio rápido: te haré 5 preguntas. Trata de responder y luego de las preguntas, te daré las respuestas.

Preguntas
1) ¿Cuál era la ocupación de Henry?
2) ¿Por qué Henry llamó al doctor?
3) ¿La familia de Henry mostró interés en su recuperación?
4) Henry no fingió su muerte. Verdadero o falso.
5) ¿Por qué Henry dejó a su familia?

Respuestas
1) Granjero de flores
2) Veneno de serpiente
3) NO
4) FALSO
5) Porque no lo querían

The Assumed Death of Henry, the Framer

In a city where everybody loved flowers, there lived an old man called Henry.

He grew exquisite flowers of rare colors and scent.

In the entire community, only a few people knew the art of farming flowers.

Henry's flowers were the most sought after because he sold only fresh and healthy flowers.

Though he was known for growing different kinds of flowers, he was popular for farming sunflowers, white lily, and red roses.

"I wonder when you're going to learn all that I try to teach you." his grandmother would say years ago when Henry was still a kid.

She was the one who had taught Henry everything about flower farming.

"You are now thirty. You must now establish your own farm." she once told Henry.

Henry had long since made a lot of fortune from his flower farming business.

He was greatly admired by everyone for his loving and generous nature.

He had a wife and five children. None of his children helped him on his farm.

To meet up with demand, he hired diligent workers who assisted him with the challenges of cultivating, weeding, growing and cutting flowers.

One day as he was going to the farm a snake, bit him.

A passerby who recognized him quickly came to his rescue and aided him home.

Henry asked to call his doctor. The doctor came soon afterward.

"I was bitten by a snake on my way to the farm yesterday" explained Henry.

"Oh! Sorry for that" said the doctor, "Your health will be restored. I am here to minimize the pain and to help you recover."

"Exactly why I wanted you here," said Henry. Henry suffered from severe pain and agony.

"You might have died if you had delayed a second in seeking my presence. You did well, Henry. You are going to be okay." assured the doctor.

Soon Henry began to recover. He was satisfied with the speed of relief he got from the doctor's treatment.

Unfortunately, his family gave him little or no attention. They were indifferent to his predicament. His wife was more interested in attending parties and social gatherings. She loved her jewelry box more than she loved her husband.

Soon Henry recovered. He was in doubt of the complete abandonment he experienced from his family. He hatched a grand plan to help him overcome his great doubt.

"Your father is dead" declared one of the farm workers who came to message Henry's wife and children about the tragedy. The worker looked confused and aggrieved.

"How did he die?" Henry's wife asked with an apparent lack of interest and sympathy.

"He slumped just as we were about to start weeding." explained one of the farmers.

The workers who brought in Henry's supposed corps clearly discovered a hidden joy and malicious happiness among members of Henry's family.

"Aha!" announced Henry suddenly rising, "I have seen it all," he said in a strong voice. His mild face immediately transformed into a stern countenance.

Deeply terrified, his wife and children looked at him in disbelief.

"Was it a plan, or are we seeing a ghost" they wondered. The workers understood what happened. It was a collective scheme.

"You have never loved me," Henry told his family, "You wanted me to die so that you could inherit my wealth. I faked it. I did it to know how much love you have for me," he said.

They all stood motionless as if they were dead and lifeless. None spoke a single word.

"And my will when written will not bear anyone of you as beneficiary. You all deserve nothing." declared Henry.

Henry later left his family and lived in the same quarters he once provided for his workers.

Exercise

Ok, let's now start a quick exercise: I am going to ask you 5 questions. Try to reply, and after the questions, I will give you the answers.

Questions
   1) What was Henry's occupation?
   2) Why did Henry ask for the medical doctor?
   3) Did Henry's family show interest in his recovery?
   4) Henry didn't fake his death. True or False?
   5) Why did Henry leave his family?

Answers
   1) Flower Farmer
   2) Snake poison
   3) No
   4) False
   5) They didn't love him

Chapter 14: La Gran Noticia

El 26 de septiembre era un día como cualquiera. Matías se levantaba a las 7 de la mañana, desayunaba y se iba al colegio. Últimamente había estado llegando tarde, ya que su mamá no podía llevarlo porque estaba embarazada y su papá trabajaba en la fábrica desde temprano. Matías debía tomar el autobús para llegar al colegio, y en esos viajes se había hecho un amigo, Kevin.

Esa mañana, Matías saltó de la cama, tomó sus carpetas y salió corriendo a la parada de autobús. Allí lo estaba esperando Kevin y estrecharon las manos como de costumbre. Kevin estaba un poco molesto ese día, lo que le causaba un poco de disgusto a Matías, que le costaba soportar.

Cuando llegó el autobús, subieron y ya estaban de camino a clase. Unas pocas cuadras antes de llegar, algo desafortunado sucedió. De casualidad, antes de doblar en una esquina, un camión cruzó rápidamente y causó un choque con otro auto. Matías y Kevin vieron la situación desde la ventana del autobús. El chofer bajó a ayudar a los conductores. Por suerte, los bomberos estaban de paso y se aseguraron de que no hubiera sucedido una desgracia. Ambos conductores se encontraban sanos, pero Kevin y Matías ya llegaban muy tarde, pero aún podían asistir a clase, por lo que bajaron del autobús y siguieron caminando.

Una vez que llegaron, le explicaron lo que había sucedido a su maestra. La maestra entendió y se puso feliz de que no hubiera víctimas. Kevin y Matías fueron a sentarse en sus pupitres.

Cuando Matías abrió su cartuchera, vio un mensaje escrito a mano que decía "Hoy recibirás una gran noticia. La luna dice que será tu mejor amiga." Matías comenzó a preguntarse '¿Qué tipo de noticia recibiré hoy?'

A Matías lo agobiaban las dudas, entonces les preguntó a sus amigos. Kevin era un poco escéptico, le dijo que quizás solo era una broma. María era un poco celosa, le dijo que él ya tenía una mejor amiga y que era ella y nadie más. Juliana era más pragmática, le dijo que la luna no hablaba. Lucas era muy pesimista, le dijo que podría ser una mala noticia.

Matías estaba lleno de curiosidad. De camino a su casa, solo pensaba en la nota. Miraba a la luna e intentaba hablar con ella. Si bien no escuchaba nada, había algo que lo llenaba de esperanzas y le confirmaba que esa tarde se iba a poner muy feliz con la noticia.

Se había sentado al lado de una señora de unos 50 años que le contaba que ella tenía un nieto de la edad de él, que se llamaba Julián y que su mamá siempre supo que sería varón. Matías se dio cuenta de inmediato de cuál sería la sorpresa. Su mamá le había contado historias similares sobre el día en que él nació. Miró a la luna, cerró los ojos, y le dio las gracias. El mensaje era cierto, era una gran sorpresa y él ya sabía cuál era. Siempre había querido una mejor amiga con quién compartir su vida. Ya sabía quién había dejado ese mensaje en su cartuchera. Bajó del autobús y fue corriendo a su casa. Había muchos autos estacionados en la calle, y su casa era la que más brillaba a la luz de la luna. Se veían muchas siluetas en las cortinas de la ventana. Sentía un clima navideño en pleno julio.

Llegó rápido, abrazó fuerte a su papá y se encontró con sus abuelos, sus dos tíos con su hija, sus primos, y su tía. Todos sus parientes estaban allí. Y detrás de todos ellos estaba su mamá. Matías se acercó llorando de felicidad y le dio un beso a su mamá. En sus brazos estaba Rocío, tan pequeña y frágil. Matías la sostuvo en sus brazos y le dijo:

"Tú serás mi mejor amiga. Te enseñaré a hacer las mejores bromas, nos divertiremos con las mejores travesuras y te cuidaré siempre." Y preguntó, "Pero mamá, ¿cómo sabías que sería niña?"

"Yo siempre lo supe, hijo. No solo fue la luna, sino que cuando deseas algo con fuerza, amor, honestidad y desinterés, tus deseos se hacen realidad."

"Si hubiera sido niño, lo hubiera querido igual."

"Lo sé, hijo."

Todos habían traído regalos. Sus tíos le trajeron ropa de todos colores: violeta, amarillo, marrón, negro, verde, celeste y naranja. Sus abuelos le trajeron un cochecito. Su tía le trajo la cuna que había prometido. Pero el que había recibido el mejor regalo de todos era Matías... Una hermanita.

Quiz
Preguntas
1) ¿Qué hizo Matías después de tomar el desayuno?
    a. Fui a jugar
    b. Fue a la cama

     c. Fue a la escuela
2) ¿Por qué no podía la madre Matías llevarlo a la escuela?
     a. Ella trabajó temprano en la fábrica
     b. Ella estaba mal
     c. Ella estaba embarazada
3) ¿Cómo se llamaba el niño que esperaba a Matías en el autobús?
     a. Ken
     b. Kevin
     c. Karen
4) ¿Qué pasó camino a la escuela?
     a. El autobús se dañó
     b. Coches chocaron
     c. Hubo fuego
5) ¿Qué regalos compraron los abuelos de Matías?
     a. Ropa de todos los colores
     b. Un cochecito
     c. Una cuna

Respuestas
- **1)** c
- **2)** c
- **3)** b
- **4)** b
- **5)** b

The Great News

September 26 was a day like any other. Matías got up at 7 in the morning, ate breakfast, and went to school. Lately, he had been late since his mother could not take him because she was pregnant, and his father worked at the factory early. Matías had to take the bus to get to school, and on those trips, he had become a friend to Kevin.

That morning, Matías jumped out of bed, took his books, and ran to the bus stop. Kevin was waiting for him there, and they shook hands as usual. Kevin was a little upset that day, which caused Matias a bit of annoyance, which was hard to bear.

When the bus arrived, they got on and were already on their way to class. A few blocks before arriving, something unfortunate happened. By chance, before turning in a corner, a truck quickly crossed and caused a crash with another car. Matías and Kevin saw the situation from the bus window. The driver went down to help the drivers. Luckily, firefighters were passing through and made sure that a misfortune had not happened. Both drivers were healthy, but Kevin and Matías were already late, but they could still attend class, so they got off the bus and kept walking.

Once they arrived, they explained what had happened to their teacher. The teacher understood and was happy that there were no victims. Kevin and Matías went to sit at their desks.

When Matías opened his holster, he saw a handwritten message that said "Today you will receive great news. The moon says she will be your best friend." Matías began to wonder 'What kind of news will I receive today?'

Matthias was overwhelmed by doubts, so he asked his friends. Kevin was a bit skeptical; he said maybe it was just a joke. Maria was a little jealous; she told him that he already had a best friend and that was she and no one else. Juliana was more pragmatic; she told him that the moon did not speak. Lucas was very pessimistic; he said it could be bad news.

Matías was full of curiosity. On the way home, he just thought about the note. He looked at the moon and tried to talk to her. Although he didn't hear anything, there was something that filled him with hope and confirmed that he was going to be very happy with the news that afternoon.

He had sat next to a lady in her 50s who told her that she had a grandson his age, that his name was Julian, and that his mother always knew he would be male. Matías immediately realized what the surprise would be. His mother had told him similar stories about the day he was born. He looked at the moon, closed his eyes, and thanked himself. The message was true, it was a big surprise, and he already knew what it was. He had always wanted a best friend with whom to share his life. He already knew who had left that message in his holster. He got off the bus and ran home. There were many cars parked on the street, and his house was the one that shone brighter in the moonlight. There were many silhouettes in the window curtains. I felt a Christmas weather in the middle of July.

He arrived quickly, hugged his dad tightly, and met his grandparents, his two uncles with his daughter, his cousins, and his aunt. All his relatives were there. And behind all of them was his mom. Matías approached crying with happiness and kissed his mother. In his arms was Rocío, so small and fragile. Matthias held her in his arms and said:

"You will be my best friend. I will teach you to make the best jokes, we will have fun with the best pranks, and I will always take care of you." And asked: "But mom, how did you know it would be a girl?"

"I always knew, son. Not only was the moon, but when you want something with strength, love, honesty, and disinterest, your wishes come true."

"If she had been a boy, I would have wanted him the same."

"I know, son."

Everyone had brought gifts. His uncles brought him clothes of all colors: violet, yellow, brown, black, green, light blue, and orange. His grandparents brought him a stroller. His aunt brought him the crib he had promised. But the one who had received the best gift of all was Matthias, a little sister.

Quiz

Question
1) What did Matías do after taking breakfast?
    a. Went to play
    b. Went to bed
    c. Went to school
2) 2. Why couldn't Matías mother take him to school?
    a. She worked early at the factory
    b. She was unwell

c. She was pregnant
3) 3. What was the name of the boy waiting for Matías on the bus?
   a. Ken
   b. Kevin
   c. Karen
4) 4. What happened on the way to school?
   a. The bus broke
   b. Cars crashed
   c. There was a fire
5) 5. What gifts did the Matías grandparents buy?
   a. clothes of all colors
   b. A stroller
   c. A crib

Answers
   1) c
   2) c
   3) b
   4) b
   5) b

Vocabulario (Vocabulary)

(Nos) divertiremos – (We) will have fun; **(Te) cuidaré** – (I) will take care of (you); **Abuelos** – Grandparents; **Agobiaban** – Overwhelmed; **Amarillo** – Yellow; **Amigo/a** – Friend; Amor – Love; **Asistir** – To be present; **Auto** – Car; **Bajaron** – Got off; **Bomberos** – Firefighters; **Brazos** – Arms; **Brillaba** – Gleamed; **Broma** – Joke; **Calle** – Street; **Cama** – Bed; **Caminando** – Walking;

Camión – Truck; **Carpetas** – Folders; **Cartuchera** – Pencil case; **Celeste** – Light blue; **Celoso/a** – Jealous; **Chofer** – (Bus) driver; **Choque** – Crash; **Cierto** – True; **Clima** – Environment; **Cochecito** – Stroller; **Colegio** – High school; **Comenzó** – Started; **Compartir** – Share; **Conductores** - (Car) drivers; **Corriendo** – Running; **Cualquiera** – Any; **Cuna** – Crib; **De camino a** – On (their) way to; **Desayunaba** – Had breakfast;- **Deseas** – Wish; **Desgracia** – Misfortune; **Desinterés** – Selflessness; **Disgusto** – Annoyance; **Doblar** – Turn; **Embarazada** – Pregnant; **Enseñaré** – Will teach; **Entendió** – Understood; **Entonces** – So; **Escéptico** – Skeptical; **Escrito a mano** – Handwritten; **Escuchaba** – Listened; **Esperanzas** – Hopes; **Esquina** – Corner; **Estacionados** – Parking; **Estrecharon** – Shaked-hands; **Fábrica** – Factory; **Felicidad** – Happiness; **Fuerza** – Strength; **Gracias** – Thanks; **Gran(de)** – Big; **Había dejado** – Had left; **Había querido** – Had wanted; **Hermanita** – Little sister; **Hija** – Daughter; **Hijo** – Son; **Hoy** – Today; **Intentaba** – Tried; **Levantaba** – Got up; **Llorando** – Crying; **Luna** – Moon; **Maestro/a** – Teacher; **Mamá** – Mom; **Marrón** – Brown; **Mejor** – Best; **Miraba** – Looked; **Molesto** – Annoying; **Naranja** – Orange; **Navideño** – Christmas; **Negro** – Black; **Nieto** – Grandson; **Niña** – Girl; **Ojos** – Eyes; **Papá** – Dad; **Parada** – Bus stop; **Parientes** – Family members; **Pequeña** – Little; **Preguntarse** – Wonder; **Primos** – Cousins; **Pupitres** – Desks; **Quizás** – Maybe; **Regalos** – Presents; **Sabía** – Knew; **Saltó** – Jumped; **Sanos** – Healthy; **Señora** – Lady; **Sentarse** – Sit down; **Siempre** – Always; **Sostuvo** – Held; **Subieron** – Got on; **Tarde** –Late; **Temprano** – Early; **Tía** – Aunt; **Tíos** – Uncles; **Travesuras** – Antics;

Últimamente – Recently; **Varón** – Boy; **Ventana** – Window; **Verde** – Green; **Vida** – Life; **Vieron** – Saw; **Violeta** – Purple.

Chapter 15: Salir con Los Amigos

Hoy es viernes y mis amigos se reúnen en un bar de deportes para ver el juego de futbol de la selección nacional. El juego empieza a las 6 pm y termina a las 8 pm. Yo voy a tomar el metro para poder llegar al área del bar. El bar está ubicado en la zona norte de la ciudad, queda como a 3 kilómetros de mi oficina. Yo no llevo el carro por que hoy tomaré tres cervezas en el bar, y si se toma licor no se debe manejar. En el metro, me reúno con otros compañeros y nos vamos hacia el bar.

Son las 5 pm, y el metro está muy congestionado; hay muchos pasajeros. La gente acaba de salir del trabajo, por lo que estamos en hora pico. A mí no me gusta usar el transporte público durante las horas pico porque todos vamos como sardinas en latas. Estamos muy apretados, yo creo que hay más de 300 personas en este vagón del metro.

Las puertas del vagón no cierran porque está muy lleno, alguien tendrá que bajarse para que cierren las puertas.

Ya llegué al bar, hay una cola de espera para entrar, el portero no me deja pasar si no hago la cola. Llamo por teléfono a mis compañeros y hablo con Víctor. Víctor sale del bar y le dice al portero que mi puesto está reservado, el portero me deja entrar. Hoy el bar está lleno, el juego de hoy es decisivo para la clasificación al mundial de Rusia. La selección juega en Santiago de Chile contra la selección Argentina.

Todos están muy emocionados, la gente de mi ciudad es muy aficionada al futbol, y siempre que juega la selección nacional, todos la quieren ver. Antes que empiece el juego, voy a pedir algo de comer, pido una hamburguesa con papas fritas, y de tomar un refresco. La mesonera es muy amable y trae la comida rápido. Me como todo, está muy sabroso.

El juego empezó, los jugadores de Argentina se ven nerviosos. Todos en el bar están emocionados. Gritan como locos cada vez que los jugadores de la selección se acercan a la portería. El juego está muy bueno. El portero de nuestra selección es el mejor, tapa todos los tiros, nadie puede meterle un gol. Después del partido, ponen música y la fiesta continúa; ahora las mujeres están bailando sobre la barra, y a la que aplaude más le regalan bebidas para todo su grupo.

La música está muy movida, el ambiente es festivo, la gente está alegre por el juego. Mi vecina está en el bar y me invita a bailar, yo bailo con ella y de repente me pregunta a qué hora me voy, yo le respondo que no lo sé. Ella me pide que por favor le dé un aventón hasta su casa cuando me vaya. Yo le digo que no tengo carro, que el carro está en la casa. Ella me dice que, por favor, cuando me vaya a mi casa le avise, y que yo la acompañe a la casa de ella, porque le da miedo irse sola en taxi.

Hangout With Friends

Today is Friday, and my friends gather at a sports bar to watch the national soccer team game. The game starts at 6 pm and ends at 8 pm. I'm going to take the metro to get to the bar. The bar is located in the north part of the city. It is about 3 kilometers from my office. I do not take the car with me because today I will drink three beers at the bar. If you drink liquor, you should not drive. In the subway, I meet with other colleagues, and we go to the bar.

It is 5 pm, and the subway is very crowded; there are too many passengers. People just got off work, so we're at rush hour. I do not like to use public transportation during rush hour because we all get packed like sardines. We are very tight. I think there are more than 300 people in this subway car.

The car doors do not close because it is too full, someone will have to get off to close the doors.

I arrived at the bar; there is a long waiting line to enter, the Bouncer will not let me pass without making the line. I call my friends and talk to Victor. Victor gets out of the bar and tells the doorman that my seat is reserved; the porter lets me in. Today the bar is full. Today's game is decisive for qualifying for the World Cup in Russia. The selection plays in Santiago de Chile against the Argentina team.

Everyone is very excited. The people of my city are very fond of soccer, and whenever the national team plays, everyone wants to see it. Before the game starts, I'm going to order something to eat. I order a hamburger with fries and a soda. The server is very friendly and brings the food fast. I eat everything; it is delicious.

The game started, Argentinian players look nervous. Everyone at the bar is thrilled. They yell like crazy every time the players of the selection approach the goal. The game is very good. The goalkeeper of our team is the best, cover all the shots, nobody can put a goal. After the game, they put on music, and the party goes on. Now the women are dancing on the bar, and the one who gets more cheers gains free drinks for her whole group.

The music is vivacious; the atmosphere is festive; people are happy for the game. My neighbor is at the bar and invites me to dance, I dance with her, and she asks me at what time I go; I reply that I do not know. She asks me to please give her a ride home when I leave. I tell her that I do not have a car that the car is at home. She tells me to let her know when I go to my house and that I accompany her to her home because she is scared to go alone in a taxi.

Quiz

Questions
1) ¿Dónde se reúnen mis amigos el viernes?
    a. Bar deportivo
    b. En el garaje
    c. Restaurante
2) ¿Por qué dejo mi auto hoy?
    a. Llegaré tarde
    b. Estaré borracho
    c. Prefiero caminar
3) ¿Por qué está lleno el metro?
    a. Tráfico vehicular
    b. Demasiados pasajeros

          c. Hubo lluvias
    4) ¿Cómo era la mesonera?
          a. Amistosa
          b. Triste
          c. Silenciosa

Answers
   1) a
   2) b
   3) b
   4) a

Vocabulario (Vocabulary)

Companion – Compañeros; **Gather** – Reunirse; **Pub** – Bar; **Sports Bar** – Bar Deportivo; **Football** – Futbol; **Beers** – Cervezas; **Food** – Comida; **Questions** – Preguntas; **Answers** – Respuestas; **Goal** – Portería.

Chapter 16: El Alfarero Sabio

Un alfarero vivía con su esposa. Hacía hermosas vasijas y vasos. En un momento, no tenía donde encontrar arcilla cruda. Se volvió pobre porque no tenia vasijas ni vasos para vender otra vez. Pronto, no pudo mantener a su familia. Un día, llamó a su esposa y le informó su decisión de buscar y reubicarse donde pudiese encontrar arcilla cruda en grandes cantidades.

"Te seguiré con gusto a donde vayas" le prometió.

Unos días después, encontró una gran cantidad de arcilla en una de las ciudades grandes. El alfarero y su esposa se reubicaron en la ciudad y el alfarero empezó a hacer hermosas vasijas y vasos.

"Nadie esta comprando mis vasijas" dijo el alfarero, muy preocupado. Empezó a ofrecer sus productos alrededor de la ciudad. "Compre hermosas vasijas y vasos" decía, "soy el mejor alfarero de todos los tiempos. Puedo hacer cualquier diseño de vasija. Sólo dígame como la quiere" decía el alfarero.

Nadie lo escuchaba. Al día siguiente continuó ofreciendo y atrayendo atención hacia su trabajo y habilidades.

"Compre hermosas vasijas de terracota y vasos de flores. No le dolerá verlos de cerca. Compre dos y llévese una gratis" decía el alfarero.

Un día, una peatona se acercó y estudió de cerca algunas de las vasijas.

"Hola señor alfarero", dijo la peatona. "No me gustan ninguna de estas vasijas. ¿Le puedo pagar para que haga vasijas a mi gusto?"

"Si señora" dijo el alfarero. Y la llevó a su taller y rápidamente le hizo el diseño de vasija que ella pidió

"Tenga señora, las vasijas están listas." Ella tomó las vasijas y le pagó al alfarero. Fue a su casa y sus amigas vieron lo hermosas que se veían las vasijas. Decidieron ir también a ver al alfarero a su taller.

"¿Puede hacer nuestro diseño de vasijas? Podemos pagar cualquier cantidad" dijo la rica mujer.

"Si, si puede. Es posible" dijo con alegría.

"Aquí, señoras. Las vasijas están listas" dijo. Las mujeres tomaron las vasijas y pagaron al alfarero una gran cantidad de dinero.

"¿Qué haré con todo este dinero?" Contempló el alfarero. "Úsalo para comprar equipos modernos para hacer las vasijas" le aconsejó su esposa.

Pronto, compró una rueda de alfarería, moldes y otras herramientas avanzadas. Hizo su tienda mas atractiva pintándola de nuevo, y reparando las herramientas abandonadas. Luego, empezó a producir vasijas que estaban bien hechas y arregladas. Producía vasijas con formas maravillosas y colores. Las vasijas eran tan atractivas que muchas personas empezaron a entrar en el taller del alfarero a pedir vasijas. El negocio del alfarero empezó a crecer y su esposa comenzó a vivir en abundancia

"Querido", dijo sonriendo, "te he enseñado el secreto del éxito en los negocios."

Ejercicio

Ok, ahora hagamos un ejercicio rápido: te haré 5 preguntas. Trata de responder y luego de las preguntas, te daré las respuestas.

Preguntas
1) ¿Qué decisión le comentó el alfarero a su esposa?
2) ¿Dónde se reubicó el alfarero?
3) ¿El alfarero era rápido haciendo sus pedidos?
4) ¿El alfarero ofreció sus trabajos?
5) ¿Quién le dijo al alfarero que comprara equipos modernos?

Respuestas
1) Que buscaría y se reubicaría donde encontrase arcilla cruda
2) En una gran ciudad
3) SÍ
4) Sí, lo hizo
5) Su esposa

The Wise Potter

A potter once lived with his wife. He made beautiful vessels and verses. There came a time when he had nowhere to find raw clay. He became poor because he had neither pots nor verses to sell again. Soon, he couldn't afford to fend for his family. One day, he called his wife and informed her of his decision to search and resettle wherever he could find raw clay in big quantities.

"I will joyfully follow you wherever you go" she promised.

A few days after, he found a big quantity of clay in one of the big cities. The potter and his wife resettled in the city, and the potter began to make beautiful vessels and verses.

"Nobody is buying my pots." said the potter deeply worried. He started hawking his products around the town. "Buy beautiful pots and verses." he would say. "I am the greatest potter of all time. I can make any design of pot. Just tell me how you want to it" said the potter.

No one listened to him. The next day he continued hawking and drawing attention to his works and skills.

"Buy beautiful terracotta pots and flower verses. It won't hurt to take a closer look. Buy two and get one free." the potter would say.

On a particular day, a pedestrian walked up to him and closely studied some of the pots.

"Hello, Mr. potter," said the pedestrian, "I do not like any of these pots here. Can I pay you to have my choice of a vessel made for me?"

"Yes, ma'am," said the potter. And the potter took her to his workshop and quickly made the design of the pots she asked requested.

"Here ma'am, the pots are ready." she collected the pots and paid the potter. She went home, and her friends saw how beautiful the pots looked. They too decided to go and see the potter in his workshop.

" Can you make our choice of pots, we are ready to pay you any amount." said the rich women?"

"Yes, you can. Yes, it is very possible," he said joyfully.

"Here, my ladies. The vessels are ready," he said. The women collected the vessels and paid the potter a very huge amount of money.

"What shall I do with all this money?" the potter contemplated. "Use it to buy modern pottery-making equipment," advised his wife.

Soon, he acquired a pottery wheel, mold, and other advanced tools. He made his shop look more attractive by repainting it and by repairing abandoned tools. Thereafter, he started producing vessels that were well treated and beautified. He produced vessels with wonderful shapes and colors. The vessels were so attractive that people started entering the potter's workshop in big numbers requesting for vessels. The potter's business started booming, and his wife began to live in abundance.

"Dearie, she said, smiling," I have taught you the secret of business success."

Exercise

Ok, let's now start a quick exercise: I am going to ask you 5 questions. Try to reply, and after the questions, I will give you the answers.

Questions
1) What decision did the potter share with the wife?
2) Where did the potter relocate?
3) Was the potter fast in delivering his services?
4) Did the potter ever hawk his works?
5) Who told the potter to buy modern equipment?

Answers
1) He would search and resettle wherever he would find raw clay
2) A big city
3) Yes
4) Yes, he did
5) His wife

Chapter 17: La Fiesta de Los Gnomos y Las Hadas

Es luna llena y Ed está viendo por su ventana en su habitación

Ha estado leyendo cuentos de aventuras de hadas y quería mucho ver las cosas por sí mismo.

Halloween había llegado y se había ido junto con su esperanza de encontrar a un elfo como del que se había disfrazado.

Ahora estaba sentado viendo con anhelo desde la ventana en su habitación.

Antes de que sus padres se mudaran a San Francisco, vivían en una gran casa en Minnesota.

Había leído muchos libros de la tierra de las hadas y magos, pero nunca había visto uno.

Y el año pasado, se mudaron a una casa más grande con torrecillas y un ático.

Su hermano mayor, Henry, le contaba historias de terror de magia y hechicería que ocurrieron en el ático y él lo escuchaba con mucho interés.

Suspiró fuertemente luego de recordarlos.

Se levantó del asiento de la ventana donde estaba, y tomó su libro de la mesa de lectura.

Mientras se volteaba para sentarse, escucho el crujir de las hojas en el jardín.

Vio alrededor y sus ojos casi saltaron de curiosidad.

Vio un gnomo llevando la mesa más pequeña que había visto en su vida, colocándola con cuidado sobre una seta.

"Debo estar soñando" murmuró.

Otro gnomo corrió pasando al primero.

"Brittle, no hagas eso. Las setas serán mesas para las hadas más pequeñas. La mesa no se suponen que sean para pararse."

Y con eso, movió la mesa de ahí y la colocó en el suelo.

"Tal vez no es un sueño. Debo bajar rápidamente."

Entonces Ed corrió hacia abajo y gentilmente abrió la puerta de la cocina, y salió al jardín.

Los gnomos temblaron cuando lo vieron.

"Esperen, no se vayan" rogó Ed.

"Los he estado viendo desde mi ventana y solo bajé para asegurarme de que no estuviese durmiendo."

"¿Para qué es la mesa?"

Brittle habló primero.

"Esta noche es una fiesta para nosotros. ¡Y estamos invitando a las hadas también!" Dijo con emoción.

"¿Nos puedes ayudar a armar todo?"

"Se nos hace tarde."

"Claro" dijo Ed, sintiendo que estaba en un sueño.

Los tres se pusieron a trabajar de inmediato con los gnomos cantando alegremente.

Ed llevó todos los muebles de los gnomos al mismo tiempo y los puso en el jardín.

Encontró unos bombillos viejos y los encendió.

Luego tomó las velas viejas que su madre quería tirar, las cortó y las puso en cada mesa.

"Muchas gracias" dijo Scurry, el otro gnomo.

Debemos vestirnos ahora, pronto estarán aquí.

"¿Te gustaría venir? A nuestros amigos les encantaría conocerte" dijo Brittle.

"¡Siiii!" Dijo Ed, muy contento.

Corrió rápidamente a vestirse para la fiesta, y cuando bajó, tuvo una gran vista frente a sus ojos.

Todo el jardín estaba lleno de pequeñas hadas y gnomos bailando alegremente y comiendo.

Todos habían llegado cuando él subió.

Se detuvo en el jardín con la boca abierta.

Y de algún lugar, vio a Brittle y Scurry saludándolo.

Fin.

Ejercicio

Ok, ahora hagamos un ejercicio rápido: te haré 5 preguntas. Trata de responder y luego de las preguntas, te daré las respuestas.

Preguntas
1) ¿Dónde vivían Ed y su familia?
2) ¿Qué historias le contaba su hermano?
3) ¿Quiénes tuvieron una fiesta en el jardín de Ed?
4) ¿Ed ayudó a los gnomos?
5) ¿Quién invitó a Ed a la fiesta?

Respuestas
1) MINNESOTA
2) Historias de magia y hechicería que ocurrían en el ático
3) Gnomos y hadas
4) Si, Ed ayudó
5) Brittle, el gnomo

The Gnomes and Fairies Party

It's the full moon and Ed is looking out from his window in his bedroom.

He has been reading tales of fairies adventures and had badly wanted to see things for himself.

The Halloween had come and gone with his hope of meeting an elf as whom he had dressed up.

Now he sat and stared longingly from his bedroom window.

Before his parents moved to San Francisco, they lived in a big house in Minnesota.

He had read lots of books on fairyland and wizards but had never seen any.

And last year, when they moved to a bigger house with turrets and an attic.

His big brother Henry would tell him scary tales of magic and sorcery that happened in the attic, and he would listen with much interest.

He sighed heavily after recalling all of these.

He rose from the window seat he had been seating on and grabbed his book from the reading table.

As he turned to sit, he heard the rustling of leaves in the garden below.

He looked out, and his eyes nearly popped out in wonder.

He saw a gnome carrying the tiniest table he had ever seen in his life and placing it carefully on a toadstool.

"I must be dreaming," he muttered.

Another gnome ran past the first one.

"Brittle, don't do that. The toadstools will be tables for the smaller fairies. The table isn't supposed to stand on it."

And with that, it moved the table from there and laid it on the bare ground.

"Perhaps, this isn't a dream. I must quickly hurry down there."

So Ed ran down and gently opened the kitchen door and was out into the garden.

The gnomes trembled when they saw him.

"Wait, don't go." Ed pleaded.

"I've been watching from my bedroom window and have just come down to be sure I wasn't dreaming."

"What's the table for?"

Brittle spoke first.

"Tonight is a party for us all. And we're inviting some fairies too!" he said excitedly.

"Can you help us set up?"

"We're almost running late."

"Sure," Ed said, gleefully still feeling like he was in a dream.

The three of them set to work immediately with the gnomes humming happily.

Ed carried all the furniture from the gnome's toolshed at once and set them in the garden.

He found some old bulbs and lighted them.

Then he took the old candles his mother had wanted to throw away, cut them, and put them on every table.

"Thank you a thousand times."

"Scurry," the other gnome said. "We must dress up now; they'd soon be here."

"Would you love to come? Our friends would love to meet you," Brittle squealed.

"Yesssss!" Ed said, most happily.

He ran up quickly to dress up for the party, and when he came down, what a sight met his eyes.

The whole garden was filled with tiny fairies and gnomes dancing happily and eating.

They had all arrived as soon as he went up.

He stood by the garden with his mouth wide open.

And from somewhere, he saw Brittle and Scurry waving to him.

The End.

Exercise

Ok, let's now start a quick exercise: I am going to ask you 5 questions. Try to reply, and after the questions, I will give you the answers.

Questions
1) Where did Ed and his family live?
2) What stories did his brother tell him?
3) Who had a party in Ed's garden?
4) Did Ed help the gnomes?
5) Who invited Ed to the party?

Answers
1) Minnesota
2) Stories of magic and sorcery that happened in the attic
3) The gnomes and fairies
4) Yes, Ed helped
5) Brittle the gnome

Chapter 18: Granja Los Villalobos

Los Villalobos, una familia de cuatro integrantes, el señor Jacobo, la señora María y sus dos hijos Luciano y Sara, viven en una granja ubicada en las afueras de Costa Rica.

Jacobo, quien hereda la granja de su padre, siempre tuvo el sueño de hacer de ella una atracción turística y siempre que podía comprar más hectáreas lo hacía para ampliar su variedad de animales.

Su hijo Luciano, quien también ama a los animales como su padre, siempre ha querido tener un espacio en la granja especialmente para sus animales favoritos, que son las aves.

Luciano tiene una pequeña colección. Tiene una pareja de aves quetzal, una pájaro campana y una guacamaya roja. Les tiene mucho aprecio ya que los heredó de su abuelo. En una mañana nublada la granja está muy tranquila, y los animales descansan un tanto perezosos debido al clima tan fresco que había. No es soleada como suele estar. A lo lejos, se acerca el vecino.

Jacobo, saludando al vecino, le hace señas para que este se acerque a la casa y disfrute de un rico chocolate caliente.

"Hola vecino, ¿qué lo trae por aquí?" Pregunta Jacobo.

El vecino responde "Solo paso a saludar y a comentarle un par de cosas, o, mejor dicho, para proponerle un negocio" dijo el vecino.

"A ver coménteme ese negocio del que habla" responde Luciano mientras sirve dos tazas de chocolate caliente.

"Lo que pasa es que mi esposa quiere mudarse a la ciudad y poder estar más pendiente del negocio que tenemos allá, entonces estoy pensando en vender mi granja" dice el vecino.

Jacobo se fue en pensamiento mientras su vecino seguía hablando. Solamente se imaginaba todo lo que iba a hacer si compraba esa granja. "¡Jacobo! ¿Me escuchaste todo lo que dije?" Pregunta el vecino exaltado.

"Sí, disculpa, es que me agrada mucho la idea y solo me estaba imaginando todos los planes que tengo para esas jugosas siete hectáreas que tienes" dice Jacobo.

"Perfecto, mañana vendré con mi abogado para que podamos hacer los papeles y llevar todo de forma legal" dice el vecino.

Se despiden ambos vecinos y Jacobo llama a sus hijos y a su esposa para contarles lo que le acaba de decir el vecino y todos los planes que tiene. "Podemos ampliar nuestro corral, nuestro establo y podemos tener una jaula grande para poder albergar tus aves, Luciano" comenta muy emocionado Jacobo.

Llega el día siguiente, esta vez sí era una mañana soleada como la mayoría, pero a Jacobo eso no le importó, y desde horas de la mañana ya estaba sentado en el frente de su casa esperando a su vecino.

"¡Vecino, vecino!" Escucha Jacobo a lo lejos, a lo que se asoma y ve a su vecino acercarse junto a un hombre con un traje negro y sosteniendo un maletín negro.

"Buenos días, Jacobo. Te presento a mi abogado que siempre me ha acompañado en todos mis negocios. Ya le comenté que quiero vender mi granja y él ha venido a hacerlo legal" dice el vecino.

"Perfecto, vamos a concretar esto" dice Jacobo. Pasaron dos horas platicando y firmando los papeles de su nueva adquisición. Finalmente, el vecino se despide con ojos llorosos debido a que acababa de vender su granja.

Pasaron dos meses durante los cuales Jacobo había dedicado tiempo para ampliar su granja, colocar nuevas jaulas y dividir por zonas los distintos animales que ya tenía y los nuevos que había comprado. Las áreas para las vacas, los cerdos, los caballos y hasta pequeños ponis estaban todos con sus respectivas cercas, áreas para comer y para la recreación de los animales. Uno de los más contentos por la nueva granja y por la nueva ampliación era su hijo Luciano, ya que finalmente tenía su espacio para sus aves.

Finalizada la ampliación de la granja, se reúnen en familia para la planificación de las áreas de atracción turística, desde una pequeña granja de contacto para los visitantes más pequeños hasta largas caminatas a caballo. En la reunión todos opinan:

"La granja de contacto tendrá animales pequeños como cerdos, ovejas y ponis para que los niños puedan jugar y alimentarlos" opina Sara.

"Buena idea; y las cabalgatas a caballo serán por el sendero norte que llegarán a la colina para ver el atardecer" dice Jacobo.

"Me parece muy romántico la idea de las cabalgatas, tienen que ser exclusivas para las parejas que nos visiten" acota la señora María.

"Estaba pensando que una actividad familiar sería que todos puedan ordeñar una vaca y que vieran el proceso de cómo se hace la leche" agrega Luciano.

Al finalizar su tarde en la granja se podrán tomar una foto de recuerdo con mis bellas aves. Al terminar la reunión familiar, planifican cuándo será la gran apertura de la granja para el público, comienzan todos los preparativos y realizan un gran cartel que anuncia el día de apertura.

Llegado el día, muchas personas emocionadas por conocer la hermosa granja de los Villalobos, se reúnen en la gran puerta de tablas de madera esperando la hora de entrada. Los Villalobos, un poco angustiados por todos los detalles para que la gran inauguración al público salga bien, se dividen las tareas del día y Jacobo dice:

"Sofía, tú te vas a encargar de los niños en la granja de contacto, asegúrate que los alimenten y jueguen con ellos. María, tú organiza la cabalgata a caballo de las parejas y Luciano, prepara la cámara para las fotos con tus aves."

Luciano pregunta "¿Y tú papá, ¿qué harás?"

"Yo prepararé a las vacas con sus respectivos becerros y cubetas para que las familias las puedan ordeñar, previo a un pequeño curso de cómo hacerlo." Responde Jacobo.

Llega la hora de abrir las puertas y entre globos y música los visitantes entran a la hermosa granja de los Villalobos. Asombrados por lo que ven, comentan:

"¡Qué hermosa es!, no puedo creer que exista un lugar tan bello y familiar en Costa Rica" Dice una mamá que visita la granja con sus dos pequeños hijos.

"Tenemos una granja de contacto donde sus pequeños hijos pueden estar con lindos animales, darles de comer y jugar con ellos" le dice Sofía a la mamá.

Los niños saltan de la emoción y corren a donde se encuentra la granja de contacto.

Muy emocionados los niños exclaman "¡Mira, mamá, un bebé cerdito y una pequeña oveja!, les daré de comer con este biberón."

"Son muy lindos, trátenlos con cuidado y amor" les dice la mamá a sus hijos.

Al otro lado de la granja la señora María reúne a las parejas asistentes y les ofrece una romántica cabalgata a caballo hasta la colina, donde verán el hermoso atardecer y al finalizar degustarán unos ricos aperitivos.

Una pareja de recién casados, interesados en el paseo, comenta "Me parece interesante ese paseo, ¿podemos escoger los caballos?" pregunta el esposo.

"Claro que sí; vengan al establo y les muestro los caballos ensillados" responde María.

Al ir al establo, encuentran unos hermosos caballos pura sangre y María se los presenta "Este caballo negro es Cometa, es muy dócil y le encanta la zanahoria; este caballo blanco de aquí es Copo de Nieve, es muy veloz y le encanta que le trencen su cola."

"¡Me gusta Copo de Nieve!, ese será mi caballo" dice la esposa entusiasmada.

"Entonces el mío será Cometa, me encantan los caballos negros" responde el esposo que visita la granja.

"Está bien, móntense en sus respectivos caballos que les espera una hermosa puesta de sol" dice María a la pareja de recién casados.

La pareja inicia la cabalgata por un hermoso sendero cubierto de un césped totalmente verde, con un clima agradable y escuchando los sonidos característicos de todos los animales que habitan en la granja.

El señor Jacobo se reúne con las familias asistentes y les dicta una breve charla de como es el proceso de obtención de leche de vaca, y pregunta a los asistentes "¿Alguien quiere ordeñar una de estas hermosas vacas mariposas?"

Y del grupo de asistentes, un padre y un hijo gritan emocionados "¡Nosotros, nosotros!"

El señor Jacobo les pide que se acerquen a donde está la vaca junto a su pequeño becerro y dice que uno de los dos se siente en un taburete de madera muy bajo, que los ayudará a alcanzar las ubres de la vaca.

El padre de familia se sienta y coloca a su hijo en su regazo, toman como les había enseñado previamente Jacobo las ubres de la vaca y empiezan a ordeñarlas.

El niño muy entusiasmado le dice al papá "¡Papá, es leche como la que como con mi cereal!"

Todas las familias asistentes se ríen y continúan observando el proceso de obtención de leche.

Mientras tanto, un grupo de jóvenes se encuentran con Luciano en el área de las jaulas de aves, y extasiados por los hermosos colores de cada especie de ave y por sus peculiares cantos, se toman fotos con cada una de ellas.

"Quiero una foto con el ave en mi cabeza" dice un joven emocionado.

"¡Mi foto será alimentando al ave azul!" exclama otra joven del grupo.

Jacobo complace a todos los presentes y les entrega su foto como recuerdo de la visita a la granja.

Al finalizar el día de apertura de la granja, toda la familia Villalobos se reúne para la cena y concluyen, que la inauguración de la granja para el público ha sido todo un éxito y que lo harían cada fin de semana de sus vidas.

Resumen

Los Villalobos son una familia de cuatro integrantes que viven en una granja en las afueras de Costa Rica. Jacobo, el padre de la familia, tiene como objetivo ampliar el tamaño de su granja, tener más animales y convertirla en una atracción turística. A Jacobo se le presenta una gran oportunidad por la venta de la granja vecina, y emprende junto al resto de su familia la remodelación de la granja para convertirla en lo que siempre quiso, un lugar con constantes visitas de familias y grupos.

The Villalobos' Farm

Los Villalobos, a family of four, Mr. Jacobo, Mrs. Maria, and their two children Luciano and Sara, live on a farm located on the outskirts of Costa Rica.

Jacobo, who inherits his father's farm, always had the dream of making it a tourist attraction, and whenever he could buy more, hectares he did so to expand his variety of animals.

His son Luciano, who also loves animals like his father, has always wanted to have a space on the farm, especially for his favorite animals, which are birds.

Luciano has a small collection. It has a pair of quetzal birds, a bellbird, and a red barnacle. He has a lot of appreciation since he inherited them from his grandfather. On a cloudy morning, the farm is very quiet, and the animals rest somewhat lazy due to the cool weather. It is not as sunny as it used to be. In the distance, the neighbor approaches.

Jacobo, greeting the neighbor, beckons him to come to the house and enjoy a delicious hot chocolate.

"Hello, neighbor, what brings you here?" Asks Jacobo.

The neighbor replies:

"I just come to say hello and to tell you a couple of things, or rather, I want to propose a business," said the neighbor.

"Let's see, tell me about that business you are talking about," Luciano replies while serving two cups of hot chocolate.

What happens is that my wife wants to move to the city and be more aware of the business we have there, so I'm thinking of selling my farm," says the neighbor. Jacobo left in thought while his neighbor kept talking. He only imagined everything he was going to do if he bought that farm. "Jacob! Did you hear everything I said?" The exalted neighbor asks.

"Yes, I'm sorry, I really like the idea and I was just imagining all the plans I have for those juicy seven hectares you have," Jacobo says.

"Perfect, tomorrow I will come with my lawyer so we can do the papers and take everything legally," says the neighbor.

Both neighbors say goodbye, and Jacobo calls his children and his wife to tell them what the neighbor just told him, and all the plans he has. "We can expand our pen, our stable and we can have a large cage to house your birds, Luciano," says Jacobo, very excited. The next day arrives, this time it was a sunny morning like most, but Jacobo didn't mind that, and from early he was already sitting in the front of his house waiting for his neighbor.

"Neighbor, neighbor!" Listen Jacobo in the distance, so he looks at and sees his neighbor approaching with a man in a black suit and holding a black briefcase. "Good morning, Jacobo. I present you to my lawyer who has always accompanied me in all my businesses. I already told him that I want to sell my farm, and he has come to make it legal," says the neighbor.

"Perfect, let's make this happen," says Jacobo. They spent two hours talking and signing the papers for their new acquisition. Finally, the neighbor says goodbye with teary eyes because he had just sold his farm.

Two months passed during which Jacobo had dedicated time to expand his farm, place new cages, and divide the different animals he already had and the new ones he had bought. The areas for cows, pigs, horses, and even small ponies were all with their respective fences, areas for eating, and the recreation of animals. One of the happiest for the new farm and the new extension was his son, Luciano, since he finally had his space for his birds.

After the extension of the farm, they meet as a family to plan the areas of tourist attraction, from a small interactive farm for smaller visitors to long walks on horseback. In the meeting everyone thinks:

"The interactive farm will have small animals such as pigs, sheep, and ponies so children can play and feed them," Sara says.

"Good idea; and horseback riding will be on the north path that will reach the hill to watch the sunset," says Jacobo.

"The idea of horseback riding seems very romantic to me, they have to be exclusive for couples who visit us," says María.

"I was thinking that a family activity would be for everyone to milk a cow and see the process of how milk is made," Luciano adds. "At the end of their afternoon at the farm, they can take a souvenir photo with my beautiful birds."

At the end of the family reunion, they plan when the grand opening of the farm will be for the public, all preparations begin, and they make a great poster that announces the opening day.

When the day arrives, many people are excited to know the beautiful farm of the Villalobos, gather at the large wooden plank door waiting for the entrance time. The Villalobos, a little distressed by all the details so that the grand opening to the public goes well, the tasks of the day are divided and Jacobo says:

"Sofia, you will take care of the children in the interactive farm, make sure they feed them and play with them. Maria, you organize the horseback riding of couples, and Luciano prepares the camera for photos with your birds."

Luciano asks:

"And you, dad, what will you do?"

"I will prepare the cows with their respective calves and buckets so that families can milk them before a small course on how to do it," Jacobo responds.

It is time to open the doors and among balloons and music, visitors enter the beautiful farm of the Villalobos. Amazed by what they see they comment:

"How beautiful it is! I can't believe there is such a beautiful and familiar place in Costa Rica," says a mother who visits the farm with her two young children.

"We have a contact farm where your little children can be with cute animals, feed them and play with them," Sofia tells the mother.

The children jump from emotion and run to where it is located the contact farm.

Very excited the children exclaim "Look, mom, a baby pig, and a little sheep! I will feed them with this bottle."

"They are very cute, treat them with care and love," the mother tells her children.

On the other side of the farm, Mrs. Maria gathers the couples who attended and offers a romantic horseback ride to the hill, where they will see the beautiful sunset, and in the end, they will taste some delicious snacks.

A just-married couple, interested in the ride, comment.

"I think that ride is interesting, can we choose the horses?" Asks the husband.

"Of course; you come to the barn, and I show you saddled horses" Maria answers.

When they go to the barn, they find beautiful thoroughbred horses, and Maria is introduced to them.

"This black horse is Cometa, it is very docile, and it loves carrots, this white horse here is Copo de nieve, it is very fast and it loves to be braided in his tail."

"I like Copo de nieve! That will be my horse," says the excited wife.

"Then mine will be Cometa; I love black horses" replies the husband who visits the farm.

"All right, get on your respective horses that a beautiful sunset awaits," Maria says to the just married couple.

The couple starts the ride on a beautiful path covered with a completely green lawn, with a pleasant climate and listening to the characteristic sounds of all the animals that inhabit the farm.

Mr. Jacob meets with the attending families and gives them a brief talk about the process of obtaining cow's milk, and asks the attendees:

"Does anyone want to milk one of these beautiful butterfly cows?"

And from the group of assistants, a father and a son shout excitedly "We, we!"

Mr. Jacobo asks them to go where the cow is next to his little calf, and since one of the two sits on a very low wooden board, that will help them to reach the udders of the cow.

The father sits down and places his son in his lap; they take as Jacobo had previously taught them the cow udders and periodically milk them.

The very excited boy tells his dad "Dad, it's milk like the one I eat with my cereal!"

All attending families laugh and continue to observe the process of obtaining milk.

Meanwhile, a group of young people meets Luciano in the area of bird cages, and ecstatic about the beautiful colors of each bird species and its peculiar songs, photos are taken with each of them.

"I want a picture with the bird in my head," says an excited young man

"My photo will be feeding the blue bird!" Exclaims another girl from the group.

Jacobo pleases everyone present and gives them his photo as a souvenir of the visit to the farm.

At the end of the farm's opening day, the whole family of Villalobos meets for dinner and concludes the inauguration of the farm for the public that has been a success and that they would do it every weekend of their lives.

Resume

The Villalobos is a family of four who lives on a farm on the outskirts of Costa Rica. Jacobo, the father of the family, aims to expand the size of his farm, have more animals and turn it into a tourist attraction. Jacobo is presented with a great opportunity for the sale of the neighboring farm and undertakes with the rest of his family the remodeling of the farm to make it what he always wanted, a place with constant visits from families and groups.

Quiz

Questions

1) ¿De quién heredó las aves Luciano?
    a. De su padre
    b. De su abuelo
    c. De su hermana
2) ¿Qué actividad planeaban para los visitantes más pequeños?
    a. Paseos a caballos
    b. Fotos con las aves
    c. Granja de contacto
3) ¿Quién organiza las cabalgatas para las parejas?
    a. María
    b. Sofía

      c. Luciano
4) ¿Qué caballo escoge el esposo que visita la granja?
      a. Copo de Nieve
      b. Cometa
      c. Guacamaya roja
5) ¿Cuándo harán más aperturas al público luego de la exitosa inauguración?
      a. Todos los días
      b. Nunca
      c. Cada fin de semana

Answers
1) b
2) c
3) a
4) b
5) c

Vocabulario (Vocabulary)

Integrantes - Members; **Granja** – Farm; **Afueras** – Outskirts; **Hereda** – Inherit; **Atracción turística** – Tourist attraction; **Hectáreas** – Hectares; **Espacio** – Space; **Aves** – Birds; **Quetzal** – (A type of bird); **Guacamaya roja** – Scarlet macaw; **Nublada** – Cloudy; **Perezosos** – Lazy; **Clima** – Weather; **Soleada** – Sunny; **Solía** – Used to; **Vecino** – Neighbour; **Saludar** – To greet; **Negocio** – Deal; **Esposa** – Wife; **Mudarse** – To move out; **Pendiente** – Attentive; **Vender** – To sell; **Imaginaba** – Imagined; **Agrada** – Pleases; **Planes** – Plans; **Abogado** – Lawyer; **Legal** – Legal; **Establo** – Barn; **Jaula** – Cage; **Albergar** – To harbor; **Frente** – Front; **Traje negro** – Black suit; **Sosteniendo** – Holding; **Maletín** – Briefcase; **Concretar** – To finalize; **Platicando** – Talking; **Firmando**

– Signing; **Adquisición** – Acquisition; **Jaulas** – Cages; **Zonas** – Areas; **Vacas** – Cows; **Cerdos** – Pigs; **Caballos** – Horses; **Ponis** – Ponies; **Cercas** – Fences; **Recreación** – Recreation; **Planificación** – Planning; **Granja de contacto** – Interactive farm/Petting farm; **Caminatas** – Walks; **Ovejas** – Sheep; **Cabalgatas** – Horseback riding; **Sendero** – Path; **Colina** – Hill; **Atardecer** – Sunset; **Romántico** – Romantic; **Parejas** – Couples; **Actividad familiar** – Family activity; **Ordeñar** – To milk; **Agrega** – Adds; **Apertura** – Opening; **Preparativos** – Preparations; **Tablas de madera** – Wooden boards; **Angustiados** – Preoccupied; **Inauguración** – Opening; **Tareas** – Tasks; **Asegúrate** – You make sure; **Cámara** – Camera; **Becerros** – Calves; **Cubetas** – Buckets; **Curso** – Course; **Globos** – Balloons; **Asombrados** – Amazed; **Darles de comer** – Feed them; **Trátenlos** – Treat them (instructions); **Cuidado** – Care; **Aperitivos** – Appetizers; **Recién casados** – Just married; **Escoger** – To choose; **Ensillados** – Saddled; **Pura sangre** – Pure blood; **Cometa** – Comet or kite; **Zanahoria** – Carrot; **Copo de Nieve** – Snowflake; **Veloz** – Fast; **Trencen** – Braid; **Caballos negros** – Black horses; **Móntense** – Mount (a horse); **Puesta de sol** – Sunset; **Césped** – Grass; **Agradable** – Nice; **Habitan** – They inhabit (Verb; habitar); **Charla** – Chat; **Proceso** – Process; **Vacas mariposas** – White cows with black spots; **Taburete de madera** – Wooden stool; **Alcanzar** – To reach; **Ubres** – Udders; **Regazo** – Lap; **Mientras tanto** – Meanwhile; **Jóvenes** – Young boys; **Especie** – Species; **Cantos** – Songs; **Complace** – Pleases; **Entrega** – Gives; **Recuerdo** – Memory; **Éxito** – Success; **Fin de semana** – Weekend.

Chapter 19: Los Piratas del Bufón Errante (Torpes en Tierra y en Mar)

Todo sucedió tan rápido que nadie sabe qué fue lo que pasó. ¿Qué pasó? Eran siete barcos piratas, anclados en una montaña en el medio de la nada, no había mar, océano, rio, riachuelo, charco, pantano ni nada que esté relacionado con el agua. Simplemente eran siete barcos en una montaña sin ningún tipo de razón o explicación alguna.

Piratas urbanos de ciudad establecieron su guarida en las montañas para permanecer ocultos. Estaban buscando un extraño tesoro que llevaba más de mil años enterrado en alguna *parte* de la ciudad. Por eso desarrollaron un sistema de ruedas y neumáticos para sus barcos y poder trasladarse desde los mares hasta las ciudades. Los 'barcos-carros/auto-barcos', navegaron por mar y tierra, de puerto en puerto, de pueblo en pueblo, de ciudad en ciudad.

El día de su llegada los piratas venían de una legendaria fiesta de corsarios por el Mar Muerto que siguió en el mar Mediterráneo. Terminaron en el mar Caribe descubriendo que el verdadero Mar Muerto en realidad queda en Puerto Rico y no en Jordania. De hecho, el Mar Muerto en Puerto Rico está vivo y bien.

Eran conocidos como los Piratas del Bufón Errante, torpes en tierra y en mar. Y estaban convencidos de que la leyenda del tesoro del Morokotongo era cierta y estaba escondido en este pequeño Pueblo de Los Andes rodeado de montañas. Cuentan los Antiguos historiadores que el tesoro de Morokotongo pertenecía al rey de los piratas, el temible Barbacoa.

En 1883, se lo robó al conde de Bermeja. Barbacoa derrochó gran parte del tesoro en sus viajes y aventuras por los siete mares. El resto lo escondió tan bien que ningún otro pirata ha podido encontrarlo. Muchos grupos de piratas *dejaron* incluso de navegar para dedicarse solo a la búsqueda de ese tesoro.

Los Piratas del Bufón Errante habían estudiado todos los errores cometidos por los piratas anteriores. Bajo juramento del código de los piratas se prometían encontrar el legendario tesoro y pasar a la historia como los únicos piratas que descifraron la coordenada del mapa del gran Barbacoa.

Pero eran un poco despistados, atolondrados y locos. Bueno todos los piratas están locos, pero estos de verdad estaban chiflados. El día que decidieron buscar el tesoro de Morokotongo fue una verdadera locura. Apenas zarparon, todo fue un caos.

"¡Se va se va la Baarcaaa …tooodos a bordooooo!" grito el capitán Jaky Esparragos.

"¿Para donde se va?" respondió el primero al mando.

"¿Qué dicen las velas?" grito el capitán.

"No dicen nada capitán, están calladas."

"¿Quién dejó entrar a estos monos?" protestaba el capitán. Monos por todos lados del barco, colgados y saltando, desordenando y rompiendo todo lo que encontraban a su paso, acabaron con las provisiones. En la pelea contra los monos, aparecieron sesenta loros y repetían lo mismo.

"Rua la la Morokotongo Morokotongo peligro peligro la la rua rua dónde dónde Morokotongo rua rua", habla los loros.

Se desató una gran tormenta y una de las velas se incendió. Un relámpago le pulverizo el sombrero al capitán. Los monos se bebieron todo el barril de cerveza y los toneles de vino y enloquecieron; los loros se alborotaron también.

Los sorprendió un bucanero y se enfrentaron a cañonazos y espadas por una hora. Así transcurrían todos sus viajes por mar y tierra. Y tenían la costumbre, como todos los piratas, de hacer retos y torneos entre ellos diciendo cosas como:

"¡Mi espada es la más rápida de todo el océano!"

"¡*Blasfemia*! ¡Mi espada es más veloz! ¡En guardia!"

"¡Ya estoy listo! ¡Te demostraré que soy el mejor con la espada! ¿Ves esa mosca que está volando sobre la botella? ¡Mira! *Agarro* mi espada y le corto las alas."

"¡Eso no es nada! ¿Ves ese mosquito que vuela sobre la gorda panza del contramaestre? ¡Presta atención! Saco mi espada y zum…"

"¡Ja Ja Ja, siguió volando; fallaste!"

"¡No fallé para nada! ¡Es cierto que siguió volando, pero no va poder tener más hijos!"

"¿Que?"

"¡Lo que escuchas tal y como te lo acabo de demostrar, que soy el mejor con la espada!"

Otro de los retos piratas era 'La Danza de La Plancha' que consistía en girar sobre tu propio cuerpo dando vueltas parado en un solo pie en el borde de la plancha sobre el olfato y la mirada de los tiburones. Todos los peligros, riesgos y retos valían la pena porque el tesoro de Morokotongo era el mayor de todos los tesoros. Dicen los que conocen la leyenda, que el tesoro del temible Barbacoa está compuesto de:

Ciento treinta toneladas de doblones de plata, dos mil ochocientos cincuenta lingotes de oro, mil ciento setenta y cinco esmeraldas, novecientos ochenta y tres rubíes, trescientos noventa y seis diamantes, dos mil cuatrocientos noventa y nueve *monedas de* oro, tres mil ciento veintitrés joyas de cristal, cuatro mil trescientos veinte esculturas de bronce y plata, ochenta espadas bañadas en oro y plata, ciento noventa y cinco dagas templadas en oro, y quinientos setenta y cinco collares de perlas preciosas.

Después de recorrer y saquear todo el pueblo, los piratas del bufón errante no tenían pista alguna del fabuloso tesoro, habían seguido las instrucciones del mapa al pie de la letra. Y no sabían que era lo que estaba mal hasta que se dieron cuenta que todo el tiempo habían estado leyendo el mapa al revés.

The Pirates of the Wandering Jester (Clumsy on Land and Sea)

Everything happened so fast that no one knows what happened. What happened? There were seven pirate ships anchored on a mountain in the middle of nowhere. There was no sea, ocean, river, stream, puddle, swamp, or anything that is related to water around. They were simply seven ships on a mountain without any kind of reason or explanation.

City urban pirates established their lair in the mountains to stay hidden. They were looking for a strange treasure that had been buried somewhere in the city. That's why they developed a system of wheels and tires for their ships to be able to move from the seas to the cities. The 'ships-cars/auto-boats,' navigated by sea and land, from seaport to seaport, from village to village, from city to city.

On the day of their arrival, the pirates came from a legendary party of pirates by the Dead Sea that flowed into the Mediterranean Sea. They ended up in the Caribbean Sea as they discovered that the true Dead Sea actually ends in Puerto Rico and not in Jordan. In fact, the Dead Sea in Puerto Rico is alive and well.

They were known as the Pirates of the Wandering Jester, clumsy on land and sea. And they were convinced that the legend of the treasure of the Morokotongo was true and was hidden in this small town in the Andes surrounded by mountains. The ancient historians say that the treasure of Morokotongo belonged to the king of the pirates, the fearsome Barbacoa.

In 1883, he stole the treasure from the Count of Bermeja. Barbacoa squandered much of the treasure in his travels and adventures on the seven seas. The rest he hid so well that no other pirate has been able to find it. Many groups of pirates even stopped sailing to dedicate themselves alone to the search for that treasure.

The Pirates of the Wandering Jester had studied all the mistakes made by the previous pirates. Under oath of the code, the pirates promised themselves to find the legendary treasure and go down in history as the only pirates who deciphered the map coordinates of the great Barbacoa.

But they were a bit clueless and mad. Well, all the pirates are crazy, but they really were nuts. The day they decided to look for the treasure, Morokotongo was full of real madness. As soon as they set sail, everything was chaotic.

"The boat is leaving! All of you aboard!" Captain Jaky Esparragos shouted.

"Where does it go?" responded the first in command.

"What do the sails say?" said the captain.

"They do not say anything, Captain. They are silent."

"Who let these monkeys in?" the captain protested. Monkeys were all over the ship, hanging and jumping, messing up, and breaking everything in their path. They ended up with provisions, and in the fight against the monkeys, sixty parrots appeared and repeated the same thing.

"Rua la la Morokotongo Morokotongo danger danger la rua rua where where Morokotongo rua rua."

A great storm broke, and one of the sails caught fire. A lightning bolt smashed the captain's hat. The monkeys drank the whole barrel of beer and wine, and the parrots went mad.

They were surprised by a buccaneer and faced guns and swords for an hour. This is how all his trips by sea and land passed. And they had the habit, like all pirates, of making challenges and tournaments between them.

"My sword is the fastest in the whole ocean!"

"Blasphemy! My sword is faster. On guard!"

"I'm ready now. I will show you that I am the best with the sword. Do you see that fly that is flying over the bottle? Look. I grab my sword and cut his wings."

"That is nothing. Do you see that mosquito that flies over the fat belly of the first mate? Pay attention! I take out my sword and zum..."

"¡Ha Ha ha, kept flying! You failed!"

"I did not fail at all! It is true that he kept flying, but he will not be able to have more children."

"What?"

"What you hear and how I just showed you is that I am the best with the sword."

Another of the pirate challenges was 'The Dance of the Plank,' which consisted of spinning on one foot on the edge of the plank above the nose and the eyes of the sharks. All the dangers risks and challenges were worth it because the treasure of Morokotongo was the greatest of all the treasures. Those who know the legend say that the treasure of the fearsome Barbacoa is composed of:

One hundred and thirty tons of silver doubloons, two thousand eight hundred and fifty gold ingots, one thousand one hundred seventy-five emeralds, nine hundred and eighty-three rubies, three hundred ninety-six diamonds, two thousand four hundred and ninety-nine gold coins, three thousand one hundred and twenty-three crystal jewelry, four thousand three hundred and twenty bronze and silver sculptures, eighty swords bathed in gold and silver, one hundred and ninety-five gold-plated daggers and five hundred seventy-five precious pearl necklaces.

After touring and plundering the entire town, the Pirates of the Wandering Jester had no clue to the location of the fabulous treasure. They had followed the instructions on the map to the letter. They did not know what was wrong until they realized that they had been reading the map upside down all the time.

Quiz

Questions

1) ¿Dónde estaban los siete barcos?
    a. Océano
    b. Mar
    c. Montaña
2) ¿Dónde habían establecido su guarida los piratas de la ciudad urbana?
    a. Montañas
    b. Mar
    c. Océano

3) ¿De dónde venían los piratas?
    a. Mar Mediterráneo
    b. Mar Muerto
    c. Montaña
4) ¿A quién fue robado el tesoro en 1883?
    a. Capitán Jaky Espárragos
    b. Conde de Bermeja
    c. Pirata Barbacoa

Answers
1) c
2) a
3) b
4) b

Vocabulary (Vocabulario)

Acabaron (ah-kah-bah-rohn) Transitive verb – They finished; conjugated form of acabar, past third person plural.

Agarró (ah-gahr-roh) Transitive verb – I grab; conjugated form of agarrar, present first person singular.

Alborotaron (ahl-boh-roh-tah-rohn) Transitive verb – They disturbed; conjugated form of alborotar, past third person plural.

Anclados (ahn-klahr) Intransitive verb – To anchor.

Anterior (ahn-teh-ryohr) Adjective – Front, previous.

Aparecieron (ah-pah-reh-seh-rohn) Intransitive verb – They appeared; conjugated form of aparecer, past third person plural.

Bajo (bah-hoh) Adjective – Short, low.

Bañada (bah-nyah-dah) Feminine noun – Bath, swim.

Bebieron (beh-beh-ehr-rohn) Transitive verb – They drink; conjugated form of beber, past third person plural.

Blasfemia (Blahs-feh-mee-ah) Feminine noun – Blasphemy.

Botella (boh-teh-yah) Feminine noun – Bottle.

Bronce (brohn-seh) Masculine noun – Bronze.

Bufón (boo-fohn) Masculine noun – Buffon, fool.

Cañonazo (kah-nyoh-nah-soh) Masculine noun – Cannon shot.

Caribe (ka-ree-beh) Proper noun – Carribean.

Cerveza (sehr-beh-sah) Feminine noun – Beer.

Charco (chahr-koh) Masculine noun – Puddle, pool.

Chiflados (chee-flahr) Transitive verb – To whistle.

Ciento noventa y cinco (see-en-toe no-vehn-tah ee sen-coh) Adjective – The number one hundred ninety-five.

Ciento treinta (see-en-toe trin-tah) Adjective – The number one hundred thirty.

Collar (koh-yahr) Masculine noun – Necklace.

Cometido (koh-meh-tee-doh) Masculine noun – Task, mission, duty.

Compuesto (kohm-pwehs-toh) Masculine noun. – Compound.

Corsarios (kohr-sah-ryoh) Masculine or Feminine noun. — Pirate.

Cristal (krees-tahl) Masculine noun — Glass, shard of glass.

Cuatro mil trescientos veinte (quat-roh mill tres-see-en-tohs ven-tea) Adjective — The number four thousand three hundred twenty.

Cuerpo (kwehr-poh) Masculine noun — Body.

Daga (dah-gah) Feminine noun — Dagger.

Dedicarse (deh-dee-kahr-seh) Pronominal verb — To do for a living.

Demostrare (deh-mohs-trah-rey) Transitive verb — I will demonstrate; conjugated form of demostrar, future subjunctive form, first person singular.

Derrocho (deh-rroh-cho) Transitive verb — I squander; conjugated form of derrochar, present first person singular

Desarrollaron (deh-sah-rroh-yahr) Transitive verb — They developed; conjugated form of desarrollar, past third person plural.

Descifraron (deh-see-frah-rohn) Transitive verb — They deciphered; conjugated form of decifrar, past third person plural.

Descubrieron (dehs-koo-breer) Transitive verb — They discovered, conjugated form of descubrir, past third person plural.

Desordenando (dehs-ohr-deh-nahn-doh) Transitive verb — to mess up.

Diamantes (dyah-mahn-tehs) Plural noun – Diamonds.

Dos mil cuatrocientos noventa y nueve (dohs mill quat-roh-see-en-tohs no-vehn-tah ee new-eh-veh) Adjective – The number two thousand four hundred ninety-nine.

Dos mil ochocientos cincuenta (dohs mill oh-cho-see-en-tohs sin-qwin-tah) Adjective – The number two thousand eight hundred fifty.

Enloquecieron (ehn-loh-keh-sehr) Transitive verb – To go crazy, to drive crazy; conjugated form of enloquecier, past third person plural.

Enterrado (ehn-teh-rrah-doh) Adjective – Buried.

Errante (eh-rrahn-teh) Adjective – Wandering.

Esmeralda (ehs-meh-rahl-dah) Feminine noun – Emeralds.

Espada (ehs-pah-dah) Feminine noun – Sword.

Estudiado (ehs-too-dyah-doh) Adjective – Studied.

Fallaste (fah-yah-steh) Intransitive verb – You failed; conjugated form of fallar, past second person singular.

Gorda (gohr-dah) Adjective – Fat, thick, big.

Joya (hoh-yah) Feminine noun – Jewel.

Juramento (hoo-rah-mehn-toh) Masculine noun – Oath.

Lingote (leeng-goh-teh) Masculine noun – Ingot, gold bar.

Loro (loh-roh) Masculine or Feminine noun – Parrot.

Mar (mahr) Masculine noun – Sea, ocean.

Mil ciento setenta y cinco (mill see-en-toe seh-tehn-tah ee seen-ko) Adjective – The number one thousand one hundred seventy-five.

Mirada (mee-rah-dah) Feminine noun – Look.

Monos (moh-noh) Masculine or Feminine noun – Monkeys.

Mosca (mohs-kah) Feminine noun – Fly.

Novecientos ochenta y tres (no-veh-see-en-tohs oh-chin-tah ee trahys) Adjective – The number nine hundred eighty-three.

Ochenta (oh-chehn-tah) Adjective – The number eighty.

Ocultos (oh-kool-toh) Adjective – Hidden.

Oro (oh-roh) Masculine noun – Gold.

Pantano (pahn-tah-noh) Masculine noun – Swampland, wetland.

Panza (pahn-sah) Feminine noun – Belly.

Perlas (pehr-lah) Feminine noun – Pearls.

Permanecer (pehr-mah-neh-sehr) Intransitive verb – To stay.

Pertenecía (pehr-teh-neh-seh-ah) Intransitive verb – To belong to; conjugated form of pertenecer, imperfect first person singular.

Plancha (plahn-chah) Feminine noun – Plank.

Preciosas (preh-syoh-sahs) Adjective – Beautiful, precious.

Protestaba (proh-tehs-tah-bah) Intransitive verb – I protested; conjugated form of protestar, imperfect first person singular.

Quinientos setenta y cinco (kee-nyehn-tohs say-ten-tah ee seen-ko) Adjective – The number five hundred seventy-five.

Relámpago (rreh-lahm-pah-goh) Masculine noun – Lightening.

Repetían (rreh-peh-tee-ahn) Transitive verb – To repeat, to do again; conjugated form of repetir, imperfect third person plural.

Tesoro (teh-soh-roh) Masculine noun – Treasure.

Riachuelo (rryah-chweh-loh) Masculine noun – Brook, stream.

Riesgos (rryehs-goh) Masculine noun – Risk.

Ruedas (rruh-eh-dahs) Intransitive verb – You roll; conjugated form of rodar, present second person singular.

Saquear (sah-keh-ahr) Transitive verb – To loot.

Sesenta (seh-sehn-tah) Adjective – The number sixty.

Templadas (tehm-plah-doh) Adjective – Lukewarm, mild.

Tesoro (teh-soh-roh) Masculine noun – Treasure.

Tiburon (tee-boo-rohn) Masculine noun – Shark.

Tipo (tee-poh) Masculine noun – Type, class, sort.

Tonelada (toh-neh-lah-dah) Feminine noun (weight) – Ton.

Tonto (tohn-toh) Adjective – Stupid, dumb, idiot.

Torpes (tohr-peh) Adjective – Clumsy, dim-witted.

Transcurrían (trahns-koo-rreer) Intransitive verb – They passed; conjugated form of transcurrir, imperfect third person plural.

Tres mil ciento veintitrés (trays mill see-en-toe beyn-tee-trehs) Adjective – The number three thousand one hundred twenty-three.

Trescientos noventa y seis (trays-see-en-tohs no-ven-tah eh sahys) Adjective – The number three hundred ninety-six.

Chapter 20: Nuevos Amigos

Ana está en la universidad. Es su primer día de clases. Estudia Derecho. Quiere convertirse en abogada penalista. Su sueño es investigar casos y defender a personas que no tienen recursos económicos.

Está en un aula muy grande con otros estudiantes. Todos hablan entre ellos. Ana no conoce a nadie. Se siente un poco solitaria. Extraña a sus amigos del pueblo.

Cuando entra el profesor, todos los estudiantes guardan silencio. El profesor empieza la clase. Habla muy rápido. Todos los estudiantes tienen bolígrafos y anotadores, y toman notas. Algunos usan sus computadoras para tomar apuntes. Ana toma su mochila, la abre y saca un anotador y un bolígrafo. Quiere escribir la fecha y tomar notas, pero su bolígrafo no funciona. ¡Qué mala suerte! El profesor sigue hablando muy rápido y Ana no puede tomar notas. No sabe qué hacer.

"¡Tchh!" dice alguien.

Ana mira a su izquierda y ve a una chica rubia con un bolígrafo en la mano.

"¿Quieres que te preste un bolígrafo?" pregunta la chica rubia.

"Sí, por favor. ¡Muchas gracias!" dice Ana.

Ana está muy contenta. Empieza a tomar notas. Cuando termina la clase, todos los estudiantes toman sus anotadores y bolígrafos y los guardan en sus mochilas. Ana llama a la chica que le prestó el bolígrafo.

"Oye, muchas gracias por prestarme el bolígrafo" dice Ana.

"¡De nada! Soy Lucía Pérez, ¿eres nueva?"

"Sí, es mi primer día. Me llamo Ana García."

"Voy a tomar un café. ¿Quieres venir a tomar un café conmigo?"

"Sí, me encantaría; me gusta mucho tomar café, ¡gracias!"

Ana y Lucía van a la cafetería de la universidad y compran café. Se sientan en el patio a tomarlo.

"¿Dónde vives?" pregunta Lucía

"Ahora, en Palermo. Antes vivía en un pueblo. ¿Y tú?"

"Yo soy de Buenos Aires de toda la vida. Vivo en Almagro. ¿Conoces el barrio de Almagro?"

"No, no lo conozco todavía."

"¿Te gusta Buenos Aires?"

"Sí, me gusta, pero extraño a mis amigos."

"Ay, sí, qué difícil. ¡Los amigos son muy importantes!"

"¿Tienes familia?"

"Sí. Vivo con mi mamá porque mis padres están divorciados. Mi mamá tiene un nuevo marido y tengo una hermana pequeña."

"Yo también tengo un hermano pequeño. Mis padres siguen juntos. Creo que se quieren mucho."

"Los míos no se querían nada. ¡Es mejor que estén divorciados!"

"¿Te gusta estudiar Derecho?"

"No sé aún. Me gustó mucho la clase, pero todavía no sé qué quiero hacer. ¿y Tú?"

"A mí me encantó la clase. Me gusta mucho el derecho. Mi sueño es ser abogada penalista."

"Ah, como mi amigo Martín. Mira, ahí viene."

"Un chico alto y de cabello castaño se acerca a la mesa donde están Ana y Lucía."

"Hola, Lucía, ¿cómo estás?" dice el chico alto.

"Hola, Martín, esta es Ana, se acaba de mudar a Buenos Aires" dice Lucía.

"Hola, Ana, ¿cómo estás?" dice Martín.

"Muy bien, gracias, ¿y tú?" pregunta Ana.

"¡Cansado! Tuve muchas clases. ¿Y ustedes?" responde Martín.

"Yo también estoy cansada. Por suerte ya terminaron nuestras clases de hoy" dice Lucía.

"Lucía, ¿vienes a mi fiesta de cumpleaños el viernes?" pregunta Martín.

"Sí, claro."

"Ana, ¿quieres venir a mi fiesta de cumpleaños? Es en mi casa, en Palermo" dice Martín.

"Sí, me encantaría, yo también vivo en Palermo", dice Ana, contenta.

"Genial. Nos vemos el viernes entonces."

"¡Nos vemos!" dicen Lucía y Ana.

Ana no lo puede creer—tiene dos nuevos amigos y una invitación a una fiesta de cumpleaños. ¡Nada mal para el primer día de clases!

New Friends

Ana is in college. It is her first day of school studying Law. She wants to become a criminal lawyer. Her dream is to investigate cases and defend people who do not have financial resources.

She is in a very large classroom with other students. Everyone talks to each other. Ana doesn't know anyone. It feels a little lonely. She misses her village friends.

When the teacher enters, all students remain silent. The teacher starts the class and speaks very fast. All students have pens and annotators and take notes. Some use their computers to take notes. Ana takes her backpack, opens it, and takes out a notebook and a pen. She wants to write the date and take notes, but her pen doesn't work. What a bad luck! The teacher keeps talking very fast, and Ana can't take notes. She does not know what to do.

"Tchh!" Says, someone.

Ana looks to her left and sees a blonde girl with a pen in her hand.

"Do you want me to lend you a pen?" Asks the blonde girl.

"Yes, please. Thank you very much!" says Ana.

Ana is very happy. Start taking notes. When the class ends, all students take their notebooks and pens and store them in their backpacks. Ana calls the girl who lent her the pen.

"Hey, thank you very much for lending me the pen," says Ana.

"You are welcome! I'm Lucía Pérez, are you new?"

"Yes, it is my first day. My name is Ana García."

"I'm going to drink a cup of coffee. Do you want to come for coffee with me?"

"Yes, I would love to. I really like having coffee, thank you!"

Ana and Lucia go to the university cafeteria and buy coffee. They sit on the patio to take it.

"Where do you live?" Asks Lucia

"Now, in Palermo. I used to live in a town. And you?"

"I am from Buenos Aires of a lifetime. I live in Almagro. Do you know the neighborhood of Almagro?"

"No, I don't know yet."

"Do you like Buenos Aires?"

"Yes, I like it, but I miss my friends."

"Oh, yes, it's difficult. Friends are very important!"

"Do you have a family?"

"Yes. I live with my mom because my parents are divorced. My mom has a new husband, and I have a little sister."

"I also have a little brother. My parents are still together. I think they love each other very much."

"Mine didn't want anything. It is better that they are divorced!"

"Do you like studying law?"

"I do not know yet. I really liked the class, but I still don't know what I want to do. And you?"

"I loved the class. I really like the right one. My dream is to be a criminal lawyer."

"Oh, like my friend Martin. Look, there he comes."

A tall boy with brown hair approaches the table where Ana and Lucia are.

"Hello, Lucia, how are you?" Says the tall boy.

"Hello, Martín, this is Ana, she has just moved to Buenos Aires" says Lucia.

"Hello, Ana, how are you?" Says Martin.

"Very well, thank you, and you?" Asks Ana.

"Tired! I had many classes. And you?" replies Martín.

"I am tired too. Luckily our classes are over today," says Lucia.

"Lucia, are you coming to my birthday party on Friday?" Asks Martin.

"Yeah, of course."

"Ana, do you want to come to my birthday party?" It's in my house, in Palermo," says Martín.

"Yes, I would love to; I also live in Palermo," says Ana, happy.

"Great. See you on Friday then."

"See you!" say Lucia and Ana.

Ana can't believe it—she has two new friends and an invitation to a birthday party. Not bad for the first day of school!

Reading Comprehension

1) Do you remember your first day in school, in college or at work? What was it like? How did you feel? Think about how Ana feels. Is she happy at the beginning of the story?

2) Make a list (in Spanish, of course) of all the school supplies mentioned in the story. Did you use any of them at school to take notes?

3) With a partner, role-play the meeting between Lucía and Ana. Do it in Spanish, of course. Use their words and phrases!

Quiz

Questions

Select only one of the options.

1) "Ana está en un aula." What is the correct translation?
   a. Ana is at school
   b. Ana is studying
   c. Ana is in a classroom
2) What is the grammatically correct sentence?
   a. Los alumnos guarda silencio
   b. Los alumno guardan silencio
   c. Los alumnos guardan silencio
3) "Lucía es rubia." What does this sentence mean?
   a. Lucía is blonde
   b. Lucía is tall
   c. Lucía is red-haired
4) What is the correct translation of "Ana misses her friends?"
   a. Ana quiere a sus amigos
   b. Ana extraña a sus amigos

c. Ana no extraña a sus amigos
5) Ana likes coffee. Is that true?
   a. Yes
   b. No
   c. She prefers tea
6) Where does Lucía live?
   a. In a small town
   b. In Palermo
   c. In Almagro
7) "Martín es amigo de Lucía." What is the correct translation of that sentence?
   a. Lucía is Martín's friend.
   b. Martín is Lucía's friend.
   c. Lucía is not Martín's friend.

8) Martín says he is "cansado." What does that mean?
   a. He is married.
   b. He is bored.
   c. He is tired.
9) When's the party?
   a. El viernes
   b. El martes
   c. El sábado
10) Where does Martín live?
    a. In the same neighborhood as Lucía
    b. In the same neighborhood as Ana
    c. Near university
11) How does Ana feel when Martín invites her to the party?
    a. Triste
    b. Cansada
    c. Contenta

12) If Martín says: "Te invito a mi fiesta," is he inviting one, two, or more persons to his party? You can use the dictionary or anything you need to answer this question.
   a. One
   b. Two
   c. More than two

Answers
1) c
2) c
3) a
4) b
5) a
6) c
7) b
8) c
9) a
10) b
11) c
12) a

Vocabulario (Vocabulary)
Universidad – College/University; **Convertirse** – Become; **Investigar** – Research; **Recursos** – Means; **Estudiantes** – Students; **Conocer** – Known; **Empieza** – Starts; **Algunos** – Some; **Bolígrafo** – Pen; **Quiere** – Wants; **Puede** – May; **Anotadores** – Notebooks.

Conclusion

I hope you have really enjoyed this Spanish Short Stories for Beginners series.

Short Stories really improve your language understanding skills while enabling you to improve your grammar.

These stories were true lessons and if you still don't feel confident and you are missing a lot of the content, then start again from the beginning.

Please keep in mind that with some hard work and dedication, you can get your English level up to par in no time. So, whether you are looking to get started with English, improve your current skills, or just brush up on some language before heading out on a trip, you will find that learning Spanish can be fun and interesting when the topic you are reading is engaging.

Thank you, and good luck!

Made in the USA
Monee, IL
28 April 2022